THE PRINTS OF John Himmelfarb

THE PRINTS OF John Himmelfarb

A CATALOGUE RAISONNÉ

1967–2004

Essays by
Michael Bonesteel and
Linda Konheim Kramer

HUDSON HILLS PRESS
NEW YORK AND MANCHESTER

Published in the United States by Hudson Hills Press LLC, 74-2 Union Street, Manchester, Vermont 05254.
Distributed in the United States, its territories and possessions, and Canada by National Book Network, Inc.
Distributed in the United Kingdom, Eire, and Europe by Windsor Books International.

Co-Directors: Randall Perkins and Leslie van Breen
Founding Publisher: Paul Anbinder

Editor: Susan Rossen
Production Manager: David Skolkin
Designer: David Skolkin / Skolkin + Chickey, Santa Fe
Typesetting: Angela Taormina
Proofreader: Laura Addison
Printed and bound by CS Graphics, Singapore
Color Separation by Pre Tech Color, Wilder, Vermont

Library of Congress Cataloging-in-Publication Data
Bonesteel, Michael.
John Himmelfarb : a catalogue raisonné, 1967-2004 / by Michael Bonesteel, Linda Konheim Kramer.— 1st ed.
p. cm.
Includes bibliographical references.
ISBN 1-55595-245-3 (alk. paper)
1. Himmelfarb, John, 1946—Catalogues raisonnés. I. Kramer, Linda Konheim. II. Title.
NE539.H55A4 2005
759.13—dc22
2005028369

FRONTISPIECE:
Detail, NO. 91, *Tabula Tabula Picta*, 1992–93.

Contents

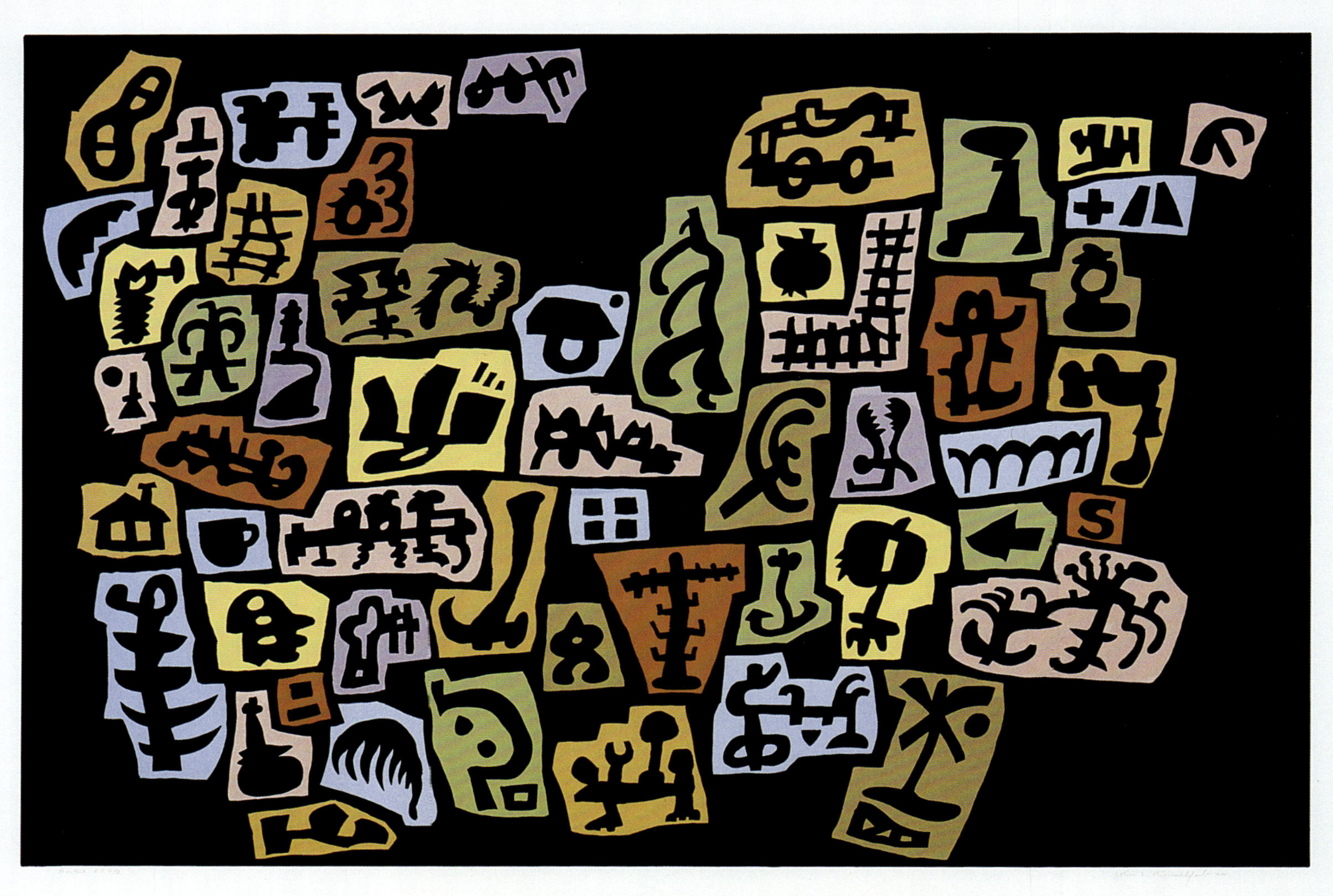

John Himmelfarb

A Life in Art

Linda Konheim Kramer,
Executive Director, Nancy Graves Foundation

John Himmelfarb derives the themes for his art from personal experience. He follows his own muse: "I'm not trying to figure out what the next step in contemporary art will be.... The drive I have seems to come from something internal."[1] Because he identifies strongly with the Midwest, he has chosen to remain in the Chicago area where he grew up. There he has found his core audience, which he has described as "a group of people curious enough to go to see art and anxious to integrate new ideas and experiences into their lives. Not necessarily people who are highly educated in the latest twist and turn of contemporary art movements."[2]

Himmelfarb's family gave him the support and encouragement he needed to pursue his chosen career. He was born in Chicago on June 3, 1946, the second child of two artists, Samuel and Eleanor Himmelfarb. His father, who died in 1976, was in many ways his role model, and he has maintained a close relationship with his mother, his older sister, Susan, and half-sister, Nell, Samuel's daughter from a previous marriage. The experiences of Himmelfarb's childhood fueled his decision to become an artist, and provided the intellectual and emotional resources that he continues to draw upon for his work. It was a time filled with trips to museums, painting and drawing sessions with his father, concerts, and violin and piano lessons. The art he saw on family trips to Europe remained imprinted upon his subconscious. He adopted his parents' progressive political views, which were at odds with those of the rural community in which they lived. The fields and woods of Winfield Township, outside Chicago, where Himmelfarb played as a youngster surrounded by pets and wild animals, are the source of many of his visual fantasies.

Always a reader, Himmelfarb has derived some of his concepts and themes from literature and reference books. Music also has played a significant role throughout his life. He was proficient enough at the violin to play in the Chicago Youth Symphony in high school, and in his college orchestra. Although

opposite page.
no. 133, *Practice*, 2001.

he had decided against a career in music before he entered Harvard University in 1964 to study liberal arts, he feels the rhythm of music in the way he makes his marks and brush strokes.

Himmelfarb had no intention of becoming an artist when, in his first year of college, he took a design course taught by Albert Alcalay. He wanted to gain some exposure to the field because his father was also a designer. (The family lived in a house that Sam Himmelfarb designed and built, inspired by Frank Lloyd Wright's Prairie Style; he also established a successful design firm in the city.) To the college freshman's surprise, an alphabet (Fig. 1), decorated with fanciful embellishments (perhaps with reference to musical ornamentation) that he had designed to fulfill an assignment for Alcalay's class, was accepted in an all-Harvard exhibition. This acknowledgment of his ability encouraged him to continue drawing on his own.

Himmelfarb's interest in design, combined with his desire to improve the world's social ills, led him to declare a major in architectural sciences and urban planning in his sophomore year. But it was through an independent study in drawing with Wil Reimann, a sculptor from whom he had taken a three-dimensional design course, that Himmelfarb came to recognize his true calling. During his last three semesters, he took drawings to Reimann each week to be critiqued; for his senior project, which the sculptor directed, he organized an exhibition of them at Adams House, a student residence. In addition to these various Bauhaus-derived design classes and a drawing course with Robert Neuman, Himmelfarb pursued noncredit study with Mirko Basadella, an artist-in-residence who taught him, and a few other students, how to etch. The delicately rendered landscapes that he made with Basadella (nos. 1–4), composed of nervous, calligraphic strokes reminiscent of the alphabet he had designed three years earlier, offer a window onto some of Himmelfarb's future endeavors.

While his formal artistic training at Harvard was limited, by the time that he graduated in 1968, Himmelfarb knew that he would be an artist. Following the example of his father, whose design business helped to support his art, he decided to earn a master's degree at Harvard's Graduate School of Education. He believed that, by teaching inner-city children, he could make a positive contribution to society while earning a living at a profession that would give him some free time to do his own work. The faux-naive style of some of his images may reflect the art of the children he worked with as a student teacher.

After Himmelfarb's graduation, his parents offered to support him so that he could concentrate fully on art for one year. They gave him a workspace in the studio they shared in Chicago, a place to sleep, a hot plate, and $100 per month. The connections he made with other artists in the building introduced him to new media that were to have a profound effect on his future artistic production. He made sculptures with the distinguished ceramist Ruth Duckworth; Misch Kohn, a well-respected printmaker, introduced him in the fall of 1970 to Jack Lemon, the master printer at Landfall Press in Chicago, with whom Himmelfarb immediately began making lithographs. He was able to live for another year on the proceeds from sales from a show he held in the studio at the end of 1971 and money he had saved during graduate school.

Himmelfarb had an immediate affinity for printmaking. The first two lithographs he executed at Landfall Press in 1970 are Giacometti-like landscapes (nos. 5–6) stylistically similar to two of the earlier etchings he had made with Basadella at Harvard. When he returned to Landfall in 1971, he made ten color lithographs (nos. 10–19) in which his signature vocabulary began to emerge. He used the technique of automatic drawing developed by the French Surrealist André Masson to fashion images of dogs, birds, fish, houses, faces, trees, bridges, armies, and arches inspired by memories of the creatures and woods of his childhood and the industrial structures of Chicago. These prints received immediate recognition. They were selected for a traveling exhibition, "Prints from Landfall Press," organized by the Smithsonian Institution in 1971, and in 1973 the Walker Art Center in Minneapolis included some in a show called "Printmakers: Midwest Invitational."

Through his sister Susan, Himmelfarb had met Molly Day in 1970. They were married in March 1972 in New York, where she was finishing a graduate degree at the Bank Street School of Education. By the time she arrived in Chicago to teach at the University of Chicago's Laboratory School, Himmelfarb had already decided to make his art *his* business. His first step was to create an affordable place in which to live. He spent the next one and one-half years renovating an old, run-down house in Pilsen, an edgy neighborhood southwest of the Loop, for use as a living and studio space. Then, he focused on finding innovative ways to get his work into the world. Between 1973 and 1977, Himmelfarb drove across the country with his prints and drawings, staging sales in the homes of family and friends who invited their friends to attend the exhibitions. Through these events—his "tupperware" parties—he created a group of devoted patrons. These contacts also led to exhibitions in galleries, cultural centers, and museums in Iowa, Missouri, and Nebraska.

Filming of "Sunny Days" (no. 20), one of the large, five-color prints he made at Landfall Press in 1972–73, was selected for the "19th National Print Exhibition" at the Brooklyn Museum in 1974–75. For Himmelfarb 1979 proved to be a banner year: he was awarded a residency at the prestigious artist colony Yaddo, in Saratoga Springs, New York; the noted dealer Terry Dintenfass gave him a one-person exhibition at her gallery in New York; and he had the first of many solo exhibitions at Bob Rogers' Gallery 72 in Omaha. In 1980 Gene Baro, curator of prints and drawings at the Brooklyn Museum, bought some of the artist's prints for the collection and included one of his drawings in the exhibition "American Drawings in Black and White: 1970–1980."

Despite these breakthroughs, the early 1980s were difficult for the Himmelfarbs. The birth of a son, Forest, in October 1979, prompted their decision to keep the studio in Pilsen and purchase a condominium in the Hyde Park, home to the University of Chicago. Unfortunately, the one-person exhibition at Terry Dintenfass Gallery was not the financial success for which Himmelfarb had hoped, perhaps because it took place at the beginning of a recession. To make ends meet, the artist took jobs rehabilitating buildings in 1980.

The problems created by the recession and the proliferation of nuclear weapons at this time affected Himmelfarb's choice of subjects and style. He moved away from constructing works with small marks and a proliferation of details to boldly conceived images of only a few forms realized in black and white. The first works in this style are his *Bone* series, followed by the *Boatman* series (see Bonesteel essay, Fig. 3), both from 1982. The *Bone* works depict a man tossing a dog a bone, a metaphor for the ways in which society fails to meet challenges honestly and substantially. The *Boatman* series features a man sitting in a boat that he fills with material possessions to the point that it eventually sinks, and the man disappears along with it.

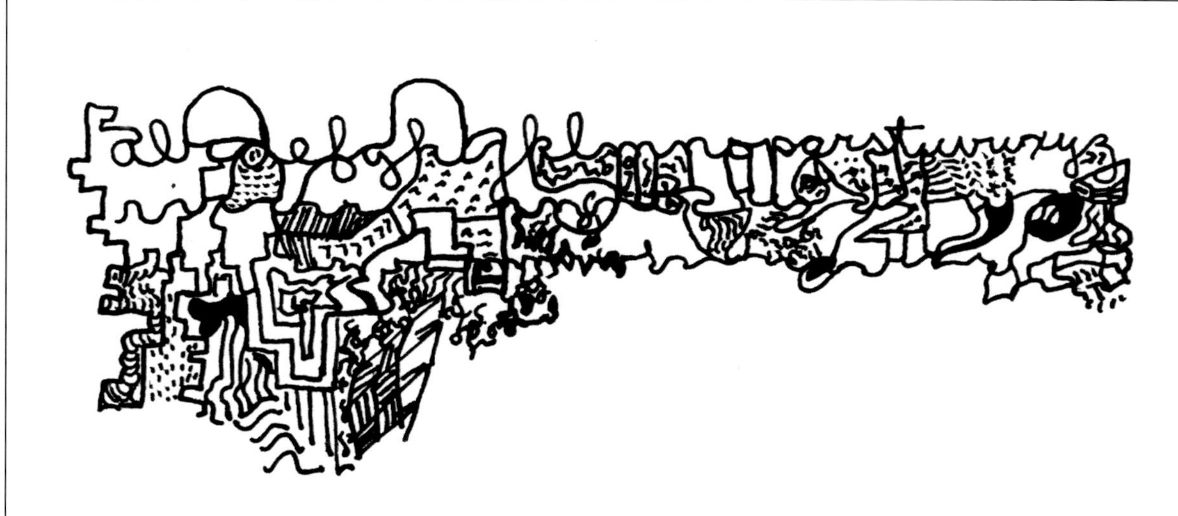

Fig. 1. *College Alphabet*, 1964. Pen and ink on paper; $4\frac{15}{16} \times 6\frac{7}{16}$ in. Collection of Eleanor Himmelfarb.

A grant from the National Endowment for the Arts for Himmelfarb's *Boatman* series allowed the Himmelfarb family to move to Molly's parents' farm in Barnesville, Maryland, for one year beginning in the fall of 1983. There, the artist developed the *Meeting* series, giant brush drawings on paper and canvas. Featuring pairs of big-lipped heads facing each other (sometimes accompanied by a dog), this group of works, which Himmelfarb likened to self-portraits, deals with confrontation and resolution.[3] When the family returned to Illinois in 1984 to a house in suburban Oak Park, they rented out the studio in the city to make ends meet. Between 1984 and 1989, Himmelfarb worked in his living room; as the scale of the *Meeting* series increased, he had to close off windows to have enough wall space to accommodate them.

The *Meeting* drawings were large enough in 1986 for Charlotta Kotik to include two in the exhibition "Monumental Drawings" at the Brooklyn Museum.[4] Even the prints belonging to this series are big. A 40 × 50-inch etching, *Serena Lane Meeting* (no. 67), named for the Himmelfarbs' second child, born in 1986, was made with Rudy Pozzatti at Echo Press at Indiana University, Bloomington. Landfall Press published a 37 × 69-inch color woodcut, *Lumber Street Meeting* (no. 68). The *Meetings* constituted a culmination of all of the artist's previous work, as evidenced by the title "Meetings in the Garden: The Art of John Himmelfarb," given to a large traveling retrospective that opened in September 1989 at the Kalamazoo Institute of Arts.

In the mid-1980s, Himmelfarb revived his interest in ceramics. He collaborated with Duckworth on a project for an animal shelter in Chicago in 1984, and included ceramics in a show of his work at Area X, a gallery in New York's East Village, in 1985. In 1984 he met Juan Gardy Llorens Artigas. His father, the ceramist Josep Llorens Artigas, had worked with Alexander Calder, Joan Miró, and others. Himmelfarb visited the younger Artigas at his studio in Gallifa, Spain, during the summer of 1984. Their friendship resulted in Himmelfarb being the first artist to be invited for a residence in the recently finished studio building at the Fundació Tallers Josep Llorens Artigas in Gallifa, for three weeks in June and July 1989. A grant from Chicago Artists Abroad paid for the trip. Inspired by the black-line murals, accented with touches of red, yellow, and blue, that Miró had made in the same studio, Himmelfarb produced *Catalan*, *Mirorim*, and *Forest*, lithographs printed in 1990–91 (nos. 72, 74–75). Soon thereafter, he made two ceramic tile murals for the Art Omaha program, fabricated at Wilson Tile in Omaha, in which he translated references to Miró's visual vocabulary into his own iconography.

The so-called "non-objective paintings" that were the subject of Himmelfarb's last solo exhibition at the Terry Dintenfass Gallery in the spring of 1991 are in fact not "non-objective," but rather cartoon-like animations of vaginas, penises, and thighs prancing and flying through the air. He intended them as a humorous, satiric commentary on the National Endowment for the Arts' shocking refusal to support artists who produce sexually explicit work.[5] This theme reappears in screenprints that he made with Norman Stewart, a master printer and publisher located in Bloomfield Hills, Michigan, with whom he worked that year for the first time.

Another side of Himmelfarb's nature, his deadpan sense of humor and love of visual and verbal puns, which one sees readily in many of his titles, is illustrated by the postcard he designed to announce the location of his new studio on South Oakley Avenue in Chicago, to which he moved in October 1991 (Fig. 2). On the front of the card, he placed his new address and phone number; on the other side, in the area on the left typically reserved for a message, appears a text using a totally fictitious alphabet, except for the artist's signature. Thus, the card also served to introduce his *Letterform* series, calligraphic fantasies rooted in the alphabet he invented during his freshman year at Harvard.

> I got the idea for this series from . . . a book by O. B. Hardison, Jr., a series of essays called *Disappearing through the Skylight* . . . in which certain parties advocated removing or weakening the meaning of specific words so they could be used in a more playful or plastic manner. That seems humorous to me. Does removing the meaning of words end the possibility of communication? But if you can take the meaning out of words, why not take words out of the text and be left with just the shell form of the text?[6]

Sometimes, Himmelfarb's fake calligraphy resembles Chinese, Japanese, or Korean script. He has been attracted to Asian writing since childhood. He took Chinese newspapers home when he went to Chinatown with his family because he liked the way they looked. In high school, a Japanese exchange student presented him with a Japanese dictionary and taught him to make characters; a college friend of Chinese background gave him lessons in making characters with a brush.[7] Himmelfarb's calligraphy can also invoke Egyptian hieroglyphs, which fascinated the youngster on his visits to Chicago's Field Museum. Musical notation influenced his calligraphic drawings as well. In one instance, he kept music paper, blank except for staff lines, along with original scores by a composer friend, on his drawing board.[8]

Letters and other written documents became the focus of many of his works on paper. Himmelfarb's 1993 screenprint *Short Order* (no. 96) is based on a restaurant or deli bill. Another from the same year, *Note of Appeal* (no. 95), looks like a fundraising letter complete with the names of board members and an official seal at the bottom; the calligraphy appears convincing but is completely invented. As the artist has stated, "I think these letters are part of a dialogue about . . . the difference between visual information and visual art, and [between] visual information about visual art and visual art about visual information!"[9] He moved on to a set of drawings in which he filled the sheet with rows of irregularly shaped boxes, each containing a pictograph. These works, which resemble cracked, ancient tablets, led Himmelfarb once again to ceramics. Pictographic images appear on plates he made for private clients. Others were exhibited in a show of plates by artists at the Fondacio Taller Artigas in the summer of 1994.

By 1995 Himmelfarb's association with Dintenfass had ended and the artist had fully immersed himself in Chicago, both in terms of his life and work. His concern for the environment and interest in the urban landscape led him to join the Board of the Friends of the Chicago River, an organization dedicated to cleaning up and revitalizing the river. He has interpreted the bands of color, or pathways, that weave in and out of the *Inland Romance* series, a theme he began to explore in 1994 in drawings, paintings, and prints, as expressions of the midwestern city's terrain. The images suggest the elevated tracks, highways, bridges, and cranes visible in and around Chicago. He has also stated that they can be read as abstract representations of aerial views of sections of the Midwest for which he has always had an affinity. The paintings and drawings in this series were shown at the Chicago Cultural Center beginning in December 1995.

Increasingly, Himmelfarb's work received attention in Chicago. Following the Cultural Center show, the Evanston Art Center exhibited "Recent Drawings by John Himmelfarb" in March; his prints were included in "Second Sight: Printmaking in Chicago 1935–1995," which opened in September at Northwestern University's Block Museum. A one-person show at the Jean Albano Gallery in September 1996 marked the beginning of a nine-year relationship with a significant Chicago dealer. It featured works from the *Inland Romance* series, drawings made during a second three-week residency at the Fundacio Taller Artigas the previous summer, as well as prints and ceramic tiles. That November Himmelfarb traveled with Chicago dealer Mindy Oh to Korea to see "Cultured Pearl," a show of works by contemporary Korean and American artists that she had organized at the Total Museum of Contemporary Art in Seoul, in which an entire room was devoted to his work.

In two brightly hued screenprints, *Crinkum* and *Crankum* (nos. 105–06),[10] large calligraphic marks merge with the industrial forms seen in the *Inland Romance* series. Wide bands of color seem to form two figures (like man and dog) that are superimposed over a background of the narrower meandering lines of the *Inland Romance* images. Like the earlier *Meetings*, the *Inland Romance* series increased in scale as it developed. As a visiting artist at the Sioux City Art Center in the summer of 1997, Himmelfarb made a 90 × 115-inch drawing, *Sioux City Fandango* (collection of the artist), on which he allowed children who visited his studio to see him work, to make additions, an acknowledgment on the artist's part of the childlike aspects of some of his own work. The art center then invited him to exhibit the *Inland Romance* paintings in November

Fig. 2. Announcement of opening of Himmelfarb's new studio at 2400 S. Oakley Ave., Chicago, 1991. Offset postcard; 4¼ × 6 in.

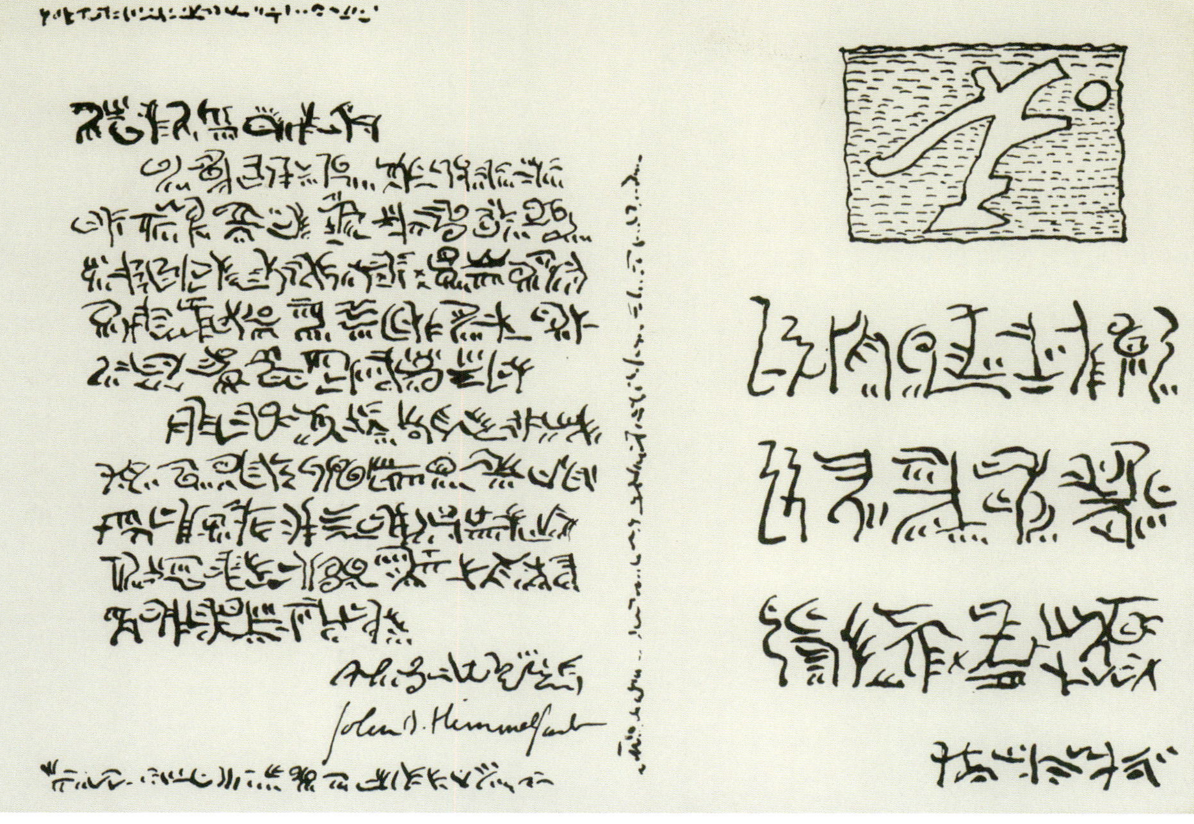

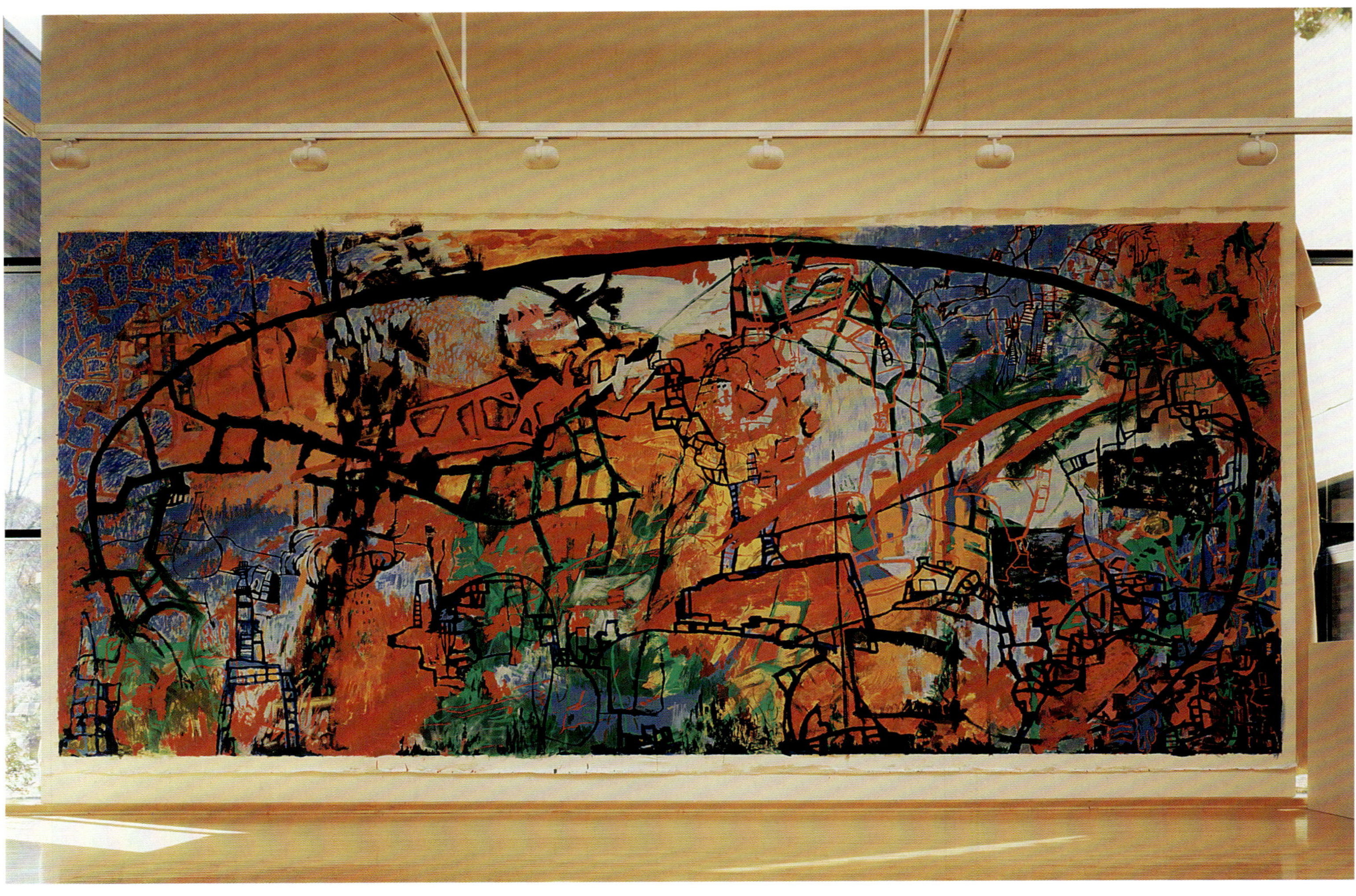

Fig. 3. *Inland Romance: Oakton Circle*, 2001. Acrylic on canvas; 136 × 305½ in. Collection of the artist.

2000. A number of these big, expressive canvases, with their brilliantly colored, swirling pathways and mazes, were displayed dramatically on the white walls of the circular balconies of the museum's three-story open rotunda. The installation was appropriately subtitled "Floor to Ceiling."

Himmelfarb found another great exhibition space for the *Inland Romance* canvases at the Centre of Contemporary Art in Christchurch, New Zealand. When in 1998 the Himmelfarbs visited friends there, the artist met the director of the art center, who offered him a show in August 2001. Himmelfarb returned to Christchurch for the installation, which included a 30-foot-long canvas, *Inland Romance: Nino Rota in Chicago* (collection of the artist). When Nathan Harpaz, curator of the art gallery at Oakton Community College in Des Plaines, Illinois, saw the mural-sized painting in the artist's studio before its departure for New Zealand, he asked the artist to produce three paintings of that style and size for a show. Before he left for New Zealand, Himmelfarb was able to finish two 12 × 30-foot *Inland Romance* paintings. The completion of the third involved the artist in a new challenge. For a month after he returned to Chicago, he staged a performance piece for Oakton College gallery-goers by creating the final work, *Inland Romance: Oakton Circle* (Fig. 3), on the spot. It was successful from every point of view: the gallery considered this an educational opportunity for visitors to learn about the creative process, and the artist found the experience stimulating. One year later, he painted in public a canvas twice that length, *Inland Romance: Gary, Indiana* (collection of the artist) for an exhibition titled "Wall to Wall: John Himmelfarb" at the IUN Gallery at Indiana University Northwest, Gary. As these paintings built up to a large, expressive, and dramatic crescendo, Himmelfarb looked to Miró once again, this time to find a new direction for his smaller works. The drawings he made in 2000 during a stay in Artigas's Paris studio comprise irregularly shaped forms resembling ceramic tiles inscribed with pictographic icons. They were first shown at the Jean Albano Gallery in the fall of that year, along with paintings.

Prints the artist made in 2001 derive from these drawings. *Uzzle* (no. 125), an intaglio print published by UNO Print Workshop at the University of Nebraska, Omaha, evokes a Native American deer hide that is covered with red and black pictographs. *Turandot's Riddles* (no. 135), printed by Richard D. Finch at his workshop in Bloomington, Illinois, for the show in New Zealand, is a perfect example of the kind of mental gymnastics that Himmelfarb enjoys. Puccini's opera was being performed in New Zealand during the run of his show; the print refers to the three riddles the princess posed to her suitors in its arrangement of three different sorts of script—hieroglyphic, pictographic, and calligraphic—in irregularly shaped boxes. Each type is grouped separately at the top and intermixed at the bottom. The screenprints *Theory* and *Practice* (nos. 131 and 133), which Himmelfarb made with Norman Stewart that year, are similar in format, but the boxes are arranged so that their outline describes a larger image. A palette evoking the natural world—ocher, tans, yellows, pale blues and greens on a black ground—is the trademark of this series.

These prints inspired a ceramic-tile mural for the University of Nebraska. The university, which had purchased a large drawing by Himmelfarb, *Imaginary Friends*, for one of its dormitories in 2002, asked him to submit an idea for a mural for the new addition to its graduate school of education. The artist sent a reproduction of *Theory*, suggesting that he could do something like it in tile with education-related icons. The result was two 6 × 12-foot murals fabricated in 2003 by Wilson Tile in Omaha. Another of Himmelfarb's tile murals, *Coast of Chicago,* has been installed recently in Chicago's Kedzie subway station (Fig. 4).[11] And, most recently, Delta Airlines commissioned two 15 × 20-foot paintings for its Terminal A at Logan Airport, Boston (Fig. 5).

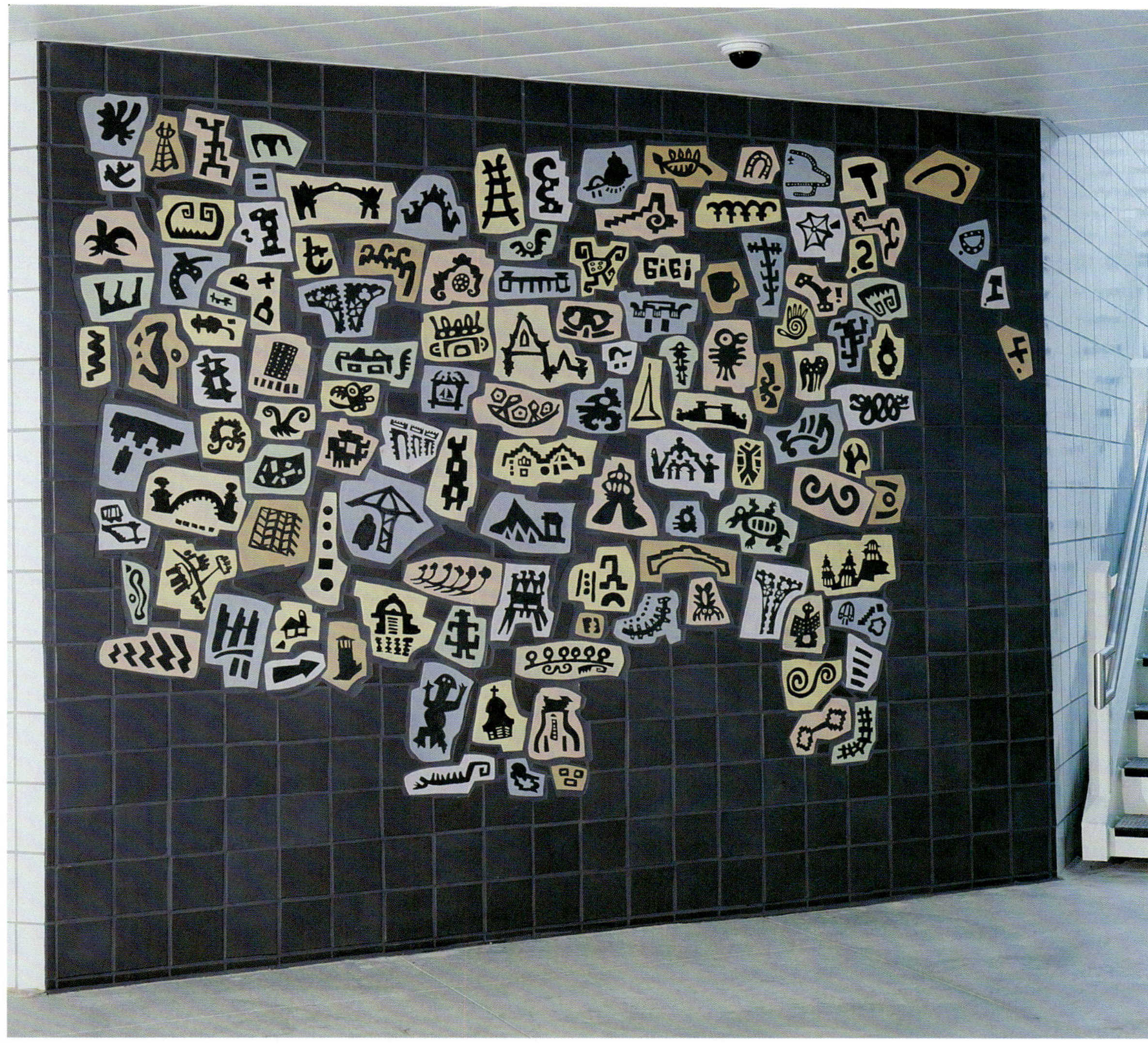

Fig. 4. *Coast of Chicago*, 2004. Ceramic tile; 108 × 144 in. Chicago Transit Authority's Kedzie station, in the 1900 block of S. Kedzie Ave., Chicago.

Each new life experience seems to suggest a fresh idea to Himmelfarb. When the library of the Laboratory School of the University of Chicago, where his wife continues to teach, recently switched to an electronic catalogue, the artist took the old library cards without knowing what he wanted to do with them.[12] He began to draw on them and now carries them along when he travels, making "diary entries," as he likes to call them, when he has to wait somewhere, or recording on them things he has seen and liked (Figs. 6–7).[13] Himmelfarb focused intensively on the cards during a 2002 visit to a cousin living in the Ecuadorian jungle. While serving as a visiting artist at the University of Wisconsin–Milwaukee in 2002, he began a lithograph called *Handbook* (no. 141), a composite image made from his drawings on two library cards—one of some of

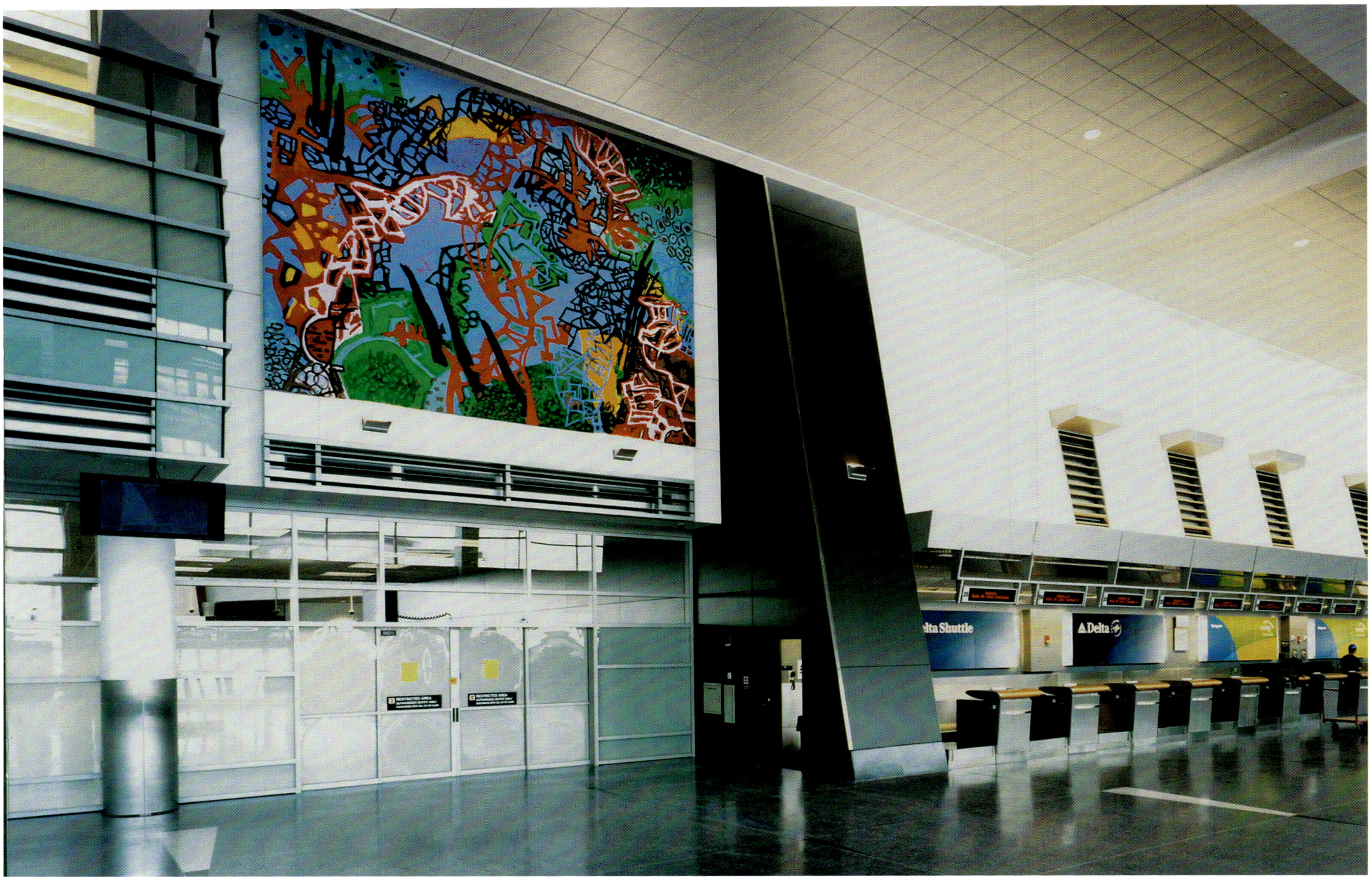

Fig. 5. *A Small Gain in Altitude*, 2005. Acrylic on canvas; 185 × 239 in. Boston, Logan Airport, Delta Airlines Terminal A.

Leonardo da Vinci's inventions, and the other of insects illustrated in a natural-history book.

Although he tends to produce in series, Himmelfarb sees every work as a step to something else. Perhaps a recollection from childhood will surface from his subconscious to inspire a new series. Maybe some national or international political event will demand protest. Yet another focus may arise after his first visit to Brooklyn since 1989 for exhibitions of his work in April 2005 at the Brooklyn campus of Long Island University and the Phyllis Stigliano Gallery. I eagerly await the surprise of seeing where John Himmelfarb's muse will lead him next.

NOTES

1. Helen Sheridan, "Interview," *Meetings in the Garden: The Art of John Himmelfarb, Kalamazoo Institute of Arts Bulletin* 75 (1989), p. 18.

2. Ibid.

3. Ibid., p. 9.

4. Around this time, I met Himmelfarb when he visited the Brooklyn Museum, where I had recently become Curator of Prints and Drawings, to show me some of his prints.

5. Conversation with the artist, August 2004.

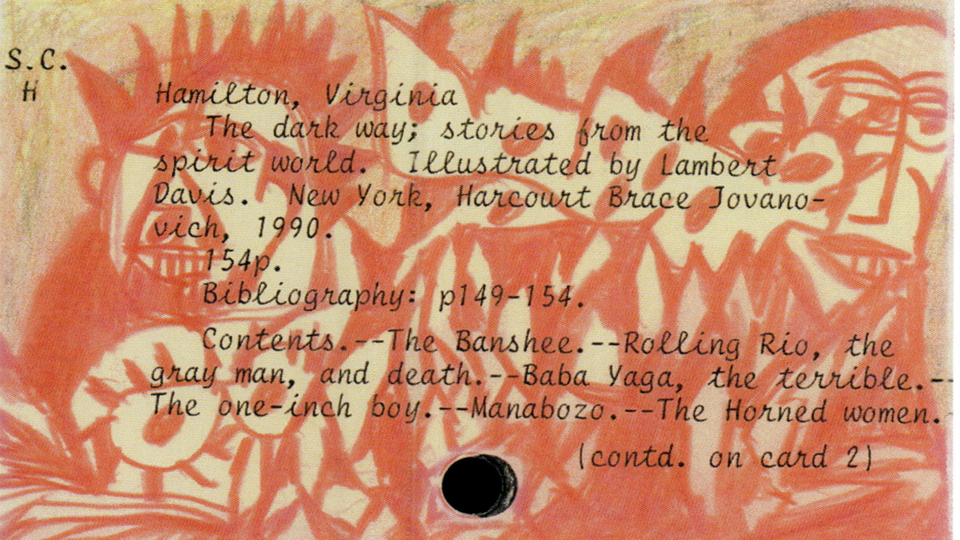

Fig. 6. *Baba Yaga*, 2003. Colored pencil on library catalogue card; 3 × 5 in. Collection of the artist.

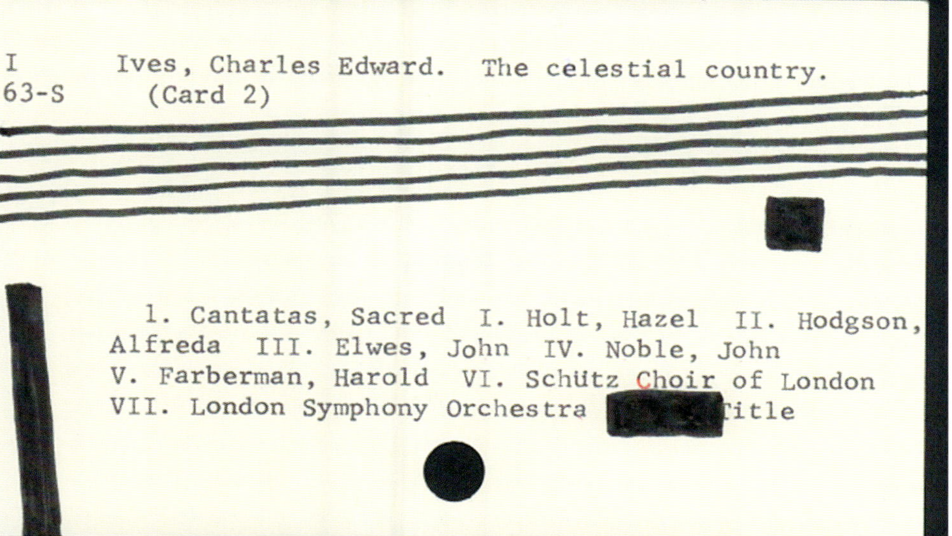

Fig. 7. *London Choir Invaded by Reds*, 2004. Pen and ink on library catalogue card; 3 × 5 in. Collection of the artist.

6. "Five New Prints by John Himmelfarb," *Journal of the Print World* 17, 1 (winter 1994).

7. Susan Stewart, interview with John Himmelfarb, in *Contemporary Impressions: Journal of the American Print Alliance* 2, 2 (fall 1994), p. 16.

8. Ibid., p. 19.

9. "John Himmelfarb, 'Fax Appeal,' 'First Draft,' 'Note of Appeal,' 'Short Order,' White Out,'" *Print Collectors Newsletter* 25, 1 (Mar.–Apr. 1994).

10. Impressions of these prints are now in the British Museum, London.

11. After seeing a photograph of these murals, my husband and I asked Himmelfarb to design a tile back-splash for the newly renovated kitchen in our New York home. It is similar in style to the Nebraska murals.

12. Email from the artist, Oct. 4, 2004.

13. The cards were the focus of an exhibition, "The Borrower's Name," held at Phyllis Stigliano Gallery in Brooklyn, New York, April 8–30, 2005.

Building on Literature, Music, and Modernism:

The Prints of John Himmelfarb

Michael Bonesteel,
Arts Writer and Critic, Chicago

. . . he seemed to see how life flowed into art: how art gives life a form and meaning and flows on into life, yet life has not stood still; that was what was always forgotten: how life transformed by art sought further meaning through art transformed by life. . . .

— MALCOLM LOWRY
Dark As the Grave Wherein My Friend Is Laid

We are just approaching the realization that past and future have no real meaning in art, or in life for that matter. How long these will remain the favorite fictions of art historians is anybody's guess.

— JACK BURNHAM
Great Western Salt Works

JOHN HIMMELFARB CAME OF AGE at a time when the supposed last gasp of modernism in the form of Abstract Expressionism was giving way to the new Minimalist schools of painting and sculpture on the one hand, and Pop Art on the other. Soon, the 1970s brought forth newer, ever more anti-romantic, cerebral, and political movements: conceptual art, earth art, feminist art, installation art, performance art, It would take another decade before the art world, starving for traditional painterly beauty, would succumb to revisiting modernism's most enduring approach in the guise of Neo-Expressionism, playing with it, of course, with a coolly ironic tongue planted firmly in its postmodern cheek. But from the beginning, Himmelfarb was on his own path, out of step with the trends of the 1970s, quietly going about his own business. The cartoon sensibility of Chicago Imagism à la the Hairy Who is echoed distantly in the caricatured realism of his early work, but it quickly evolved into a raw, unpolished, and unselfconscious expressionism that cannot quite be called "Neo," and further still, in more experimental directions. There is little that is postmodern about Himmelfarb's art. Even when he professes to have been responding to deconstructionism in the early 1990s with his abstract Asian calligraphic work, his response is pure, sincere Mark Tobey–style Abstract Expressionism.

Beginning as a late modernist in the last quarter of the twentieth century, Himmelfarb has now taken the movement into the twenty-first century. And it ain't necessarily so that, once we have passed into a new era, what is past automatically becomes passé. Artists who chose to work in a modernist mode can continue to make vital and interesting art, just as those committed to traditional realism or any other older school can revitalize it with vision and originality. If there is anything truly postmodern about Himmelfarb's art, it is the fact that he has transcended the modernist obsession with "making it new." Or as he observed, he has not rebelled against what previous modernists

opposite page.
NO. 144, *Xtra Xtra*, 2003–04.

accomplished, but instead, has built on those accomplishments.[1]

Himmelfarb's print oeuvre from 1967 to 2004, much like his paintings and drawings over these years, can be separated roughly into a half-dozen succinct, but sometimes related, bodies of work: Landscapes and Cityscapes, Individuals and Groups, Grid Works, Letterform Works, Maps and Bridges, and Narrative Puzzle Pieces. They are for the most part enduring journeys and explorations that continually lead to new discoveries, even when returned to years later and embarked upon once again. To be sure, Landscapes and Cityscapes and Individuals and Groups are two common genres that have supported entire careers of many artists. Himmelfarb's Letterform series, like the Grid Works and Maps and Bridges, constitutes a foray into abstraction, but one that proved more fertile and productive for his prints. There are occasional anomalies, like his Abstract Expressionist pieces, although even in his figurative works, the lure of the non-representational is always lurking in the background, just pulling at the edges of the picture plane; conversely, his abstractions often threaten to resolve themselves into figuration.[2] And there are certain hybrids: his anthropomorphic abstract works, which draw from both Landscapes and Cityscapes and Individuals and Groups; and the Narrative Puzzle Pieces, which combine aspects of his Letterform Works with Individuals and Groups.

Landscapes and Cityscapes

One of the first prints Himmelfarb made as an undergraduate at Harvard University, *College Etching* (no. 1), reflects a significant bend toward abstraction that has reappeared and evolved throughout his career. This 1967 piece is basically a study in curvilinear parallel lines describing space. Unfolding organically, the work builds on repeated contours reminiscent of water ripples, wood grains, or plaits of combed hair. He took care to keep his lines from overlapping or creating cross-hatching, an exercise that would become habitual in his later works, such as his *Meeting* series (nos. 57–58, 66–71) and in *Lava Flow Part II* (no. 65). Ultimately, the study is a purely decorative exercise, yet it betrays an intuitive quality that relates to Himmelfarb's abiding interest in Surrealist automatism. As in his later works, this abstract composition suggests the figurative in the way that configurations of abstract shapes such as clouds or tree bark seem to invite the reading-in of animals, facial features, or human appendages. This student piece foreshadows the artist's attraction to Asian calligraphy and pictograms: one can almost see the possibility of a Chinese dragon collecting itself within the image's linear folds. The hiding of natural, animal, human, and man-made elements within what initially appears to be an abstract composition was an inclination that Himmelfarb would actualize and refine in much of his subsequent work.

Another print of the same year, *Millock Mountain* (no. 4), depicts an actual landscape. The slope of a hill covered by scumbled markings and shadings occupies nearly half of the composition on the left. In the center, a triangular mountain is described with fewer marks, as if located in the far, hazy distance. The white space of the sky takes up more than one-third of the total sheet, while other patches of white occupy the immediate foreground and the triangular suggestion of what appears to be a body of water midway up on the far right. *Millock Mountain* is in many respects a study of textures, as Himmelfarb assembled a vocabulary of marks to describe rock formations and foliage. One can just begin to distinguish fissures, crevices, and outcroppings from shrubs and grasses. While this is a straightforward, realistic rendering of a landscape, without the slightest hint of anthropomorphic forms, such forms are only sleeping, hibernating so to speak, as latent possibilities within the organic shapes that abound here.

A third print completed during Himmelfarb's college years, *Industrial Etching* (no. 2), is a linear rendering of the kind of early-twentieth-century industrial structures and machinery one can still see when traveling between Chicago and Gary, Indiana: elevated bridges, towers, smokestacks, pipelines, warehouses, oil refineries, storage tanks, and railroad tracks. Although more realistic and simplified than the 1999 lithograph *Boca* (no. 118), which recalls *Industrial Etching* in spirit and subject matter, it represents a third interest that would preoccupy Himmelfarb for the duration of his career: man-made environments.

Industrial Etching marks the first appearance of Himmelfarb's practice of compiling figurative images. As mentioned above, he was aware of

Surrealist automatism, but he was not really attempting to implement that procedure in any formal way. It was more a matter of trying to draw as rapidly as possible without thinking too much. Things seem to have tumbled out onto the drawing surface in stream-of-consciousness fashion. This approach, akin to playing a game of mental and visual free-association, consistently threads its way through much of Himmelfarb's subsequent figurative work, right up to the recent Narrative Puzzle Pieces.

After completing his formal education, the young artist returned to his hometown, Chicago, where he tried his hand at making lithographs with Jack Lemon at Landfall Press. By his own admission, Himmelfarb has recalled, he did not even know what a lithograph was. Lemon showed him how to draw on decal transfer paper and slide it off onto a lithographic stone. In the three years that had ensued since the fledgling artist's first undergraduate experiments with printmaking and his next foray into the medium, his drawing and painting skills had grown considerably. Each of the three works executed at Landfall in 1970—*Untitled*, *Landfall Two*, and *Crane Mountain*—exhibit an increasing confidence gained from having spent time in the studio working on pen-and-ink drawings.

There is a stylized quality to Himmelfarb's approach in each of these three works, which he has described as "industrial/rural landscapes." In fact, he would never again—except for a singular throwback etching, *Unknown View* (no. 28) in 1976—incorporate such a highly stylized approach, but rather would move inexorably toward expressionism, both figurative and abstract. While the 1970 lithographs appear from a distance to be highly detailed, unpopulated land formations, upon closer inspection we discover unexpected figurative elements. In *Untitled (Landfall)* (no. 5), emerging from the tangle of lines appearing to be rocks, foliage, and areas of white space delineating hills and valleys are objects resembling eyeballs, breasts, the cartoonish profile of a face, and the inside of a rowboat. *Landfall Two* (no. 6) contains somewhat smaller details and is a less exact, sketchier rendering. Both lithographs suggest rambling fragments of land, selective "islands" that may or may not be surrounded by water. *Crane Mountain* (no. 7), on the other hand, fills nearly all of the surface except for white space above a variegated horizon line and various "empty" pockets or outcroppings in the landscape. The entire composition appears alive, teeming and bristling with dense detail. Abstract forms are piled chock-a-block with building facades, towers, roofs, stairways, tunnels, bridges, roads, and other industrial forms. The work's title derives from the tiny depiction of an electromagnetic crane located at the bottom left.

At this point, Himmelfarb's artist father, Samuel, suggested that his son attempt a traditional black-crayon lithograph, so he created *Ether Ore* (no. 8). Highly detailed like his first three Landfall prints, this 1971 work is an all-over, wall-to-wall tangle of shapes and marks. The use of a litho crayon gives it a loose, even "scribbly," expressionistic texture. There is a suggestion of representational forms, but nothing is delineated in any recognizable way. While technically the lithograph can still be called a "landscape," it is a highly abstract one. As I have written elsewhere, "*Ether Ore* is basically an orchestrated jumble of doodling, and yet, however abstract, it appears to be something. Certainly, it is organic; perhaps a topographical view of a jungle or a slice of mud on a microscope slide. The punning title indicates that it is a precious component of a transcendent dimension."[3] This print marks the beginning of what would become a trademark approach for Himmelfarb, that of using puns in his titles, reflecting his interest in writing and literature. Many years later, in the 1990s, he would indulge that interest visually in his *Pictogram* series.

Himmelfarb's first print dealer, William van Straaten, warned him that customers generally shy away from black-and-white work; nevertheless, van Straaten's Chicago gallery immediately sold a number of his black-and-white Landfall Press prints. Soon, Lemon set about showing the young artist how to do his first color lithograph, using different plates for each shade and creating secondary hues by printing one primary color over another. *Salad* (no. 9) is a thicket of abstract and figurative puzzle-piece shapes in bright colors that amounts to a kind of whimsical still life influenced by Pop Art, which Himmelfarb had been looking at. The absence of the keyline around each form, revealing the slightly overlapping registrations, lends the image a cartoon-like and deliberately unresolved quality. By drawing shapes and filling them in with color, Himmelfarb was attempting to approximate in printmaking the kind of approach he was employing in his paintings, applying bright and unmodulated areas of color within his figurative forms. He would later return to the use of broad, flat areas of color in several larger, ever more ambitious, and clearly figurative lithographs executed in 1973 (*Filming of "Sunny Days"*; no. 20), 1975 (*The Clock and the Rose*; no. 22), and 1981 (*Storyteller*; no. 40). They comprise the biggest and brightest among the collective body of work referred to as Landscapes and Cityscapes.

Ten Prints from Dark As the Grave

Next, Himmelfarb embarked upon a ten-print suite at Landfall Press loosely based upon Malcolm Lowry's posthumously published novel, *Dark As the Grave Wherein My Friend Is Laid* (1968). Just as he had admired Lowry's beautiful and tortured masterpiece, *Under the Volcano*, Himmelfarb was attracted to *Dark As the Grave*'s intensity and use of language.

In this print series, Himmelfarb cut loose with a flurry of various styles and approaches, using litho crayons on some, brush and tusche on others; he seems to have worked in a frenzied attack mode in certain works and in a more contemplative pen and ink style in others.[4] In this ten-part journey, which occupied the artist for about one year, he explored many avenues of expression that he would return to and develop later on. As I have noted, "Like the aesthetic woodsman that he is, we find him backtracking throughout his career, moving forward into new territory, then retreating to an old trail; blazing that one a bit further, then returning to the first path any number of years later."[5]

Apparently, Himmelfarb's working method was not unlike that of Lowry when writing *Dark As the Grave*. Douglas Day, in his preface to the first edition, observed that the novel is divided into three distinct texts. Nonetheless, Day wrote, "We found out very quickly that Lowry had not really worked through the three texts consecutively—that, instead, he had done an uncommon amount of backing and filling, of retracing his steps, of setting off on false starts, and even of throwing in a good deal of material that belonged elsewhere, in other novels and stories ('just for safekeeping,' as he would say)."[6] Himmelfarb found the title of each work in the 1971 series in the first sentence of *Dark As the Grave*. Here is the original opening text, with the artist's selections boldfaced:

> The **sense of speed**, of gigantic **transition**, of going southward, downward, over **three countries**, the tremendous mountain ranges, the sense at once of **descent**, tremendous **regression**, and of moving, not moving, but in another way dropping straight down the **world**, straight down the **map**, as the **imminence** of something great, phenomenal, and yet the **moving shadow** of the plane below them, the eternal moving cross, less fleeting and more substantial than the dim shadow of the significance of **what they were actually doing** that Sigbjorn held in his mind. . . .[7]

Himmelfarb took a few liberties with Lowry's vocabulary, however: lifting "world" and "map" out of context, putting them together, and converting the first word into a pun ("whirled").

The first print, *Descent* (no. 10), the only litho line engraving in Himmelfarb's oeuvre, is drawn with a stylus over a gummed stone. In this image, creatures resembling dinosaurs prowl across a convoluted landscape defined in muted peacock blues. He followed this with *Imminence* (no. 11), an almost graffiti-like work in yellow and green, executed with felt-tip on acetate. *What They Were* (no. 12) seems to address the subject of violence and war. The combination here of dark-blue expressionist figures over patches of light blue and yellow is breathtaking: one figure appears to grow out of another or seems simply to rip through the loose tapestry of forms and patterns to accost the viewer, like the tank/armored-car operator in the lower center of the composition.

Sense of Speed (no. 13) is a scribble-fest in yellow, orange, and pink that explores Abstract Expressionist action-drawing techniques like those of Cy Twombly. *Regression* (no. 14) contains cartoonish figures executed in bold, dark-blue lines. *Actually Doing* (no. 16) and *Whirled Map* (no. 17) are mylar drawings transferred to photosensitive plates. The first is more abstract, featuring a riot of intersecting blue, yellow, red-orange, green, and purple linear forms. The similar size of the shapes, as well as the absence of solid patches of underlying color, gives the image a flattened appearance. The liberating influence of Paul Klee's and Joan Miró's whimsical work can be felt strongly here for the first time. Himmelfarb had previously sought to achieve such effects in his India-ink drawings, but was not satisfied with his efforts until he completed these two prints. Several years later, he attempted to respond to color-field paintings like those of Brice Marden in a 1975 mylar transfer work called *Home* (no. 25). Using a palette similar to that of *Actually Doing*, he created a larger, more complex, and more abstract image (except for an occasional face or head emerging from the tangle of multicolored lines).

Recognizable figures emerge in *Whirled Map*: cartoonish birds, fish, and mammals. The artist laid down an initial run of flat, green patches, allowing for generous pockets of white; then, a layer of small, lime-green linear forms; and finally over these larger, dark-blue linear shapes. All three colors are distributed evenly across the busy surface. The resulting impression is one of figures populating a landscape that suggests palpable, three-dimensional depth. Around the same time, Himmelfarb executed *Moving Shadow* (no. 15), a meditation on a tasteful array of colors he had encountered while jogging along Lake Michigan: silver, light blue, and green. These he scribbled or applied solidly inside organic forms evocative of the lakefront's large rocks.

Printed in black on a blue-white background, *Transition* (no. 18), an almost perfect amalgamation of abstract and representational forms, seems to best capture the moody atmosphere and somber surrealism of *Dark As the Grave*. Himmelfarb used a litho crayon, pen and autographic ink, and negro pencil to create a washlike effect in this murky, rather gothic, landscape. The topsy-turvy viaducts and arches appearing to careen dangerously downward evoke the figurative and literal direction taken by the novel's opening sentence. *Transition* seems like a warped version of a vaulted construction by G. B. Piranesi. Himmelfarb noted in conversation that a modern civilization burying itself in its own garbage is not unlike the eighteenth-century printmaker's romantic evocations of a fallen Rome. Thus, in *Transition* the artist found a voice for his social perspective and planted a subliminal message in his imagery about the capacity of civilization to implode upon itself.

The last work in the series, *Three Countries* (no. 19), is a dramatic departure from the others. Utilizing a rainbow roll, Himmelfarb created three horizontal bands of color: pink at the top, yellow on the bottom, and an orange-red combination of the two where they blend in the middle. Boldly drawn with brush and ink on acetate over each of the three zones are rows of fanciful animals marching in single file. The extremely primitive manner in which they are depicted evokes the faux Art Brut style of Jean Dubuffet. Like the French artist, Himmelfarb responds to the work of both academically and self-taught artists, to the modernist avant-garde and idiosyncratic visionary work. Thus, one finds in Himmelfarb's art, as one does in that of Dubuffet and such CoBrA artists as Pierre Alechinsky and Karel Appel (both of whom the artist admires), a technical sophistication informing spontaneous, intuitive expression. Of course, this is the creative process for many artists, but perhaps more so for old-fashioned (pardon the oxymoron) modernists and their spiritual heirs like Himmelfarb.

Lithos on a Roll

After non-stop printmaking throughout 1971, it is not surprising that Himmelfarb devoted himself to painting and drawing for the next few years. In 1974 he returned to the printmaking studio to create his large-scale *Filming of "Sunny Days"* (no. 20), a work that, as already mentioned, harks back to his 1971 print *Salad* and reflects the direction his paintings were taking at this time.

One night that year, he found that he was "on a roll." He stayed up until dawn to draw two very different, yet intricate and highly complex, lithographs: *Blue Bird* (no. 24) in dark blue and white, and the black and white *March* (no. 21).[8] *Blue Bird* is a landscape cluttered with Himmelfarb's typical vocabulary of a multitude of curiously juxtaposed elements: a building whose windows provide a view of the outdoors, a toilet seat, a refrigerator—everything but (yet probably including) the kitchen sink—surrounding a classic image of an odalisque just left of center. Reclining on a bed, which sits on a tiled floor, the woman holds a female symbol—a circle topped with a cross—in her raised hand, and a duck rests

Fig. 1. *7/9/1976* (detail), 1976. Pen and ink on paper; 24 × 24 in. Present whereabouts unknown.

on her shoulder. In this homage to feminism, as Himmelfarb has interpreted it, the woman is fully in control of her surroundings, even though the scene seems totally chaotic.

Finishing *Blue Bird* in the middle of the night, but still feeling energized and eager, he took up another aluminum plate and attacked it with a litho crayon. This work, which he titled *March*, is in some ways just that: a steady, rhythmic, and orchestrated parade of forms and variations moving from top to bottom across the picture plane. A violinist and pianist, Himmelfarb has always maintained an intimate connection with music. Although he stopped playing the piano upon entering Harvard, he continued performing in the first-violin section of the college orchestra until about the time he decided to concentrate on visual art. A practice he developed early on required that he prepare to make work by reading and/or listening to music of Bach, Beethoven, and Brahms, or, as the mood suited him, the Beatles, Doors, or Procol Harem.

Unlike *Blue Bird*, *March* reveals the artist taking a far more formal and controlled approach. He began with very small shapes, densely packed together at the top, gradually increasing their size as he moved toward the bottom. This was in part because in the course of working so intensely, he had developed blisters on one of his fingers and was anxious to finish. With objects appearing larger and closer in the foreground and gradually receding into smaller forms in the distance, the image offers the distinct impression of looking at a "city" of rounded buildings, bridges, viaducts, tables, and abstract forms, all appearing as though they had been shaped from slabs of rock, like one would see in a "Flintstones" television cartoon show from the 1960s. Or, more aptly, they resemble the stonelike formations of Dubuffet's walk-through sculpture *Winter Garden* (1968–70; Paris, Musée d'Art Moderne, Centre Pompidou), or the architectural environments he built on his property in Périgny-sur-Yerres, *Closerie* and *Villa Falbala* (1971–76), both examples of his Hourloupe style.

In 1976 Himmelfarb did several prints with Stone Roller Press in Chicago: the previously mentioned *Unknown View* and two black-and-white lithographs containing numerous, barely recognizable figurative shapes embedded in cross-hatching, *Flag* (no. 26) and the larger, denser *Single Cell* (no. 27). Using pen and autographic ink on the aluminum plate required quick and constant movement so that the ink would not pool. After it dried, he went back in and built up light and dark areas with hatching. Although he had incorporated this technique in his work from the very beginning, it is more evident in these two prints than in any he had done before.

That same year, Himmelfarb executed three very different black-and-white images that might be seen as forerunners to the Individuals and Groups category: *Rider* (no. 29), *16 Cases* (no. 30), and *Skateboard* (no. 31). The only precedent to this type of work was the keyline print originally meant to outline the 1974–75 lithograph *The Clock and the Rose* (no. 22), but that was printed separately as a simpler black-and-white piece, *Shades* (no. 23). However, because it corresponds to the colored shapes of *The Clock and the Rose*, *Shades* is carefully delineated, whereas

Rider, *Skateboard*, and *16 Cases*—featuring very loose execution with overlapping doodled lines—are almost Thurber- or Calder-esque in their whimsy, featuring a far more loose execution. In all three works, Himmelfarb's human and animal caricatures are presented in a straightforward, uncomplicated way.

Early Riser (no. 32), of 1976–77, is the artist's only soft-ground etching and the first etching since *Millock Mountain*. It is divided into a series of fifty-four separate, framed panels arranged horizontally, six across and nine down. The print looks at first to be a take-off on a comic book, but upon closer inspection, one notices that there is no real narrative progression, just the suggestion of one. The only device connecting the little images is a number of figures and objects that start in one panel and continue into the adjoining one. Himmelfarb has noted that this work grew out of a number of previous drawings containing columns and rows of boxes that were abstract at first, and then later became more narrative with the addition of anthropomorphic forms (see Fig. 1). The impulse for these drawings was the program notes for a concert Himmelfarb attended of music by Bach, which illustrated the first four bars of one of the works performed. The notes explained that the entire composition was a play on those first four bars. It occurred to the artist that he might do something similar: he could draw four panels or boxes, each containing a certain vocabulary of marks or images that he would then rearrange in subsequent panels. *Early Riser* also reflects his admiration for the ability of novelists to create dense narratives with deep layers of meaning. The approach he used here led him directly to his Grid Works and later to the Narrative Puzzle Pieces.

Expressionism Unleashed; Grid Works Revived

The New York dealer Terry Dintenfass began representing Himmelfarb in 1977 and offered to give him a one-person exhibition in 1979. Dintenfass encouraged the artist to paint whatever he wanted for the show, which liberated him to a great degree. He bought a number of cans of cheap house paint and began to make some of the most wildly uninhibited figurative images of his career. This body of work proved to be a harbinger of the kind of painting that would soon become cutting-edge in New York. The first of these canvases, *Egos* (Fig. 2), featuring two

Fig. 2. *Egos*, 1978. Acrylic on canvas; 48 × 96 in. Private collection, New York.

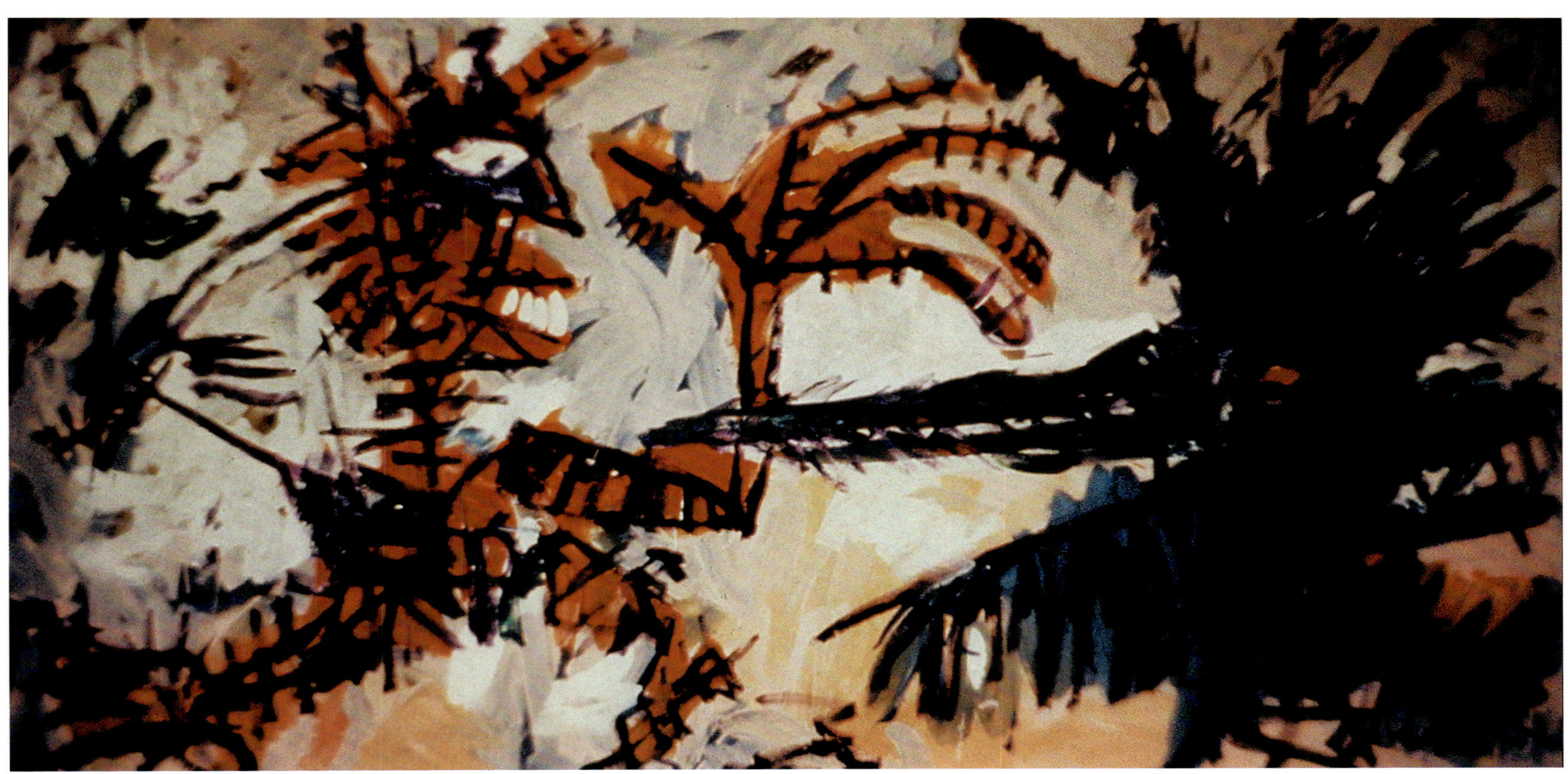

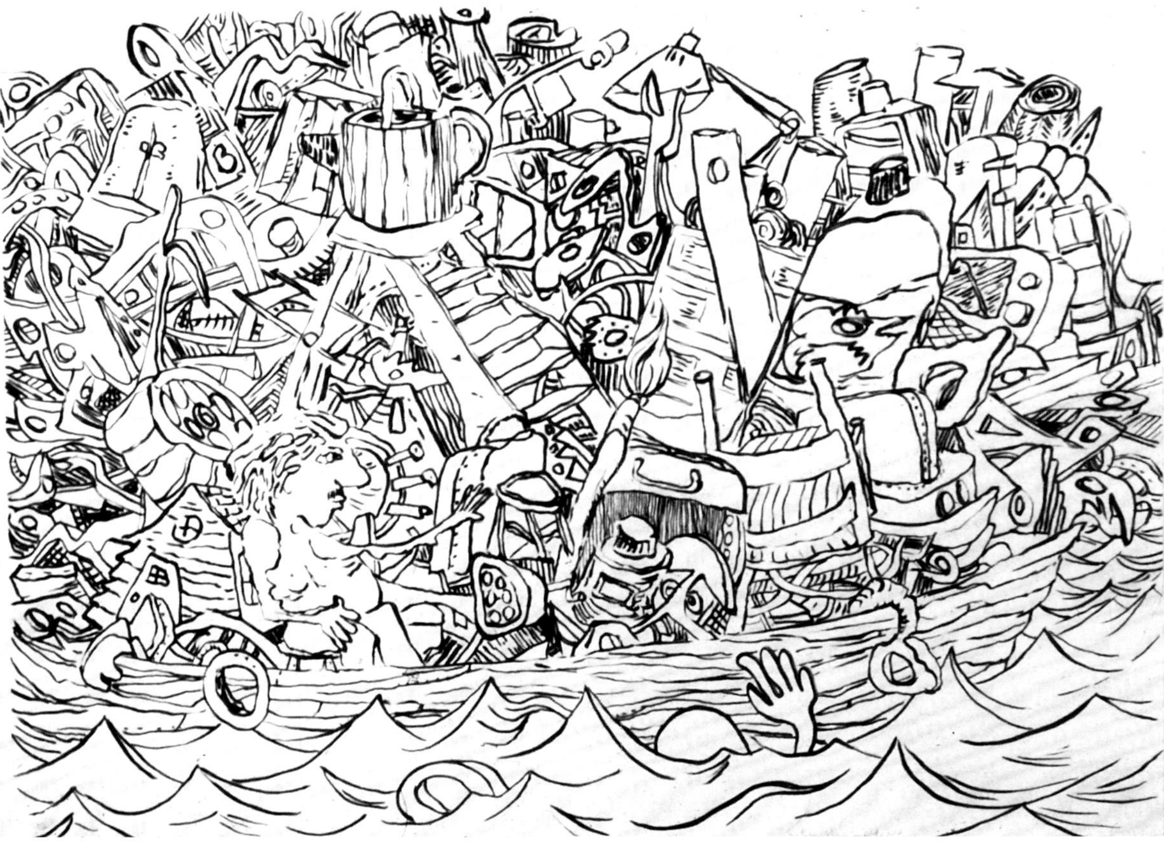

Fig. 3. *Underway*, 1982. From the *Boatman* series. Brush and ink on paper; 22 × 30 in. Collection of Molly Day.

figures facing each other in a threatening manner, inaugurated a series that he would later refine in his prints *Bone* (no. 44), *Principle of Uncertainty* (no. 49), and *Balance Sheet* (no. 42). He had been exploring the idea of two figures meeting face-to-face in a number of images in the mid-1970s, all rendered in a tight, controlled manner. With *Egos*, Himmelfarb found a new direction and the centerpiece for his display at Dintenfass. But, alas, the exhibition that he envisioned never took place.

Before the show opened, Dintenfass took a leave of absence and temporarily turned over the operation of her gallery to someone who did not care for the development called Neo-Expressionism, and disliked Himmelfarb's *Egos* in particular. Attempting to come up with something that would appeal to his sensibility, Himmelfarb decided to produce a number of prints along the lines of grid-style drawings he had made during his fall 1979 residency at Yaddo, an artist's retreat in Saratoga Springs, New York. At that time, he had embarked upon a series of black-and-white drawings in the manner of Agnes Martin or Jennifer Bartlett, incorporating grids divided up in different ways, some completely abstract, others containing iconic forms. As the grids became denser with cross-hatching, they began to suggest shapes and resemble folds in fabric.

Grid prints initiated in 1979—*Similar Sounds* (no. 35), *Plot Outline* (no. 37), and *Night Life* (no. 36)—evolved from drawings such as his 1978 *Should I Have Said More?* (collection of the artist). In another print, *Words Cannot Describe* (no. 33), the grid looks more like a series of horizontal bars filled with parallel lines slanting in different directions. Vague geometric and figurative forms are hinted at, but the image is extremely subtle and, for the most part, abstract. *Short Story* (no. 38) presents a grid of thirty-six rectangles filled with a looser pattern of noodle shapes suggesting faces or caverns encrusted with stalactites. Although not many of the drawings or prints in the exhibition sold, several institutions made purchases, including the Brooklyn Museum and the Rose Art Museum at Brandeis University.

Individuals and Groups

With the large-scale color lithograph *Storyteller* (no. 40), made in 1981 at Plucked Chicken Press, operated in Chicago by Will Peterson and his wife, Cynthia Archer, one begins to notice a definite shift from Himmelfarb's Landscapes and Cityscapes to the category identified here as Individuals and Groups. *Storyteller* is actually a combination of the two: it is a landscape of sorts like a number of his previous works, but one populated by people, most notably, several couples. Virginia Woolf's *To the Lighthouse* and Charles Dickens's *Our Mutual Friend* served as inspirations for some of the images in this piece. A rowboat plays a significant role in both these novels. In the latter, a man dredges a river looking for bodies and ends up filling his boat with all sorts of strange objects he has pulled up. In the former, a family takes a long-awaited day trip on a boat. Although little is said during this excursion, the charged atmosphere Woolf described reminded Himmelfarb of the term "emotional baggage." Thus, in *Storyteller*, a rowboat contains a number of items. Soon this image would take center stage in his *Boatman* series (see Fig. 3).

Back in 1976, Himmelfarb had created, as we have seen, a trio of prints dominated by figures: *Rider*, *16 Cases*, and *Skateboard*. He now repeated this experiment with three related group portraits. These, and most of the other prints he did in 1981–82, focus on a single interchange rather than multiple ones. Two couples and a threesome—all nude and caricatured in a Picasso-esque way—appear to be talking and, perhaps, dancing in *Home and Garden* (no. 39), *Trio* (no. 41), and *Bridge* (no. 45). *Home and Garden* and *Trio* resemble brush drawings, but the artist actually achieved this look with a liquid ground of asphaltum. The artist's 1981 painting *Night Return* (Fig. 4) set the tone—literally black and white—for much of his work in 1982. Between 1981 and 1983, Himmelfarb made ten black-and-white (as well as two prints in color) at Plucked Chicken.

The *Boatman* series contains a number of black-and-white, brushed-ink–like paintings depicting a man in a boat loaded with objects. With each successive canvas, the boat's contents increase, to the point that it finally sinks. Two prints made in response to the *Boatman* paintings are: *Boatman* (no. 43), which shows the titular figure with gritted teeth weighed down by material possessions to the point that the boat's hull is barely visible above the waves; and its companion piece, *Clearing* (no. 46), comprised of elements like hands, eyes, and teeth jumbled together, apparently depicting the flotsam and jetsam on the surface of the water after the boat has sunk. The print's title indicates the artist's wish to suggest the end of an apocalyptic, even biblical, event.

Another group of related prints that Himmelfarb made at Plucked Chicken in 1982 includes *Bone* (no. 44), *Principle of Uncertainty* (no. 49), and *Balance Sheet* (no. 42). The image common to all three sprang from *Egos*, which, as noted above, features two people confronting each other. In *Bone* a primitive figure on the right, its complexity bordering on the ornate, tosses a many-pronged rib bone to an equally eccentric dog on the left. Based on Himmelfarb's observation of a stray dog gnawing on a bone in the alley behind his studio, the image, according to the artist, symbolizes the meaningless gestures of the power elite toward the needy, offering scraps rather than substantive help.

In *Principle of Uncertainty* and *Balance Sheet*, Himmelfarb juxtaposed two recent themes: the confrontation of *Bone* and the chaos of *Clearing*. Both lithographs are, in a sense, vertical diptychs, each containing two separate images: in a narrow horizontal bottom panel, one finds the *Bone* figures motif, above which floats a wider horizontal zone enclosing a landscape. In *Principle of Uncertainty*, the bottom panel is rendered in a more exacting manner than in either *Bone* or *Balance Sheet*; it features a man with gritted teeth and facial features that seem to prefigure some of Jean-Michel Basquiat's heads of the 1980s. The upper panel, similarly detailed and richly worked, suggests depth with its assortment of abstracted stairways, bridges, fences, grates, barred windows, tennis racquets, faces, and eyeballs. The lower panel of *Balance Sheet* is a very crude and rough rendering in deep black of the *Bone* figures, while the upper panel features delicate lines executed with brush and tusche and litho pencil, which give it a range of tones, from gray to black, and achieve the look of a pencil drawing. There are many recognizable objects floating in undulating waves of water: a car fender, tires, cogs, an octopus tentacle, an erect penis, a face, and a stretched canvas.

A significant work from 1982 is the lithograph *Self-Portrait* (no. 50), which features a huge, wide face with thick lips and close-set eyes embedded in and merging with a thicket of cross-hatched patterns and vague forms: a house, slide, railing, and railroad

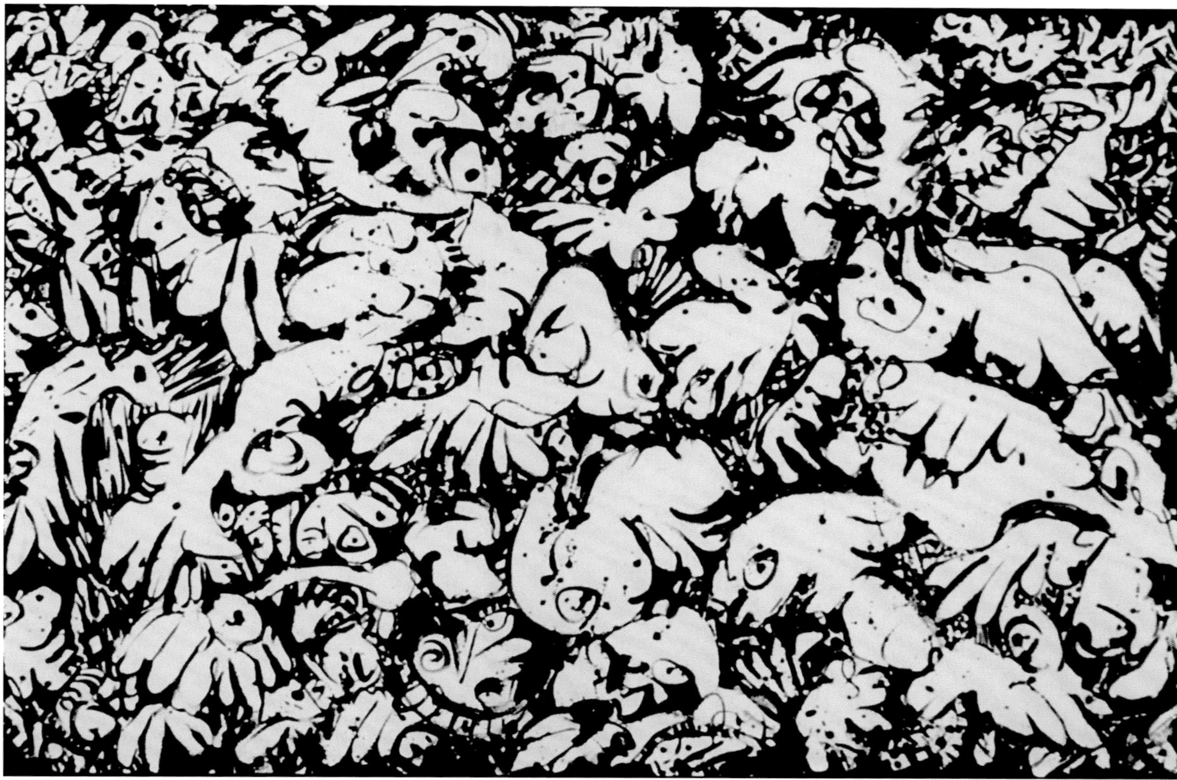

Fig. 4. *Night Return*, 1981. Acrylic on unprimed canvas; 40 × 60 in. Jenner and Block, Chicago.

tracks. The artist would later repeat this face more sparely in the woodcut *Up Front* (no. 61) and reprise it in his *Meeting* series. Himmelfarb also executed at Plucked Chicken in 1982 *Isn't Life Wonderful* (no. 48), a delicate and detailed landscape of organic forms whose title is taken from a chapter in Lowry's *October Ferry to Gabriola*; and *Dust Engenders* (no. 47), composed of organic forms, defined with heavy, black lines, which are somewhat reminiscent of the cross-hatched configurations in his Grid Works. The last print Himmelfarb made at the studio, *Physical* (no. 51), was part of a portfolio of works by Chicago-area artists. This Art Brut–like work continues his exploration of confrontation. In this case, he was inspired by a visit he made with his son to a doctor. Perhaps, the child's young age prompted Himmelfarb to take in this print a somewhat soft and childlike approach and to choose a bright palette. The physician wields a hypodermic needle in one hand and a mallet for testing knee reflexes in the other. The child also holds a mallet, with which he hits his own knee. This image of a physical examination, conducted amid a hailstorm of pink and green slashes, evokes both fear and reassurance.

Fig. 5. *Meeting*, 1982.
Brush and ink; 9 × 12¼ in.
Collection of Molly Day.

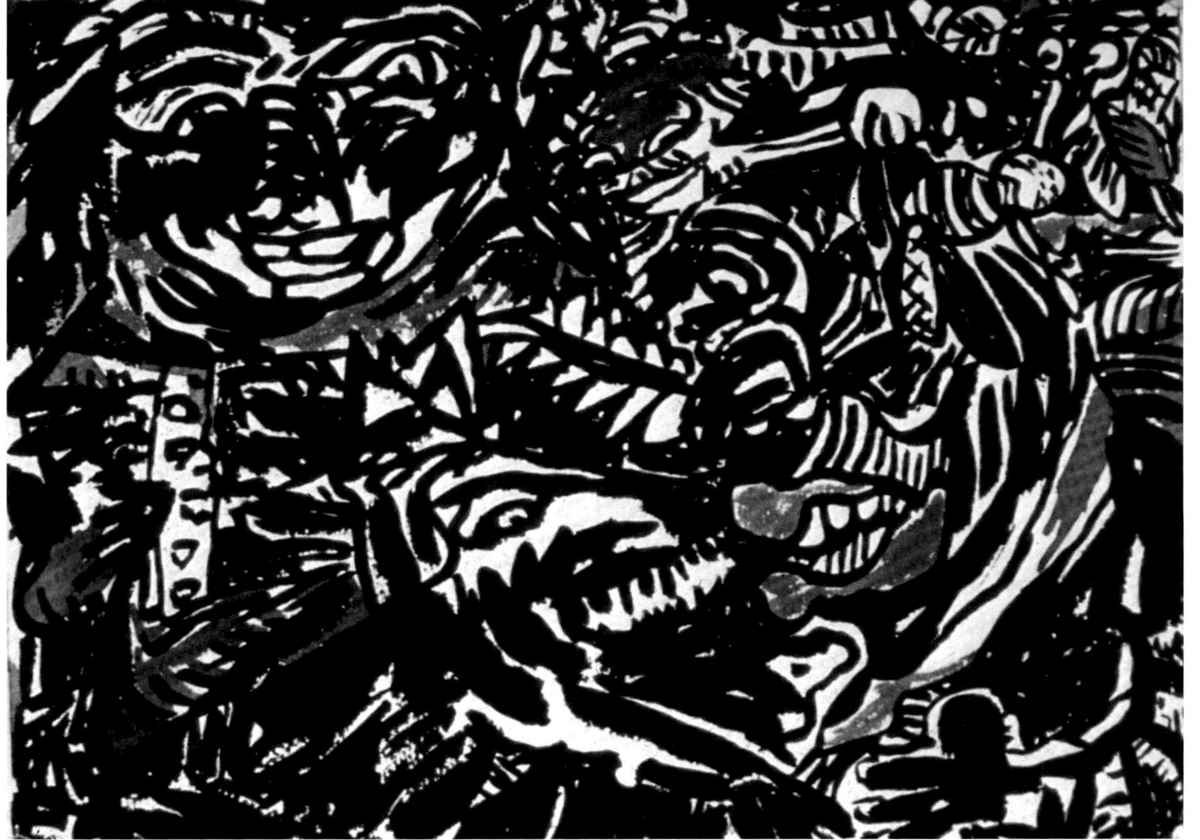

The fossil-like forms of *Face to Face* (no. 53), a 1983 stone lithograph using a crayon and scratch-through process produced at Four Brothers Press for another portfolio of Chicago artists' prints, evoke the spirit of *Bone*, even though the two prints are very different from each other. Two skeletal heads, with large mouths opened to reveal tongues and teeth, face off in the left and center portions of the composition. On the right, rough patterns suggest a landscape with a road going over a bridge. Another print that evokes the confrontational spirit of *Bone* is the 1984 *No Danger No Delay* (no. 55), Himmelfarb's first color screenprint, originally commissioned as part of a subscribers' portfolio by ARZ NOVA for the Goodman Theatre production of Nigerian political dissident Wole Soyinka's *The Road* in Chicago. *Coast to Coast* (no. 56), a black-and-white version of *No Danger No Delay*, looked so much like a woodcut to Himmelfarb that eventually he tried his hand at this process in the above-mentioned *Up Front*.

Also published by ARZ NOVA in 1984, *Profiles Blue*, *Green*, and *Red* (nos. 54a–c) are screenprints utilizing three variations of the same five screens. Loopy, organic lines suggesting arms, fingers, birds, fish, leaves, and amoebas are printed in interchangeable colors of yellow, red, blue, green, and purple. As abstract and abstruse as their titles, the trio evokes the playfulness of a work by Alexander Calder or Miró.

Meeting *Series*

A body of work that would occupy Himmelfarb for many years and that came to be known as the *Meeting* series began in 1982 with some large experimental brush-and-ink drawings (see Fig. 5). When the artist realized that he was not achieving what he wanted on the larger sheets, and wasting expensive paper in the process, he started over with smaller prototypes and gradually felt confident enough to work bigger and bigger.

Once Himmelfarb arrived at the final design of the series, he proceeded to execute numerous versions as drawings, paintings, prints, and even bronze reliefs. The prints' compositions are almost always the same (they are the mirror image of the drawings): on the left, a head in profile, mouth open to reveal teeth; in the center, a dog, its teeth bared, facing the profiled figure; and, on the right, a face gazing out at the viewer. Frequently, foliage fills the space above the canine and between the profiled and full face. It is as if the artist combined here two previous themes in one composition: from *Bone*, *Principle of Uncertainty*, and *Balance Sheet* are the men and dogs confronting one another; from *Self-Portrait* comes the outward-looking face of the artist.

In *First Meeting UNI* (no. 58) and *Illustration without Words (I.W.W.)* (no. 59), both of which were begun the same day in 1985 at the University of Northern Iowa, Cedar Falls, but printed some five years apart, the dog faces the viewer. Other *Meeting* prints include the combination lithograph and screenprint *Grand Street Meeting* (no. 57), the sugar-lift etching *Serena Lane Meeting* (no. 67) and two monumental woodcuts, the 6-foot-long *Lumber Street Meeting* (no. 68) and the 8-foot-long *Lengthy Meeting* (no. 66). Himmelfarb had already been working large, having produced two brush-and-ink-on-paper drawings, the 12-foot-long *Giant's Meeting* (1985; collection of the artist) and the 32-foot-long *Meeting in the Attic* (1986; collection of the artist).

A variation on the *Meeting* theme occurs in four sugar-lift prints utilizing the same etching plate with different ink and paper color combinations: *Summerlight Meeting* (no. 69), *Mid-Meeting Break* (no. 71), *Lava Flow* (no. 64), and *Lava Flow Part II* (no. 65). They feature a closed-mouth, profiled head confronting another head, seen in a three-quarter view (the dog has been eliminated). The sugar-lift process, with its "solarized" appearance, gives these prints such a highly abstract quality that at first it is hard to discern the facial features. Of course, there is a certain deliberateness in this. No doubt Himmelfarb was once again up to his old tricks of hiding figuration in abstraction. While the artist maintains that he attached no conscious symbolism to his *Meetings*, he has mentioned that they can be seen as images of a whole, integrated person (full face) under attack by an inner voice that is critical (profile) and protected by another voice (dog). Nevertheless, he insists that they are open to wider interpretation.

View and Review (no. 62) and *Covert Activity* (no. 63), printed at Southern Illinois University, Carbondale, are color and black-and-white versions of the same plate depicting a line of eight figures. *Parallels* (no. 60), printed by Richard D. Finch at Illinois State University, Normal, displays a similar group of figures. Himmelfarb has referred to these as "a human circus." *Talking Heads Meeting* (no. 70), printed in red on white paper, presents a very different scenario, with a new cast of characters and a more delicate drawing style. A skeletal figure with a detailed face, possibly a self-portrait, holds his pen like a wand, evidently in the process of creating along the horizon a line of railroad cars topped by disembodied heads; other detached heads seem to roll out of the sky and down the page.

Moving into Abstract Expressionism

Himmelfarb's visit to Juan Gardy Llorens Artigas's ceramic workshop in Gallifa, just outside of Barcelona, in 1989 ushered in a new era of fairly abstract work. The workshop was originally that of Artigas's father, where Joan Miró, and others, did ceramics and murals, some of which Himmelfarb saw there. After returning home, he completed three works that reflect a visual dialogue with Miró's art. He executed *Mirorim* (no. 74) at Tandem Press in Madison, Wisconsin, and then printed it with David Jones at Anchor Graphics in Chicago. The witty title is a self-referencing palindrome. The slightly hesitant, jerky movements of the brush on white paper create thick straight and curved black lines that suggest stark tree branches with red, yellow, and blue birds or flags perched on them. Flecks of black throughout act as random accents. *Forest* (no. 75) is similar to *Mirorim*, except the black "branches" are denser and the only other color is red. *Catalan* (no. 72), conceived in much the same vein as his Gallifa drawings of this period, boasts an ornate configuration of abstract black forms that occasionally resolve themselves into figurative elements such as a horse, ladder, and heart, all silhouetted against hand-painted background washes of beige and blue patches intersected by pencil markings.

In 1989 Himmelfarb executed a series of paintings he dubbed "non-objective." Laying his canvases on the floor, he drew organic forms using heavy black lines. Then he pinned the paintings to the wall and applied color to the open areas. Finally, he returned them to the floor and proceeded to drip and splatter more black accents to lend the works a feeling of spontaneity. A related series of prints from 1991—*Earth Dwellers/Fox Trot* (no. 77); its black-and-white version, *Earth Dwellers/Line Dance* (no. 78); and *Earth Dwellers/Mambo* (no. 79)—exhibits similar lines, but the forms, unlike those of the paintings, are slightly more anthropomorphic: abstracted figures or hieroglyphs, composed of disguised body parts, set in vague landscapes. In creating the sexualized, organic forms of the print *Jongleurs' Dell* (no. 85), Himmelfarb thought of a character with the suggestive name "Dewy Dell" in William Faulkner's novel *As I Lay Dying*. Around this time, members of the United States Congress were critical of the National Endowment for the Arts for funding art they deemed obscene and/or religiously irreverent. Himmelfarb's response was to hide abstracted penises and vaginas in the puffy, spotted foliage of *Jongleurs' Dell*. Other prints in this 1992 series—*Juggler on Stage* (no. 86) and its black-and-white version, *Juggler* (no. 87), as well as *Yellow Rose* (no. 88) and its black-and-white counterpart, *Stolen Glance* (no. 89)—move closer to figuration.

Letterform Works

Himmelfarb's Letterform pieces evolved from his interest in non-representational art. Precursors to this body of work are a number of Sumi-e–like calligraphic drawings that he executed in the late 1980s. Related to these is *Hi-Go* (no. 90) of 1992. Part calligraphic hieroglyph and part anthropomorphic figure, it was drawn as an elaborate gesture with a photocopy toner on an aluminum plate. The artist created his first Letter Drawings in 1991, although he had produced prototypes much earlier, in 1979. In fact, the concept of dividing a page into rows and columns had been present in Himmelfarb's art since his Grid Works. The Letter Drawings assume the format of a formal business communication, but contain lines comprised of invented calligraphic alphabets that appear to be Asian or Middle Eastern. They also recall the Chinese newspapers that intrigued Himmelfarb when, as a youngster, he and his family made excursions to Chicago's Chinatown neighborhood. Playing with notions of deconstruction, the artist created a text without actual words. With the line between visual art and visual language increasingly blurring in the contemporary art scene, Himmelfarb donned the mantle of a conceptual artist in order to come up with a new perspective on the old adage that a picture is worth a thousand words.

Letter to Ray (no. 84), a 1992 collaboration with Ray E. George of Illinois State University, Normal, is an etching on a 10⅞ × 8⅜-inch blue- and red-lined sheet that imitates the appearance of notebook paper, right down to the punched holes. Like a working model for his Letter Drawings written entirely in invented script, it contains a sketch of a cartoonlike landscape he had made in 1991, the lithograph *Untitled (anthropomorphic)* (no. 80), as if he were providing directions about how to print it. *Shop Notes* (no. 82) of 1991–92 is a larger etching in a format similar to that of *Letter to Ray*, but here rectangles are placed on the page as fake color samples and sketches for future works.

Proof Copy (no. 83), a lithograph/transfer etching, incorporates the same text as *Shop Notes*, but adds an all-over background of small white calligraphic lines. The words "PROOF COPY" in industrial letters are included at the bottom. Several of the rectangles contain industrial lettering offering variations on the spelling of "WORD." Lines with arrows, resembling pencil marks, point to different parts of the copy with notes like "redraw details" and "rust characters." *Proof Copy*'s background would be printed on its own, in black on gray paper, as *Tabula Tabula Picta* (no. 91) in 1992–93 .

In 1993 Himmelfarb began another series that combines various layers of new calligraphy. *White Out* (no. 97) is basically a block of white lines printed on gray paper. *First Draft* (no. 94) presents another calligraphic design, in blue, printed over a repeated, stamped pattern in gray that reads: "NOT YOUR BASIC." *Fax Appeal* (no. 93) reprises the formal Letter Drawing format, complete with a narrow column of smaller script running down the left side of the piece and a round calligraphic "seal" at the bottom. The Letter Drawing in blue is printed over a brown block of scribbled forms neatly divided into seventeen horizontal rows, a kind of throwback to the artist's Grid Works. *Note of Appeal* (no. 95) combines virtually all the components in *White Out*, *First Draft*, and *Fax Appeal*, and uses transparent layers of pale orange and white as subtle framing devices.

Throughout the 1990s and into 2000, Himmelfarb improvised on various approaches to his Letterform works. He allowed himself to submit to the simple pleasure of making calligraphic symbols that look beautiful together on a page, evoking a range of effects from faded scrolls or worn tablets, which appear to have been made and left by ancient civilizations, to neon-bright advertising signs inspired by modern-day Seoul, which Himmelfarb visited in 1996. Sometimes, he produced large-format prints filled with glyphs, such as the 1994 *Top This* (no. 100) and *Understatement* (no. 101), and the 2000 series *RGB Cool*, *RGB Good*, *RGB Happy*, and *RGB Mine* (nos. 120–23). More often he executed smaller works like *Short Order* (no. 96), *Female Voice-Male* (no. 102), *Lecture Notes* (no. 116), *Just Follow These…* (no. 114), *Easy Assembly* (no. 115), *Plank* (no. 117), and *In Other Words* (no. 124).

Maps and Bridges

In 1994 Himmelfarb initiated what he referred to as his *Inland Romance* series. He saw these pieces as equivalents to pathways, maps, bridges, and ironwork. Were his calligraphic marks to be greatly enlarged and interconnected, they would begin to resemble, on a very different scale, these artworks. In a sense, it seems as if Himmelfarb were attempting to transform his pictographic imagery into landscapes, albeit rather abstract, geometric ones.

Two companion screenprints, *Glyph Notes* (no. 99) and *Cipher* (no. 98), feature three or four strata of text: one or two layers of tiny writing in the background; larger, shadowy glyphs borrowed from *Top This* and *Understatement* printed above that; and, over these, linked, glyphlike white silhouettes outlined in black. With two other sets of screenprints, *Crinkum* and *Crankum* (nos. 105–06) and *Gizmo* and *Whiz-Bang* (nos. 112–13), he simplified his approach by using solid colors and streamlining the cartographic glyphs into pipelike configurations of various widths. A small linoleum cut from 1999, *18th in Summer* (cat. 119), echoes *Gizmo*'s and *Whiz-Bang*'s patterns in a very different format. The artist achieved the latticework pattern of *Suspension* (no. 129) in a very different way, using a MacPaint 88 computer program to create the drawing, which he then transferred to a litho plate.

Expressionism and Abstraction Revisited

In 1996, while still immersed in the Letterform Works, Himmelfarb drifted back into figurative expressionism with *Quiz* (no. 103), a chine-collé etching printed at Normal Editions Workshop in Normal, Illinois. Here, a man in profile, open-mouthed, stares at a domed building, a stack of tires, and a flower. In 1997–98 he created *Key Note Speech* (no. 107). At the risk of reading too much into this work, the artist may have intended to suggest that the keynote speaker (aptly pictured with a key in his head) was a politician or another authority figure with a by-the-numbers, unimaginative way of thinking. A voice balloon emerging from his mouth does not contain words, but rather tiny pictograms. He is trying to persuade a central figure with a vertical line running down the center of his face, as if he is of two minds about what he is hearing. Meanwhile, the person on the right, oblivious to the presenter, is a free-thinker, with his own ideas flowering spontaneously from his head. The element of confrontation between two or three characters recalls Himmelfarb's powerful *Meeting* series of nearly a decade before. Other expressionist-style prints followed: *Astronomer* (no. 108), *Silencio* (no. 110; titled *Colorado* [no. 109] when printed with reddish brown ink) and *Cow Phone* (no. 126). A more Abstract Expressionist work is *Eyeland* (no. 111), inspired by a business card Himmelfarb saw that depicted a map of an Italian hill town. It also reminded him, he said, of one of Philip Guston's late-style paintings of a head with a bandage wrapped over one eye, while the other stares disconcertingly at us.

In an attempt to see whether he could still draw the way he had in college, Himmelfarb made *Boca* (no. 118), a black-ink-on-gray-paper lithograph that, as observed earlier, harks back to his 1967 *Industrial Etching*. *Boca* depicts a Rube Goldberg–like construction of pipelines informed by his *Inland Romance* series, depicting the industrial typography of midwestern cities. Another reference to an earlier approach can be found in *Actually Undoing* (no. 137), recalling both *Actually Doing*, from 1971, and *Home*, from 1975, as well as the *Profiles*, from 1984. Like those works, *Actually Undoing* is a largely abstract, multicolored composition of line drawings punctuated here and there by figuration, but now the lines are more geometric and clipped, less gestural and expressionistic, as if they are about to morph into calligraphy, but not quite.

Two completely Abstract Expressionist inkjet prints related to some of the larger murals and installations Himmelfarb completed from 2000 to 2003 are *Portrait of Molly* (no. 127), named for his wife, and *Zone* (no. 128). To create these colorful works, he manipulated the color, width, and texture of each line on a computer. *Zone*, a denser piece, contains some of the same elements as *Portrait of Molly*.

Narrative Puzzle Pieces

Himmelfarb's most recent body of work is referred to here as his Narrative Puzzle Pieces. In these, asymmetrically shaped "containers" are stacked or assembled in diverse configurations against a black background. Each receptacle contains one or several abstract iconographic shapes. Thus, the Narrative Puzzle Pieces are related to the Letterform Works in that they feature pictograms, but now placed in a new context. The first Narrative Puzzle Pieces appeared in 1997 as drawings, and then were realized as paintings. In one of the first prints of the group, *Uzzle* (no. 125), light-brown compartments contain interlocked black and red pictograms. In *Turandot's Riddles* (no. 135), the pieces do not fit together, but float separately against a black background, and contain scribbled writing as well as pictograms.

However, in the screenprints *Theory* (no. 131) and *Practice* (no. 133), and in a number of other works in this group, each element is a different color than the adjoining one and holds only one fat black silhouetted icon. *Theory* resembles a pile of puzzle parts, but the overall configuration of *Practice* anthropomorphizes into a dog with curling tail and open mouth. Similarly, the computer-drawn and printed *Order Form* (no. 130) looks like a map of the United States with too many states. By 2003 the artist was fully engaged in figuration within and without the Narrative Puzzle Pieces. In *Apple Tail Double Dog* (no. 147), for example, the shapes assume a canine form; the second dog, to which the title refers, appears inside one of them; in others one finds a chair, a key, and a car.[9]

Later permutations of the Narrative Puzzle Pieces include *Chapeau* (no. 140), with compartments and pictographs comprising fully delineated and detailed figurative line drawings on beige paper, framed by a zone of stubbly black dashes and a golden-brown "wash," as well as light-blue and green accents. *Zklee* (no. 145), the title of a 2003–04 etching, is a play on the name of the giclée inkjet printing process, as well as that of artist Paul Klee, whose images are evoked in this complex Narrative Puzzle Piece. Set against a speckled surface of red and black spots, the containers appear three-dimensional—thick, irregularly shaped planar tiles imprinted with sketches of people and elements borrowed from Klee, Picasso, and Roy Lichtenstein. The profile of the cartoon hero Dick Tracy that appears here was actually inspired by a Lichtenstein piece which incorporates the face of the famed detective created originally by cartoonist Chester Gould. Tantamount to a postmodern comic-book splash page with appropriated images extending from panel to adjoining panel—a device Himmelfarb initiated back in 1977 with *Early Riser—Zklee*, in this respect, brought the artist nearly full circle, proving yet again that one can always build on the past, especially one's own.

Literature, Music, and Art

If we return once again to the first three directions taken by Himmelfarb in his prints—abstract composition, nature, and constructed environments—we can trace how these fundamental prototypes manifest themselves to a greater or lesser degree in each subsequent body of Himmelfarb's work. The organic aspects of the natural world and the more structured and geometric character of man-made spaces are represented, respectively, in his Landscapes and Cityscapes. Individuals and Groups are an expressionistic outgrowth of the natural world, while Grid Works, Letterform Works, and Maps and Bridges push into partial or pure abstraction.

The Narrative Puzzle Pieces are a true amalgamation of the artist's three major concerns. They represent a kind of abstract framing of soft- and hard-edged, figurative and non-representational elements, all in one hybrid composition. In combining the three directions that he had explored separately in previous works, the artist has perhaps found the means to express himself more completely than ever before.

Another way to think about the evolution of Himmelfarb's oeuvre is to compare his use of natural, man-made, and abstract components to his love of literature and music. To tell a story, he needs figures and/or pictographs, as seen in such narratives as his *Boatman* and *Meeting* series. He turns to calligraphy, letters, and imaginary languages to evoke the mystery and power of literary structure in his Letterform pieces. But to capture the sweeping emotions of music, he surrenders to the abstract aspects of his expressionistic *Boatman* and *Meeting* images, and in a more calculated way, to the geometric structures of his *Inland Romance* compositions. While a certain body of work may lend itself to one approach more readily than to another, he melds the realms of figuration and abstraction, literature and music to varying degrees in each of his efforts.

The Narrative Puzzle Pieces are not, so to speak, string quartets or jazz combos, to which one can liken the *Boatman* and *Inland Romance* series, but veritable symphonic orchestras and big bands. To use another metaphor, they are not poems or short stories, but novels and *Bildungsromane*. Indeed, John Himmelfarb has taken his compositions to new levels of richness and complexity.

NOTES

1. This and other observations by John Himmelfarb mentioned throughout this essay derive from several conversations with the artist in August 2004 and April 2005.

2. Frederick Ted Castle, "John Himmelfarb at Terry Dintenfass and John Nichols," *Art in America* 75 (Dec. 1987), p. 161. "While he is not the only artist observing a truce in the war between representation and non-representation, Himmelfarb is one of the best."

3. Michael Bonesteel, "Tracking the Backtracker: John Himmelfarb in the Garden," in "Meetings in the Garden: The Art of John Himmelfarb," *Bulletin of the Kalamazoo Institute of Arts* 75 (1989), p. 4.

4. Himmelfarb, interview with the author, August 1, 2004: "Because I didn't go to art school, I didn't know you were supposed to make 'bodies of work.' Yet they come together in the way I use space. It was just a natural development, that the eye not be stagnant, that things lead the eye on a journey through the piece. Follow the yellows through a piece, follow the blues, follow the linear staccato. Work the surface into an active experience."

5. Bonesteel (note 3).

6. Douglas Day, "Preface" to Malcolm Lowry, *Dark As the Grave Wherein My Friend Is Laid*, ed. by Douglas Day and Margerie Lowry (New York: New American Library, 1968), p. xv.

7. Ibid. p. 1.

8. In fact, while *March* was printed pretty quickly thereafter, *Blue Bird* was produced a number of months later.

9. Himmelfarb also made black-and-white versions of a number of the above works, which he retitled.

5.

Untitled (Landfall)

Date begun: 10/13/1970

Date finished: 10/14/1970

Medium: lithograph

Paper size: 20 × 15 in.

Image size: 18 × 12½ in.

Paper type: Rives BFK White

Publisher: artist

Press: Landfall Press

Printer: Jerry Raidiger

Edition: 25

Proofs: 1 cancellation, 2 Landfall Press, 2 printer, 1 ready to print

Signature location: LR

Chop location: LR

Job number and location: JH70–151, reverse LL

Color printing order, execution of printing elements:

1. Aluminum printed with black. Image drawn with pen and zincographic ink.

6.

Landfall Two

Date begun: 12/29/1970

Date finished: 1/2/1971

Medium: lithograph

Paper size: 15 × 19½ in.

Image size: 11⅝ × 16 in.

Paper type: German Etching

Publisher: artist

Press: Landfall Press

Printer: Jack Lemon

Edition: 25

Proofs: 1 cancellation, 2 Landfall Press, 2 press, 1 ready to print

Signature location: LR

Chop location: LR

Job number and location: JH70–156, reverse LL

Color printing order, execution of printing elements:

1. Stone printed with black. Image drawn on transfer paper with pen and tusche.

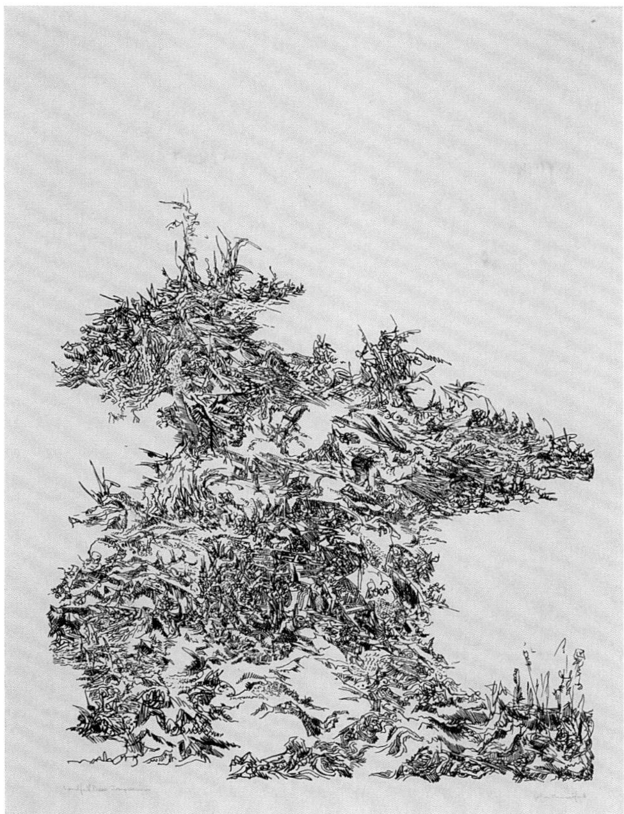

5

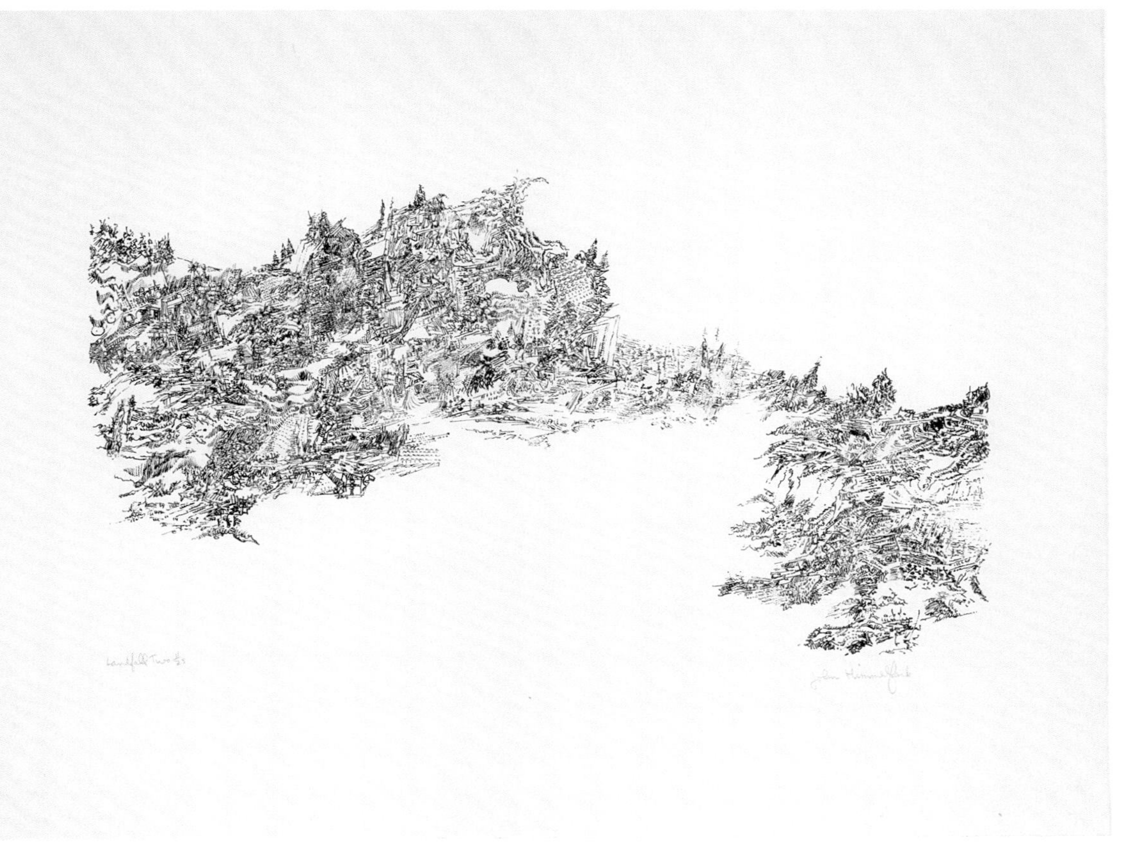

6

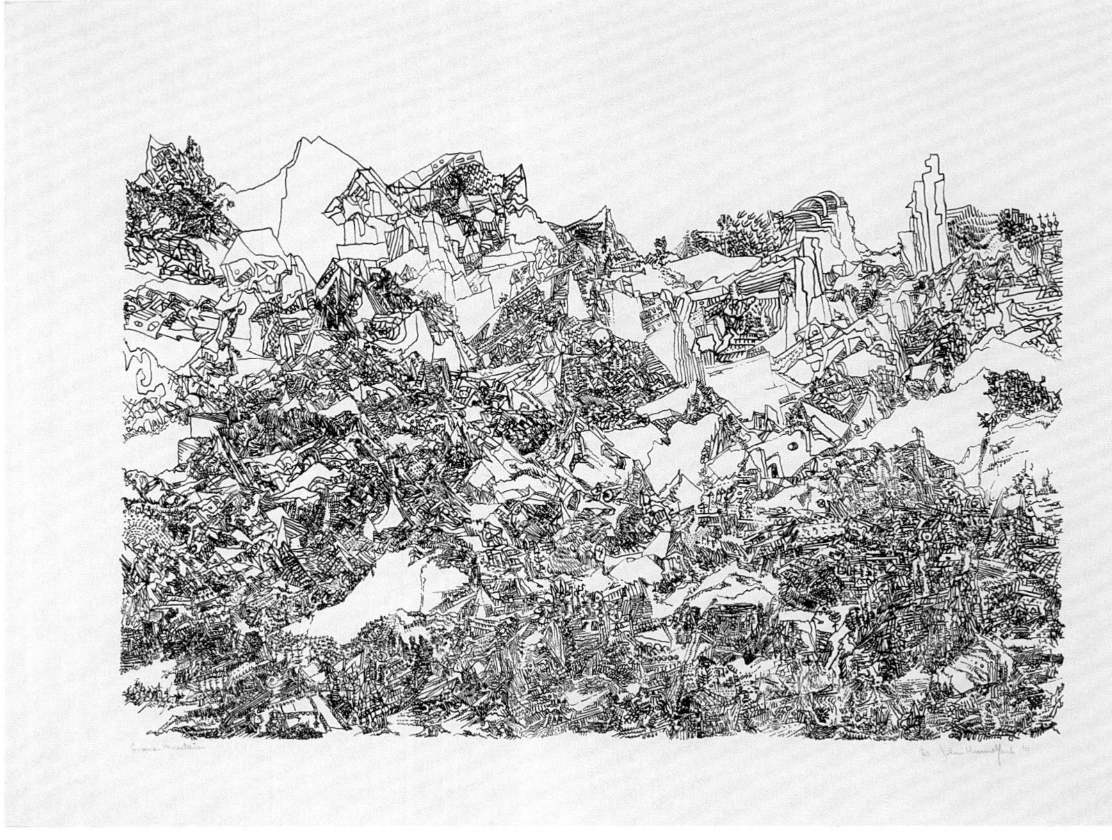

7

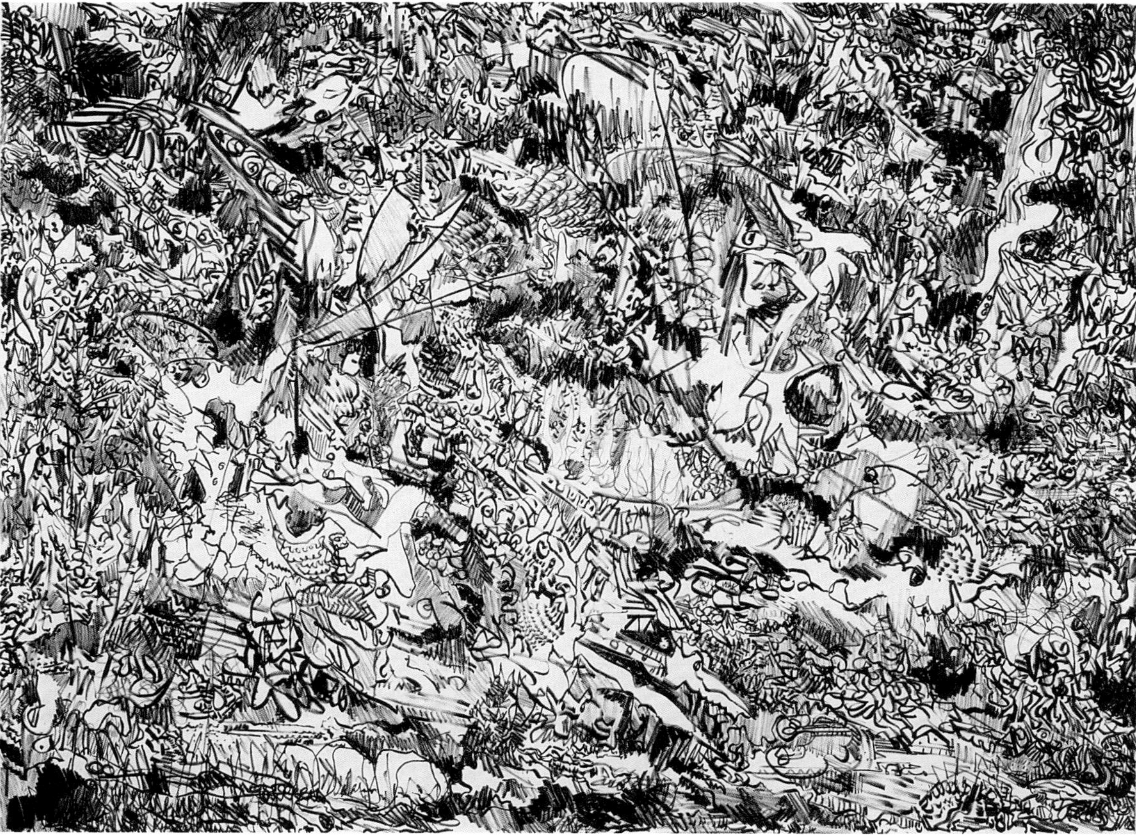

8

7.

Crane Mountain

Date begun: 12/1970

Date finished: 1/14/1971

Medium: lithograph

Paper size: 14½ × 20 in.

Image size: 9½ × 15 in.

Paper type: German Etching

Publisher: artist

Press: Landfall Press

Printer: Robert Hicks

Edition: 25

Proofs: 1 cancellation, 2 Landfall Press, 2 press, 1 ready to print

Signature location: LR

Chop location: Jack Lemon, LR

Job number and location: JH71–160, reverse LL

Color printing order, execution of printing elements:

1. Stone printed with black. Image drawn on transfer paper with pen and tusche.

8.

Ether Ore

Date begun: 1/1971

Date finished: 2/27/1971

Medium: lithograph

Paper size: 15 × 20 in.

Image size: same

Paper type: German Etching

Publisher: artist

Press: Landfall Press

Printer: Jack Lemon

Edition: 50

Proofs: 1 cancellation, 2 Landfall Press, 2 press, 1 ready to print

Signature location: LR

Chop location: none

Job number and location: JH71–161, reverse LL

Color printing order, execution of printing elements:

1. Aluminum printed with black. Image drawn with litho crayon.

9.

Salad

Date begun: 1/25/1971

Date finished: 4/17/1971

Medium: lithograph

Paper size: 15 × 20 in.

Image size: same

Paper type: German Etching

Publisher: artist

Press: Landfall Press

Printer: Jack Lemon

Printer's assistants: D. R. Holman, Jerry Raidiger

Edition: 95

Proofs: 5 artist, 1 cancellation, 2 Landfall Press, 3 unknown

Signature location: reverse LR

Chop location: Jerry Raidiger, LL

Job number and location: JH71–165, publisher stamp, reverse LL

Color printing order, execution of printing elements:

1. Aluminum printed with blue.
2. Aluminum printed with orange.
3. Aluminum printed with red.
4. Aluminum printed with yellow.

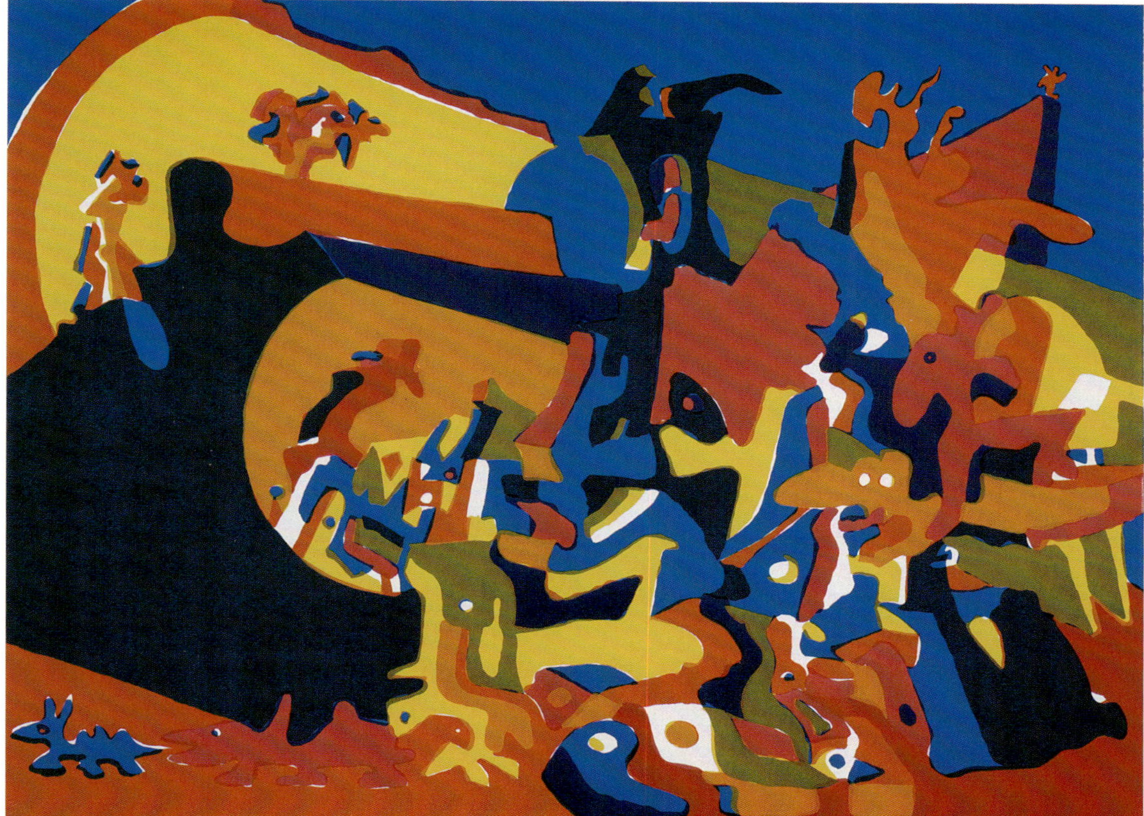

9

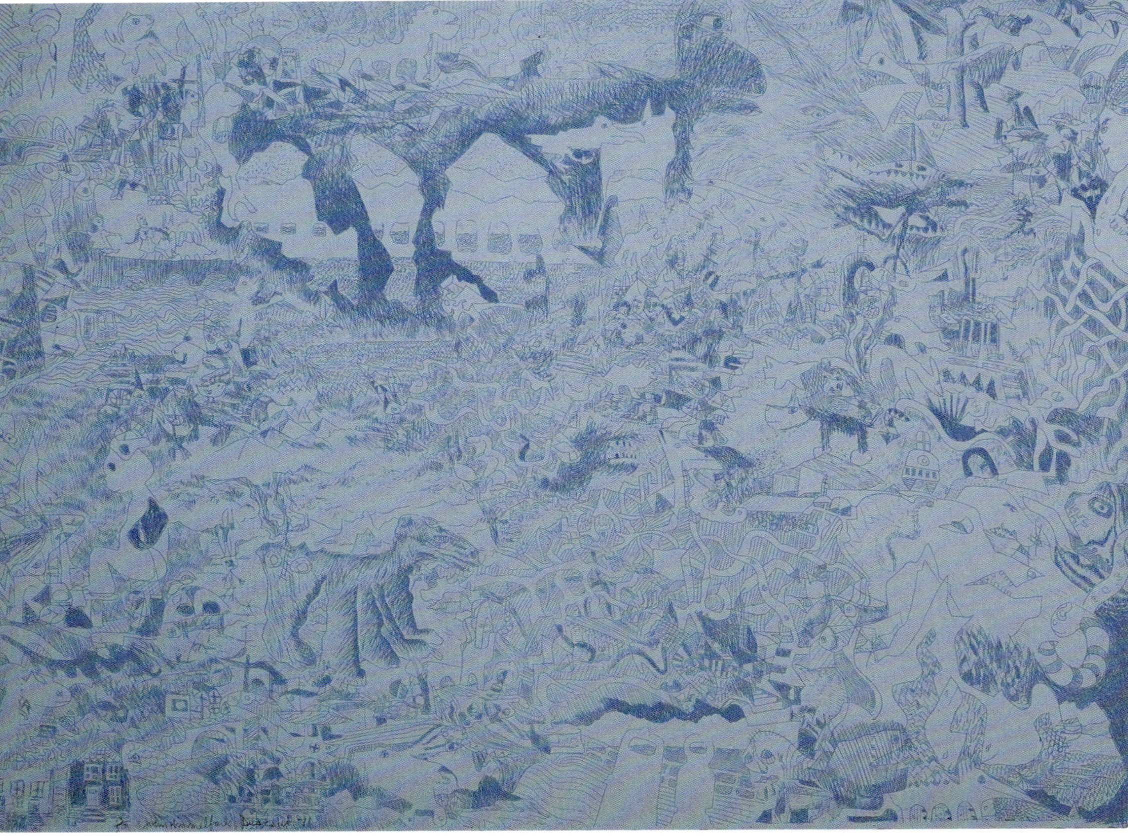

10

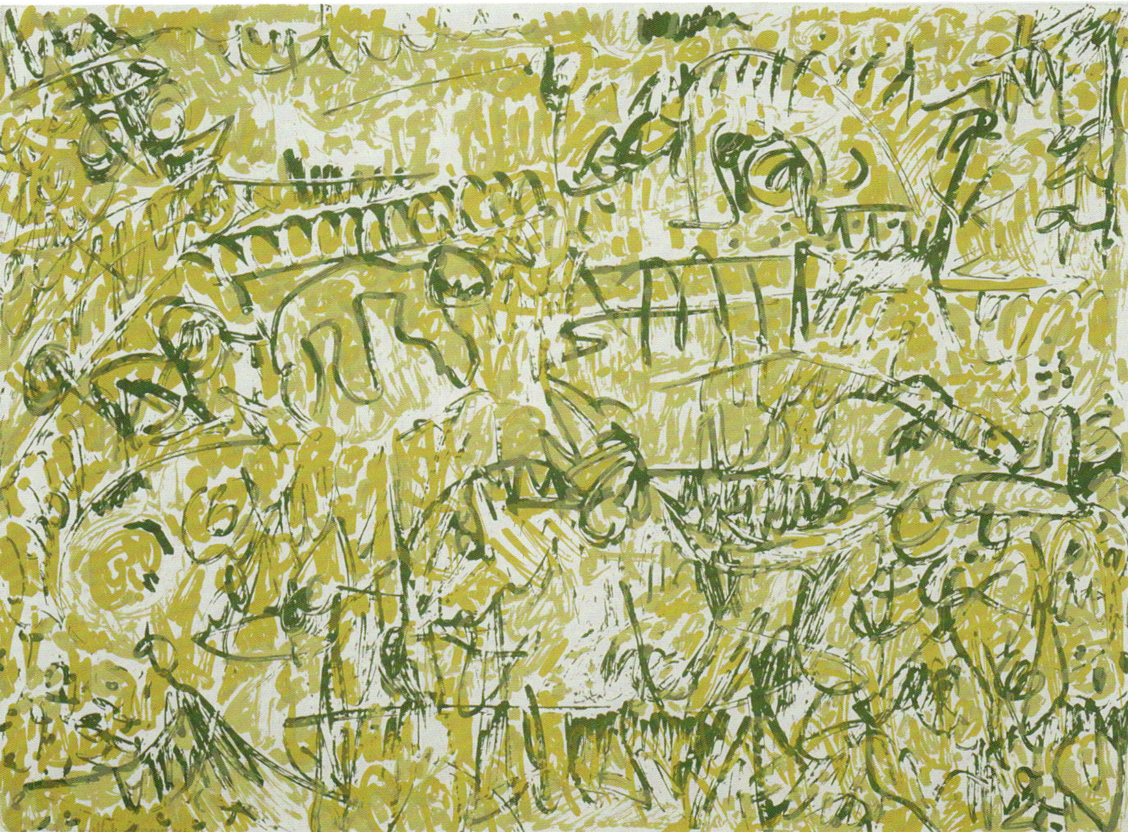

11

10.

Descent

Date begun: 4/8/1971

Date finished: 5/14/1971

Medium: lithograph

Paper size: 15 × 20 in.

Image size: same

Paper type: German Etching

Publisher: artist

Press: Landfall Press

Printers: D. R. Holman, Jerry Raidiger

Edition: 50

Proofs: 1 cancellation, 2 Landfall Press, 2 press, 1 ready to print; 1 trial, 1 trial printed on pea-green flat with line engraving printed in cyan green, 1 trial printed in fire red on Rives BFK White

Signature location: LL

Chop location: Jerry Raidiger, LL

Job number and location: JH71–198, reverse LL

Color printing order, execution of printing elements:

1. Stone printed with light blue. Flat-rolled on dry plate.

2. Stone printed with cyan blue. Image drawn with stylus on gummed stone (line engraving).

11.

Imminence

Date begun: 4/8/1971

Date finished: 5/19/1971

Medium: lithograph

Paper size: 15 × 20 in.

Image size: same

Paper type: German Etching

Publisher: artist

Press: Landfall Press

Printers: D. R. Holman, David Keister, Joe Williams

Edition: 50

Proofs: 1 cancellation, 2 Landfall Press, 2 press, 1 ready to print, 1 trial

Location of signature: LL

Chop location: Jerry Raidiger, LL

Job number and location: JH71–203, reverse LL

Color printing order, execution of printing elements:

1. Aluminum printed with green. Image drawn with felt-tip marker on acetate, transferred to photosensitive plate.

2. Aluminum printed with light yellow-green. Image drawn with felt-tip marker on acetate, transferred to photosensitive plate.

3. Aluminum printed with light green. Image drawn with felt-tip marker on acetate, transferred to photosensitive plate.

12.

What They Were

Date begun: 4/8/1971

Date finished: 5/20/1971

Medium: lithograph

Paper size: 15 × 20 in.

Image size: same

Paper type: German Etching

Publisher: artist

Press: Landfall Press

Printers: Jerry Raidiger, Joe Williams

Edition: 50

Proofs: 1 cancellation, 2 Landfall Press, 2 press, 1 ready to print; 1 trial like the edition, 1 trial printed with dark blue, purple, dark green, 1 trial printed with blue from *Salad* (no. 9), chrome yellow, dark blue, 1 trial printed from *Salad* run #1

Signature location: lower edge, C

Chop location: Jerry Raidiger, LL

Job number and location: JH71–200, reverse LL

Color printing order, execution of printing elements:

1. Aluminum printed with light blue. Image drawn with pen and ink on acetate, transferred to photosensitive plate.

2. Aluminum printed with light yellow. Image drawn with pen and ink on acetate, transferred to photosensitive plate.

3. Aluminum printed with cyan blue. Image drawn with pen and ink on acetate, transferred to photosensitive plate.

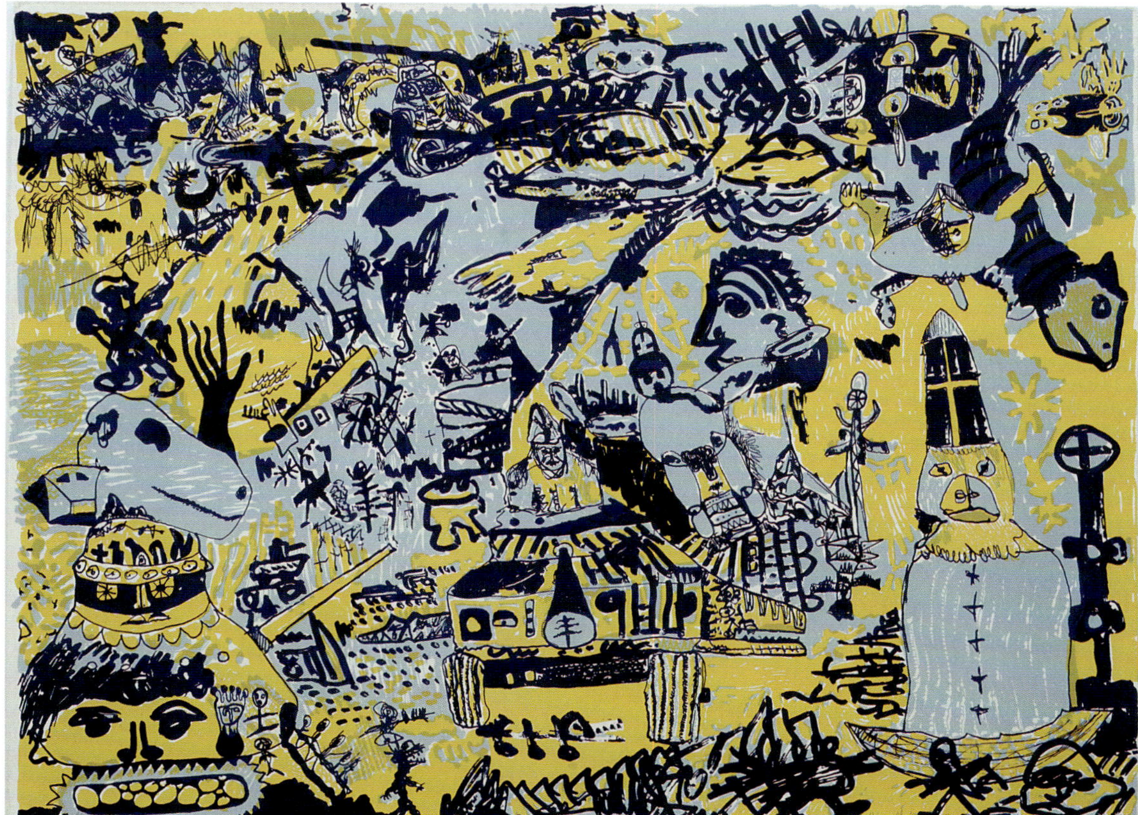

12

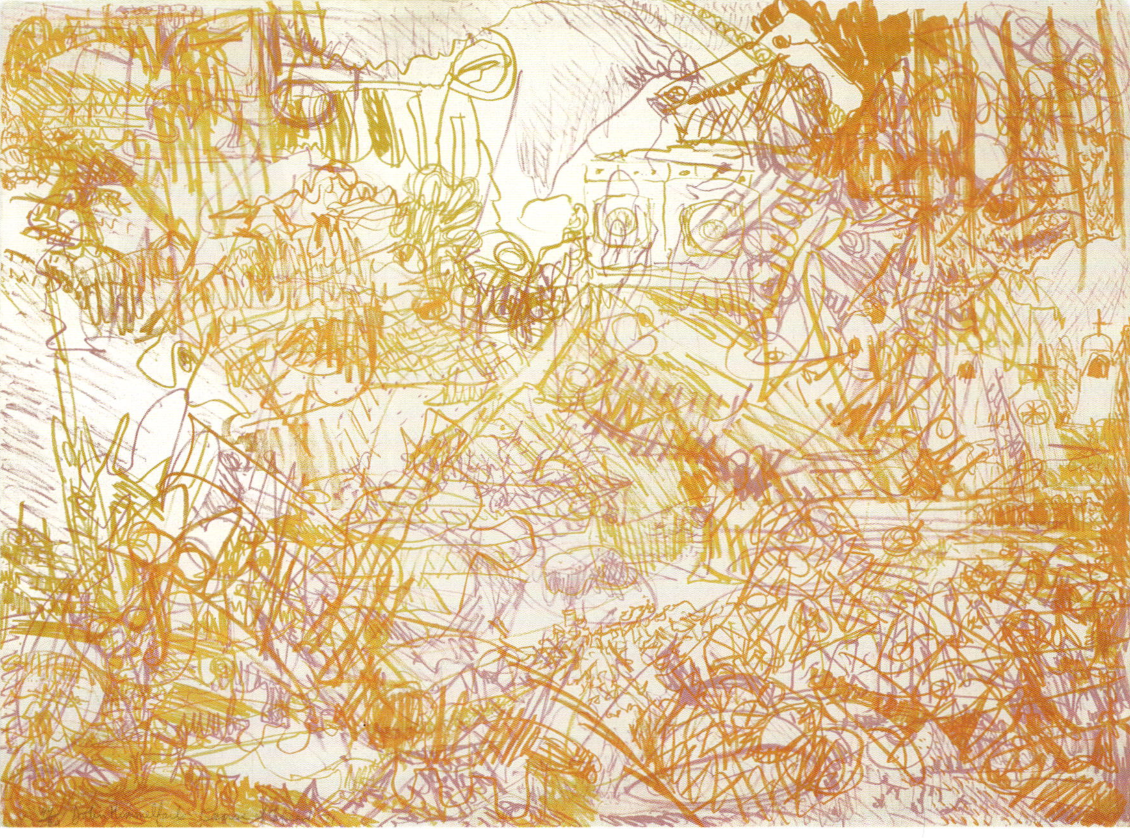

13

13.

Sense of Speed

Date begun: 4/8/1971

Date finished: 5/22/1971

Medium: lithograph

Paper size: 15 × 20 in.

Image size: same

Paper type: German Etching

Publisher: artist

Press: Landfall Press

Printers: D. R. Holman, David Keister, Joe Williams

Edition: 50

Proofs: 1 cancellation, 2 Landfall Press, 2 press, 1 ready to print; 1 trial like the edition, 1 trial in which run #1 printed in pink, run #2 in yellow, and run #3 in orange

Signature location: LL

Chop location: Jerry Raidiger, LL

Job number and location: JH71–196, reverse LL

Color printing order, execution of printing elements:

1. Aluminum printed with pink. Image drawn with litho pencil.

2. Aluminum printed with orange. Image drawn with litho pencil.

3. Aluminum printed with yellow. Image drawn with litho pencil.

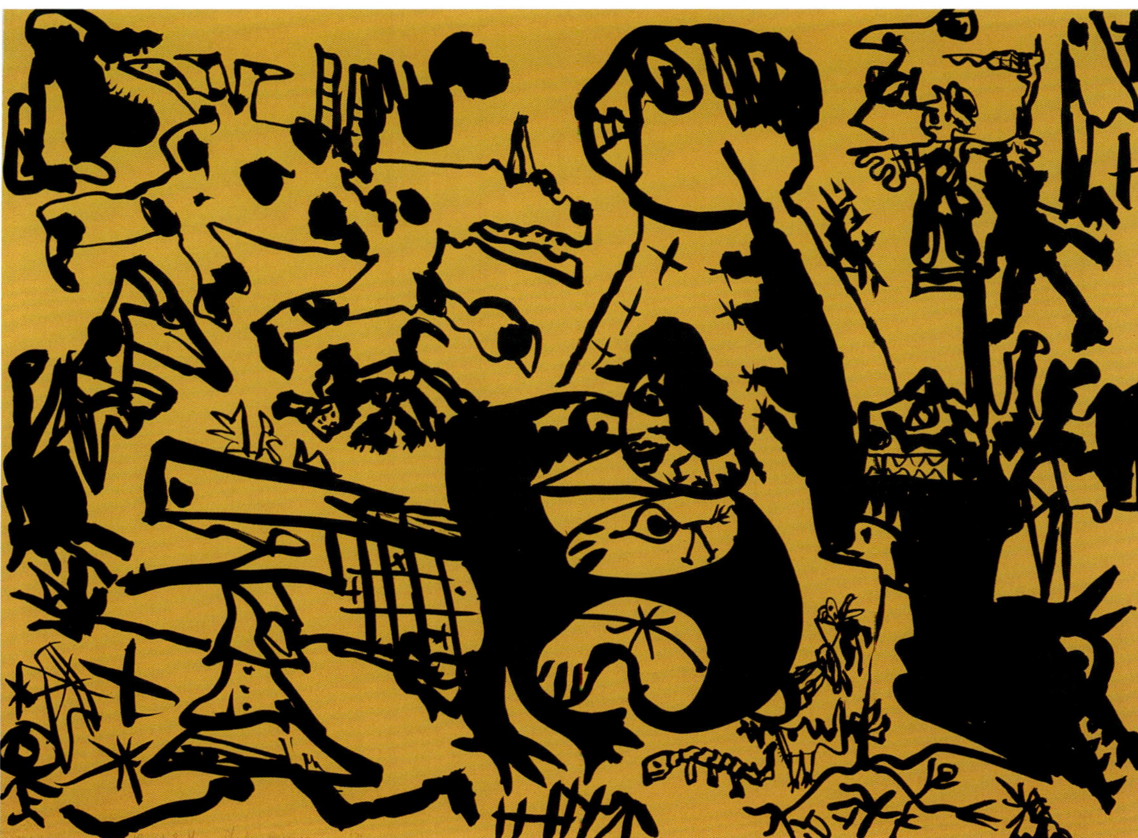

14

14.

Regression

Date begun: 4/8/1971

Date finished: 5/25/1971

Medium: lithograph

Paper size: 15 × 20 in.

Image size: same

Paper type: German Etching

Publisher: artist

Press: Landfall Press

Printers: D. R. Holman, Jerry Raidiger, Joe Williams

Edition: 50

Proofs: 1 cancellation, 2 Landfall Press, 2 press, 1 ready to print; 1 trial printed on yellow flat like edition in run #1 and cyan green in run #2, 1 trial printed in cyan green in run #1 on light pea-green flat printed in run #2

Signature location: LL

Chop location: Jerry Raidiger, LL

Job number and location: JH71–197, reverse LL

Color printing order, execution of printing elements:

1. Aluminum printed with yellow. Flat-rolled on dry plate.

2. Aluminum printed with dark blue-green. Drawn with brush and tusche.

15.

Moving Shadow

Date begun: 4/8/1971

Date finished: 6/4/1971

Medium: lithograph

Paper size: 15 × 20 in.

Image size: same

Paper type: German Etching

Publisher: artist

Press: Landfall Press

Printers: D. R. Holman, David Keister, Jack Lemon, Jerry Raidiger

Edition: 50

Proofs: 1 cancellation, 2 Landfall Press, 2 press. 1 ready to print; 1 trial like the edition, 1 trial like the edition with a fourth color (orange,) 1 trial in which runs #1 and #2 are like the edition but run #3 is printed in dark green and run #4 is in orange

Signature location: LL

Chop location: UR

Job number and location: JH7–204, reverse UR

Color printing order, execution of printing elements:

1. Aluminum. Image drawn with negro pencil and ink set-offs made from plate. Plate then discarded.

2. Aluminum printed with silver. Image drawn with litho pencil, crayon, rubbing ink, negro pencil.

3. Aluminum printed with light blue. Image drawn with litho pencil, crayon, rubbing ink, negro pencil

4. Aluminum printed with green. Image drawn with litho pencil, crayon, rubbing ink, negro pencil.

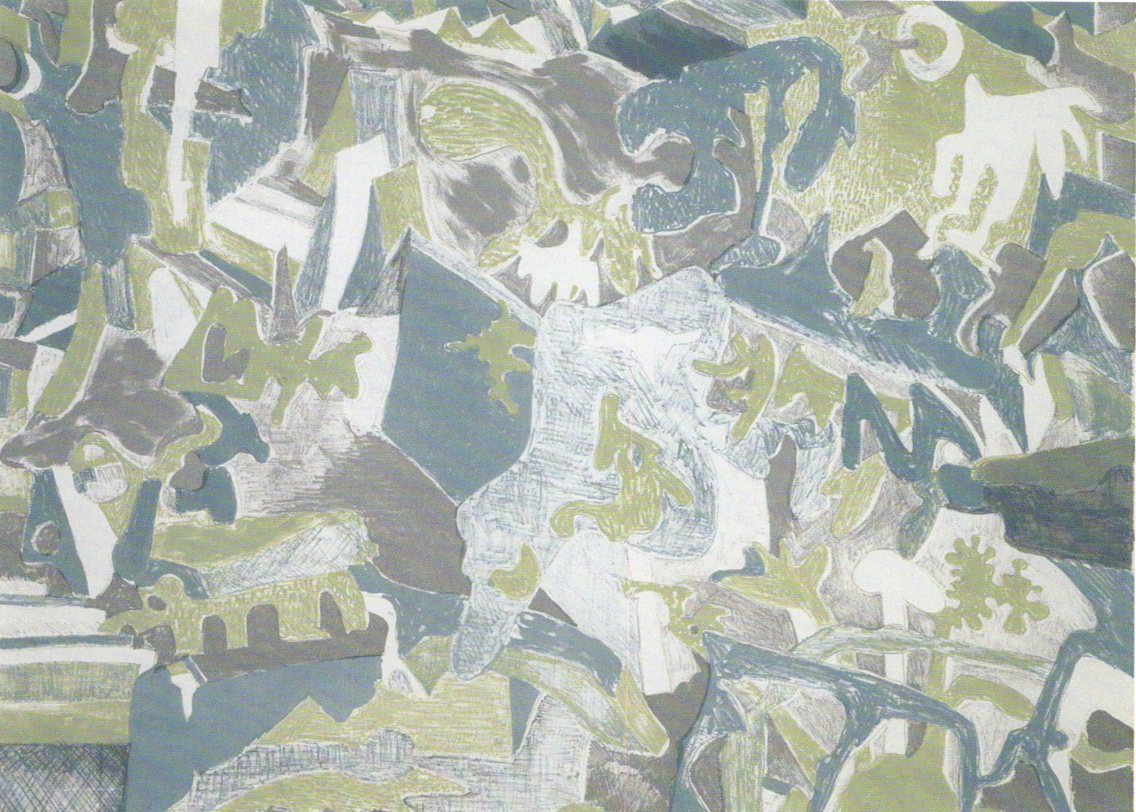

15

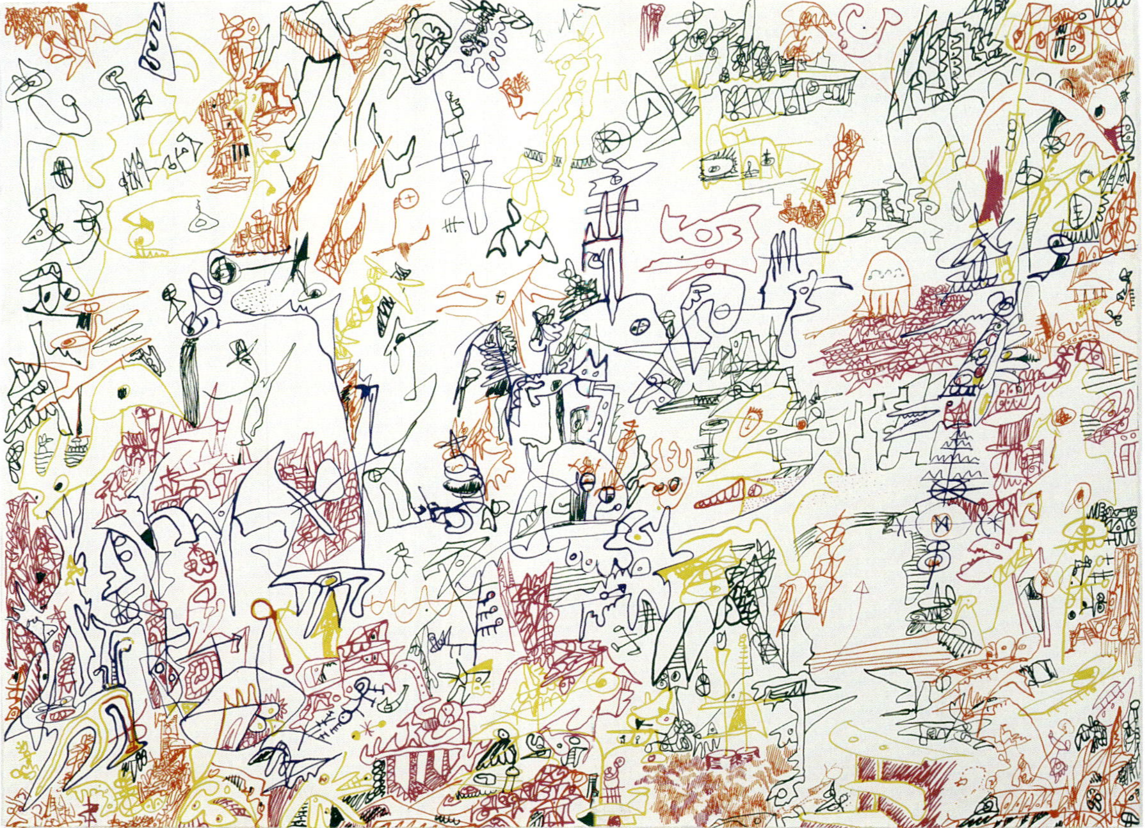

16

16.

Actually Doing

Date begun: 4/8/1971

Date finished: 6/24/1971

Medium: lithograph

Paper size: 15 × 20 in.

Image size: same

Paper type: German Etching

Publisher: artist

Press: Landfall Press

Printers: Jack Lemon, Jerry Raidiger.

Printers' assistants: D. R. Holman, Mike Rottman

Edition: 50

Proofs: 1 cancellation, 2 Landfall Press, 2 press, 1 ready to print; 2 trial like the edition, 1 trial printed with blue and yellow only, 1 trial printed with blue, yellow, red-orange

Signature location: LC

Chop location: Jerry Raidiger, LL

Job number and location: JH71–203, reverse LL

Color printing order, execution of printing elements:

1. Aluminum printed with blue. Image drawn with pen and ink on mylar, transferred to photosensitive plate.

2. Aluminum printed with yellow. Image drawn with pen and ink on mylar, transferred to photosensitive plate.

3. Aluminum printed with red-orange. Image drawn with pen and ink on mylar, transferred to photosensitive plate.

4. Aluminum printed with green. Image drawn with pen and ink on mylar, transferred to photosensitive plate.

5. Aluminum printed with purple. Image drawn with pen and ink on mylar, transferred to photosensitive plate.

17.

Whirled Map

Date begun: 4/8/1971

Date finished: 7/1/1971

Medium: lithograph

Paper size: 15 × 20 in.

Image size: same

Paper type: German Etching

Publisher: artist

Press: Landfall Press

Printers: D. R. Holman, Jack Lemon

Edition: 50

Proofs: 1 cancellation, 2 Landfall Press, 2 press, 1 ready to print; 1 trial like the edition without dark-blue additions, 1 trial printed on light-green flat like the edition without dark-blue additions

Signature location: lower edge, C

Chop location: Jerry Raidiger, LL

Job number and location: JH71–205, reverse LL

Color printing order, execution of printing elements:

1. Aluminum printed with light green. Image drawn with pen and ink on mylar, transferred to photosensitive plate.

2. Aluminum printed with green. Image drawn with pen and ink on mylar, transferred to photosensitive plate.

3. Aluminum printed with blue. Image drawn with pen and ink on mylar, transferred to photosensitive plate. Additions: plate counter-etched and reworked with pen and autographic ink.

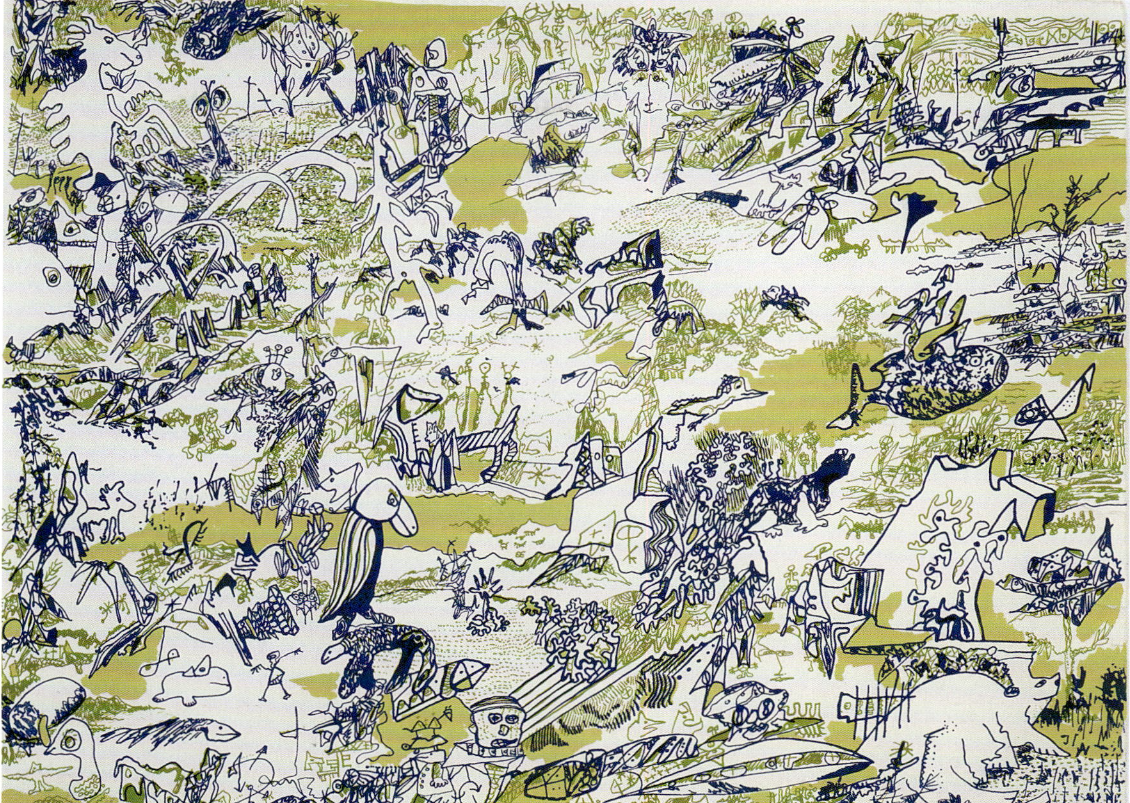

17

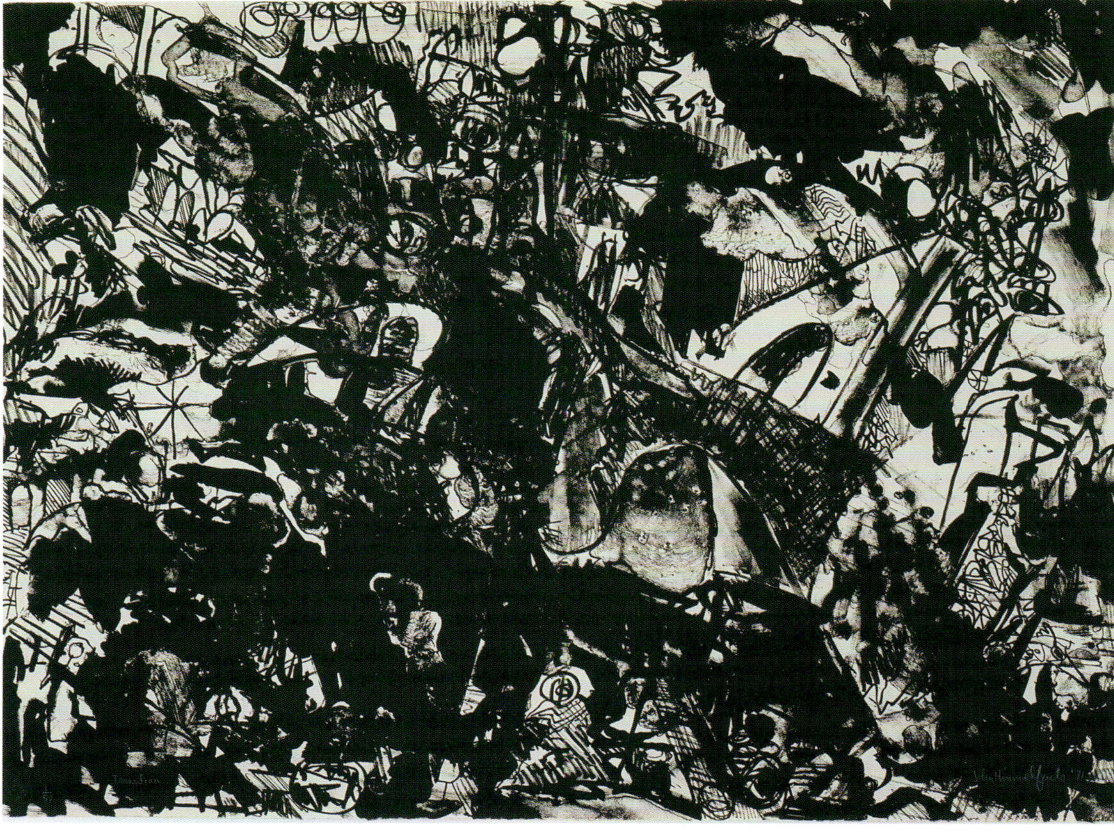

18

18.

Transition

Date begun: 4/8/1971

Date finished: 7/10/1971

Medium: lithograph

Paper size: 15 × 20 in.

Image size: same

Paper type: German Etching

Publisher: artist

Press: Landfall Press

Printers: D. R. Holman, Jerry Raidiger

Printers'assistant: Mike Rottman

Edition: 50

Proofs: 1 cancellation, 1 dead, 2 Landfall Press, 2 press, 1 ready to print: 1 trial printed with dark purple on yellow, 1 trial printed with black on cover stock

Signature location: LR

Chop location: Jerry Raidiger, LL

Job number and location: JH71–207, reverse LL

Color printing order, execution of printing elements:

1. Aluminum printed with blue-white. Flat-rolled on dry plate.

2. Aluminum printed with black. Images drawn with litho crayon, pen and autographic ink, and negro pencil.

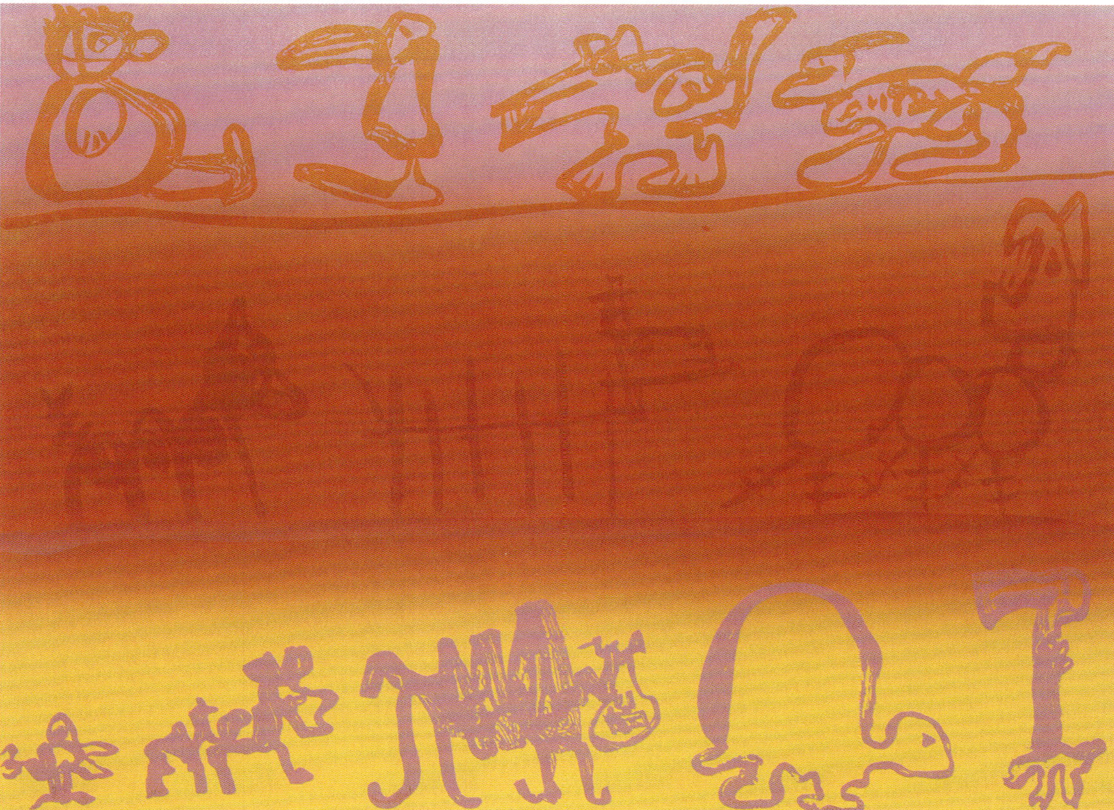

19

19.

Three Countries

Date begun: 4/1971

Date finished: 11/13/1971

Medium: lithograph

Paper size: 15 × 20 in.

Image size: same

Paper type: German Etching

Publisher: artist

Press: Landfall Press

Printers: Bill Coons, Jerry Raidiger

Edition: 45

Proofs: 5 artist, 1 cancellation, 2 Landfall Press, 2 press, 1 ready to print

Signature location: lower edge in pink area, CL

Chop location: Jerry Raidiger, LL

Job number and location: JH71–201, reverse LL

Color printing order, execution of printing elements:

1. Aluminum printed with rainbow roll with pink on top third, sun-orange on middle third, yellow on bottom third. Flat-rolled on dry plate from split fountain.

2. Aluminum printed with rainbow roll with standard orange on top third, sun-orange on middle third, and pink on bottom third. Image drawn with brush and ink on acetate, transferred to photosensitive plate.

20.

Filming of "Sunny Days"

Date begun: 1/31/1974

Date finished: 7/26/1974

Medium: lithograph

Paper size: 30 × 40 in.

Image size: same

Paper type: Special Arjomari

Publisher: artist

Press: Landfall Press

Printer: David Keister

Printer's assistants: Tom Cvikota, David Panosh

Edition: 50

Proofs: 1 artist, 1 cancellation, 2 Landfall Press, 2 press, 1 ready to print, 8 trial

Signature location: lower edge, LC

Chop location: LL

Job number and location: JH72–224, reverse LL

Color printing order, execution of printing elements:

1. Aluminum printed with blue. Image drawn with litho crayon.

2. Aluminum printed with green. Image drawn with litho crayon.

3. Aluminum printed with red. Image drawn with litho crayon.

4. Aluminum printed with pink. Image drawn with litho crayon.

5. Aluminum printed with yellow. Image drawn with litho crayon.

21.

March

Date begun: 4/8/1974

Date finished: 4/22/1974

Medium: lithograph

Paper size: 18 × 24 in.

Image size: same

Paper type: Arches Cover White

Publisher: artist

Press: Landfall Press

Printer: David Keister

Printer's assistant: Ronald E. Wyffels

Edition: 50

Proofs: 1 cancellation, 2 Landfall Press, 2 press, 1 ready to print

Signature location: LR

Chop location: LL

Job number and location: JH74–482, reverse LL

Color printing order, execution of printing elements:

1. Aluminum printed with black. Image drawn with litho crayon.

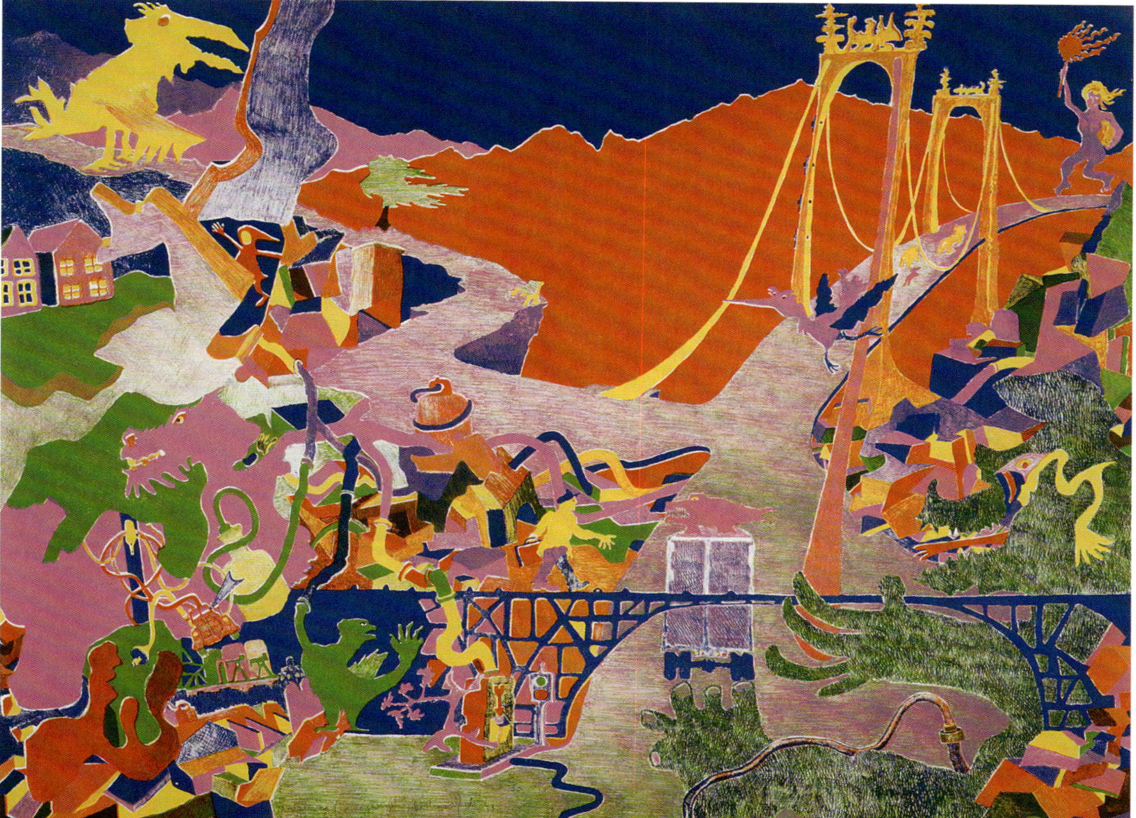

20

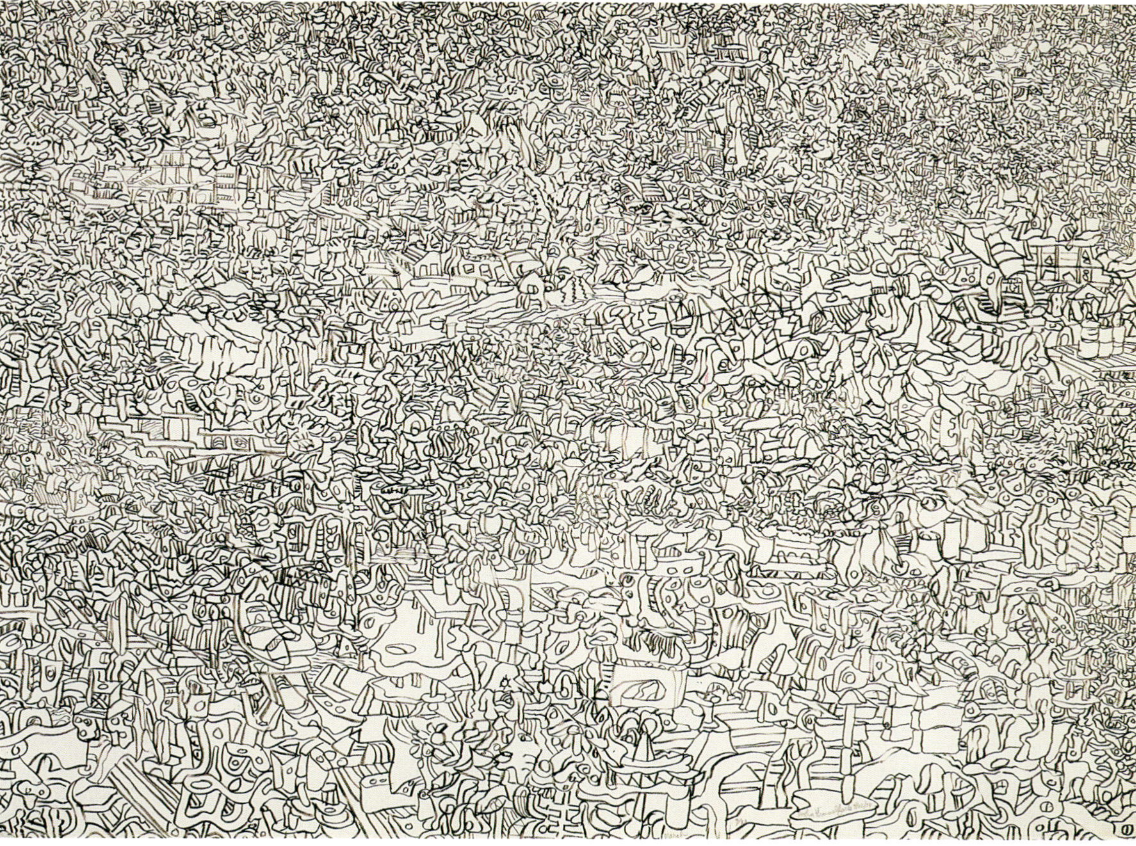

21

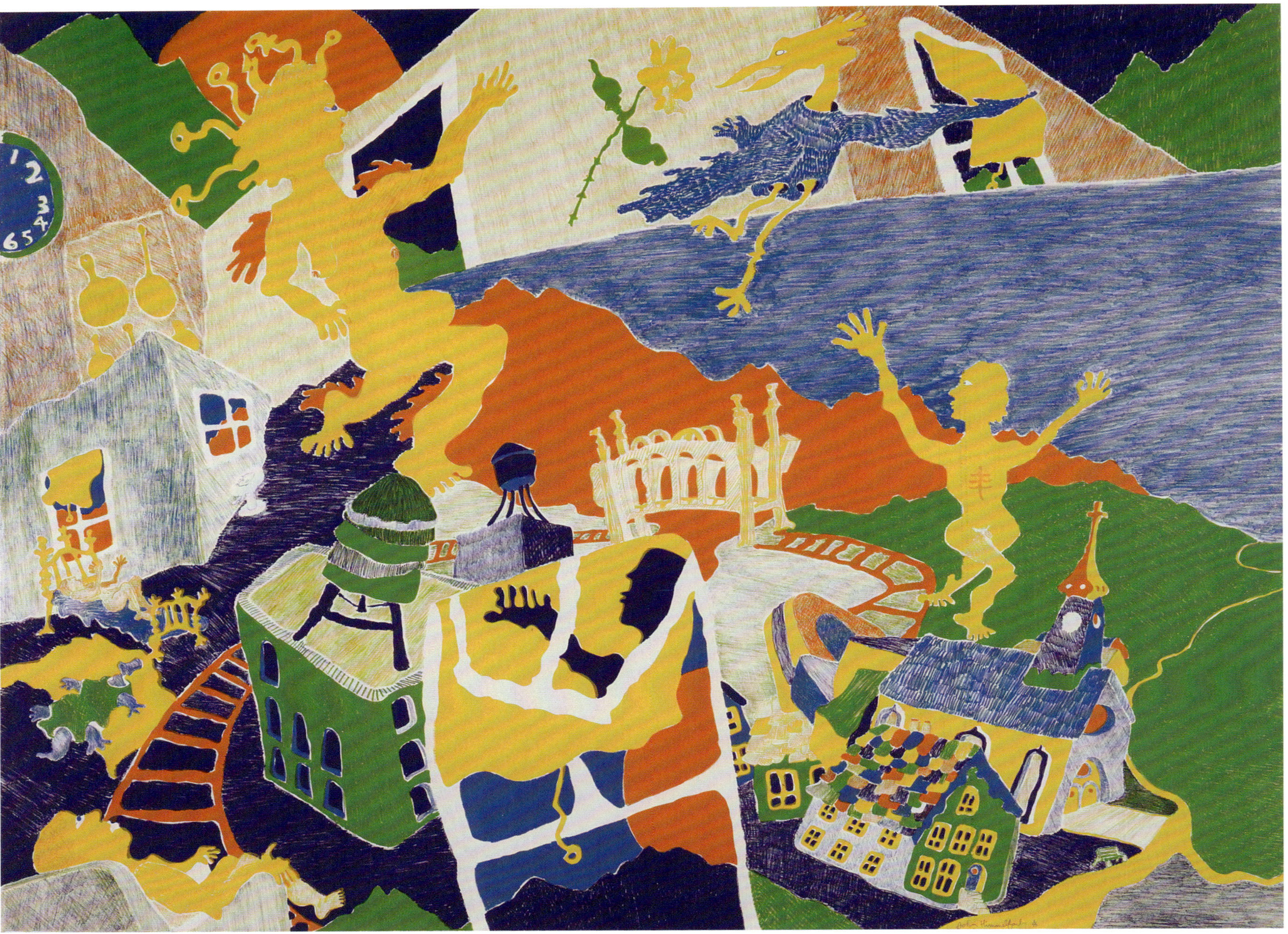

22

22.

The Clock and the Rose

Date begun: 7/22/1974

Date finished: 4/16/1975

Medium: lithograph

Paper size: 29¾ × 40 in.

Image size: same

Paper type: Arches Cover White

Publisher: artist

Press: Landfall Press

Printers: Jack Lemon, Ronald E. Wyffels

Printers' assistants: John Begley, David Keister

Edition: 95

Proofs: 1 artist, 1 cancellation, 2 Landfall Press, 2 press, 1 ready to print

Signature location: LR

Chop location: LL

Job number and location: JH74–508, reverse LL

Color printing order, execution of printing elements:

1. Aluminum printed with dark blue. Image drawn with litho crayon.

2. Aluminum printed with light blue. Image drawn with litho crayon.

3. Aluminum printed with green. Image drawn with litho crayon.

4. Aluminum printed with orange. Image drawn with litho crayon.

5. Aluminum printed with yellow. Image drawn with litho crayon.

23.

Shades

Date begun: 7/22/1974

Date finished: 3/31/1975

Medium: lithograph

Paper size: 30 × 40 in.

Image size: same

Paper type: Rives BFK White

Publisher: artist

Press: Landfall Press

Printer: David Keister

Printer's assistant: Ronald E. Wyffels

Edition: 50

Proofs: 1 cancellation, 2 Landfall Press, 2 press, 1 ready to print

Signature location: LR

Chop location: LL

Job number and location: JH74–513, reverse LL

Color printing order, execution of printing elements:

1. Aluminum printed with black. Image drawn from chalk tracing of key-line drawing used in *The Clock and the Rose* (no. 22), with pen and autographic ink.

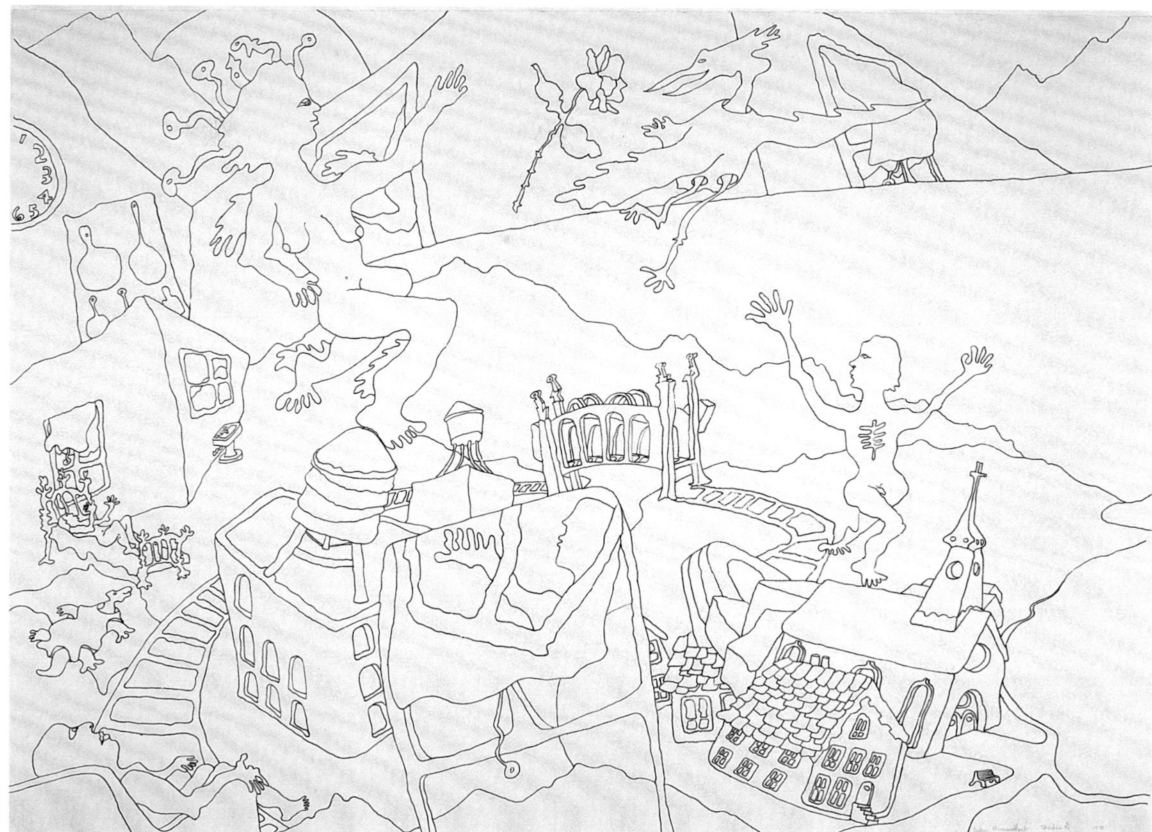

23

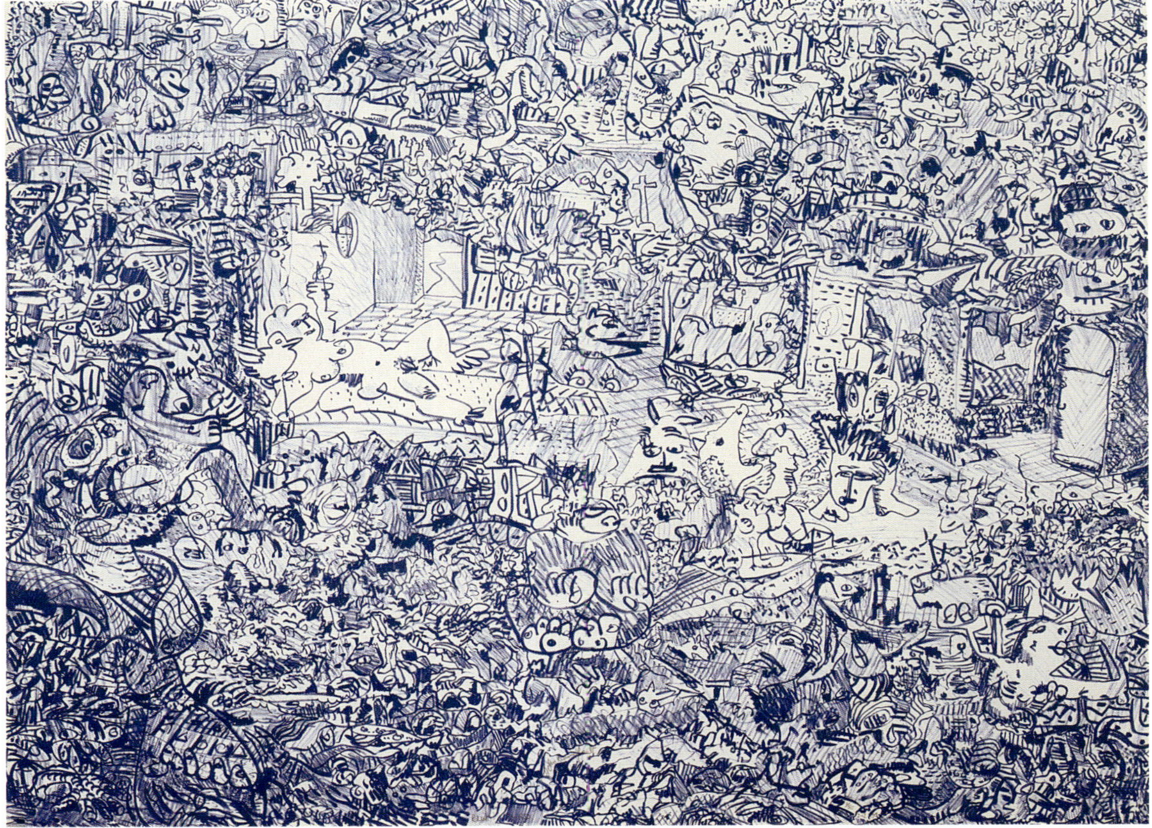

24

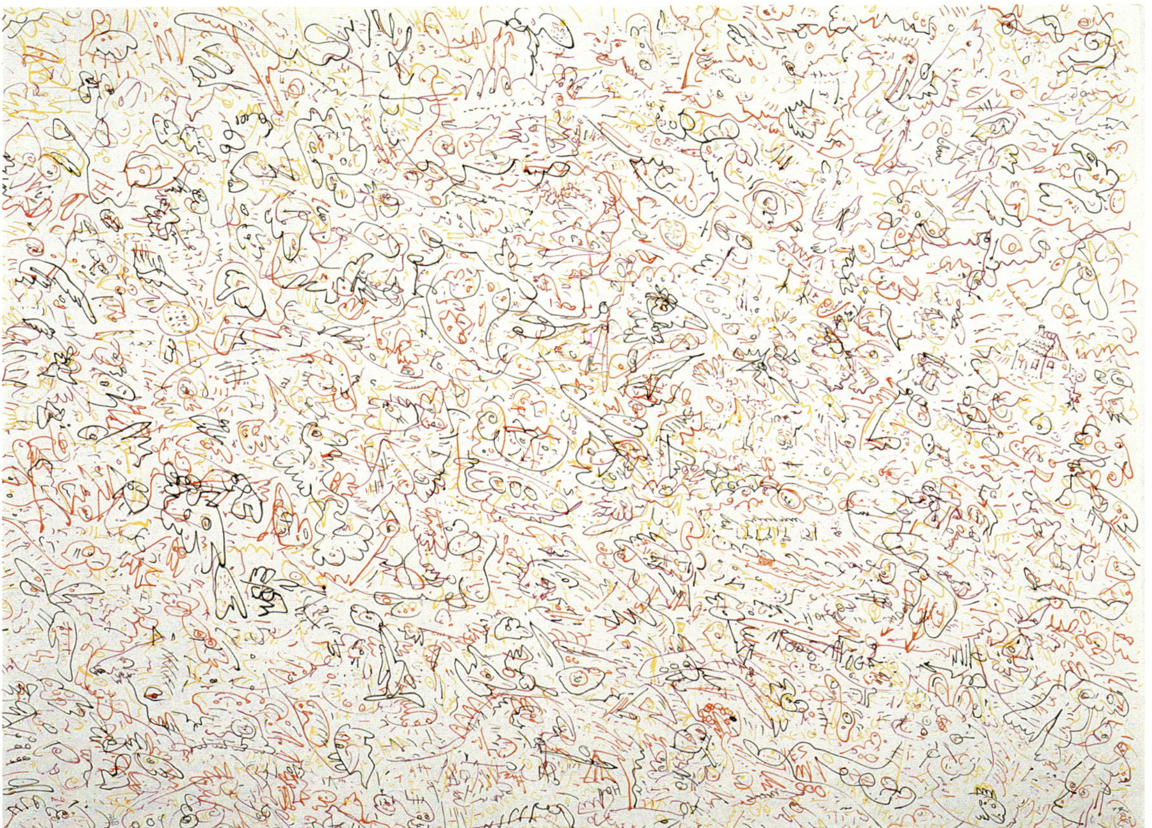

25

24.

Blue Bird

Date begun: 10/17/1974

Date finished: 2/12/1975

Medium: lithograph

Paper size: 18 × 24 in.

Image size: same

Paper type: Arches Cover White

Publisher: artist

Press: Landfall Press

Printer: Ronald E. Wyffels

Printer's assistant: Tom Hayduk

Edition: 50

Proofs: 1 cancellation, 2 Landfall Press, 2 press, 1 ready to print

Signature location: LC

Chop location: printer, LL

Job number and location: JH74–503, reverse LL

Color printing order, execution of printing elements:

1. Aluminum printed with blue. Image drawn with litho crayon.

25.

Home

Date begun: 11/1974

Date finished: 7/14/1975

Medium: lithograph

Paper size: 18 × 24 in.

Image size: same

Paper: Arches Cover White

Publisher: artist

Press: Landfall Press

Printer: Ronald E. Wyffels

Printer's assistant: David Keister

Edition: 50

Proofs: 1 cancellation, 2 Landfall Press, 2 press, 1 ready to print

Signature location: LL

Chop location: LL

Job number and location: JH74–514, reverse LL

Color printing order, execution of printing elements:

1. Aluminum printed with yellow. Image drawn with pen and ink on mylar, transferred to photosensitive plate.

2. Aluminum printed with red. Image drawn with pen and ink on mylar, transferred to photosensitive plate.

3. Aluminum printed with green. Image drawn with pen and ink on mylar, transferred to photosensitive plate.

4. Aluminum printed with purple. Image drawn with pen and ink on mylar, transferred to photosensitive plate.

26.

Flag

Date begun: 12/3/1975

Date finished: 1/9/1976

Medium: lithograph

Paper size: 16 × 20 in.

Image size: 13 × 17 in.

Paper type: Arches Cream

Publisher: artist

Press: Stone Roller

Printer: Ronald E. Wyffels

Printer's assistant: Mary Ann Kelly

Edition: 50

Proofs: 1 artist, 1 cancellation, 1 presentation, 2 press

Signature location: LR

Chop location: LL

Job number and location: JH75–009, reverse LL

Color printing order, execution of printing elements:

1. Stone printed with black. Image drawn with pen and autographic ink.

27.

Single Cell

Date begun: 1/12/1976

Date finished: 2/26/1976

Medium: lithograph

Paper size: 34 × 46 in.

Image size: 31 × 43 in.

Paper type: Process Art Paper

Publisher: artist

Press: Stone Roller

Printer: Ronald E. Wyffels

Printer's assistant: Mary Ann Kelly

Edition: 50

Proofs: 4 artist, 1 presentation, 2 press, 1 ready to print, 1 Stone Roller, 1 trial

Signature location: LR

Chop location: LL

Job number and location: JH76–013, reverse LL

Color printing order, execution of printing elements:

1. Aluminum printed with black. Image drawn with pen and autographic ink.

26

27

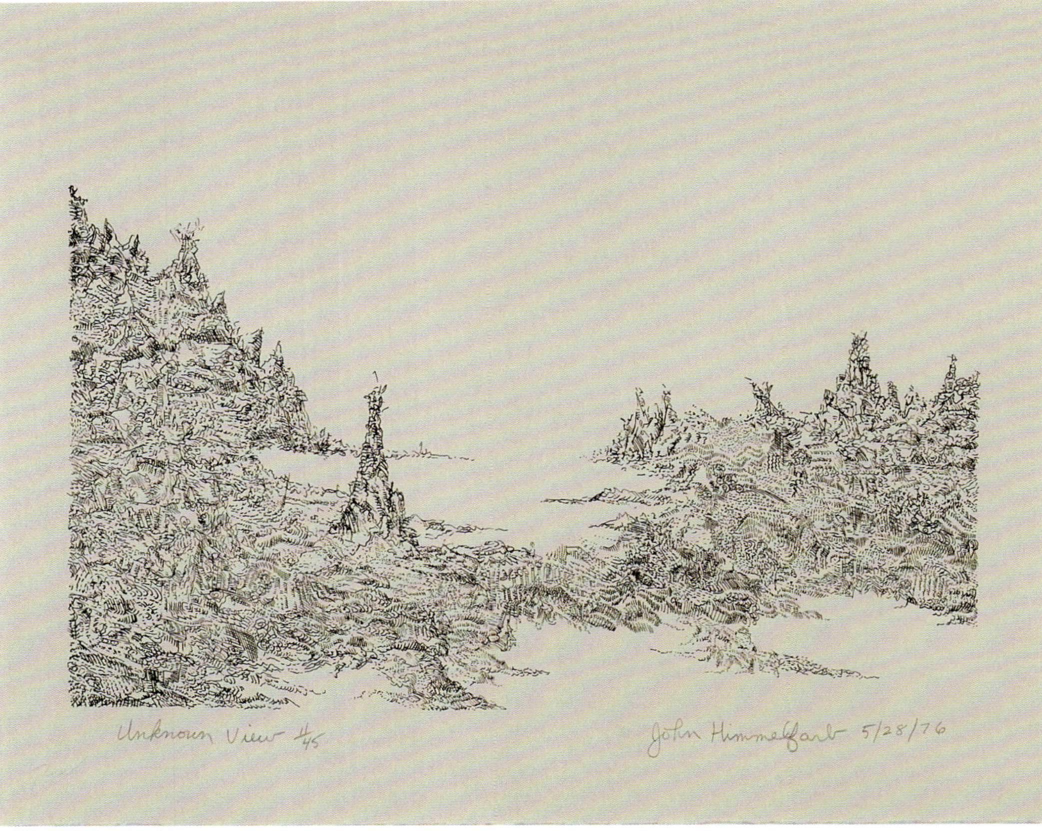

28

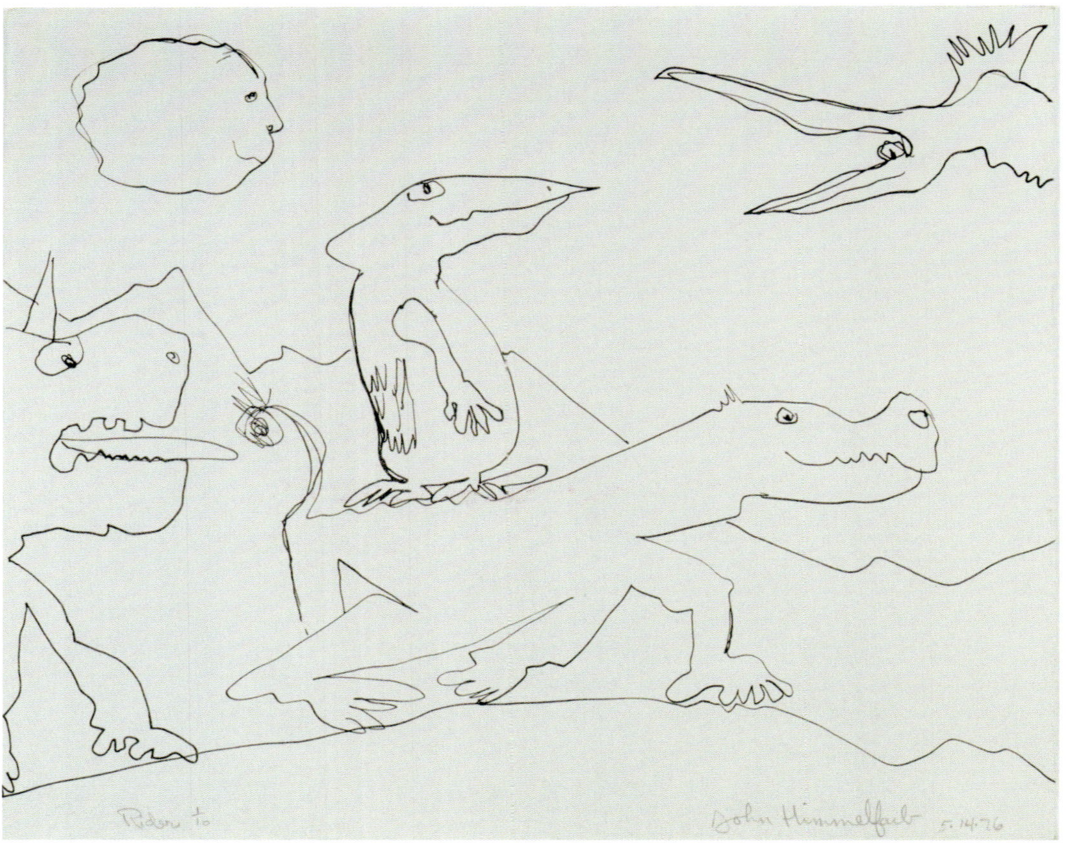

29

28.

Unknown View

Date begun: 5/6/1976

Date finished: 5/28/1976

Medium: lithograph

Paper size: 8 × 10 in.

Image size: 6¼ × 8½ in.

Paper type: Arches Buff

Publisher: artist

Press: Stone Roller

Printer: Ronald E. Wyffels

Printer's assistant: Mary Ann Kelly

Edition: 45

Proofs: 1 cancellation, 1 press, 1 Stone Roller

Signature location: LR

Chop location: LL

Job number and location: JH76–027, reverse LL

Color printing order, execution of printing elements:

1. Stone printed with black. Image drawn with pen and autographic ink.

29.

Rider

Date begun: 5/7/1976

Date finished: 5/13/1976

Medium: lithograph

Paper size: 8 × 10 in.

Image size: same

Paper type: Arches White

Publisher: artist

Press: Stone Roller

Printer: Ronald E. Wyffels

Printer's assistant: Mary Ann Kelly

Edition: 10

Proofs: 1 Stone Roller

Signature location: LR

Chop location: LL

Job number and location: JH76–028, reverse LL

Color printing order, execution of printing elements:

1. Aluminum printed with black. Image drawn with pen and autographic ink.

30.

16 Cases

Date begun: 5/7/1976

Date finished: 5/13/1976

Medium: lithograph

Paper size: 8¼ × 10 in.

Image size: same

Paper type: Arches White

Publisher: artist

Press: Stone Roller

Printer: Ronald E. Wyffels

Printer's assistant: Mary Ann Kelly

Edition: 10

Proofs: 1 Stone Roller

Signature location: lower edge, CR

Chop location: LL

Job number and location: JH76–030, reverse LL

Color printing order, execution of printing elements:

1. Aluminum printed with black. Image drawn with pen and autographic ink.

31.

Skateboard

Date begun: 5/7/1976

Date finished: 5/13/1976

Medium: lithograph

Paper size: 8 × 10 in.

Image size: same

Paper type: Arches White

Publisher: artist

Press: Stone Roller

Printer: Ronald E. Wyffels

Printer's assistant: Mary Ann Kelly

Edition: 10

Proofs: 1 press

Signature location: LL

Chop location: LL

Job number and location: JH76–029, reverse LL

Color printing order, execution of printing elements:

1. Aluminum printed with black. Image drawn with pen and autographic ink.

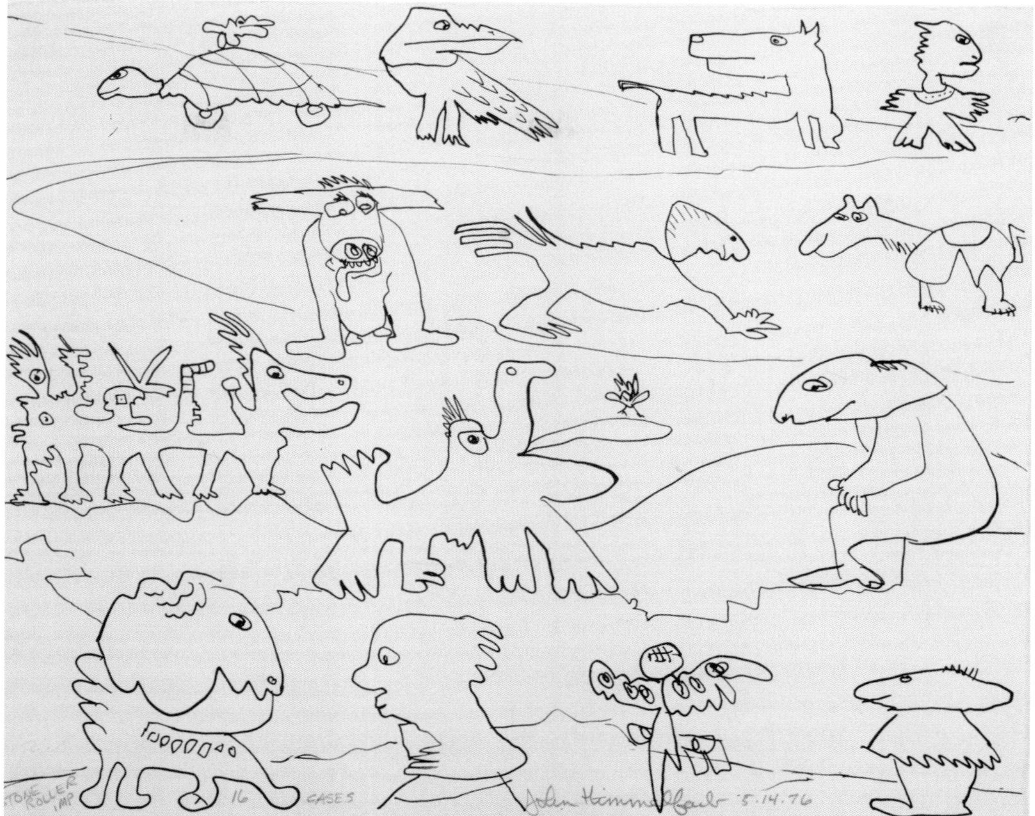

30

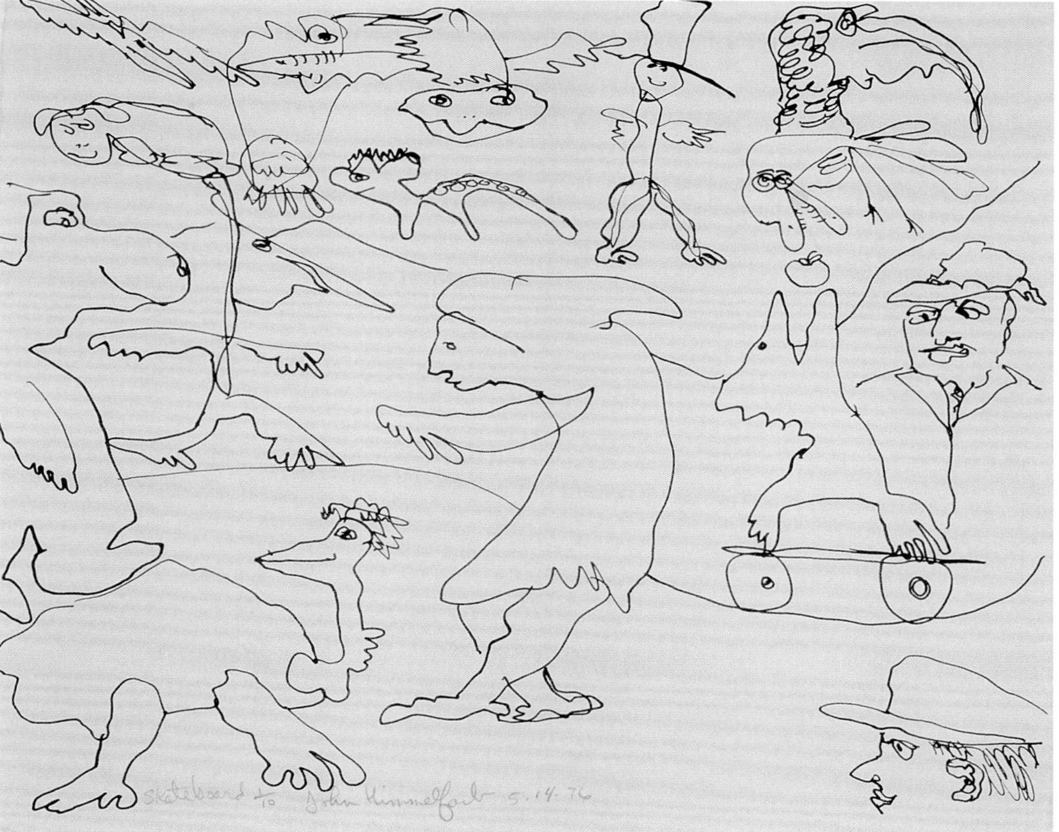

31

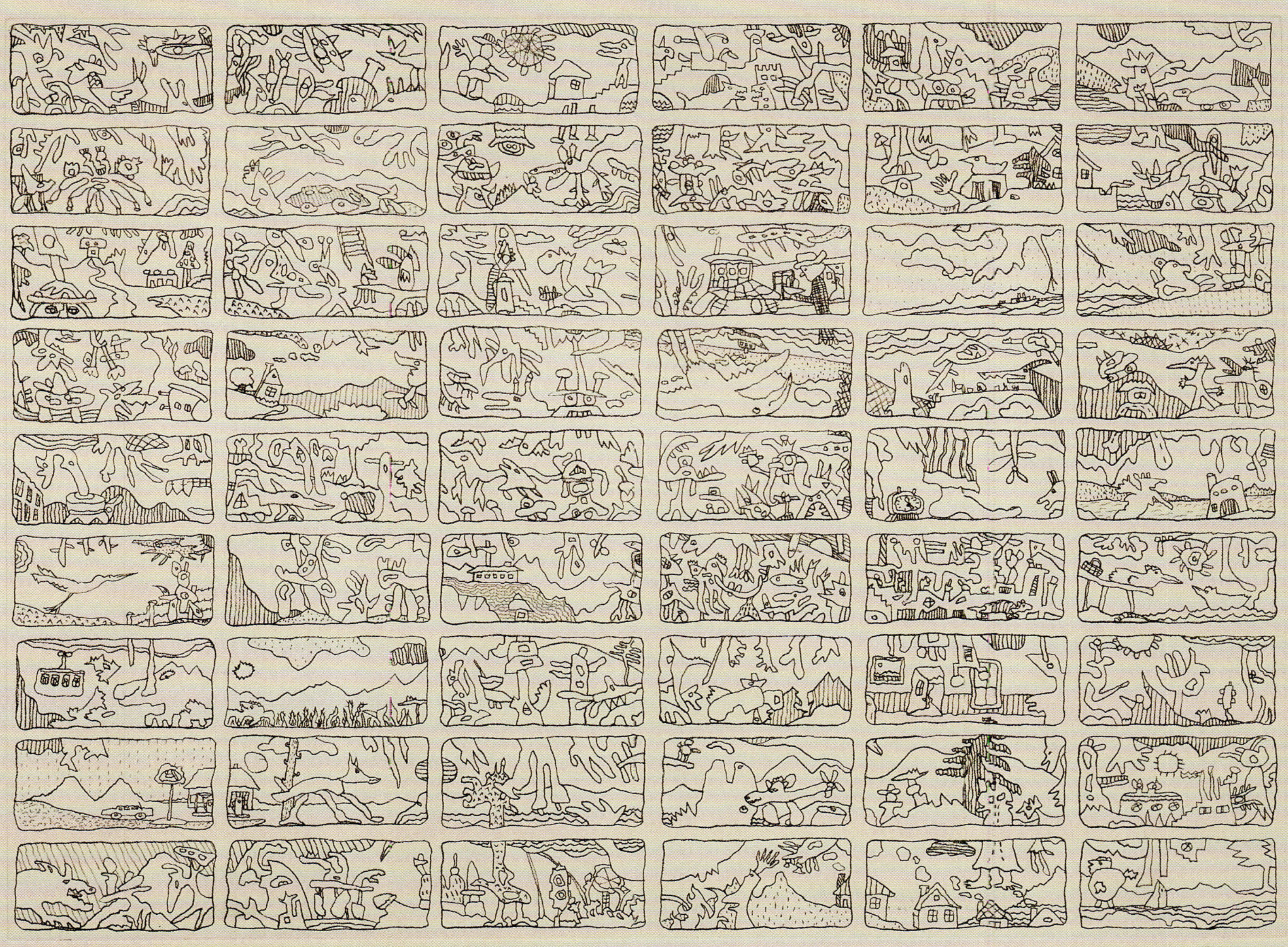

32

32.

Early Riser

Date begun: 12/14/1976

Date finished: 2/7/1977

Medium: intaglio

Paper size: 22 × 30 in.

Image size: 18 × 24 in.

Paper type: Arches Cream

Publisher: artist

Press: Teaberry Press

Printer: Timothy Berry

Edition: 40

Proofs: 1 presentation, 1 press, 1 ready to print, 1 Teaberry Press, 2 trial

Signature location: LR

Chop location: stamp, reverse LL

Job number and location: TPJH76–060, reverse LL

Color printing order, execution of printing elements:

1. Copper printed with black. Image drawn with pencil on tracing paper over soft ground.

33.

Words Cannot Describe

Date begun: 4/16/1979

Date finished: 6/18/1979

Medium: lithograph

Paper size: 38¼ × 24¾ in.

Image size: 31½ × 21¼ in.

Paper type: Sugikawa

Publisher: artist

Press: Landfall Press

Printer: Jack Lemon

Printer's assistant: Thomas Blackman

Edition: 50

Proofs: 5 artist, 1 cancellation, 2 Landfall Press 2 press, 1 ready to print

Location of signature: LR

Chop location: none

Job number and location: JH79–752, reverse LL

Color printing order, execution of printing elements:

1. Aluminum printed with white-brown. Image drawn with pen and ink on mylar, transferred to photosensitive plate.

33

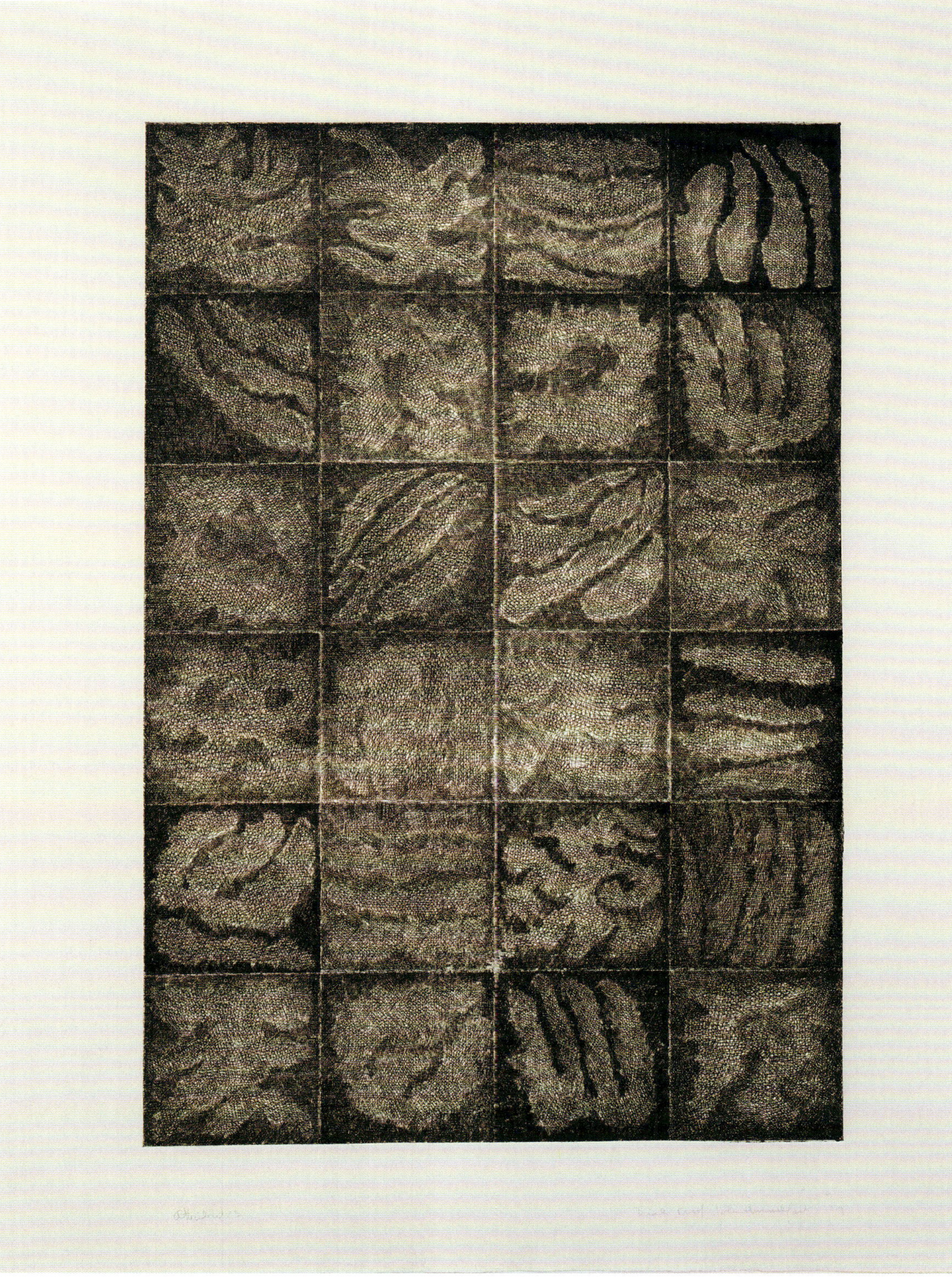

34

34.

Attributes

Date begun: 1979

Date finished: 1979

Medium: etching

Paper size: 30 × 22¼ in.

Image size: 23⅝ × 15⅝ in.

Paper type: Arches Cover White

Publisher: artist

Edition: none

Proofs: 5 or fewer

Signature location: LR or LL

Chop location: none

Job number and location: none

Color printing order, execution of printing elements:

1. Copper printed with black. Image drawn with line-etching technique.

35.

Similar Sounds

Date begun: 1979

Date finished: 1979

Medium: etching

Paper size: 30 × 22¼ in.

Image size: 23⅞ × 15⅞ in.

Paper type: Arches Cover White

Publisher: artist

Edition: none

Proofs: 2 artist, 2 trial

Signature location: LR or LL

Chop location: none

Job number and location: none

Color printing order, execution of printing elements:

1. Copper printed with black. Image drawn with line-etching technique.

Note: May have been exhibited also as *Memories*.

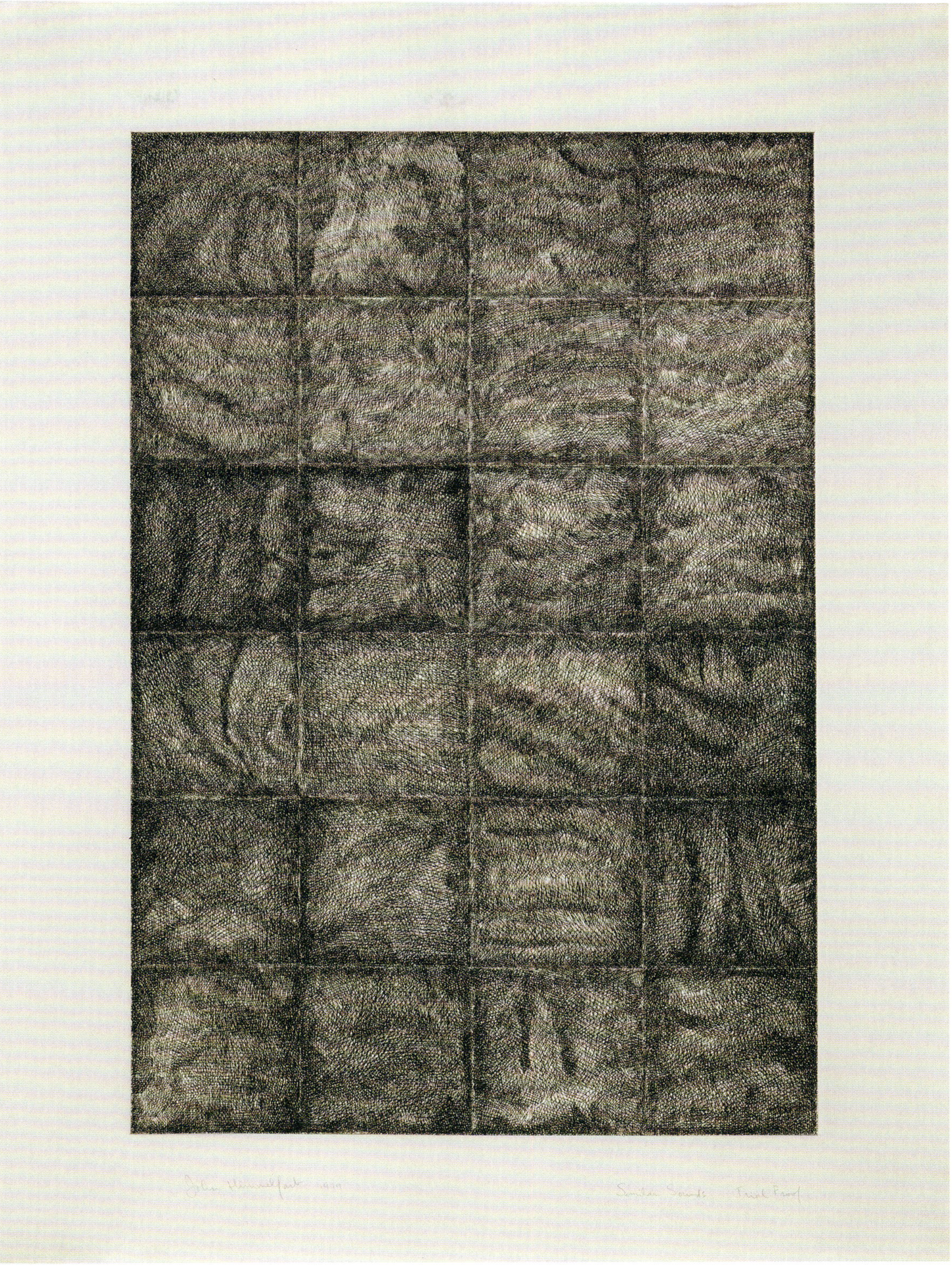

35

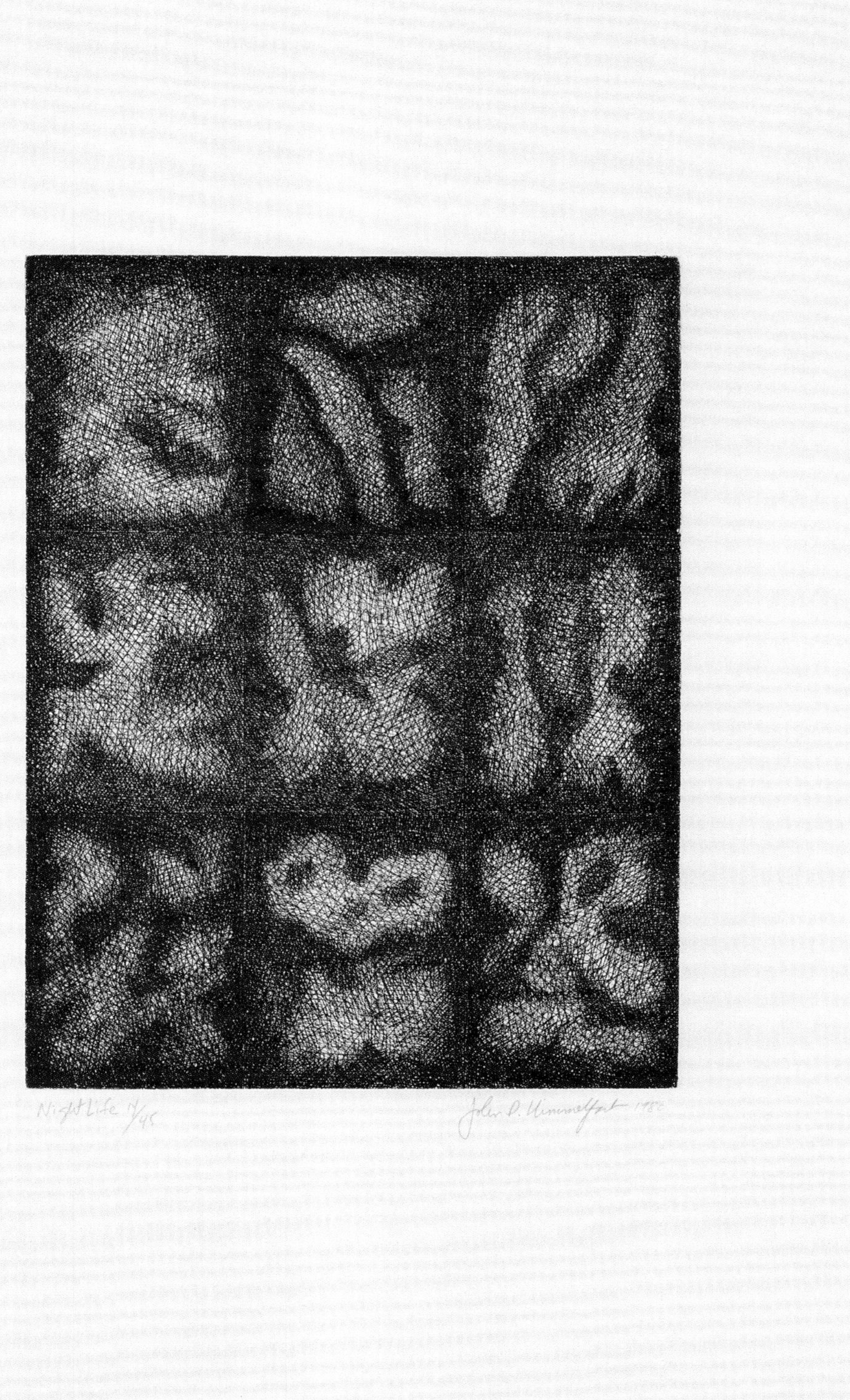

36.

Night Life

Date begun: 1979

Date finished: 1–13: 1980; 14–45: 2004

Medium: etching

Paper size: 1–13: 16 × 13 in.; 14–45: 22¼ × 15 in.

Image size: 12 × 9 in.

Paper type: 1–13: not known; 14–45: Arches Cover White

Publisher: artist

Presses: 1–13: Ruth Bauman; 14–45: Peck School of the Arts, University of Wisconsin–Milwaukee

Printers: 1–13: Ruth Bauman; 14–45: Brian Novak

Edition: 45

Proofs: 5 or fewer

Signature location: LR

Chop location: information not available

Job number and location: information not available

Color printing order, execution of printing elements:

1. Copper printed with #514 bone black.

37.

Plot Outline

Date begun: 1979

Date finished: 1–10: 1980; 11–45: 2004

Medium: etching

Paper size: 1–10: 16 × 13 in.; 11–45: 22¼ × 15 in.

Paper type: Arches Cover White

Publisher: artist

Presses: 1–10: Ruth Bauman; 11–45: Peck School of the Arts, University of Wisconsin–Milwaukee

Printers: 1–10: Ruth Bauman; 11–45: Brian Novak

Edition: 45

Proofs: 5 or fewer

Signature location: LR

Chop location: none

Job number and location: none

Color printing order, execution of printing elements:

1. Copper printed with #514 bone black. Image drawn with line-etching technique.

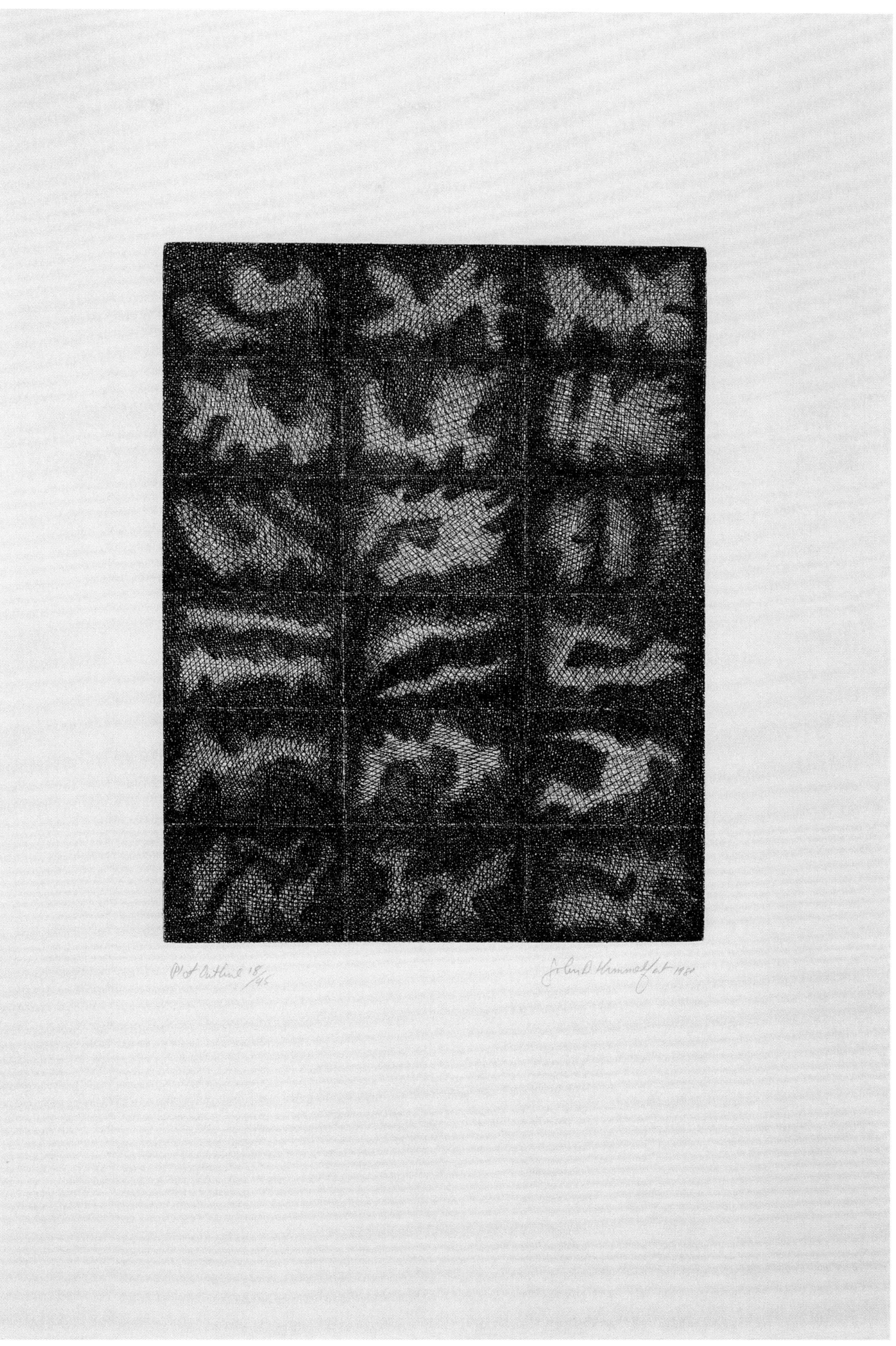

37

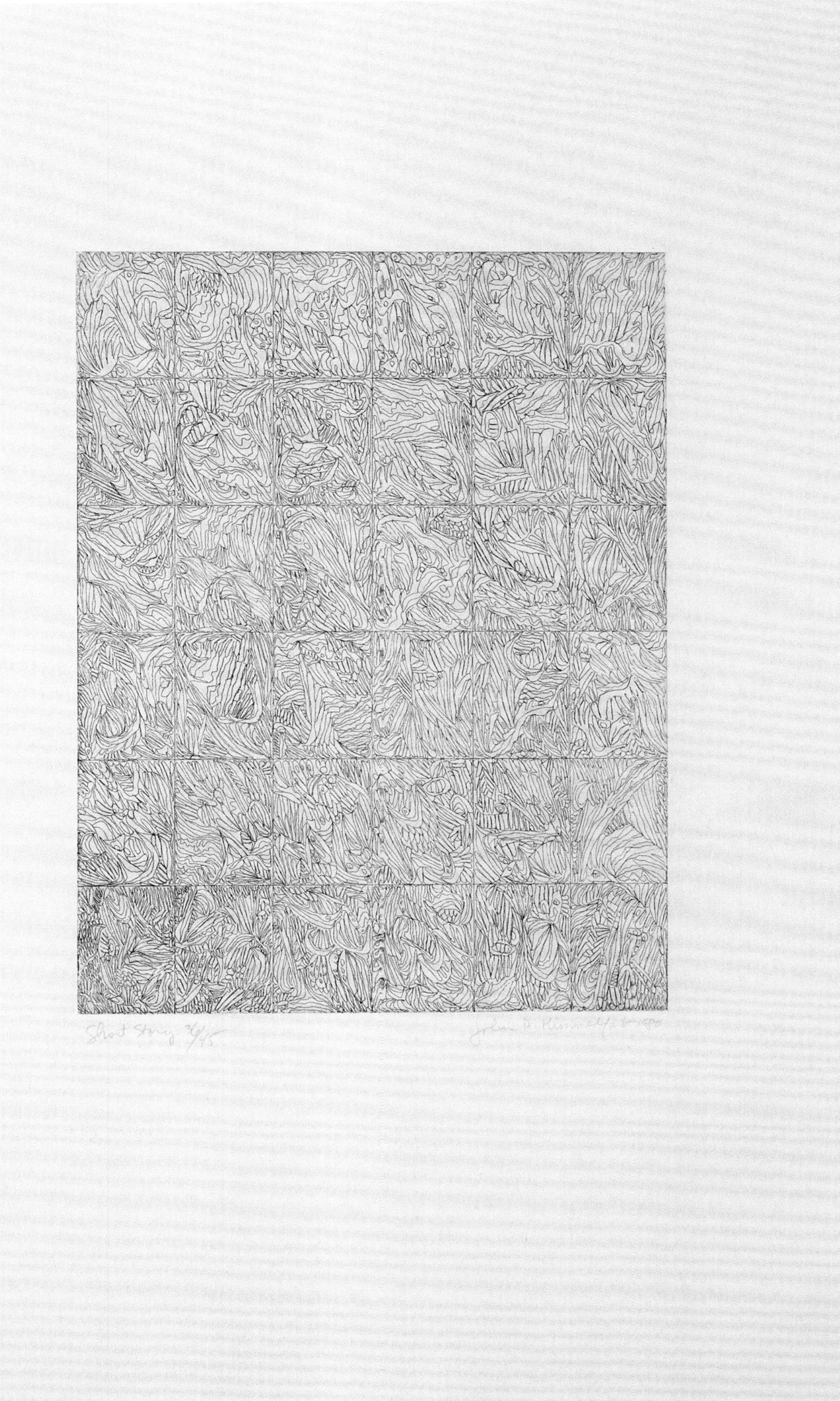

38.

Short Story

Date begun: 1979

Date finished: 1–10: 1980; 11–36: 2004

Medium: intaglio

Paper size: 1–10: 16 × 13 in.; 11–36: 22¼ × 15 in.

Image size: 12 × 9 in.

Paper type: Arches Cover White

Publisher: artist

Presses: 1–10: Ruth Bauman; 11–36: Peck School of the Arts, University of Wisconsin–Milwaukee

Printers: 1–10: Ruth Bauman; 11–36: Brian Novak

Edition: 36

Proofs: 2 artist, 5 press (Roman numerals)

Signature location: LR

Chop location: none

Job number and location: none

Color printing order, execution of printing elements:

1. Copper-printed with #514 bone black. Image drawn with line-etching technique.

Note: While an edition of 45 was planned, no more than 36 prints were made, as the plate broke down.

39.

Home and Garden

Date begun: 1981

Date finished: 1981

Medium: lithograph

Paper size: 25 × 37 in.

Image size: 22¼ in. × 30 in.

Paper type: Moriki Gray

Publisher: artist

Press: Plucked Chicken Press

Printers: Cynthia Archer, Will Petersen

Edition: None

Proofs: 5 artist (?), 1 on tan paper (not Moriki)

Signature location: LR

Chop location: LL

Job number and location: none

Color printing order, execution of printing elements:

1. Aluminum printed with black. Image drawn with brush and asphaltum.

40.

Storyteller

Date begun: 1981

Date finished: 1981

Medium: lithograph

Paper size: 30 × 40 in.

Image size: same

Paper type: Arches Cover White

Publisher: artist

Press: Plucked Chicken Press

Printers: Cynthia Archer, Will Petersen

Edition: 50

Proofs: 2 artist, 2 Plucked Chicken Press, 2 press, 2 trial

Signature location: lower edge, CR

Chop location: LL

Job number: HIM781–A

Color printing order, execution of printing elements:

1. Aluminum printed with reflex blue mixed with white. Image drawn with litho crayon.
2. Aluminum printed with pthalo green mixed with yellow. Image drawn with litho crayon.
3. Aluminum printed with flame red. Image drawn with litho crayon.
4. Aluminum printed with lemon yellow mixed with white. Image drawn with litho crayon.
5. Aluminum printed with rhodamine red mixed with white. Image drawn with litho crayon.

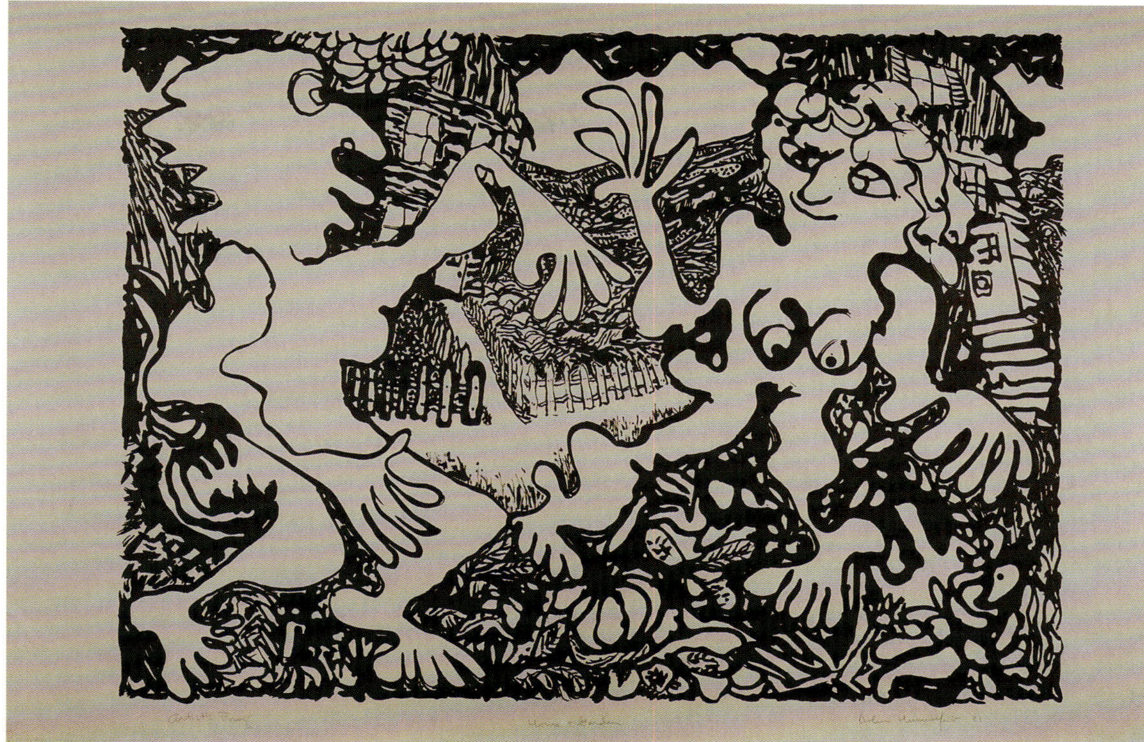

39

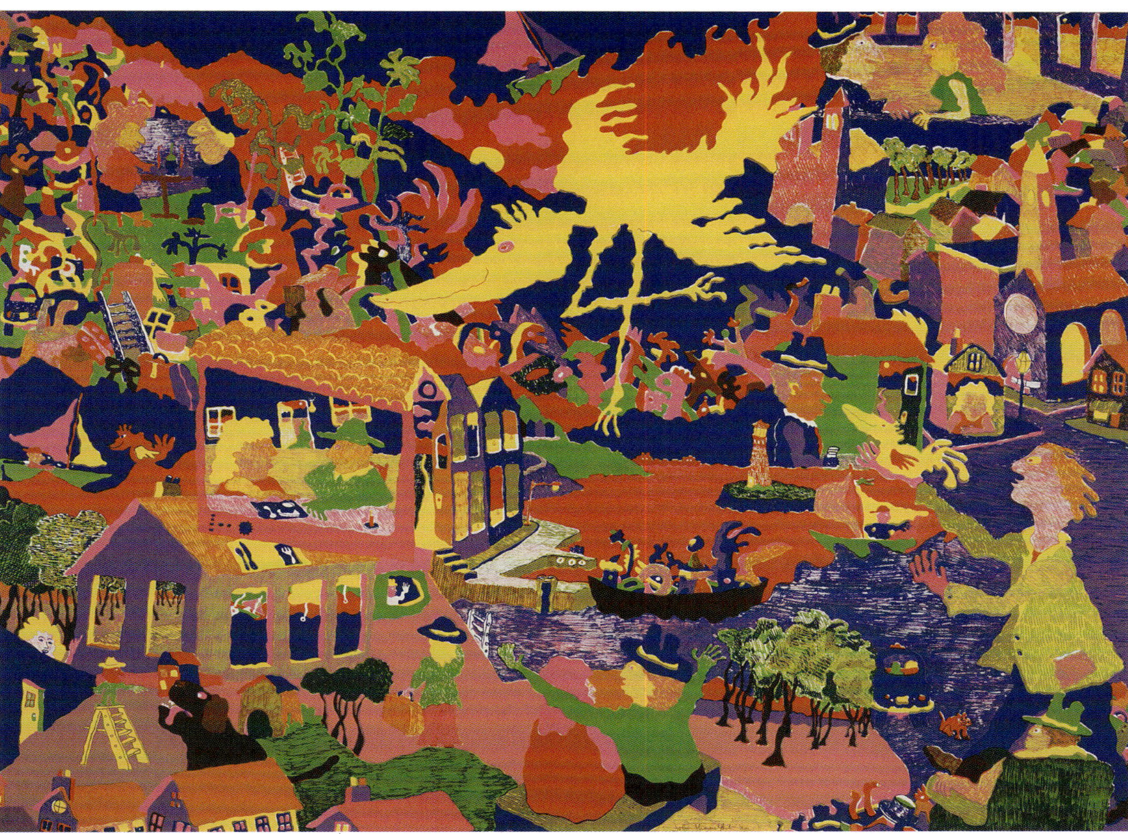

40

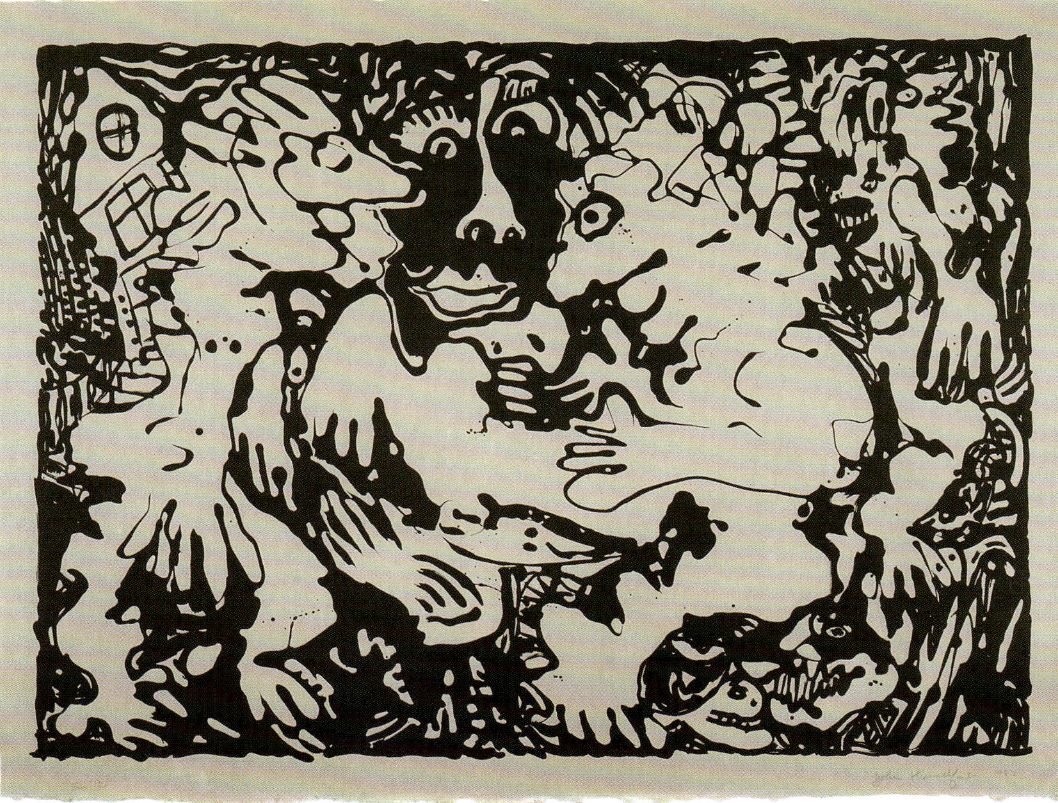

41

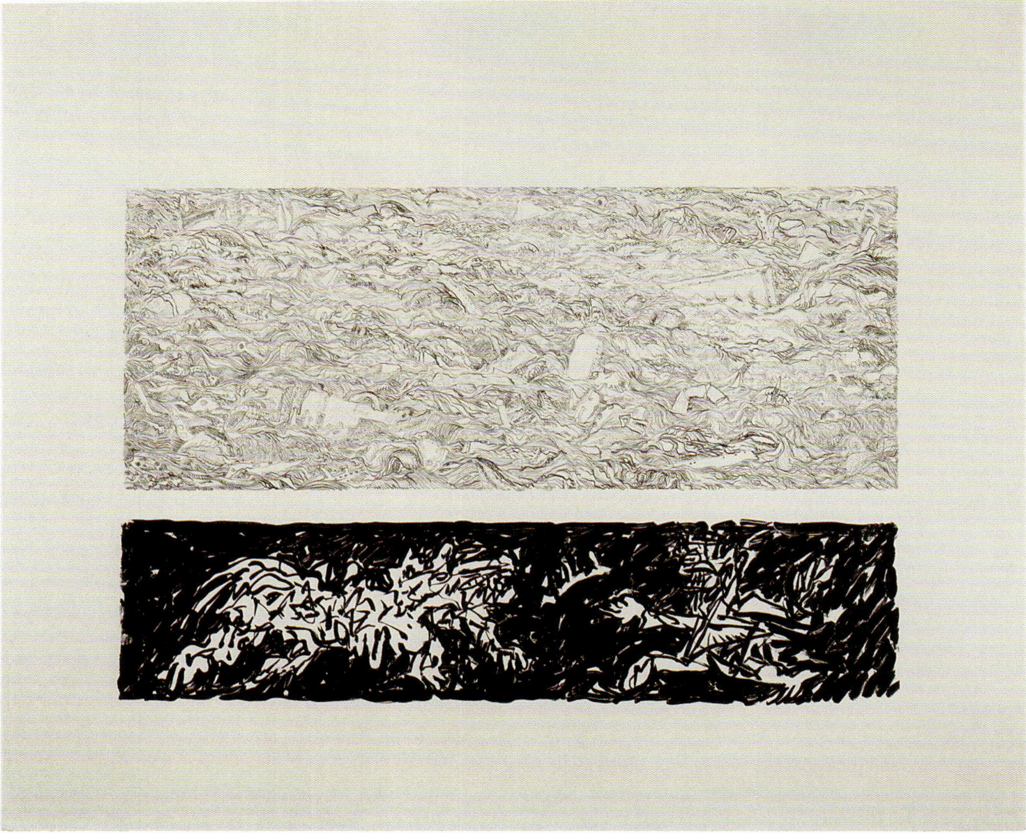

42

41.

Trio

Date begun: 1981

Date finished: 1/1982

Medium: lithograph

Paper size: 25 × 32½ in.

Image size: 22½ × 30¼ in.

Paper type: Moriki Gray

Publisher: artist

Press: Plucked Chicken Press

Printers: Cynthia Archer, Will Petersen

Edition: 25

Proofs: 2 artist, 1 press

Signature location: LR

Chop location: LL

Job number and location: none

Color printing order, execution of printing elements:

1. Aluminum printed with black ink warmed with blue-purple. Image drawn with brush and asphaltum.

42.

Balance Sheet

Date begun: 1982

Date finished: 1982

Medium: lithograph

Paper size: 27½ × 33 in.

Image size: 17 × 25¼ in.

Paper type: Rives BFK Gray

Publisher: artist

Press: Plucked Chicken Press

Printers: Cynthia Archer, Will Petersen

Edition: 25

Proofs: 2 artist (1 printed on 28¾ × 32 in. paper), 2 Plucked Chicken Press, 2 press

Signature location: LL

Chop location: LL

Job number and location: none

Color printing order, execution of printing elements:

1. Stone printed with black. Image drawn with brush and tusche and litho pencil.

43.

Boatman

Date begun: 1982

Date finished: 1982

Medium: lithograph

Paper size: 23 × 37 in.

Image size: 20½ × 34½ in.

Paper type: Rives BFK Gray

Publisher: artist

Press: Plucked Chicken Press

Printers: Cynthia Archer, Will Petersen

Edition: 25

Proofs: 3 artist on Arches Cover White, Moriki Gray, and Rives BFK Gray, 1 Plucked Chicken Press on Moriki Gray (Roman numeral), 2 press, 2 trial on Arches Cover White and Arches Text

Signature location: LR

Chop location: LL

Job number and location: none

Color printing order, execution of printing elements:

1. Aluminum printed with black. Image drawn with brush and autographic ink on transfer paper.

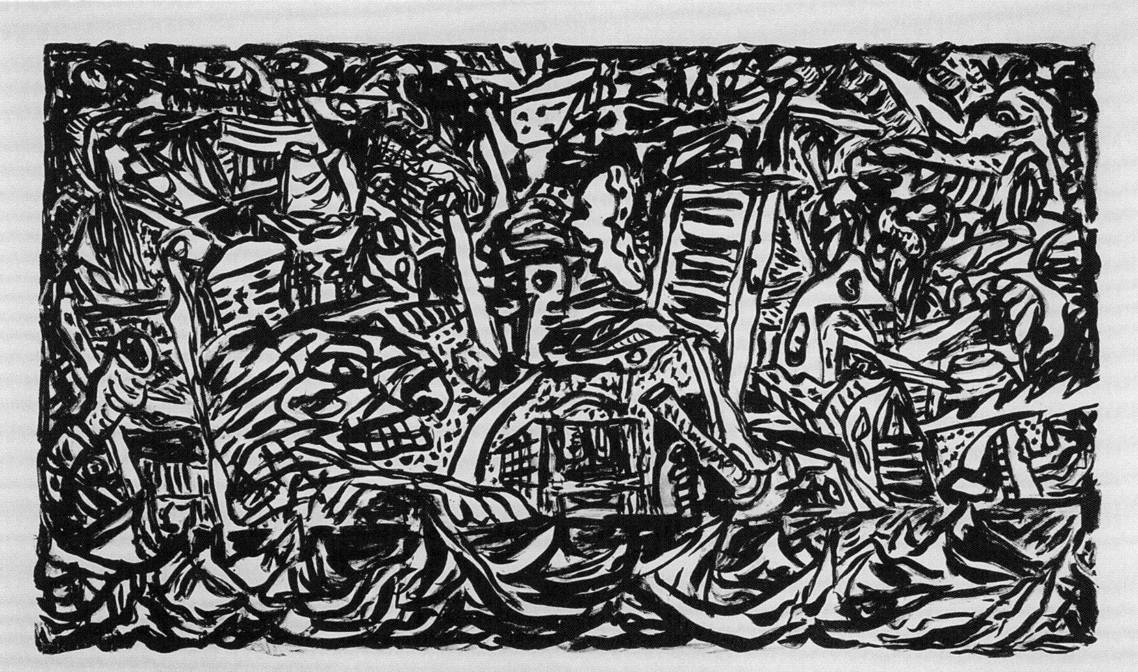

43

44.

Bone

Date begun: 1982

Date finished: 1982

Medium: lithograph

Paper size: 18½ × 32½ in.

Image size: 15¼ × 31 in.

Paper type: Shojigami

Publisher: artist

Press: Plucked Chicken Press

Printers: Cynthia Archer, Will Petersen

Edition: 25

Proofs: 1 artist, 2 Plucked Chicken Press (Roman numerals; II on Moriki Gray), 2 press

Signature location: LR

Chop location: LL

Job number and location: none

Color printing order, execution of printing elements:

1. Aluminum printed with black. Image drawn with brush and autographic ink on transfer paper.

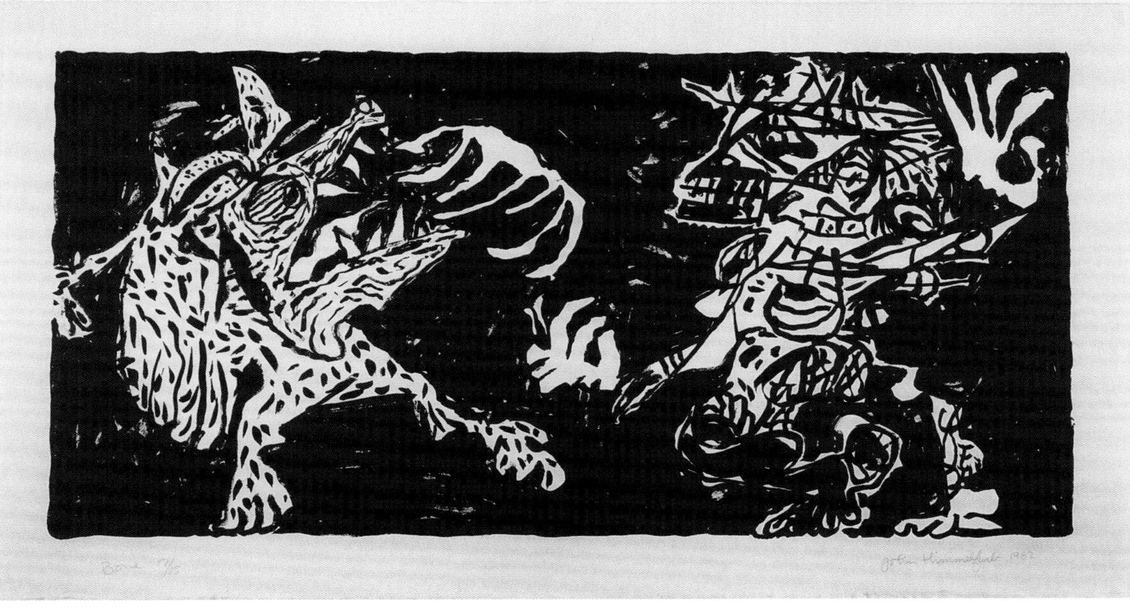

44

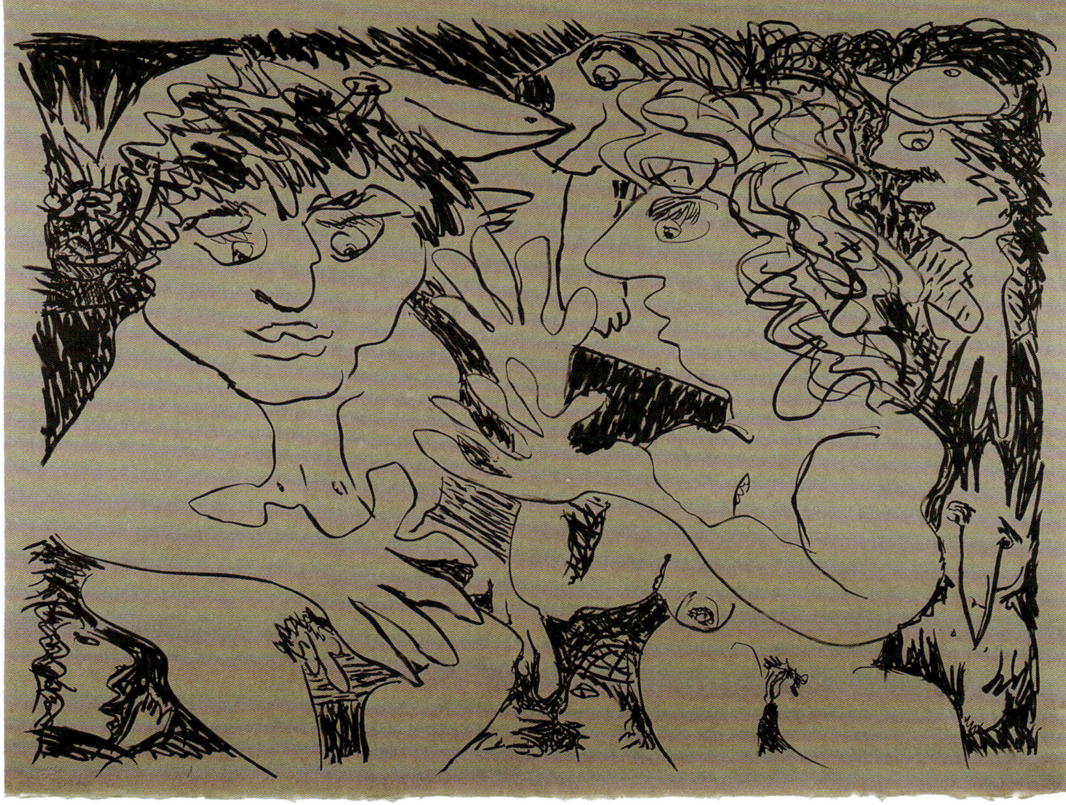

45

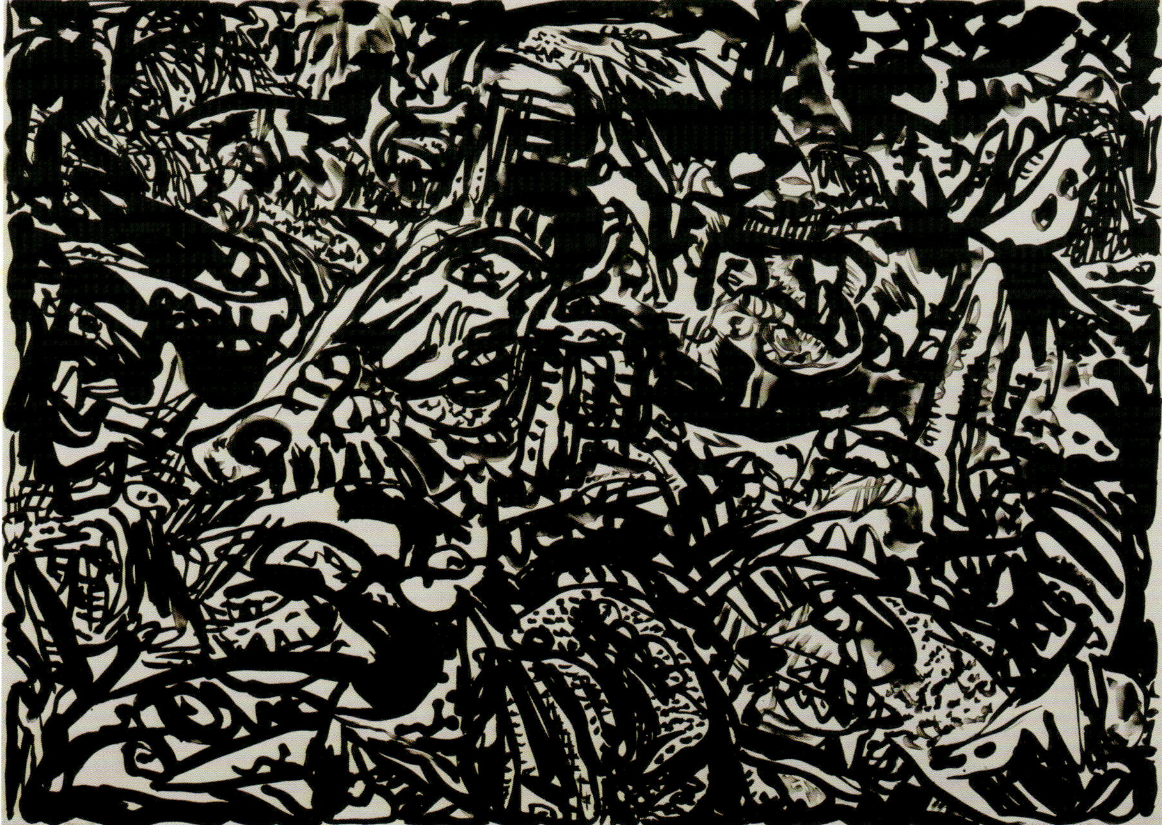

46

45.

Bridge

Date begun: 1982

Date finished: 1982

Medium: lithograph

Paper size: 24½ × 32 in.

Image size: 23¼ × 31¼ in.

Paper type: Moriki Gray

Publisher: artist

Press: Plucked Chicken Press

Printers: Cynthia Archer, Will Petersen

Edition: 25

Proofs: 2 artist, 1 press, 2 Plucked Chicken Press (Roman numerals; II on a lighter-value Moriki)

Signature location: LR

Chop location: LL

Job number and location: none

Color printing order, execution of printing elements:

1. Aluminum printed with black. Image drawn with litho crayon.

46.

Clearing

Date begun: 1982

Date finished: 1982

Medium: lithograph

Paper size: 22¼ × 30 in.

Image size: same

Paper type: Arches Buff

Publisher: artist

Press: Plucked Chicken Press

Printers: Cynthia Archer, Will Petersen

Edition: 50

Proofs: 2 Plucked Chicken Press, 2 press

Signature location: LR

Chop location: LL

Job number and location: none

Color printing order, execution of printing elements:

1. Aluminum printed with black. Image drawn with brush and tusche.

47.

Dust Engenders

Date begun: 1982

Date finished: 1982

Medium: lithograph

Paper size: 13 × 15 in.

Image size: 9 × 11 in.

Paper type: Arches White

Publisher: artist

Press: Plucked Chicken Press

Printer: Cynthia Archer

Edition: 25

Proofs: 2 Plucked Chicken Press, 2 press, 1 studio

Signature location: LR

Chop location: LL

Job number and location: none

Color printing order, execution of printing elements:

1. Stone printed with black. Image drawn with litho crayon.

48.

Isn't Life Wonderful

Date begun: 1982

Date finished: 1982

Medium: lithograph

Paper size: 8½ × 18 in.

Image size: 5 × 15 in.

Paper type: Rives BFK Gray

Publisher: artist

Press: Plucked Chicken Press

Printer: Will Petersen

Printer's assistant: Cynthia Archer

Edition: 47

Proofs: 3 artist, 3 Plucked Chicken Press, 2 press, 1 ready to print

Signature location: LR

Chop location: LR

Color printing order, execution of printing elements:

1. Stone printed with black modified with purple. Image drawn with litho crayon and litho pencil.

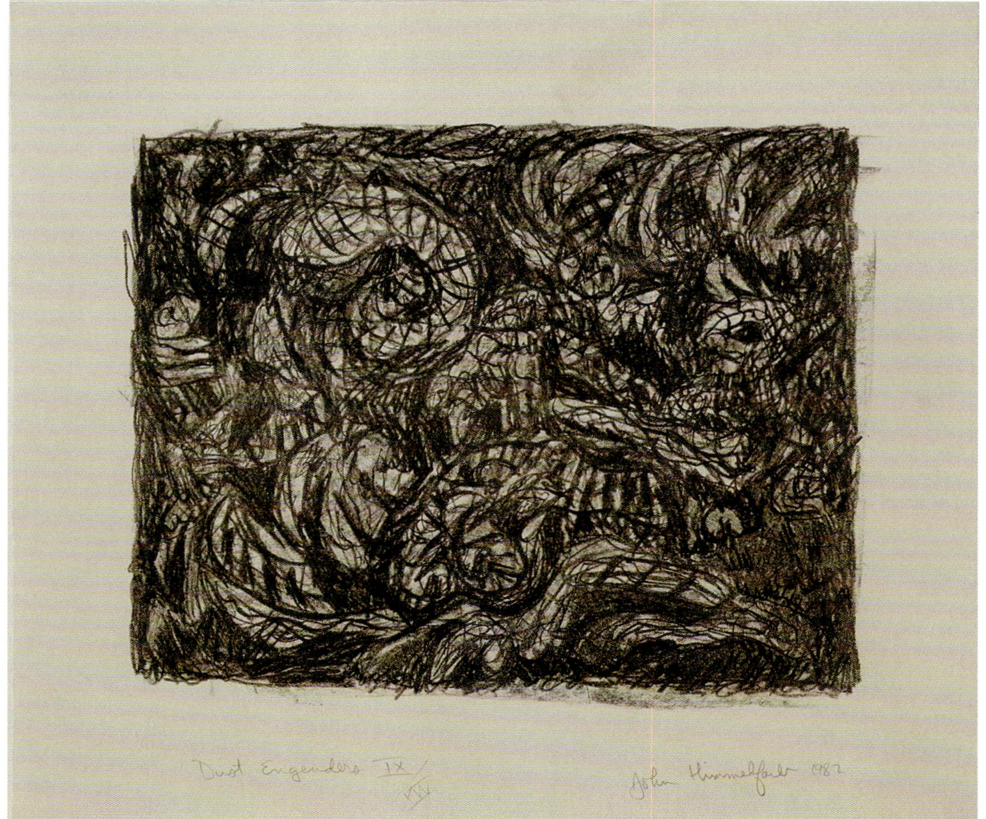

47

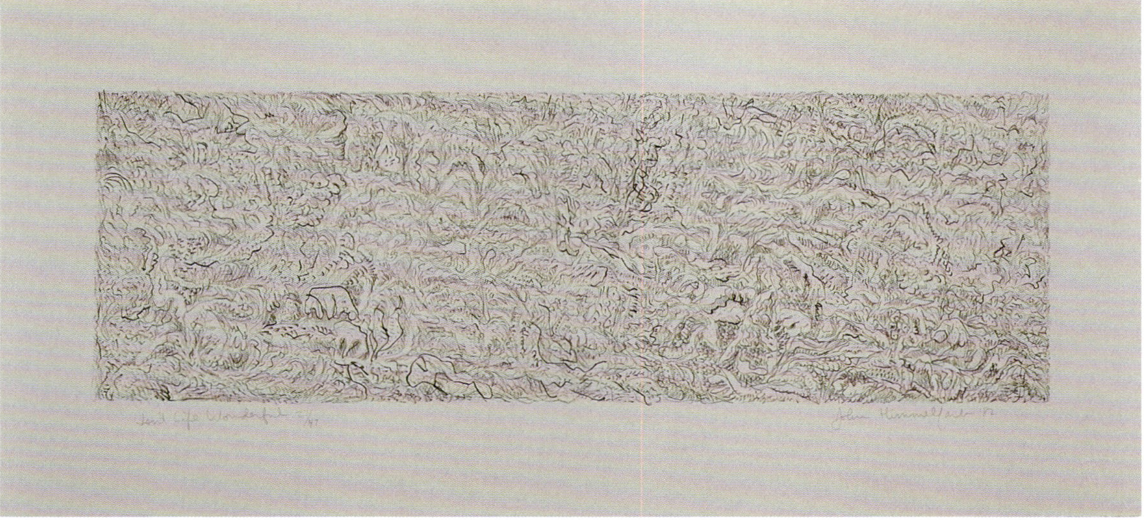

48

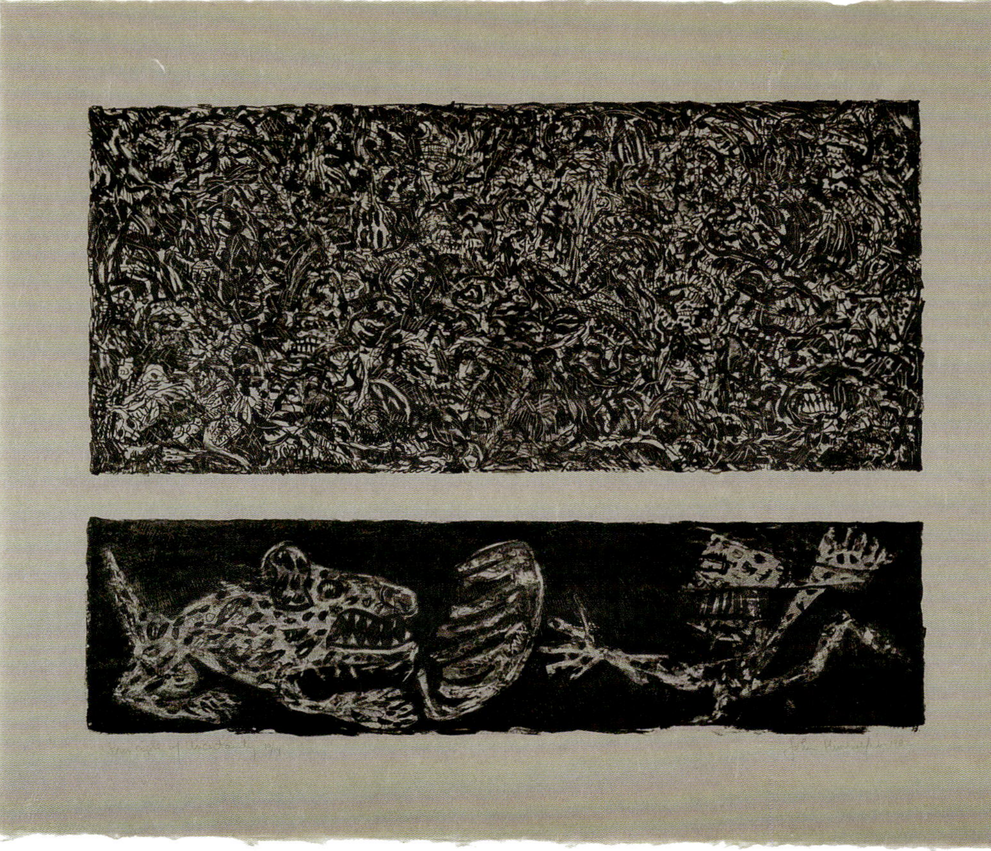

49

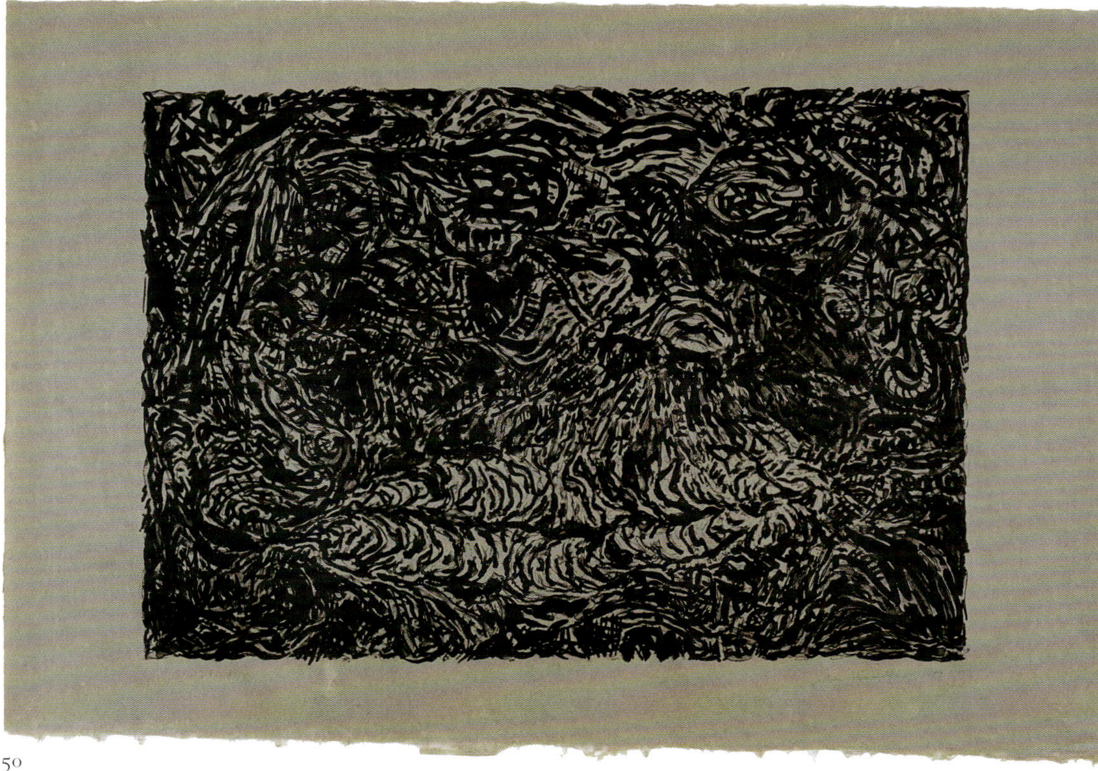

50

49.

Principle of Uncertainty

Date begun: 1982

Date finished: 1982

Medium: lithograph

Paper size: 25 × 29¼ in.

Image size: 18¾ × 24 in.

Paper type: Light Moriki Gray

Publisher: artist

Press: Plucked Chicken Press

Printers: Cynthia Archer, Will Petersen

Edition: 14

Proofs: 1 press

Signature location: LR

Chop location: LL

Job number and location: none

Color printing order, execution of printing elements:

1. Stone printed with black. Image drawn with litho crayon and tusche.

50.

Self-Portrait

Date begun: 1982

Date finished: 1982

Medium: lithograph

Paper size: 24¾ × 36 in.

Image size: 19 × 27 in.

Paper type: Dark Moriki Gray

Publisher: artist

Press: Plucked Chicken Press

Printers: Cynthia Archer, Will Petersen

Edition: 15

Proofs: 1 press

Signature location: LR

Chop location: LR

Job number and location: none

Color printing order, execution of printing elements:

1. Aluminum printed with black. Image drawn with brush and tusche.

51.

Physical

Date finished: 2/16/1983

Medium: lithograph

Paper size: 22 × 30 in.

Image size: same

Paper type: Somerset White

Publisher: Plucked Chicken Press

Press: Plucked Chicken Press

Printers: Cynthia Archer, Will Petersen

Edition: 40: 30 Arabic numerals, 10 Roman numerals

Proofs: 2 press, 1 state (2nd)

Signature location: lower edge, C

Chop location: LR

Job number and location: none

Color printing order, execution of printing elements:

1. Aluminum printed with orange. Image drawn with chunks of litho crayon.
2. Aluminum printed with pink. Image drawn with chunks of litho crayon.
3. Aluminum printed with green. Image drawn with chunks of litho crayon.
4. Aluminum printed with red. Image drawn with chunks of litho crayon.
5. Aluminum printed with blue. Image drawn with chunks of litho crayon.

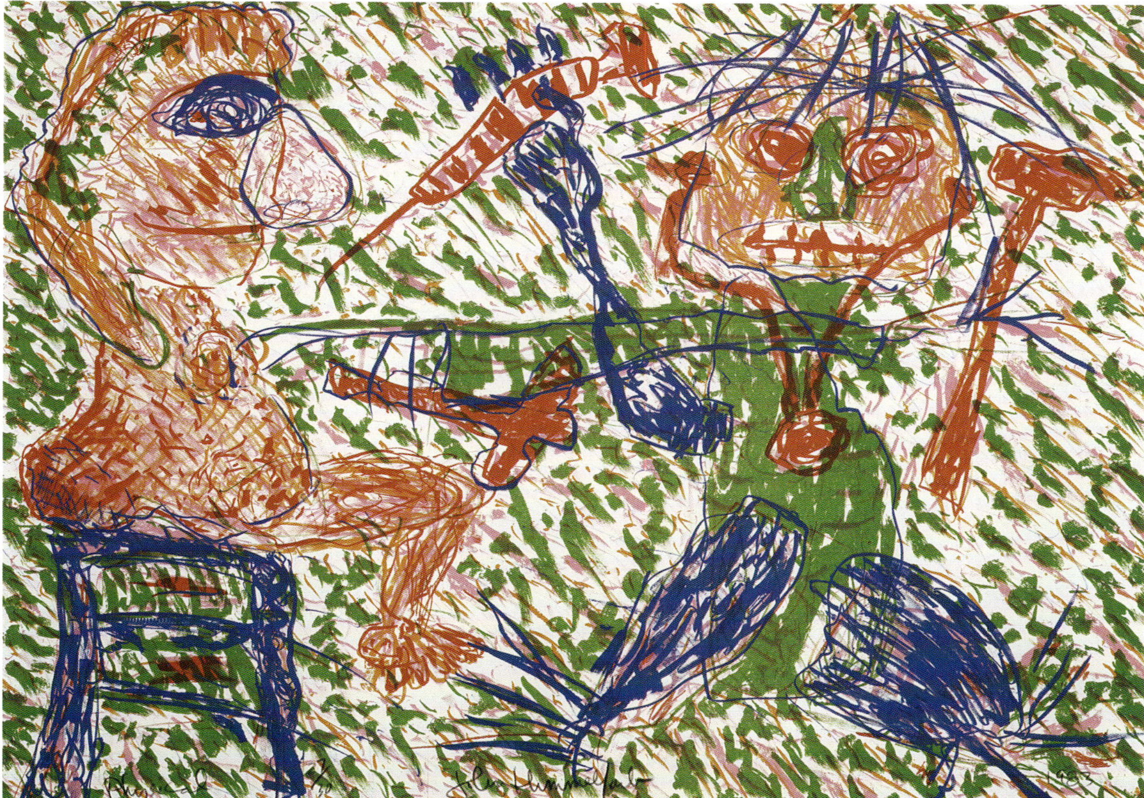

51

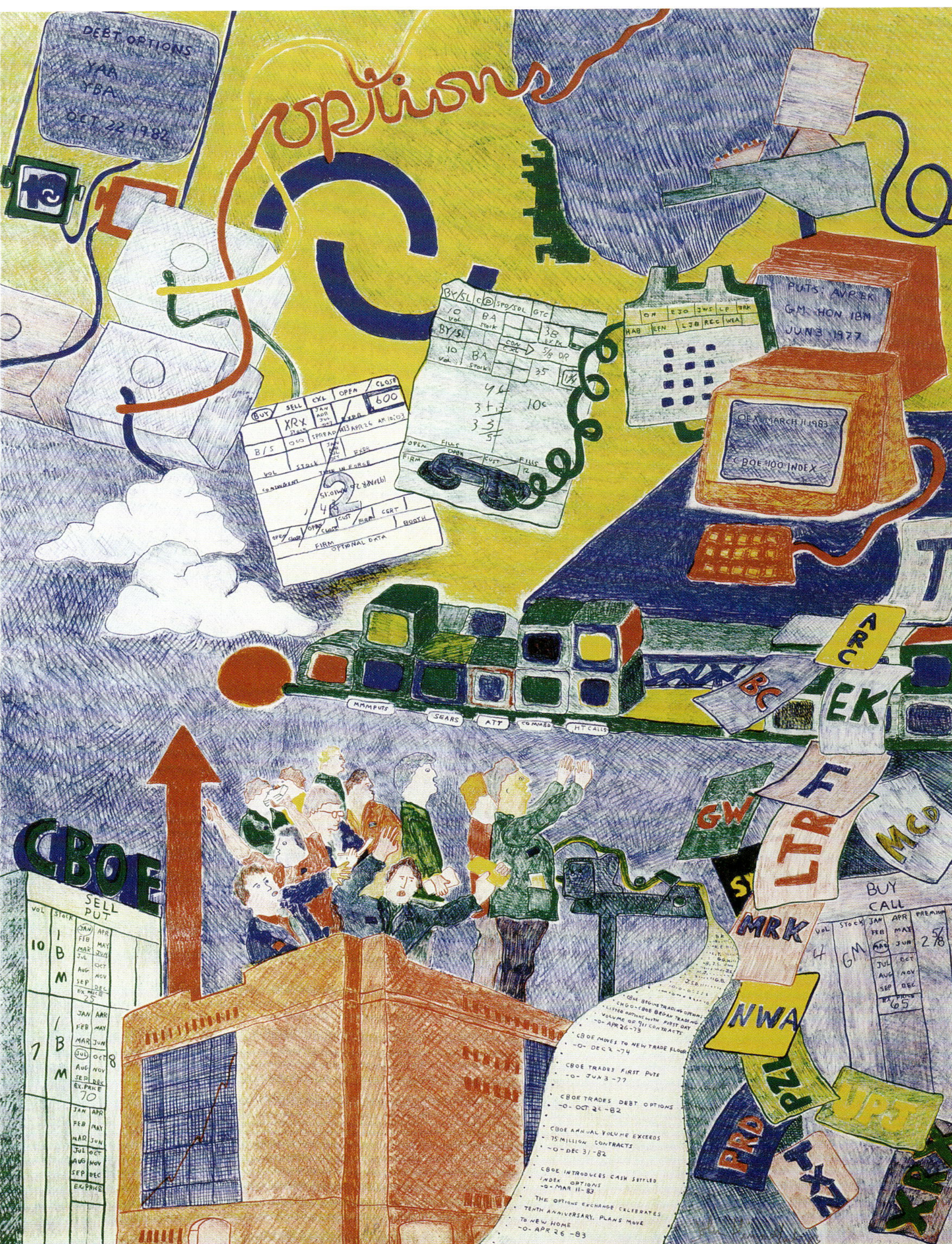

52

52.

Tenth Anniversary CBOE

Date begun: 1/1983

Date finished: 4/10/1983

Medium: lithograph

Paper size: 30 × 22¼ in.

Image size: same

Paper type: Arches Cover White

Publisher: Chicago Board Options Exchange

Press: Four Brothers Press

Printer: Frederick K. Gude

Printer's assistant: Warren Nisley

Edition: 250

Proofs: 15 artist, 3 Four Brothers Press, 2 press, 1 ready to print, 5 trial

Signature location: LR

Chop location: LL

Job number and location: JH02–83–052, reverse LL

Color printing order, execution of printing elements:

1. Aluminum printed with green. Image drawn with litho crayon.

2. Aluminum printed with yellow. Image drawn with litho crayon.

3. Aluminum printed with blue. Image drawn with litho crayon.

4. Aluminum printed with red. Image drawn with litho crayon.

53.

Face to Face

Date begun: 1/1983

Date finished: 7/26/1983

Medium: lithograph

Paper size: 22½ × 30 in.

Image size: same

Paper type: Arches White

Publisher: Four Brothers Press

Press: Four Brothers Press

Printer: Frederick K. Gude

Printer's assistant: Warren Nisley

Edition: 50

Proofs: 3 Four Brothers Press, 2 press, 1 ready to print, 1 trial

Signature location: LR

Chop location: LL

Job number and location: JH01–83–054, reverse LL

Color printing order, execution of printing elements:

1. Stone printed with black. Image drawn with litho crayon, rubbed onto rag that is applied to surface and scratched with stylus.

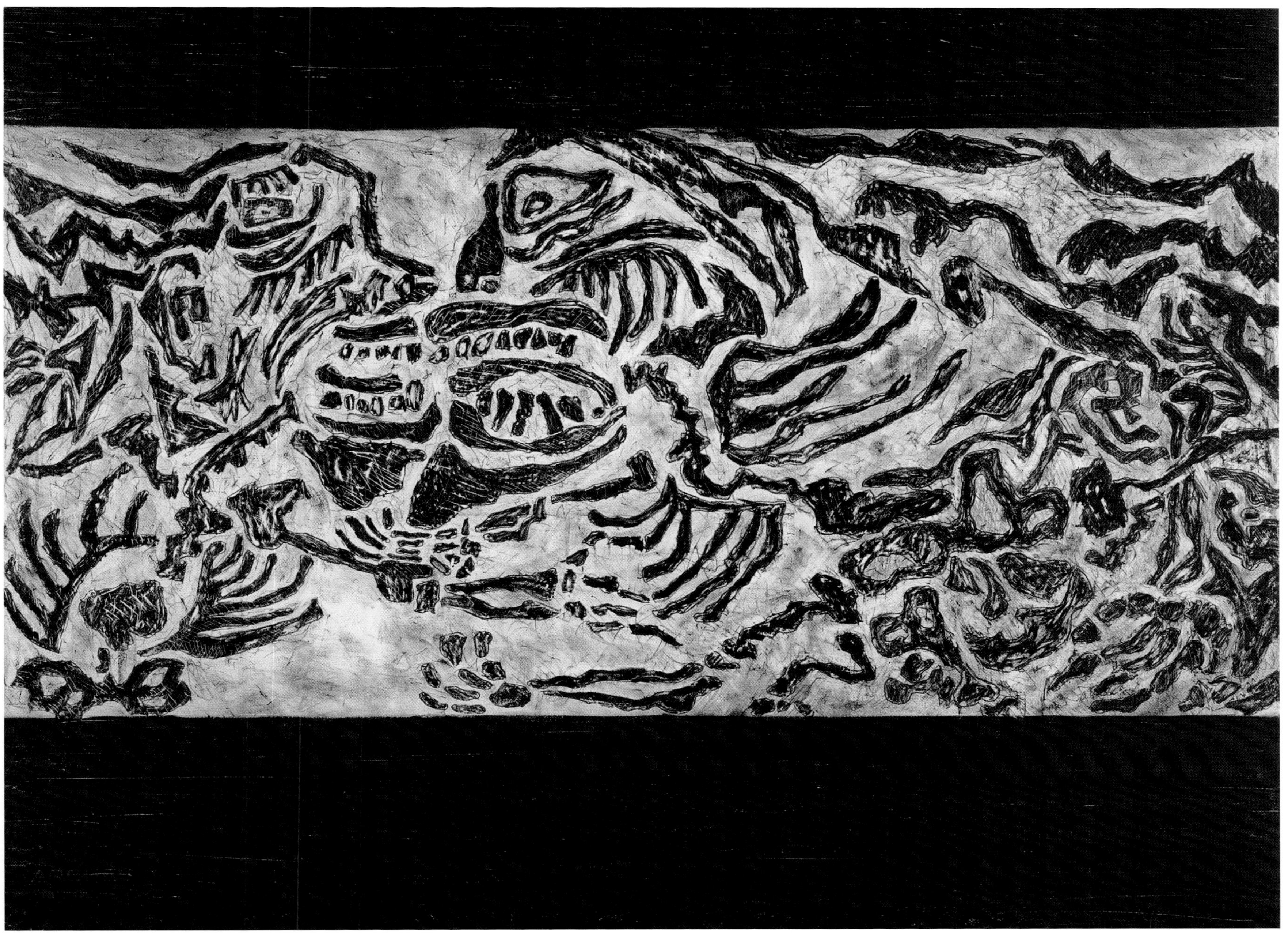

53

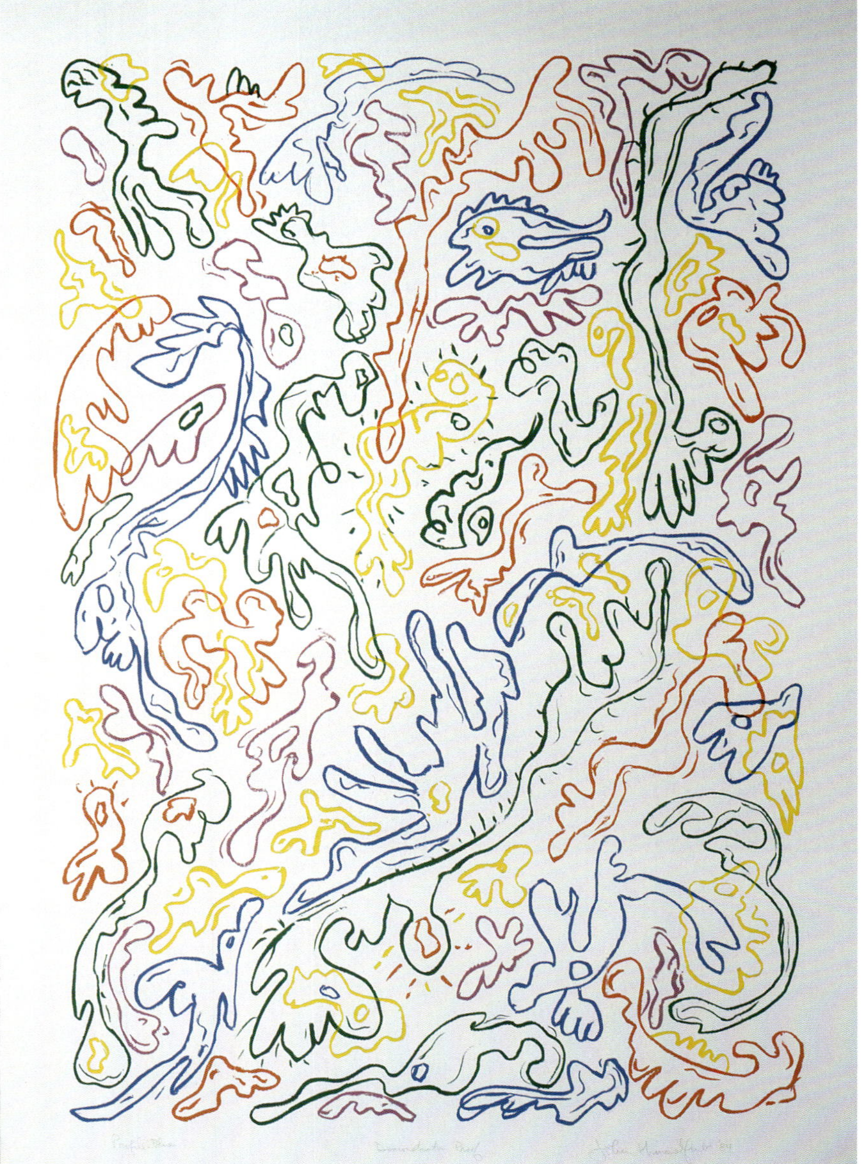

54a

54.

Profiles:

a. Blue

b. Green

c. Red

Date finished: 10/1984

Medium: screenprint

Paper size: 42½ × 30½ in.

Image size: 38 × 26 in.

Paper type: Arches 88

Publisher: ARZ NOVA

Press: Proto Grafix, Ltd.

Edition: 45 each

Proofs: 4 demonstration each, 2 presentation each, 25 progressives divided among the 3 editions

Signature location: LR

Chop location: none

Job number and location: none

Color printing order, execution of printing elements:

1. Yellow

2. Red

3. Blue

4. Green

5. Purple

Color screens shifted for each edition. Image drawn with pen and ink on mylar, transferred to photosensitive screen.

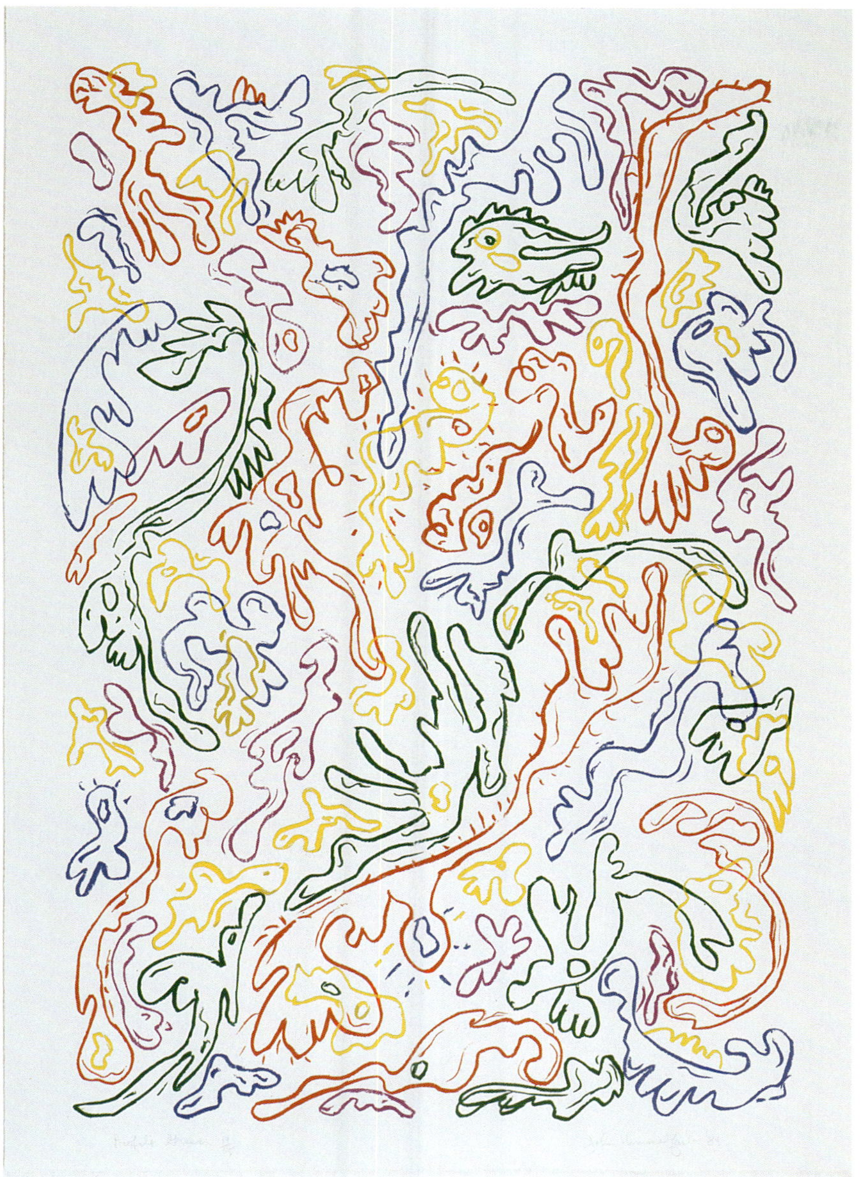

54b

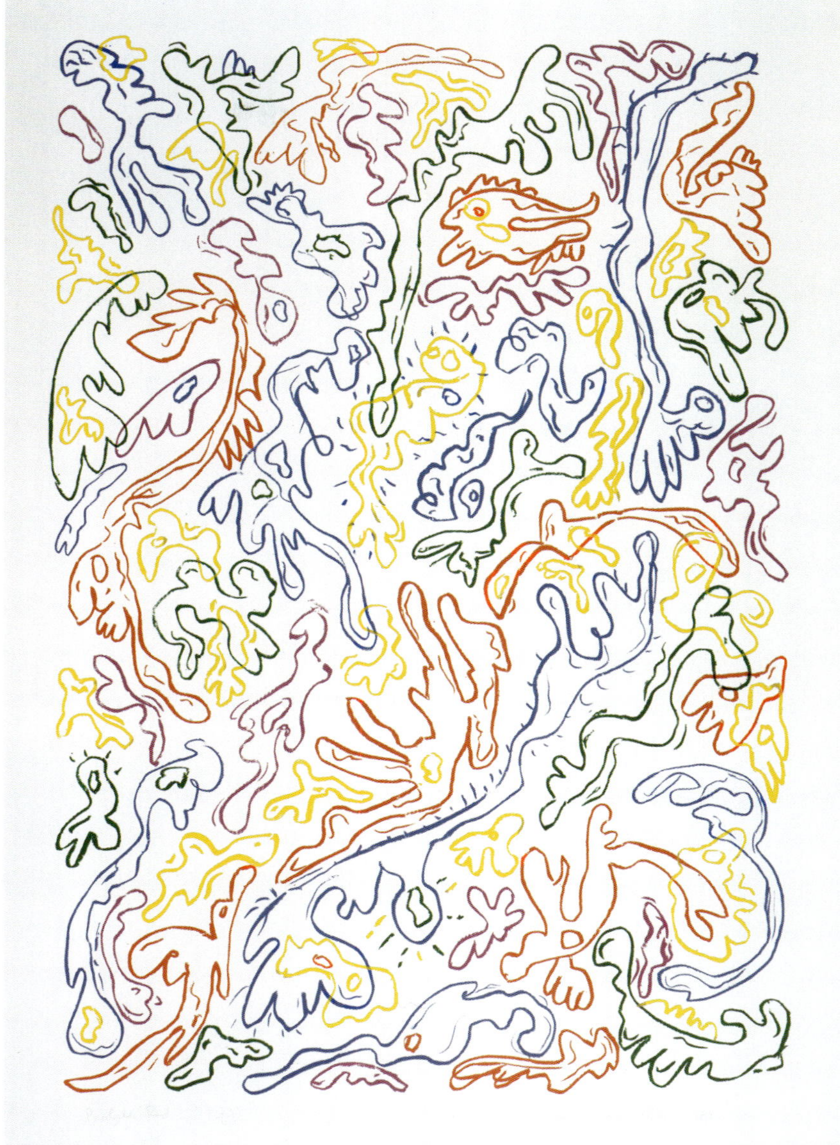

54c

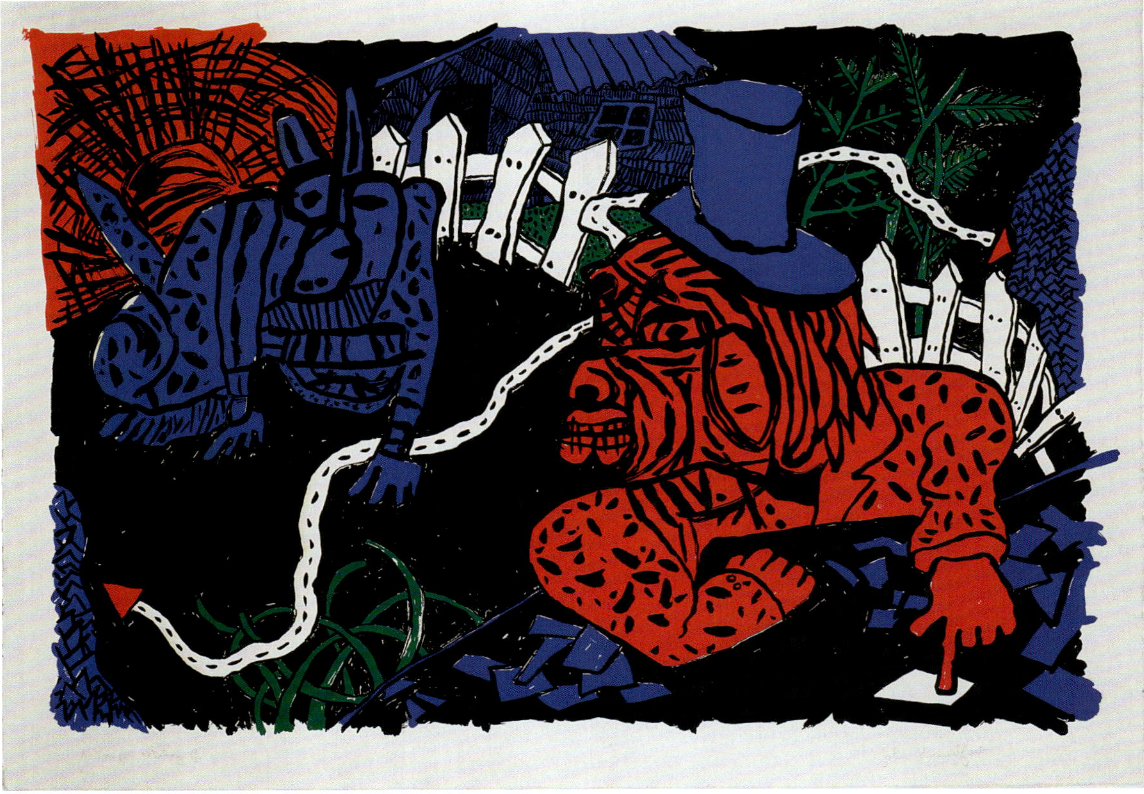

55

55.

No Danger No Delay

Date begun: 1984

Date finished: 1984

Medium: screenprint

Paper size: 30 × 42 in.

Image size: 22¼ × 40 in.

Paper type: Arches 88

Publisher: ARZ NOVA

Press: Proto Graphix, Inc.

Printer: unknown

Edition: 75

Proofs: 3 artist, 2 presentation

Signature location: LR

Chop location: none

Job number and location: none

Color printing order, execution of printing elements:

1. Four screens printed either with red, blue, green, or black. Image drawn with brush and ink on mylar, transferred to photosensitive screens.

Note: Black screen used to print white screen in *Coast to Coast* (no. 56).

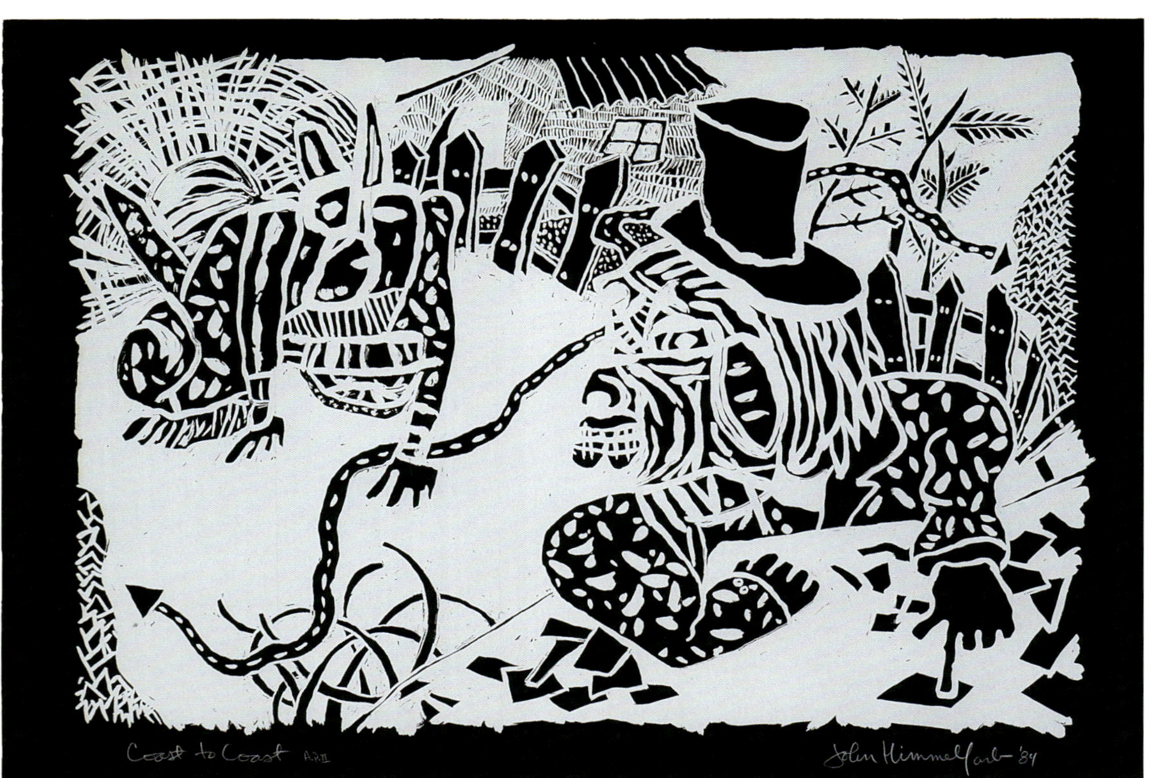

56

56.

Coast to Coast

Date begun: 1984

Date finished: 1984

Medium: screenprint

Paper size: 30 × 44 in.

Image size: 38½ × 27½ in.

Paper type: Arches Cover Black

Publisher: ARZ NOVA

Press: Proto Grafix, Ltd.

Edition: 12

Proofs: 4 artist, 2 press, 1 publisher

Signature location: LR

Chop location: none

Job number and location: none

Color printing order, execution of printing elements:

1. Screenprinted with white. Printing element drawn with brush and ink on mylar, transferred to photosensitive screen.

Note: Printing elements used in *No Danger No Delay* (no. 55).

57.

Grand Street Meeting

Date begun: 6/1985

Date finished: 9/1985

Medium: lithograph and screenprint

Paper size: 30 × 42 in.

Image size: same

Paper type: Arches 88

Publisher: John Nichols

Press: John Nichols

Printers: Nend Bozic, Arnold Brooks, Barbara Neff, John Nichols

Edition: 65

Proofs: 10 artist, 1 color, 1 dedication, 14 working

Signature location: LR

Chop location: LR

Job number and location: none

Color printing order, execution of printing elements:

1. Screenprinted with pthalo blue. Image drawn with litho crayon on mylar, transferred to photosensitive screen.

2. Screenprinted with red-brown. Image drawn with brush and ink on mylar, transferred to photosensitive screen.

3. Aluminum printed with chrome oxide. Image drawn with litho crayon.

4. Aluminum printed with violet. Image drawn with litho crayon.

5. Screenprinted with cobalt blue. Image drawn with litho crayon on mylar, transferred to photosensitive screen.

6. Screenprinted with yellow. Image drawn with brush and ink on mylar, transferred to photosensitive screen.

7. Aluminum printed with pthalo blue. Image drawn with litho crayon.

8. Screenprinted with green oxide. Image drawn with litho crayon on mylar, transferred to photosensitive screen.

9. Screenprinted with rubine red. Image drawn with litho crayon on mylar, transferred to photosensitive screen.

10. Screenprinted with transparent green oxide. Image drawn with litho crayon on mylar, transferred to photosensitive screen.

11. Aluminum printed with red. Image drawn with litho crayon.

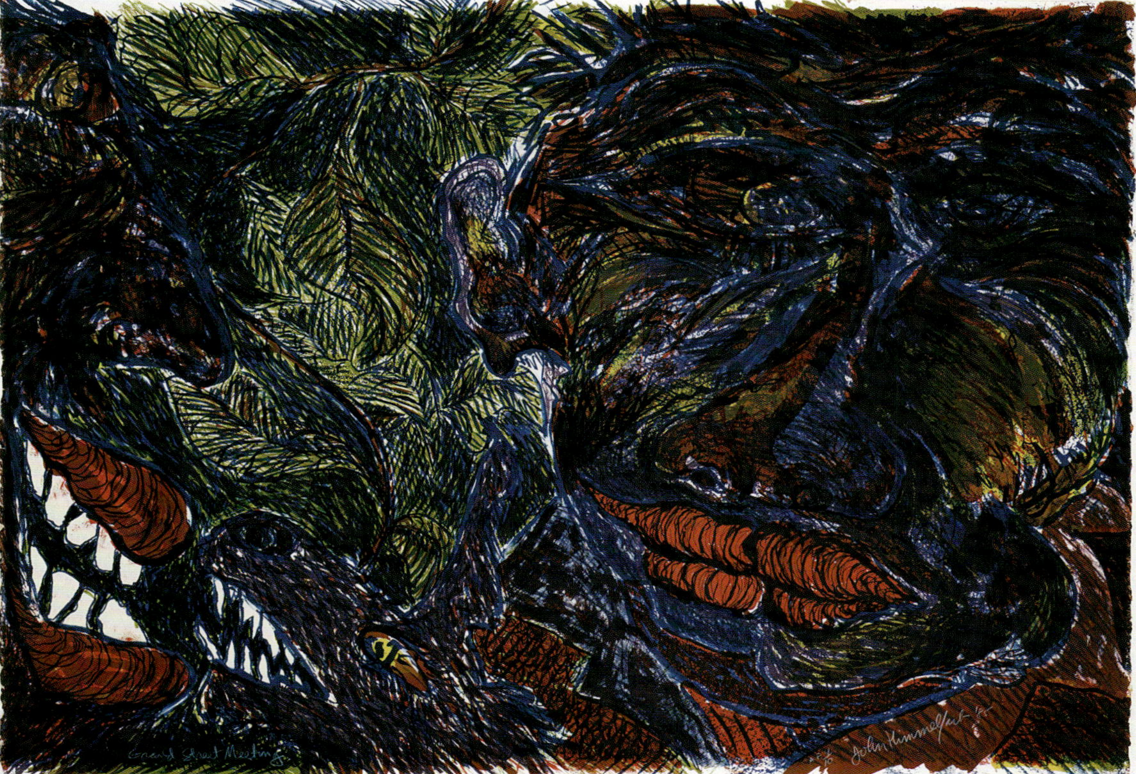

57

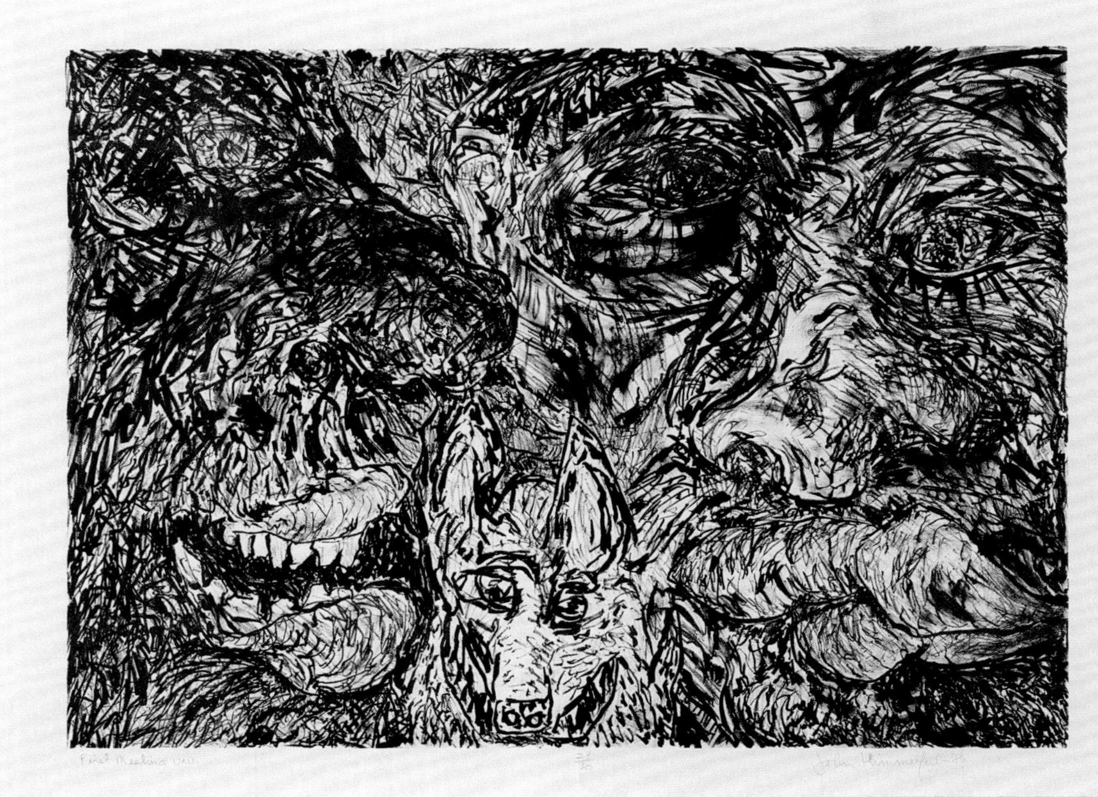

58

58.

First Meeting UNI

Date begun: 1985

Date finished: 1986

Medium: lithograph

Paper size: 17¼ × 24 in.

Image size: 15 × 24 in.

Paper type: Somerset White (?)

Publisher: artist

Press: Art Department, University of Northern Iowa

Edition: 30

Proofs: not known

Signature location: LR

Chop location: none

Job number and location: none

Color printing order, execution of printing elements:

1. Aluminum printed with black. Image drawn with litho crayon.

Note: Image drawn at same time as *Illustration without Words (I.W.W.)* (cat. 59).

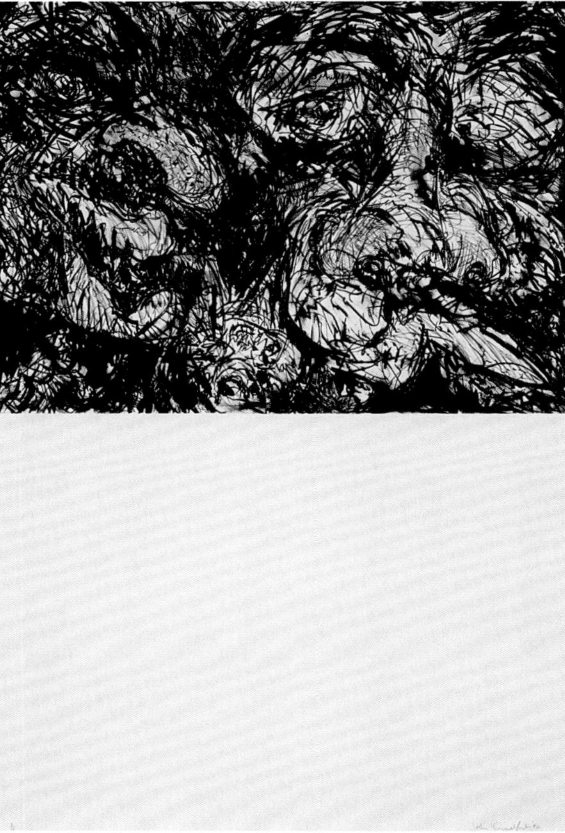

59

59.

Illustration without Words (I.W.W.)

(some proofs titled *Second Meeting at the Plate*)

Date begun: 1985

Date finished: 2/3/1990

Medium: lithograph

Paper size: 30 × 20⅞ in.

Image size: 15 × 20⅞ in.

Paper type: Rives BFK White

Publisher: Tandem Press

Press: Tandem Press

Printer: Andrew Rubin

Printer's assistants: various graduate students

Edition: 14

Proofs: 1 archive, 5 artist, 1 press, 1 publisher, 1 scholarship, several trial on smaller sheets (see Note)

Signature location: LR

Chop location: LL

Job number and location: none

Color printing order, execution of printing elements:

1. Aluminum printed with black. Image drawn with litho crayon.

Note: Image drawn in 1985 at the University of Northern Iowa, where small trial proofs were pulled. Edition printed at Tandem Press in 1990.

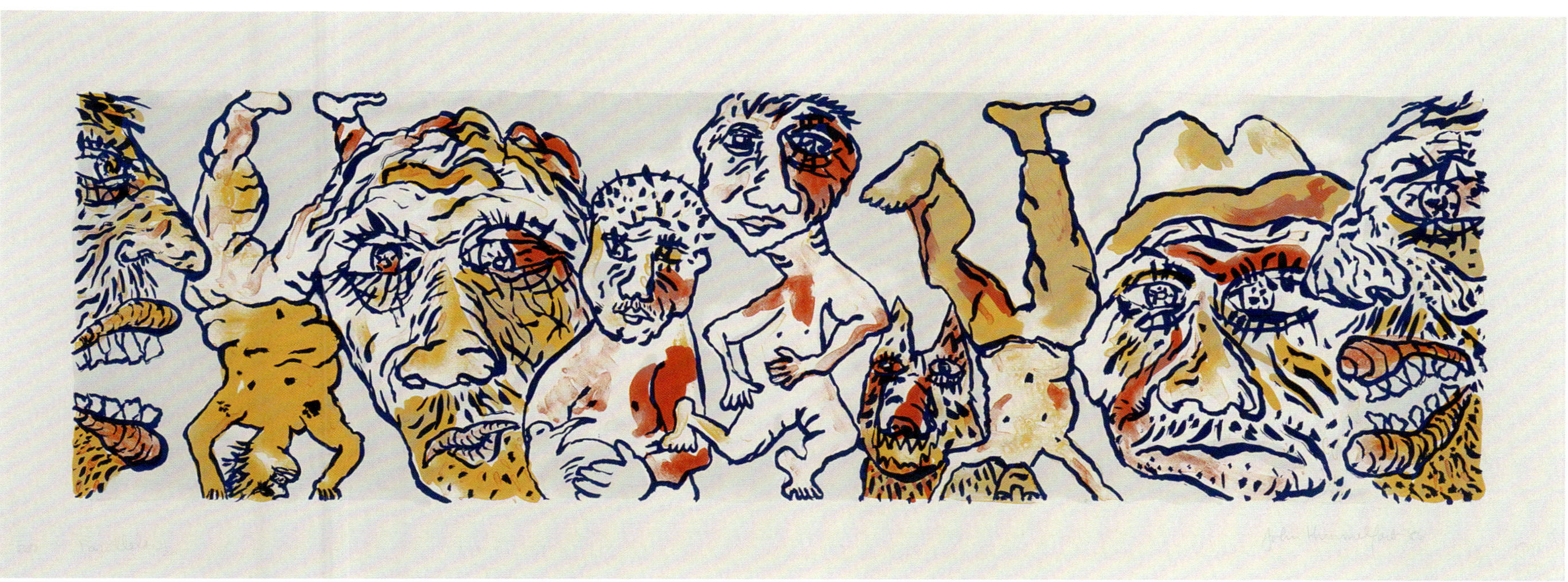

60.

Parallels

Date begun: 9/4/1986

Date finished: 10/13/1986

Medium: lithograph

Paper size: 11 × 30 in.

Image size: 8 × 27 in.

Paper type: Arches Cover White

Publisher: Normal Editions Workshop, Illinois State University

Press: Normal Editions Workshop, Illinois State University

Printer: Richard D. Finch

Printer's assistants: Todd DeVriese, Craig Martin

Edition: 32: 20 Arabic numerals, 12 Roman numerals

Proofs: 1 bon à tirer, 2 Illinois State University, 2 press, 1 publisher

Signature location: LR

Chop location: publisher, LL margin; printer, LR margin

Job number and location: 86–104, reverse LL

Color printing order, execution of printing elements:

1. Aluminum printed with orange (transparent base, lemon yellow, policy orange, opaque white, bismarck brown). Image drawn with brush and tusche.

2. Aluminum printed with red (transparent base, fire red, rubine red). Image drawn with brush and tusche.

3. Aluminum printed with light blue (transparent base, opaque white, pthalo blue-red, rubine red). Image drawn with brush and tusche.

4. Aluminum printed with pthalo blue-red. Image drawn with brush and autographic ink.

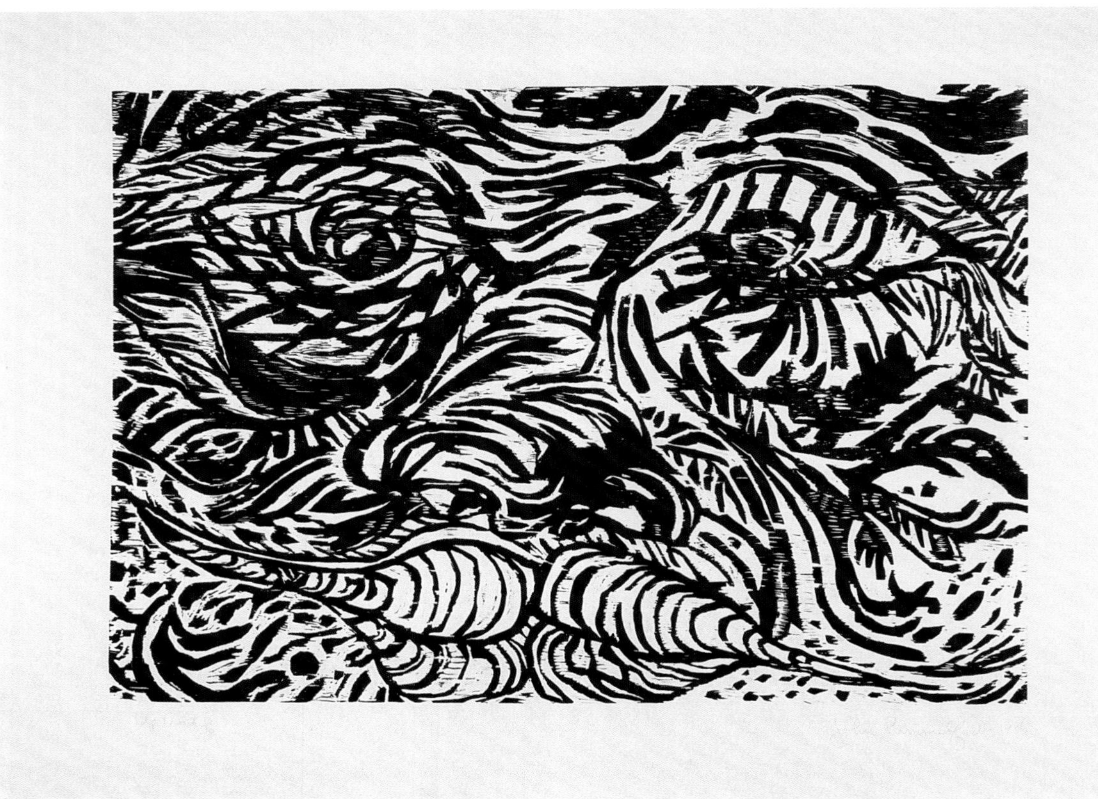

61

61.

Up Front

Date begun: 1986

Date finished: 1986

Medium: woodcut

Paper size: 31 × 42¼ in.

Image size: 23⅝ × 34 in.

Paper type: Copperplate White

Publisher: artist

Printer: Anita Jung

Edition: 10

Proofs: 1 trial on Lana Pura Cover White, 1 trial on Lana Pura Cover White (26 × 38 in.)

Signature location: LR

Chop location: none

Job number and location: none

Color printing order, execution of printing elements:

1. Woodblock printed with black.

62.

View and Review

Date begun: 11/18/1986

Date finished: 5/15/1987

Medium: intaglio

Paper size: 11 × 30 in.

Image size: 5⅝ × 23¾ in.

Paper type: Arches White

Publisher: artist

Press: Allyn Print Shop, Department of Art, Southern Illinois University

Printer: Edward H. Shay

Printers' assistants: Michael Buesking, Jaimee Kohn, Rich Kryczka, Arthur Blake Pearce, Jean Sanders, Janet Schill, Kim Treger

Edition: 18

Proofs: 2 artist

Signature location: LR

Chop location: none

Job number and location: none

Color printing order, execution of printing elements:

1. Zinc inked with pink (cadmium-red light mixed with white), wiped with tarlatan, then blue with white, reduced, surface-rolled. Image drawn with sugar-lift and aquatint techniques.

Note: Printing element used in *Covert Activity* (no. 63).

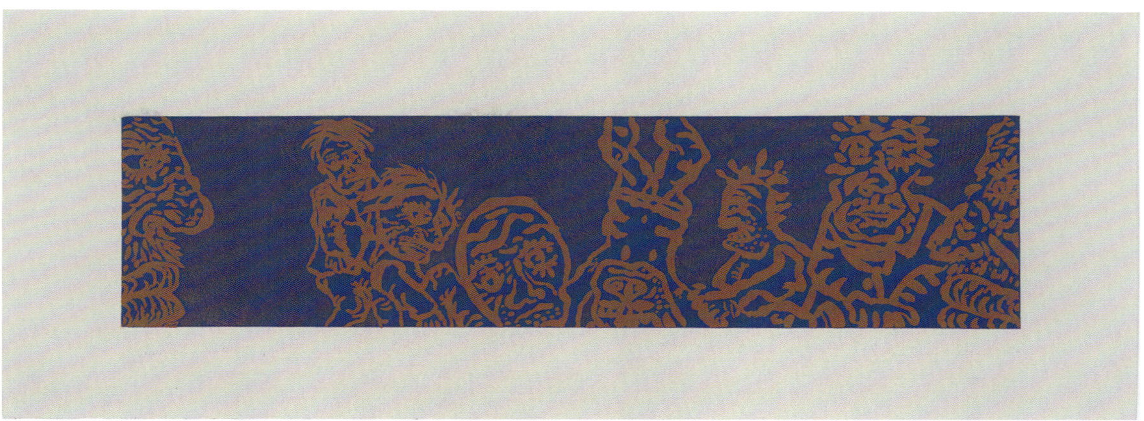

62

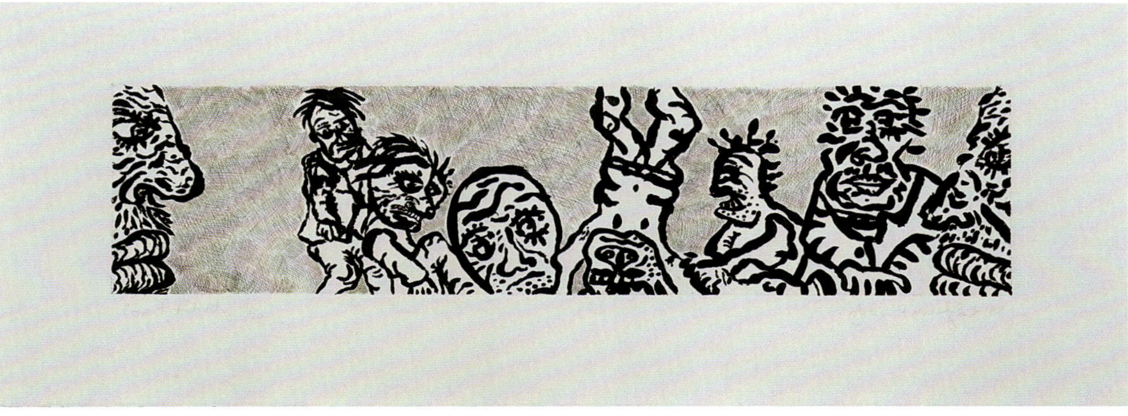

63

63.

Covert Activity

Date begun: 1/18/1986

Date finished: 7/1988

Medium: intaglio

Paper size: 11 × 30 in.

Image size: 5⅝ × 23¾ in.

Paper type: Rives BFK White

Publisher: artist

Press: Griffin Etching Press at Allyn Print Shop, Department of Art, Southern Illinois University

Printer: Arthur Blake Pearce

Edition: 20

Proofs: none

Signature location: LR

Chop location: none

Job number and location: none

Color printing order, execution of printing elements:

1. Zinc printed with Daniel Smith #99 intense black modified with David Smith Miracle Gel. Image drawn with etching and sugar-lift techniques.

Note: Printing element reused from *View and Review* (no. 62).

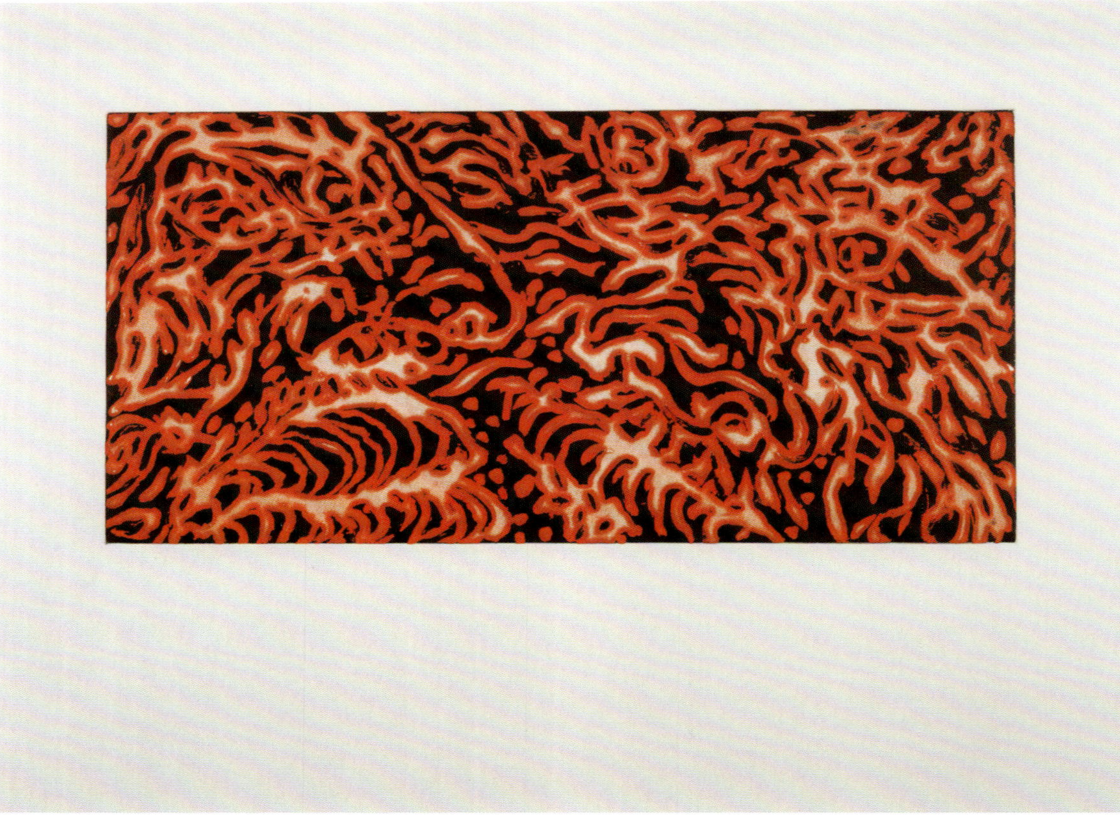

65

64.

Lava Flow

Date begun: 11/1986

Date finished: 5/1987

Medium: intaglio

Paper size: 22 × 30 in.

Image size: 11¾ × 23¾ in.

Paper type: Arches White

Publisher: artist

Press: Allyn Print Shop, Department of Art, Southern Illinois University

Printer: Edward H. Shay

Printer's assistants: Michael Buesking, Jaimee Kohn, Rich Kryczka, Arthur Blake Pearce, Jean Sanders, Janet Schill, Kim Treger

Editions: 8 red, 4 blue, 4 orange

Proofs: 2 Allyn Print Shop (blue 2/4, 3/4), 8 artist, 1 bon à tirer, 1 press (orange 2/4)

Signature location: below image, LR

Chop location: none

Job number and location: none

Color printing order, execution of printing elements:

1. Red: zinc printed with cadmium-red light (wiped) and black (surface-rolled). Image drawn using sugar-lift and aquatint techniques.

2. Blue: zinc printed with mixture of 12 parts cadmium-red light and 1 part magenta (wiped), and black (surface-rolled). Image drawn using sugar-lift and aquatint techniques.

3. Orange: zinc printed with mixture of 6 parts cadmium-red light and 1 part cadmium orange (wiped), and black (surface-rolled). Image drawn using sugar-lift and aquatint techniques.

Note: Printing element used in the following: *Lava Flow Part II* (no. 65), *Mid-Meeting Break* (no. 71), and *Summerlight Meeting* (no. 69).

Photograph not available.

65.

Lava Flow Part II

Date begun: 11/1986

Date finished: 5/1987

Medium: intaglio

Paper size: 22 × 30 in.

Image size: 11¾ × 23¾ in.

Paper type: Arches White

Publisher: artist

Press: Allyn Print Shop, Department of Art, Southern Illinois University

Printer: Arthur Blake Pearce

Edition: 8

Proofs: none

Signature location: below image, LR

Chop location: none

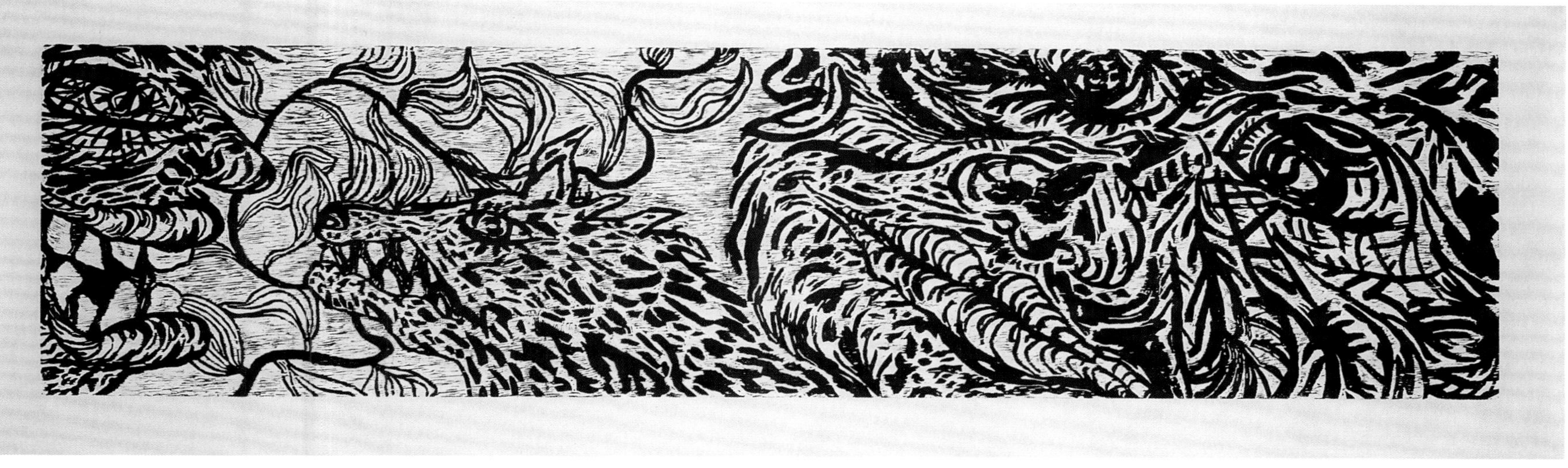

66

Job number and location: none

Color printing order, execution of printing elements:

1. Zinc printed with cadmium-red light (wiped) and black (surface-rolled).

Note: Printing element reused from *Lava Flow* (no. 64). The printing in *Lava Flow* was variable, as many students participated. *Lava Flow II* is a richer and more consistent rendering of the same image.

66.

Lengthy Meeting

Date begun: 1986

Date finished: 1986: 1–10; 1990: I–X

Medium: woodcut

Paper size: 32 × 104¼ in.

Image size: 23⅝ × 95⅞ in.

Paper type: Japanese

Publisher: artist

Press: 1–10: none; I–X: Landfall Press

Printers: 1–10: Anita Jung; I–X: Barbara Spies

Printer's assistant: I–X: Heidijo Lemon

Edition: 20: 10 Arabic numerals, 10 Roman numerals

Proofs: 2 artist on Goyu paper (printed by J. Nebraska Gifford and John Nichols at John Nichols Printmakers and Publishers)

Signature location: LR

Chop location: none

Job number: none

Color printing order, execution of printing elements:

1. Woodblock printed with black.

Note: 1–10, printed by hand with spoon, show more wood grain; I–X, printed on intaglio press, exhibit denser black in image area.

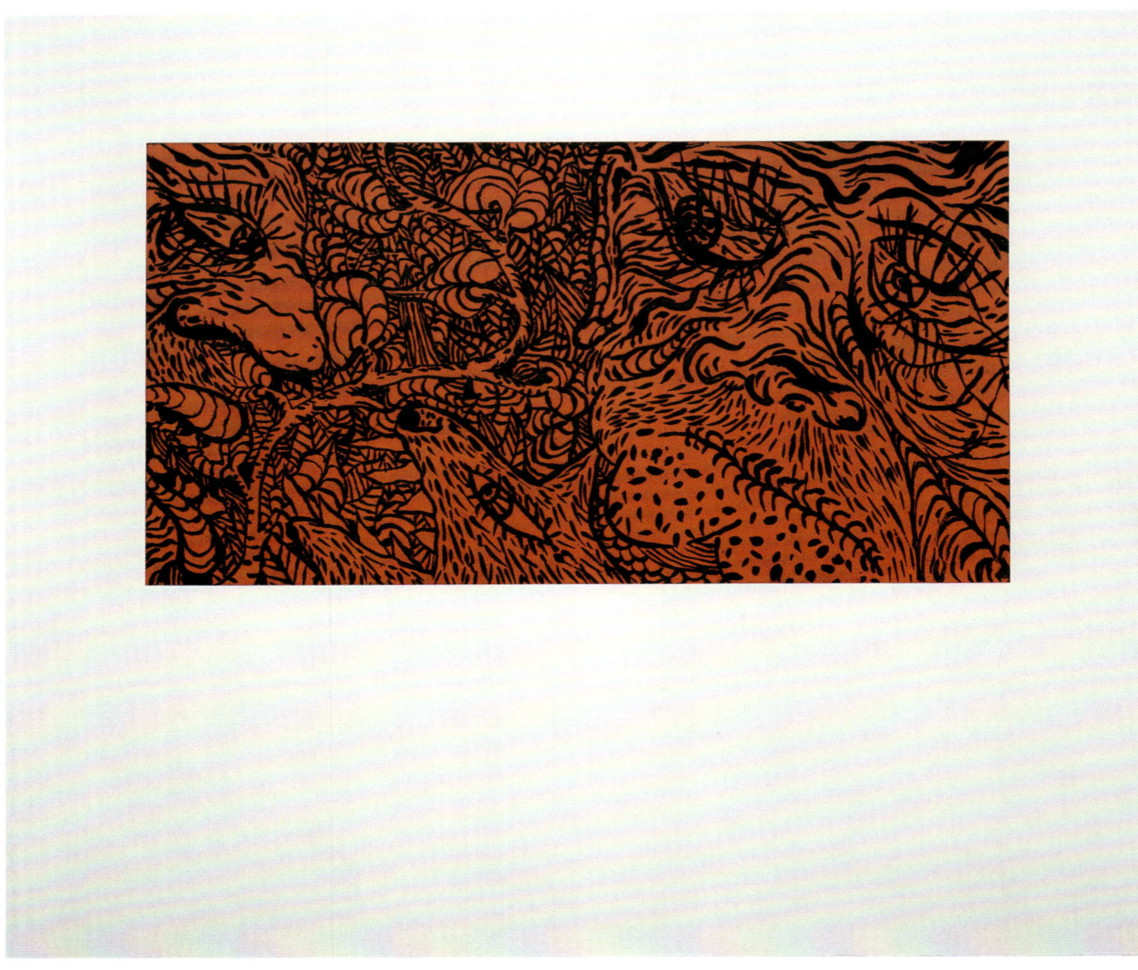

67

67.

Serena Lane Meeting

Date begun: 12/1987

Date finished: 7/1988

Medium: intaglio

Paper size: 42 × 49 in.

Image size: 19¾ × 37¾; cut to 19 × 37 in. in order to collage

Paper type: Arches Cover White

Publisher: Echo Press

Press: Echo Press

Printers: David Calkins, Rudy Pozzatti

Edition: 12

Proofs: 1 archive, 2 artist, 1 color, 3 press, 1 publisher, 1 ready to print

Signature location: sideways along L edge

Chop location: LL

Job number and location: JDH–87–445, reverse LL

Color printing order, execution of printing elements:

1. Printed red-orange as a relief flat.
2. Printed black intaglio as a sugar-lift aquatint.

Image drawn with sugar-lift and aquatint techniques. Paper was then cut to 19 × 37 in. and collaged onto a sheet of 42 × 49 in. Arches Cover White.

68.

Lumber Street Meeting

Date begun: 1987

Date finished: 9/22/1988

Medium: woodcut

Paper size: 37 × 69 in.

Image size: 30 × 62 in.

Paper type: Suzuki

Publisher: Landfall Press

Press: Landfall Press

Printers: David Jones, Barbara Spies

Printers' assistants: Fred Baehr, Heidijo Lemon

Edition: 20

Proofs: 5 artist, 1 copyright, 2 press, 1 ready to print, 5 subscriber (Roman numerals)

Signature location: LR

Chop location: none

Job number and location: JH87–966W, reverse LL

Color printing order, execution of printing elements:

1. Woodblock printed with dark blue. Image traced from pattern onto block and cut.

2. Woodblock printed with orange. Image traced from pattern onto block and cut.

3. Woodblock printed with purple. Image traced from pattern onto block and cut.

4. Woodblock printed with blue. Image traced from pattern onto block and cut.

5. Woodblock printed with black. Image drawn on wood with brush and ink and cut.

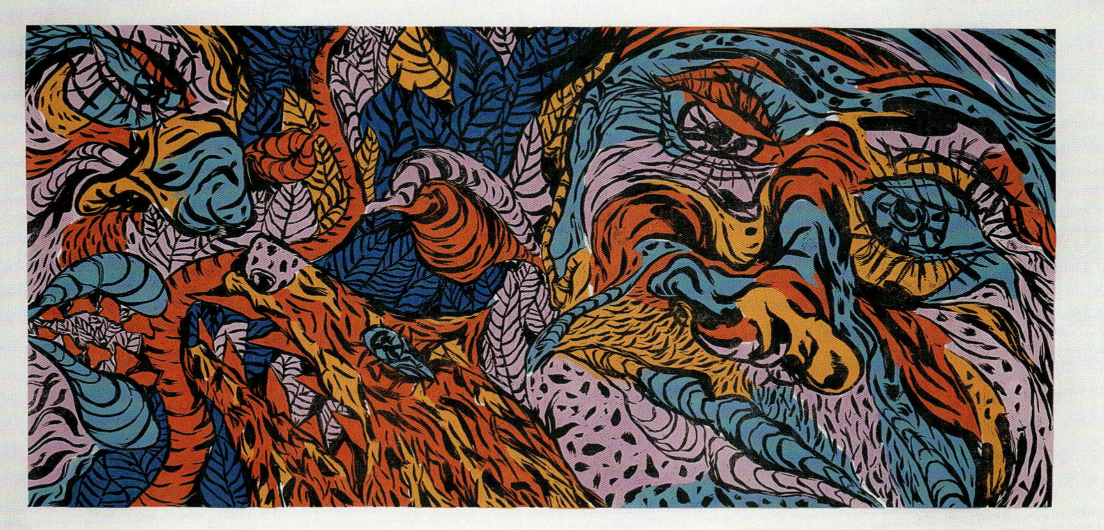

68

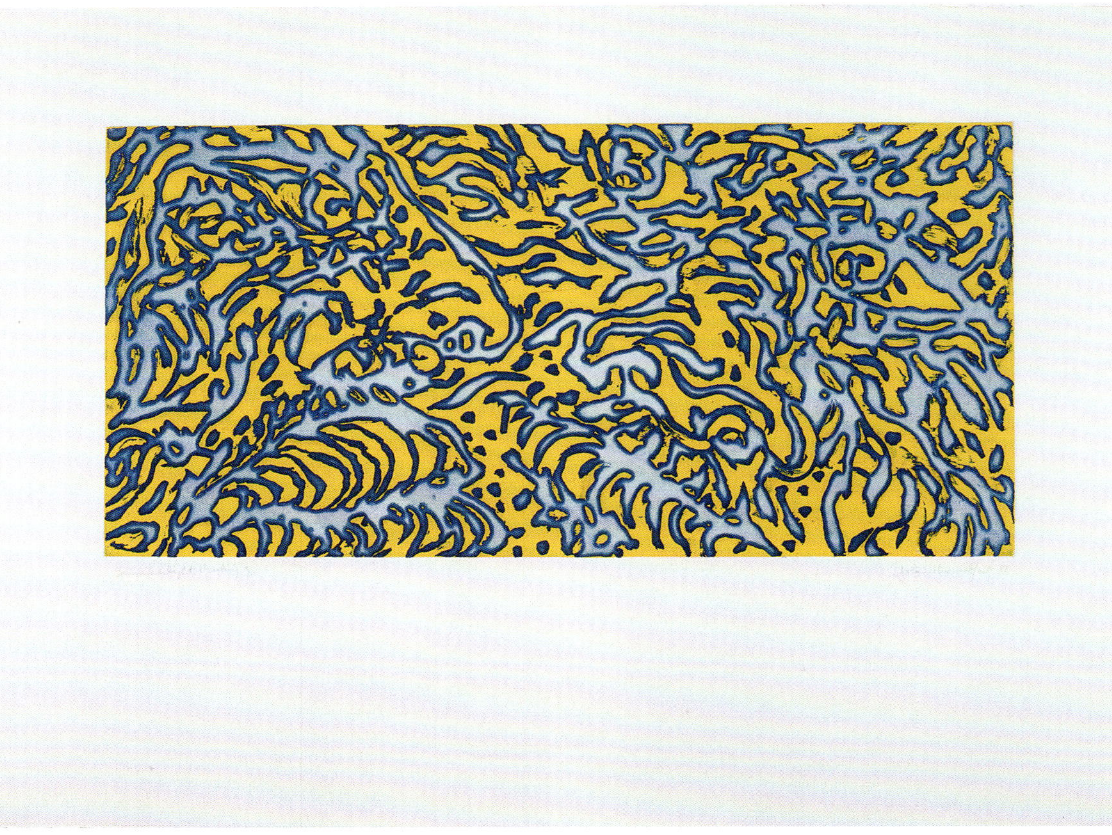

69

69.

Summerlight Meeting

Date begun: 7/1988

Date finished: 8/1988

Medium: intaglio

Paper size: 22 × 30 in.

Image size: 11¾ × 23¾ in.

Paper type: Rives BFK White

Publisher: artist

Press: Allyn Print Shop, Department of Art, Southern Illinois University

Printer: Arthur Blake Pearce

Edition: 10

Proofs: none

Signature location: below image, LR

Chop location: none

Job number and location: 8–88

Color printing order, execution of printing elements:

1. Zinc printed with Handschy sky blue #T3016 modified with Graphic Chemical Easy Wipe Compound, Daniel Smith Miracle Gel, and magnesium carbonate (wiped). Image drawn with brush and sugar-lift technique.

2. Daniel Smith process yellow etching #6697 modified with Hanco Setswell Compound (surface-rolled).

Note: Printing element reused from *Lava Flow* (no. 64).

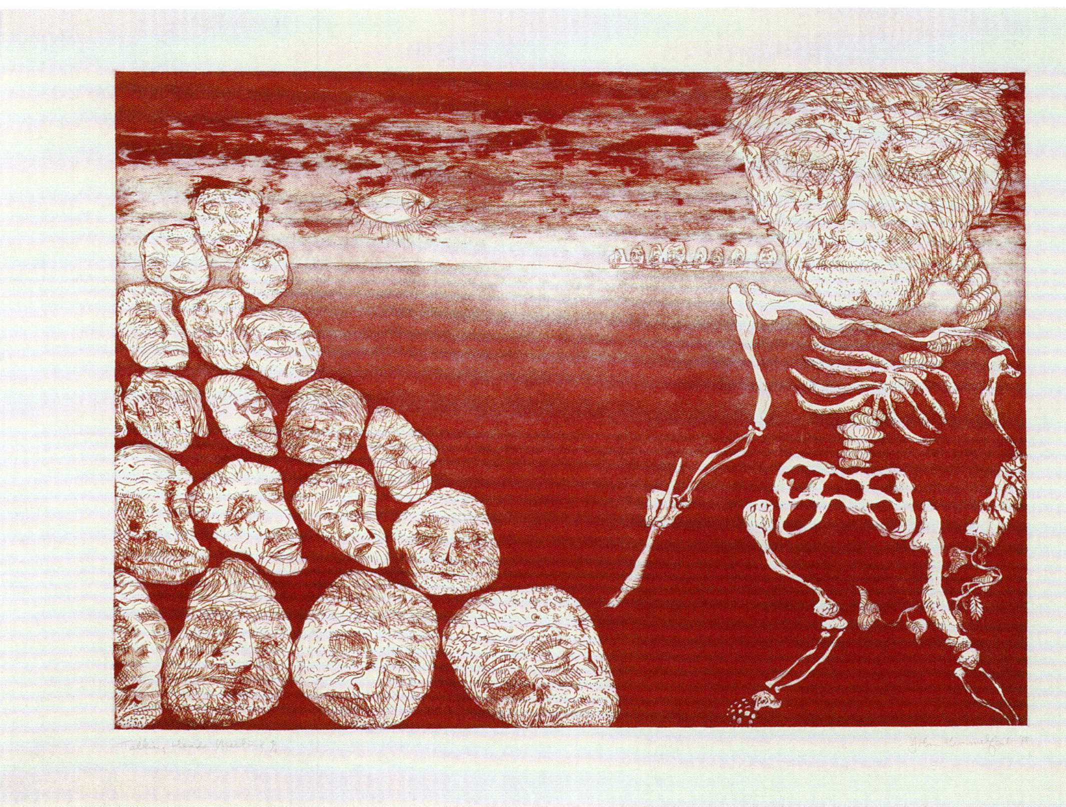

70

70.

Talking Heads Meeting

Date begun: 1988

Date finished: 1988

Medium: intaglio

Paper size: 22 × 30 in.

Image size: 17½ × 23⅞ in.

Paper type: Arches Cover White

Publisher: artist

Press: Griffin Etching Press at Allyn Print Shop, Department of Art, Southern Illinois University

Printer: Edward H. Shay

Printer's assistants: Michael Buesking, Jaimee Kohn, Rich Kryczka, Arthur Blake Pearce, Jean Sanders, Janet Schill, Kim Treger

Edition: 9

Proofs: 1 trial (black)

Signature location: LR

Chop location: none

Job number and location: none

Color printing order, execution of printing elements:

1. Zinc printed with red. Etched with line etching, aquatint, and white ground.

71.

Mid-Meeting Break

Date begun: 7/1988

Date finished: 1989

Medium: intaglio

Paper size: 22 × 30 in.

Image size: 11¾ × 23¾ in.

Paper type: Rives BFK White

Publisher: artist

Press: Allyn Print Shop, Department of Art, Southern Illinois University

Printer: Arthur Blake Pearce

Color printing order, execution of printing elements:

1. Zinc printed with Handschy sky blue #T3016 modified with Graphic Chemical Easy Wipe Compound, Daniel Smith Miracle Gel, magnesium carbonate (wiped), and Daniel Smith process yellow etching #6697 modified with Hanco Setswell Compound (surface-rolled). Image drawn with brush and sugar-lift technique.

2. Screenprinted with black to form border around image.

Note: Printing element reused from *Lava Flow* (no. 64). *Mid-Meeting Break* is identical to *Summerlight Meeting* (no. 69), except that the latter has no black border.

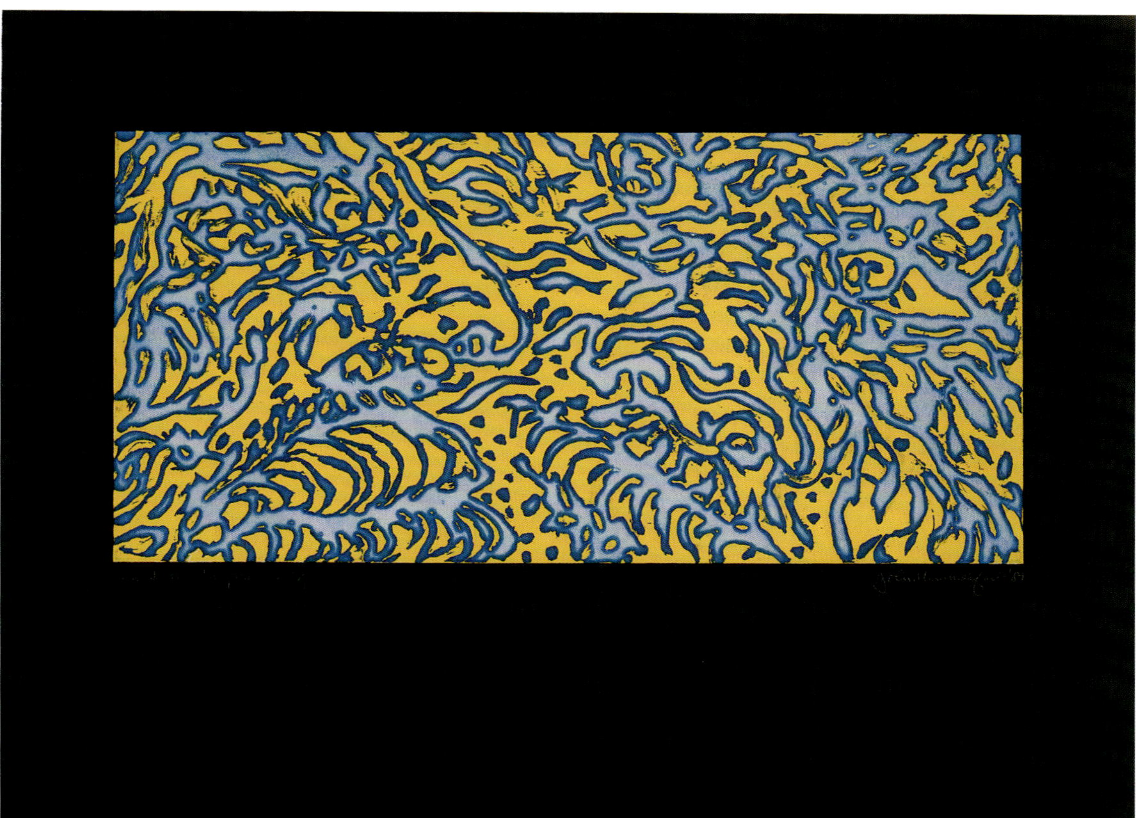

71

72.

Catalan

Date begun: 2/8/1990

Date finished: 2/10/1990

Medium: lithograph

Paper size: 22¼ × 30 in.

Image size: same

Paper type: Rives BFK White

Publisher: Tandem Press

Press: Tandem Press

Printer: Andrew Rubin

Printer's assistants: graduate students

Edition: 34

Proofs: 1 archive, 1 artist, 2 presentation, 1 publisher, 1 scholarship, 3 trial

Signature location: LL

Chop location: LR

Job number and location: JH90–74

Color printing order, execution of printing elements:

1. Drawn with pencil on each sheet followed by blue and warm beige, brushed with acrylic wash.

2. Aluminum printed with black. Image drawn with brush and ink on mylar, transferred to photosensitive plate.

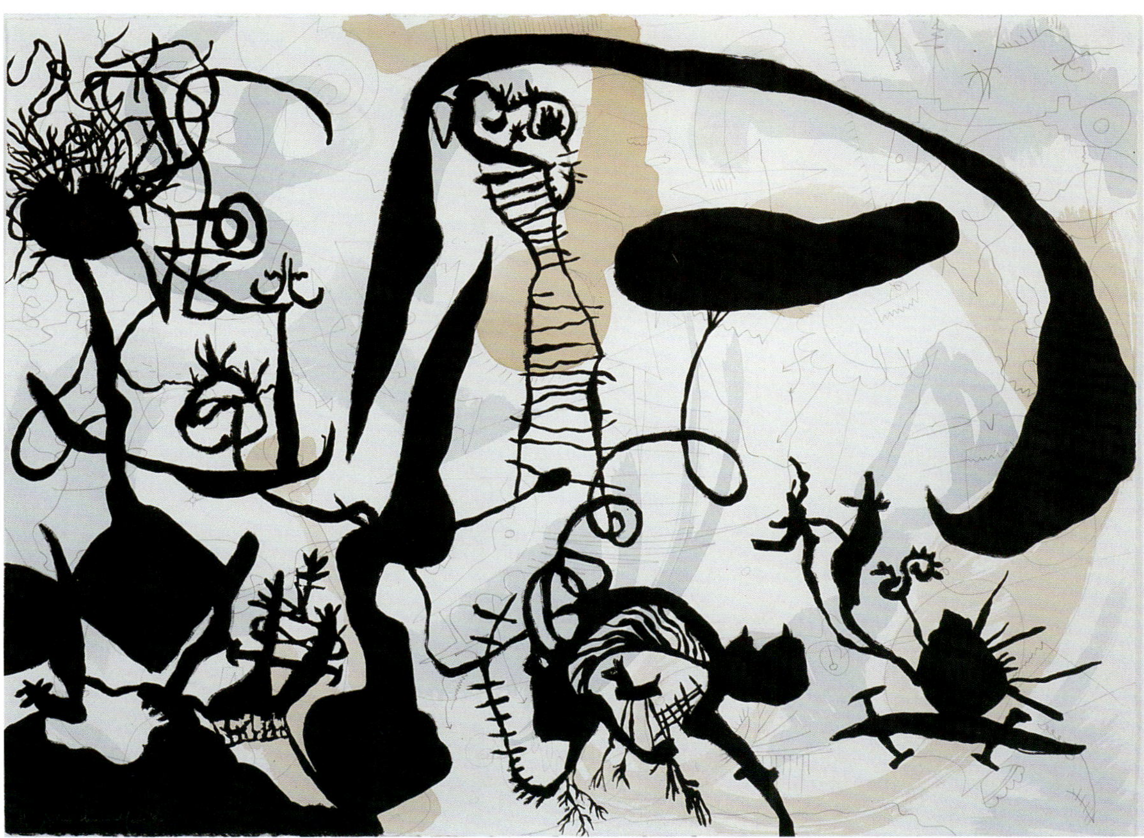

72

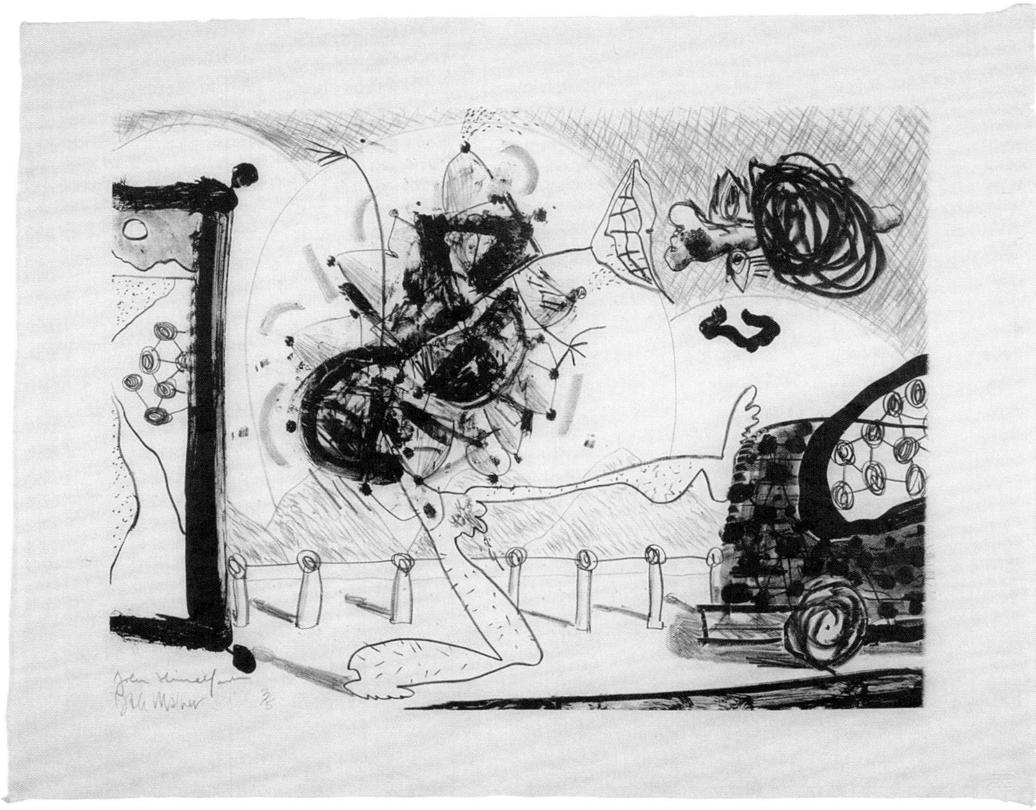

73

73.

Hill + Dale (with Dale Malner)

Date begun: 1990

Date finished: 1990

Medium: lithograph

Paper size: $19\frac{3}{8} \times 24\frac{5}{8}$ in.

Image size: 15×20 in.

Paper type: handmade Japanese paper, white

Publisher: Andrew Rubin

Press: Tandem Press

Printer: Andrew Rubin

Edition: 5

Proofs: none

Signature location: artist and collaborator, LL

Chop location: LR

Job number and location: none

Color printing order, execution of printing elements:

1. Aluminum printed with black. Image drawn with litho crayon and rubbing crayon.

74.
Mirorim

Date begun: 7/22/1990

Date finished: 9/6/1991

Medium: lithograph

Paper size: 19¾ × 41¼ in.

Image size: same

Paper type: BFK Rives White

Publisher: artist

Press: Anchor Graphics

Printer: David Jones

Printer's assistants: Jesse Murphy, Tom Sedsely, Reuben Shafer

Edition: 20

Proofs: 4 Anchor Graphics, 4 artist, 4 press, 1 ready to print, 1 trial

Signature location: LR

Chop location: LR

Job number and location: JH91–23

Color printing order, execution of printing elements:

1. Aluminum spot-printed with blue, red, and yellow. Image photo-transferred from carved woodblock.

2. Aluminum printed with black. Image drawn with brush and tusche.

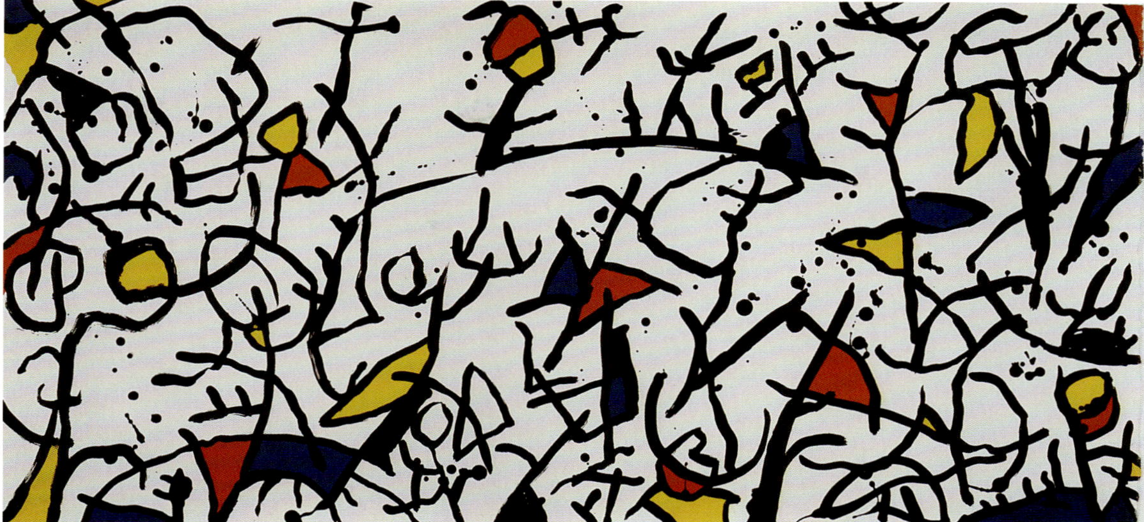

74

75.
Forest

Date begun: 9/1990

Date finished: 2004

Medium: lithograph

Paper size: 20 × 41 in.

Image size: same

Paper type: Rives BFK White

Publisher: artist

Press: Normal Editions Workshop, Illinois State University

Printer: Veda Rives

Printer's assistants: Richard D. Finch, Brandon Gunn, Jason Judd

Edition: 12

Proofs: 1 bon à tirer, 2 Illinois State University, 1 press, 1 proof (stamped, reverse), 1 ready to print, 1 trial (black)

Signature location: LR

Chop location: press, LL; printer, LR

Job number and location: 04–104, reverse LL

Color printing order, execution of printing elements:

1. Aluminum printed with red. Image drawn with brush and autographic ink.

2. Aluminum printed with black. Image drawn with brush and tusche.

Note: Print drawn and proofed at Tandem Press in 1990 and printed at Normal Editions Workshop in 2004.

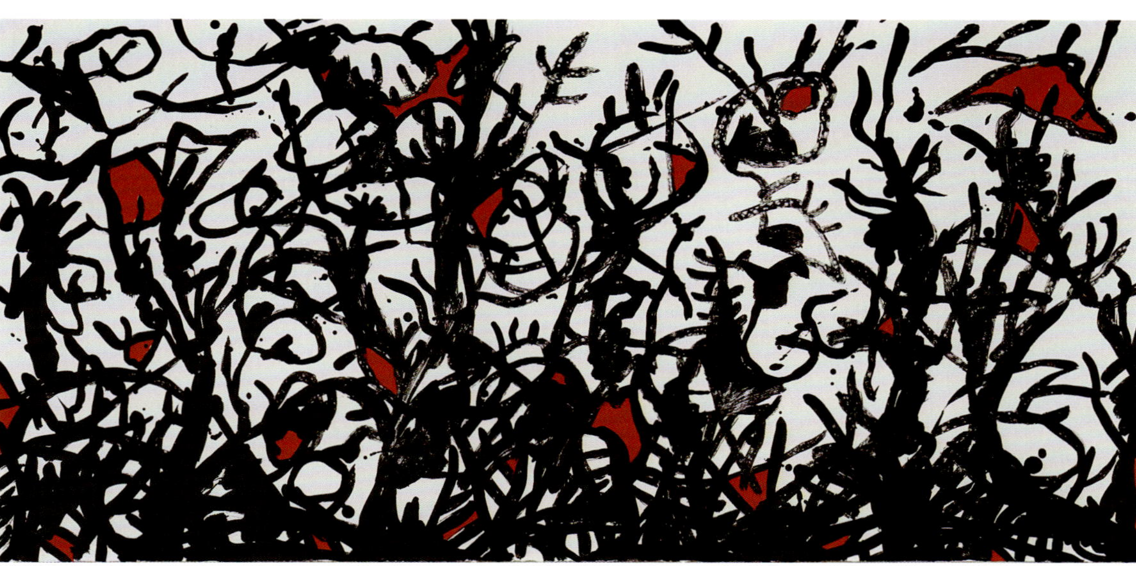

75

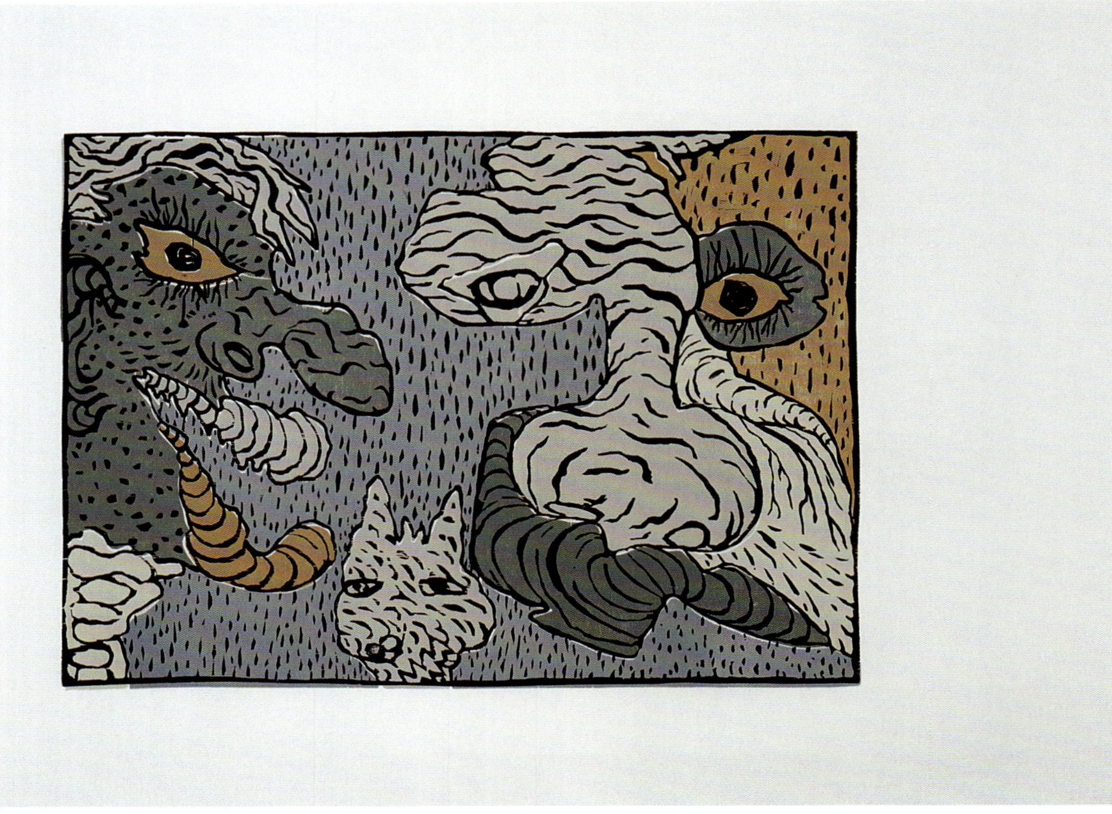

76

76.

Noon Day Rain

Date begun: 1990

Date finished: 2005

Medium: woodcut

Paper size: 16⅛ × 22$\frac{3}{16}$ in.

Image size: same

Paper type: Stonehenge Warm White

Publisher: UNO Print Workshop

Press: UNO Print Workshop

Printer: Julie Sopcak

Edition: 20

Proofs: 1 artist, 1 bon à tirer, 3 press, 1 Tandem Press (see Note)

Signature location: LL

Chop location: none

Job number and location: none

Color printing order, execution of printing elements:

1. Design drawn on woodblock, cut into jigsaw-puzzle pieces, which were inked with the following colors according to design, reassembled, and printed: light green (white, reflex blue, yellow), dark green (reflex blue, process yellow, opaque white, pthalo green), blue (white, reflex blue, yellow, cerulean blue, fire red), brown (rubine red, process blue, yellow, white, raw umber, magenta), gray (white, black, reflex blue, yellow, cerulean blue, fire red).

2. Woodblock printed with black. Image drawn on block with brush and ink.

Note: Print drawn and cut at Tandem Press in 1990 and finished at UNO Print Workshop in 2005.

77.

Earth Dwellers/Fox Trot

Date begun: 11/1991

Date finished: 11/8/1991

Medium: screenprint

Paper size: 41 × 28 in.

Image size: 36¾ × 24¾ in.

Paper type: Rives BFK White

Publisher: Stewart & Stewart

Press: Stewart & Stewart

Printer: Norman Stewart

Printer's assistant: Joe Keenan

Edition: 34

Proofs: 4 artist, 1 documentation, 1 printer, 4 publisher

Signature location: below image, LR

Chop location: LR corner

Job number and location: © John Himmelfarb stamp in black, reverse LL

Color printing order, execution of printing elements:

1. Black
2. Blue
3. Green
4. Orange
5. Brown
6. Pink
7. Darker green
8. Satin black

Each original color separation drawn on mylar, then screenprinted using an indirect sensigraphic stencil system.

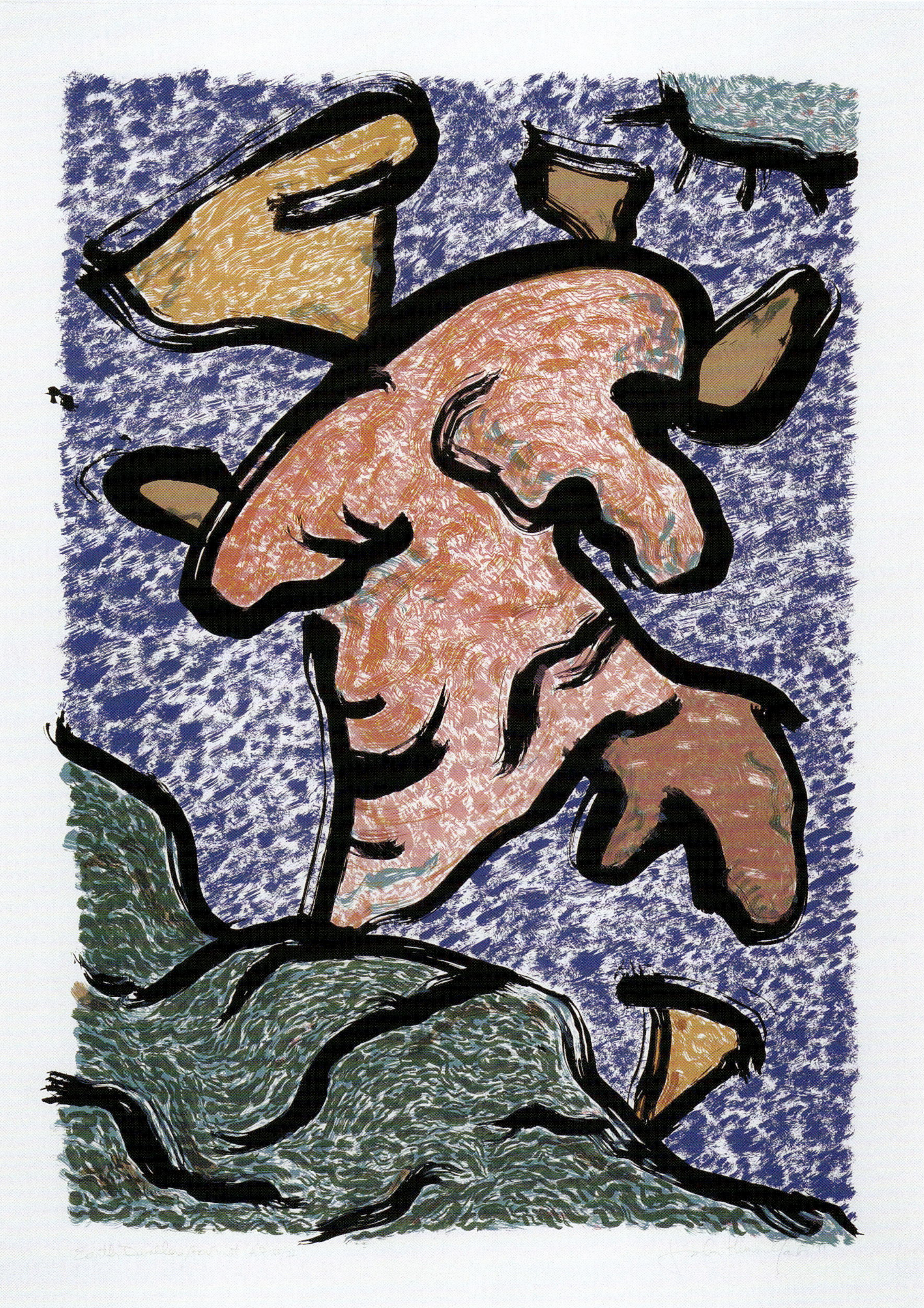

77

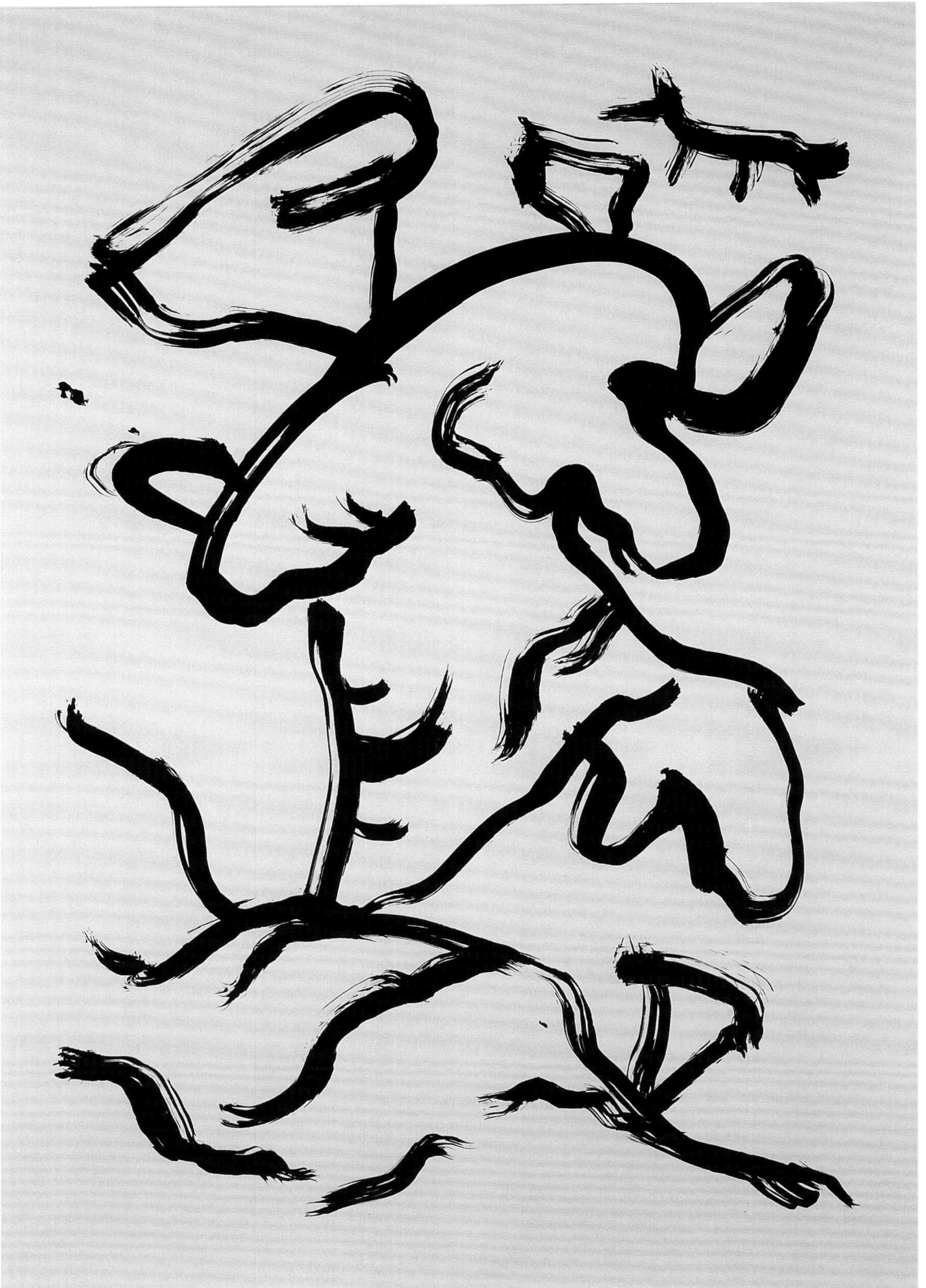

78.

Earth Dwellers/Line Dance

Date begun: 11/1991

Date finished: 11/8/1991

Medium: screenprint

Paper size: 41 × 28½ in.

Image size: 36¾ × 24¾ in.

Paper type: Rives BFK White

Publisher: Stewart & Stewart

Press: Stewart & Stewart

Printer: Norman Stewart

Printer's assistant: Joe Keenan

Edition: 4

Proofs: 1 artist, 1 publisher

Location of signature: below image, LR

Chop location: LR corner

Job number and location: © John Himmelfarb stamp in black ink, reverse LL

Color printing order, execution of printing elements:

1. Black

2. Satin black

Each original color separation drawn on mylar, then screenprinted using an indirect sensigraphic stencil system.

79.

Earth Dwellers/Mambo

Date begun: 11/1991

Date finished: 11/8/1991

Medium: screenprint

Paper size: 41 × 28½ in.

Image size: 37 × 25¼ in.

Paper type: Rives BFK White

Publisher: Stewart & Stewart

Press: Stewart & Stewart

Printer: Norman Stewart

Printer's assistant: Joe Keenan

Edition: 37

Proofs: 4 artist, 1 documentation, 1 printer, 4 publisher

Signature location: below image, LR

Chop location: LR corner

Job number and location: © John Himmelfarb stamp in black, reverse LL

Color printing order, execution of printing elements:

1. Black
2. Blue
3. Sienna
4. Brown
5. Green
6. Pink
7. Orange
8. Transparent blue

Each original color separation drawn on mylar, then screenprinted using an indirect sensigraphic stencil system.

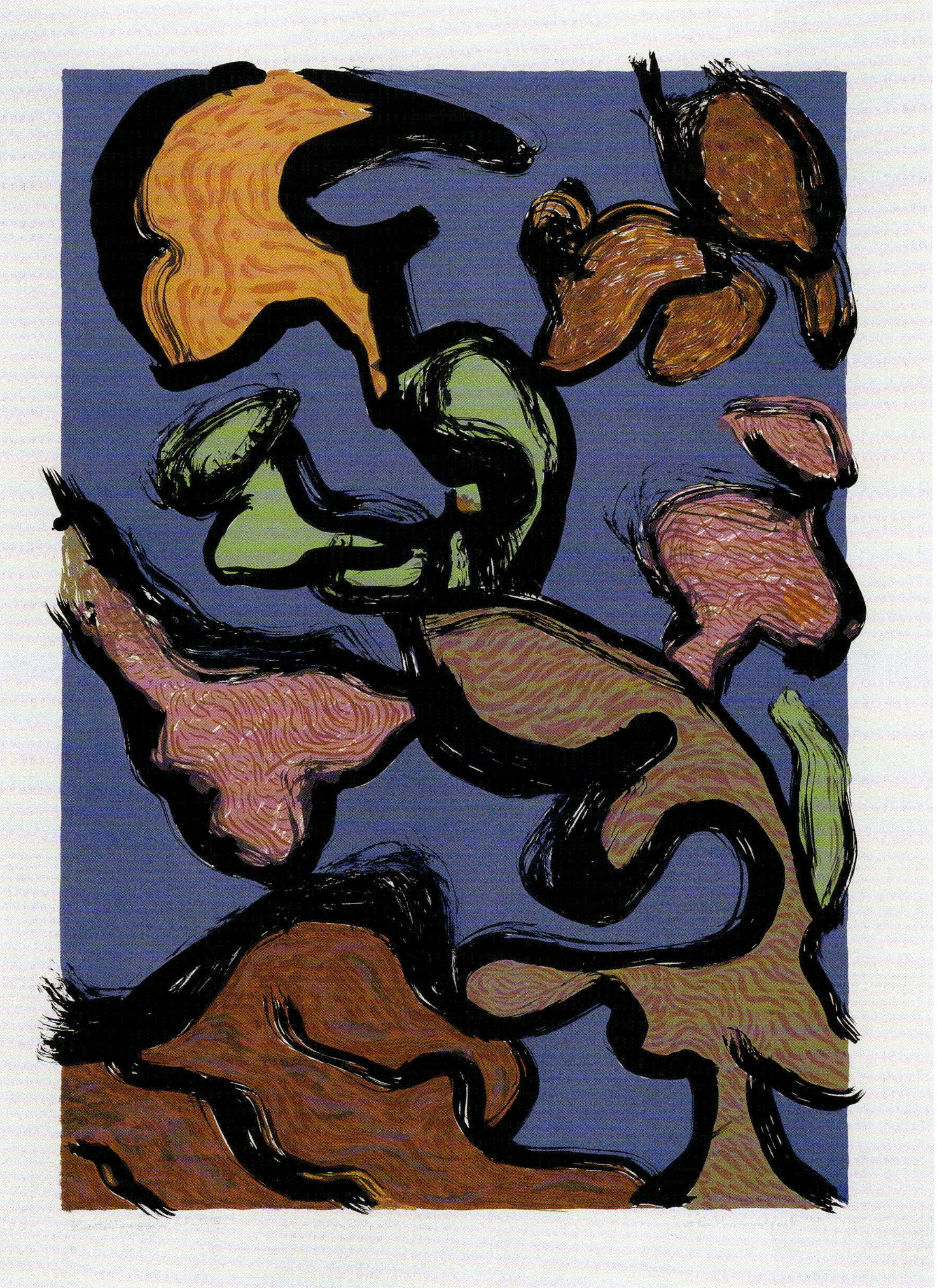

79

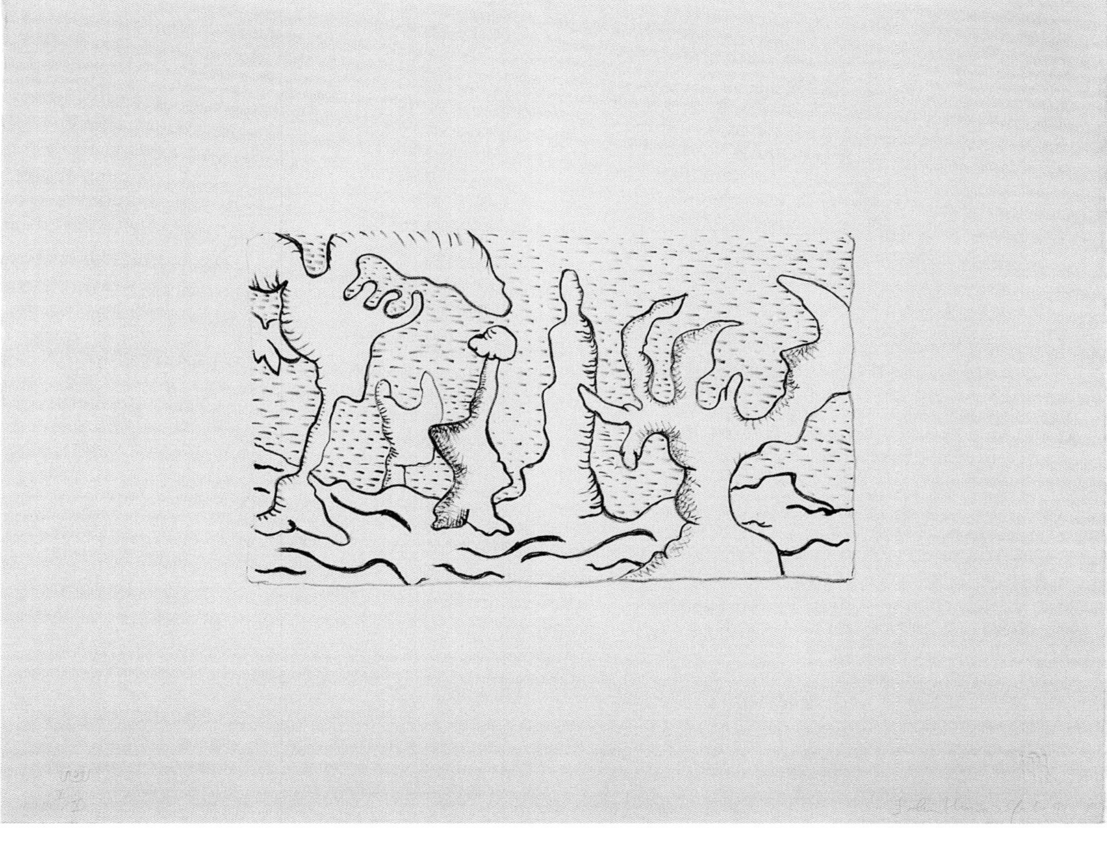

80

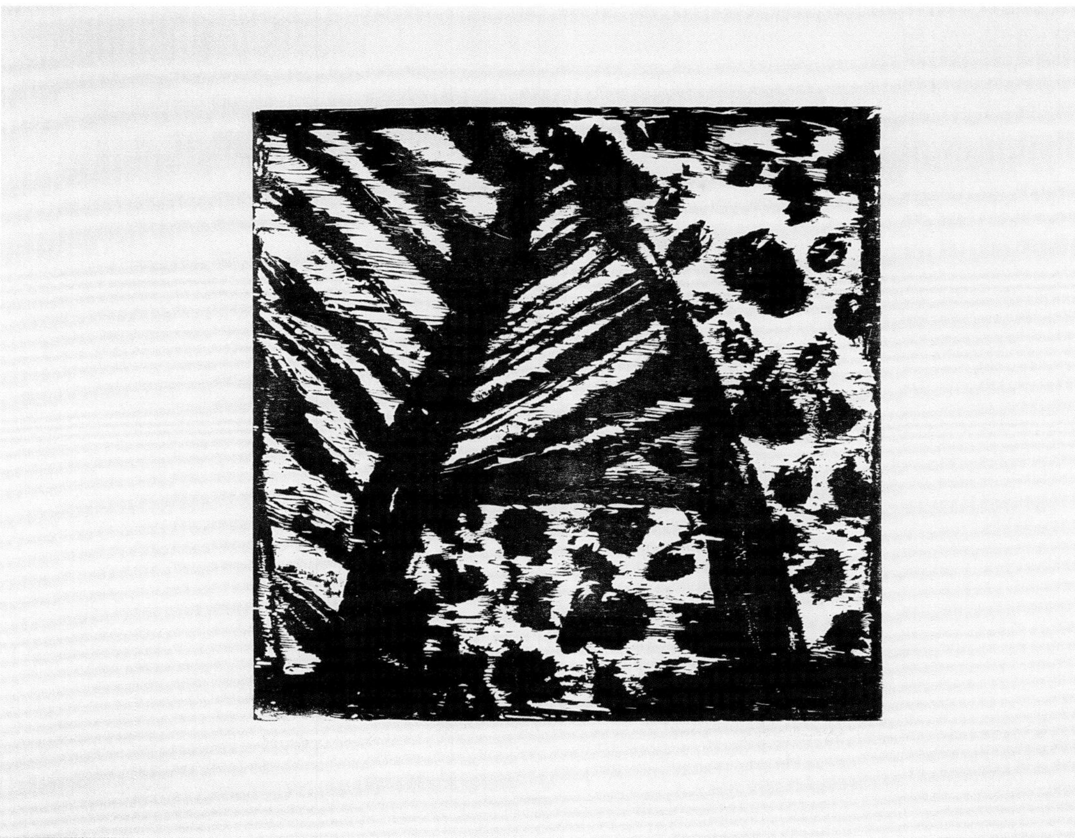

81

80.

Untitled (anthropomorphic)

Date begun: 11/20/1991

Date finished: 11/25/1991

Medium: lithograph

Paper size: 12⅛ × 15⅝ in.

Image size: 5⅛ × 8½ in.

Paper type: Rives BFK Gray

Publisher: Normal Editions Workshop, Illinois State University

Press: Normal Editions Workshop, Illinois State University

Printer: Richard D. Finch

Printer's assistant: Veda Rives

Edition: 22

Proofs: 10 artist (Roman numerals), 1 bon à tirer, 2 Illinois State University, 3 press, 1 publisher, 1 trial

Signature location: LR

Chop location: publisher, LL; printer, LR

Job number and location: 91–102, reverse LL

Color printing order, execution of printing elements:

1. Stone printed with black. Image drawn with litho pencil.

81.

Alpha or **Know Your ABC's**

Date begun: 1991

Date finished: 1991

Medium: woodcut

Paper size: 30 × 40 in.

Image size: 22 × 22 in.

Paper type: Rives BFK White

Publisher: artist

Edition: 11

Proofs: 4 printer

Signature location: below image, LR

Chop location: none

Job number and location: none

Color printing order, execution of printing elements:

1. Woodblock printed with black. Image drawn on block with brush and ink by artist; cut by Paul Schneider.

82.

Shop Notes

Date begun: 11/18/1991

Date finished: 1/29/1992

Medium: intaglio

Paper size: 39 × 27¼ in.

Image size: 35¾ × 23¾ in.

Paper type: Rives BFK Tan

Publisher: Normal Editions Workshop, Illinois State University

Press: Normal Editions Workshop, Illinois State University

Printers: Larry Bemm, Carey Deering, Richard D. Finch, Lloyd Wassenaar

Printers' assistants: Theresa Gall, Ray George, Meda Rives, Veda Rives

Edition: 12

Proofs: 2 Illinois State University, 4 presentation, 4 press, 1 publisher

Signature location: LR

Chop location: LL

Job number and location: 91–101, reverse LL

Color printing order, execution of printing elements:

1. Zinc printed with etching black #514. Image drawn with soft-ground etching technique.

Note: Print element used in *Proof Copy* (no. 83).

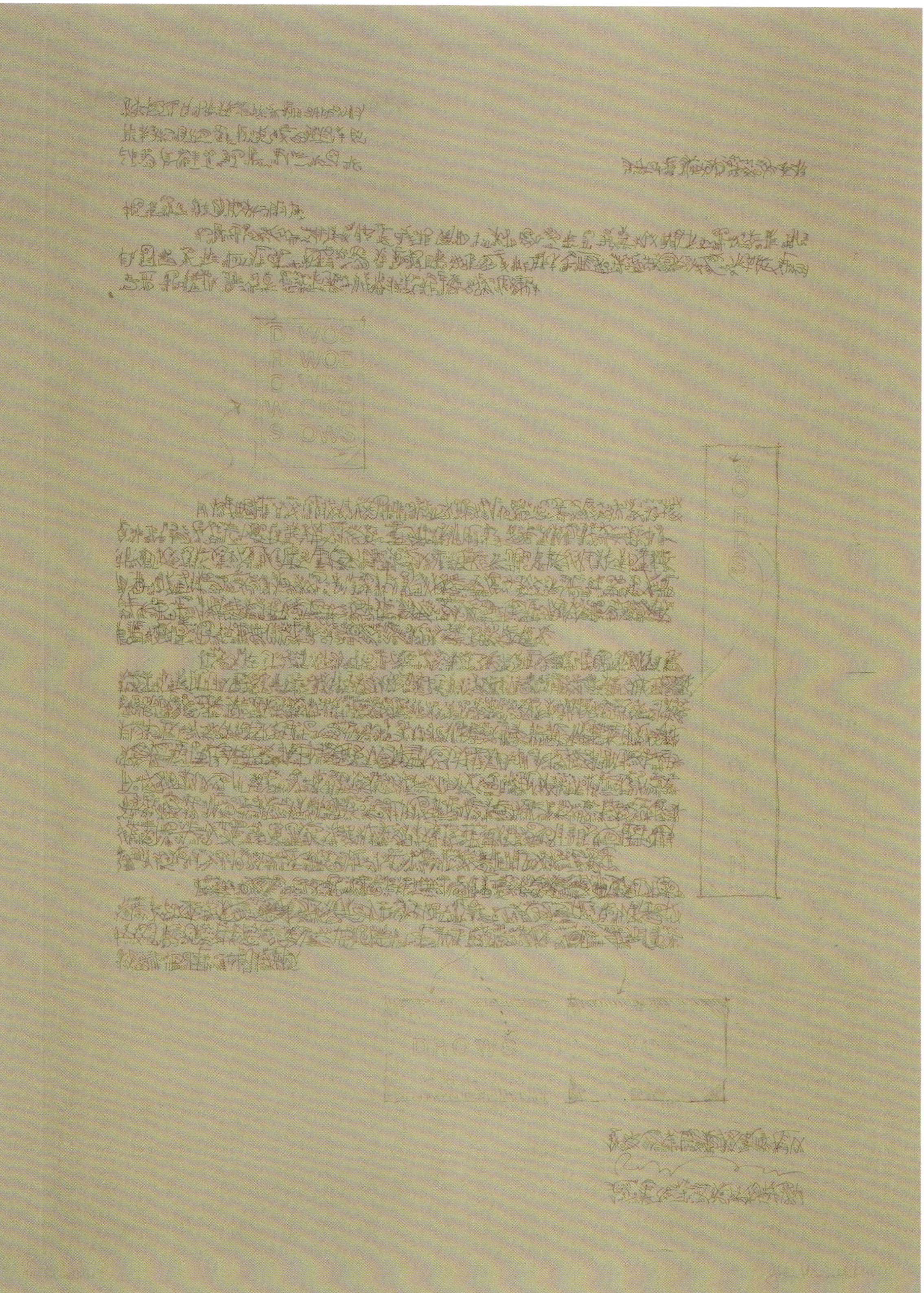

82

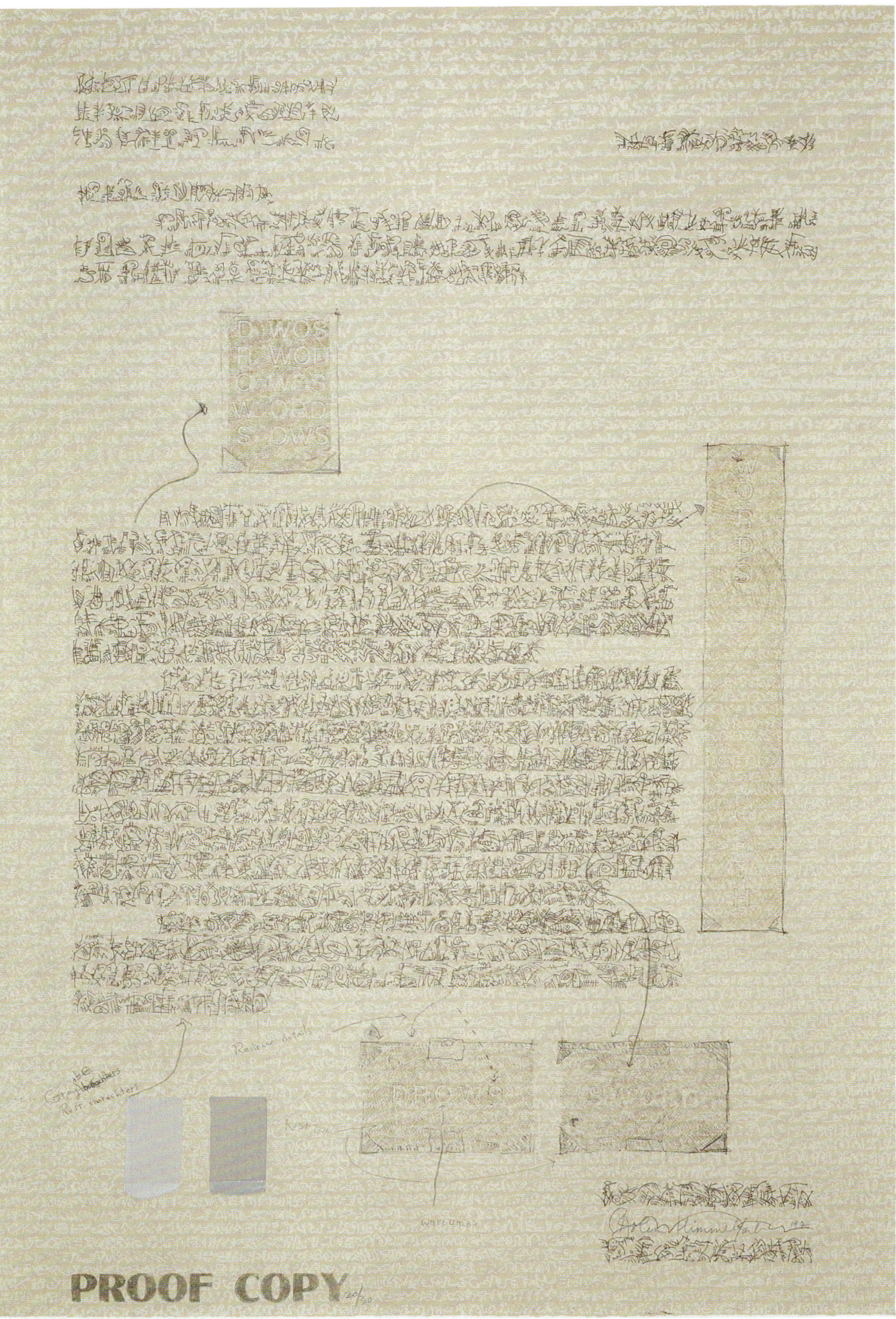

83.

Proof Copy

Date begun: 2/17/1992

Date finished: 5/13/1992

Medium: lithograph

Paper size: 36 × 24 in.

Image size: same

Paper type: Rives BFK Gray

Publisher: Normal Editions Workshop, Illinois State University

Press: Normal Editions Workshop, Illinois State University

Printer: Richard D. Finch

Printer's assistants: Larry Bemm, Meda Rives, Veda Rives

Edition: 30

Proofs: 3 artist, 1 bon à tirer, 2 Illinois State University, 1 presentation, 3 press, 1 publisher, 1 working

Signature location: LR

Chop location: publisher, LL; printer, LR

Job number and location: 92–103, reverse LL

Color printing order, execution of printing elements:

1. Aluminum printed with pale orange. Image drawn with technical pen filled with plate etch.

2. Aluminum printed using split fountain: red-gray, ocher, light brown, purple-gray. Image drawn with litho pencil.

3. Aluminum printed with warm black. Image transferred from zinc etching plate (*Shop Notes*, no. 82).

4. Aluminum printed with gray. Image drawn with litho pencil.

5. Light and dark grays in LL corner applied by hand to paper as "draw-downs."

Note: Print element in run #1 used in *Tabula Tabula Picta* (no. 91).

84.

Letter to Ray

Date begun: 2/1992

Date finished: 5/1992

Medium: intaglio and offset

Paper size: 10⅞ × 8⅜ in.

Image size: same

Paper type: Arches Cover White

Publisher: Normal Editions Workshop, Illinois State University

Press: Normal Editions Workshop, Illinois State University

Printer: Larry Bemm

Printer's assistant: Ray E. George

Edition: 20

Proofs: 3 artist (Roman numerals), 1 bon à tirer, 2 Illinois State University, 1 press

Signature location: LR

Chop location: none

Job number and location: 92–104, reverse LL

Color printing order, execution of printing elements:

1. Blue and red line-printed by offset.

2. Copper printed with black. Image drawn using line-etching technique.

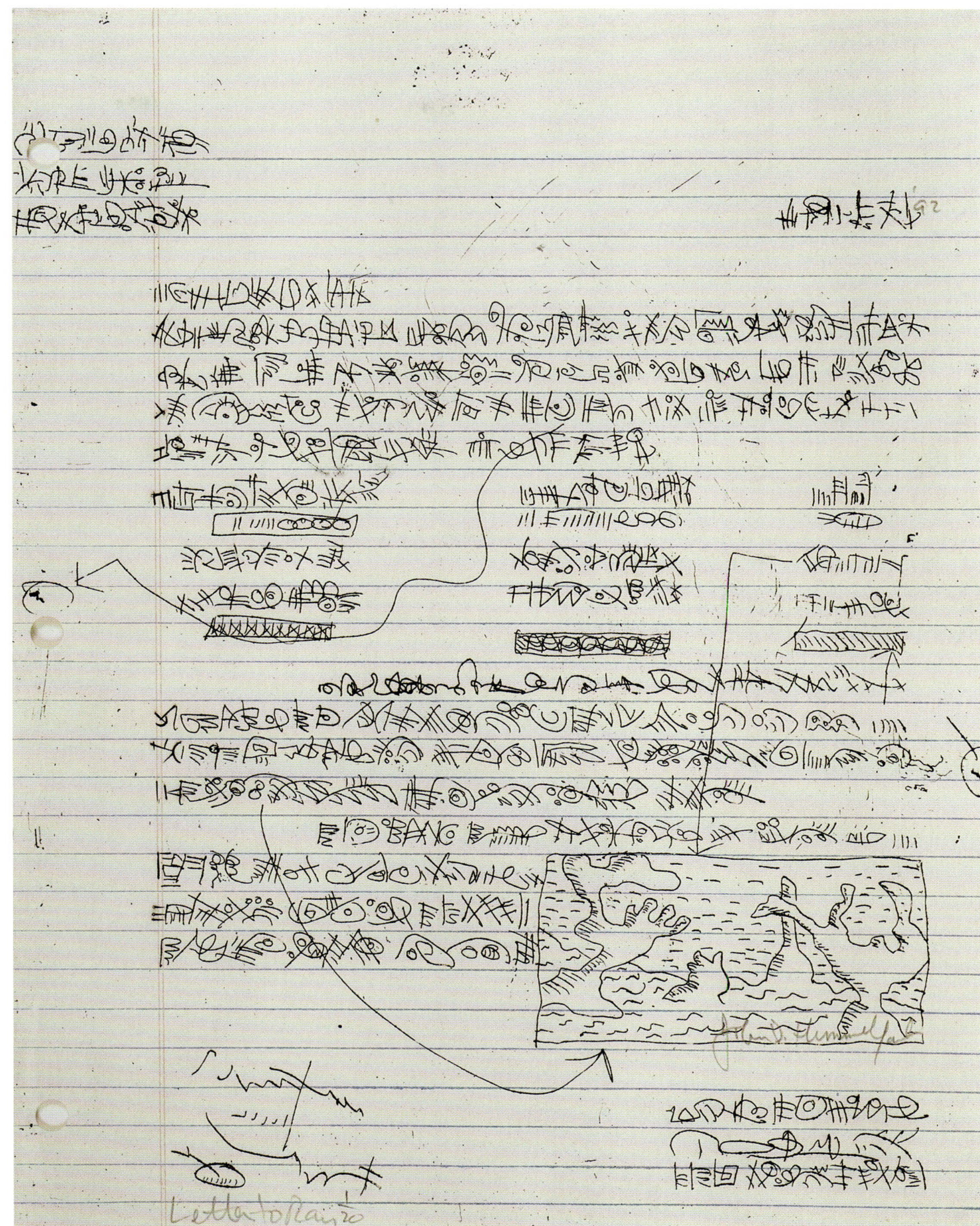

84

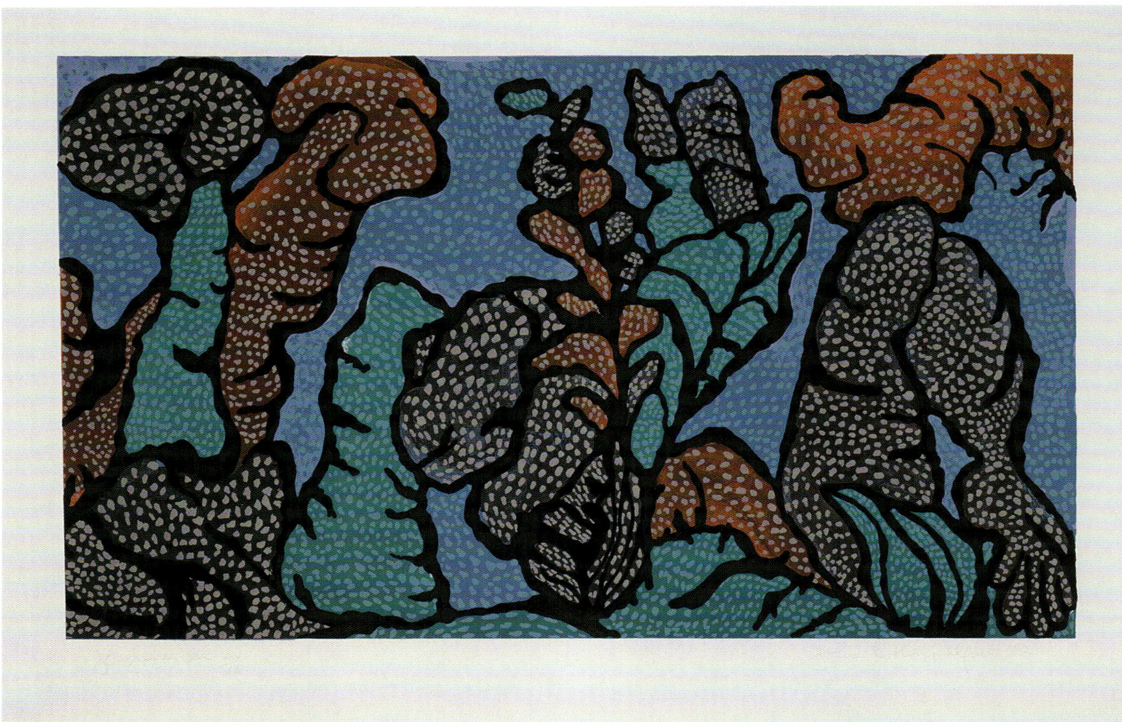
85

85.

Jongleurs' Dell

Date begun: 1992

Date finished: 8/10/1992

Medium: lithograph

Paper size: 25 × 38 in.

Image size: 20 × 33¾ in.

Paper type: Rives BFK White

Publisher: Full Court Press

Press: Full Court Press

Printer: Eric Robbins

Edition: 50: 25 Arabic numerals, 25 Roman numerals

Proofs: 2 press

Signature location: LR

Chop location: LL

Job number and location: none

Color printing order, execution of printing elements:

1. Green (transparent, pthalo green, pthalo blue, opaque white).
2. Blue (white, bronze blue, cerulean blue).
3. Brown (transparent, western brown, white, pthalo green).
4. Red (coral red, western brown, white, pthalo green).
5. White (opaque white, western brown).
6. White (opaque white, western brown).
7. Black (Senefelder's black, pthalo blue).

Aluminum plates drawn on with brush and tusche. Plates proofed, reworked, and printed.

86.

Juggler on Stage

Date begun: 10/11/1992

Date finished: 11/2/1992

Medium: screenprint

Paper size: 41 × 28½ in.

Image size: 36¾ × 25 in.

Paper type: Rives BFK White

Publisher: Stewart & Stewart

Press: Stewart & Stewart

Printer: Norman Stewart

Printer's assistant: Joe Keenan

Edition: 24

Proofs: 3 artist, 1 documentation, 1 printer, 3 publisher

Signature location: below image, LR

Chop location: LR corner

Job number and location: © John Himmelfarb stamp in black, reverse LL

Color printing order, execution of printing elements:

1. Orange
2. Yellow
3. Midnight blue with black
4. Black

Each original color separation drawn on mylar, then screenprinted using an indirect sensigraphic stencil system.

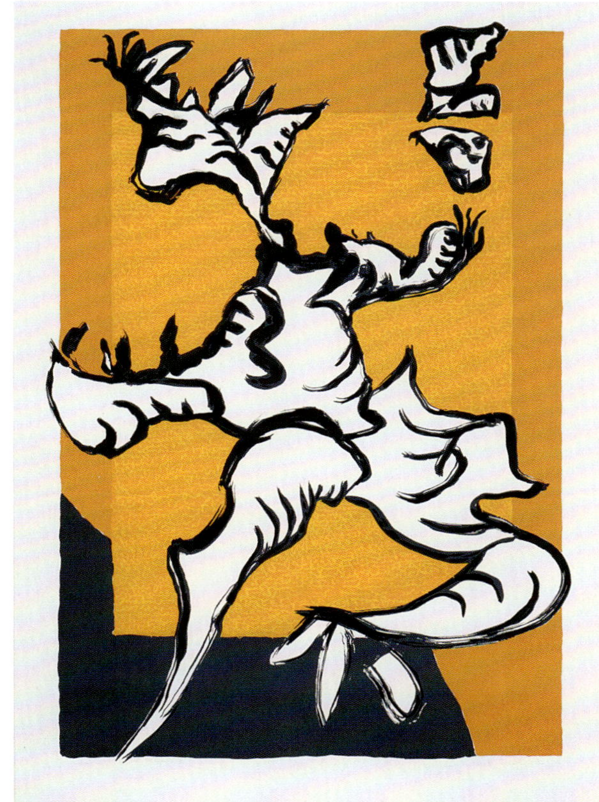

86

87.

Juggler

Date begun: 10/11/1992

Date finished: 11/2/1992

Medium: screenprint

Paper size: 41 × 28½ in.

Image size: 36¾ × 25 in.

Paper type: Rives BFK White

Publisher: Stewart & Stewart

Press: Stewart & Stewart

Printer: Norman Stewart

Printer's assistant: Joe Keenan

Edition: 11

Proofs: 2 artist, 1 documentation, 1 printer, 2 publisher

Signature location: below image, LR

Chop location: LR corner

Job number and location: © John Himmelfarb stamp in black, reverse LL

Color printing order, execution of printing elements:

1. Black with red
2. Black

Each original color separation drawn on mylar, then screenprinted using an indirect sensigraphic stencil system.

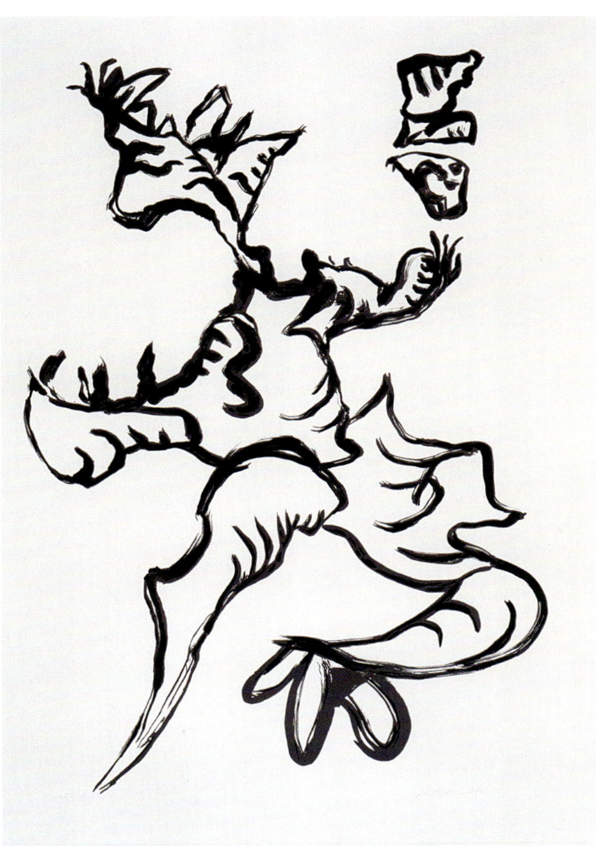

87

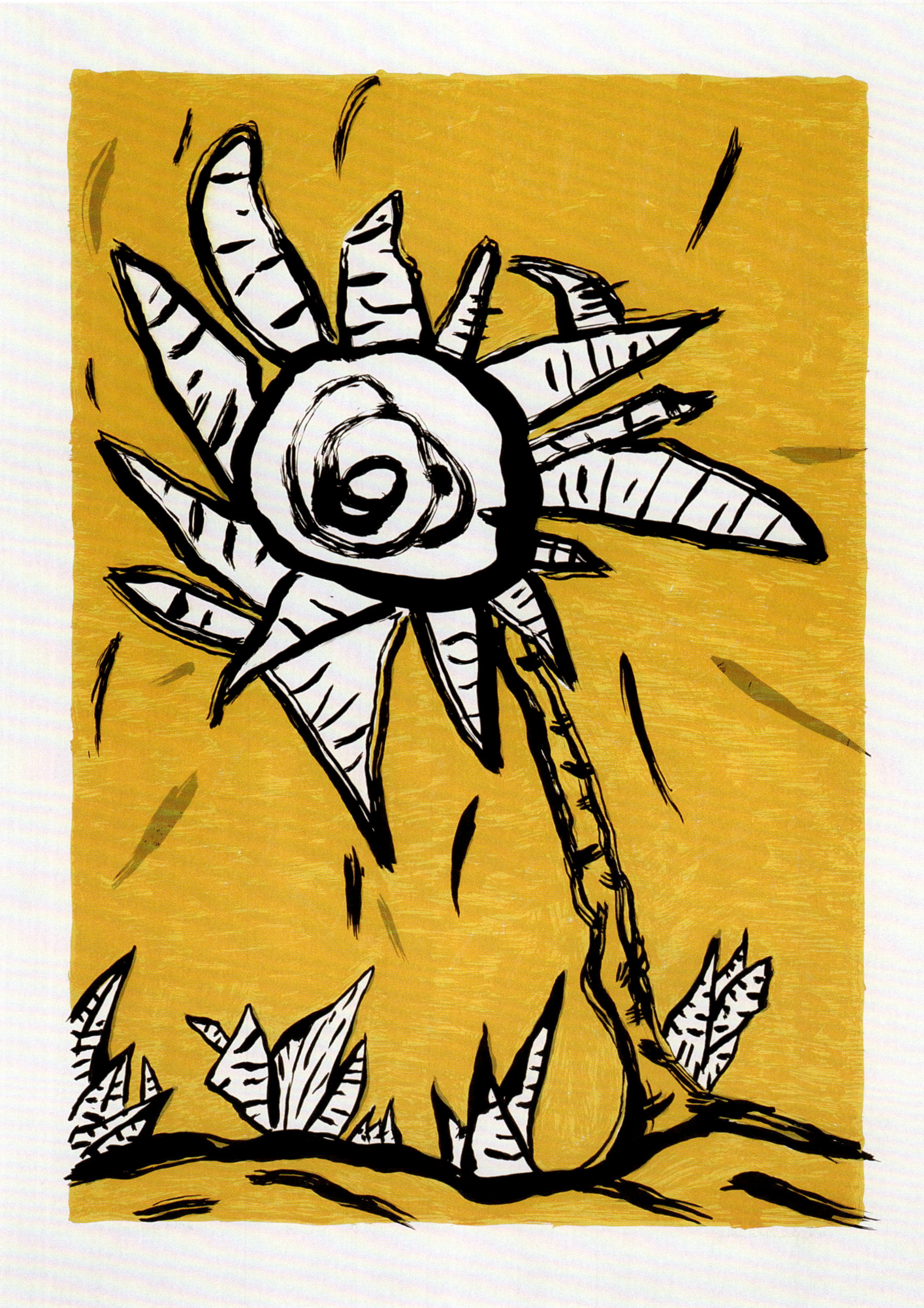

88

88.

Yellow Rose

Date begun: 10/11/1992

Date finished: 11/2/1992

Medium: screenprint

Paper size: 41 × 28½ in.

Image size: 36¼ × 24¾ in.

Paper type: Rives BFK White

Publisher: Stewart & Stewart

Press: Stewart & Stewart

Printer: Norman Stewart

Printer's assistant: Joe Keenan

Edition: 25

Proofs: 3 artist, 1 documentation, 1 printer, 3 publisher

Signature location: below image, LR

Chop location: LR corner

Job number and location: © John Himmelfarb stamp in black, reverse LL

Color printing order, execution of printing elements:

1. Cool black
2. Primrose yellow
3. Cadmium yellow
4. Black

Each original color separation drawn on mylar, then screenprinted using an indirect sensigraphic stencil system.

Note: Print element in run #4 used in *Stolen Glance* (no. 89).

89.

Stolen Glance

Date begun: 10/11/1992

Date finished: 11/2/1992

Medium: screenprint

Paper size: 41 × 28½ in.

Image size: 36¼ × 24¾ in.

Paper type: Rives BFK White

Publisher: Stewart & Stewart

Press: Stewart & Stewart

Printer: Norman Stewart

Printer's assistant: Joe Keenan

Edition: 10

Proofs: 2 artist, 1 documentation, 1 printer, 2 publisher

Signature location: below image, R

Chop location: LR corner

Job number and location: © John Himmelfarb stamp in black, reverse LL

Color printing order, execution of printing elements:

1. Cool black

2. Black

Each original color separation drawn on mylar, then screenprinted using an indirect sensigraphic stencil system.

Note: Print element used in *Yellow Rose* (no. 88).

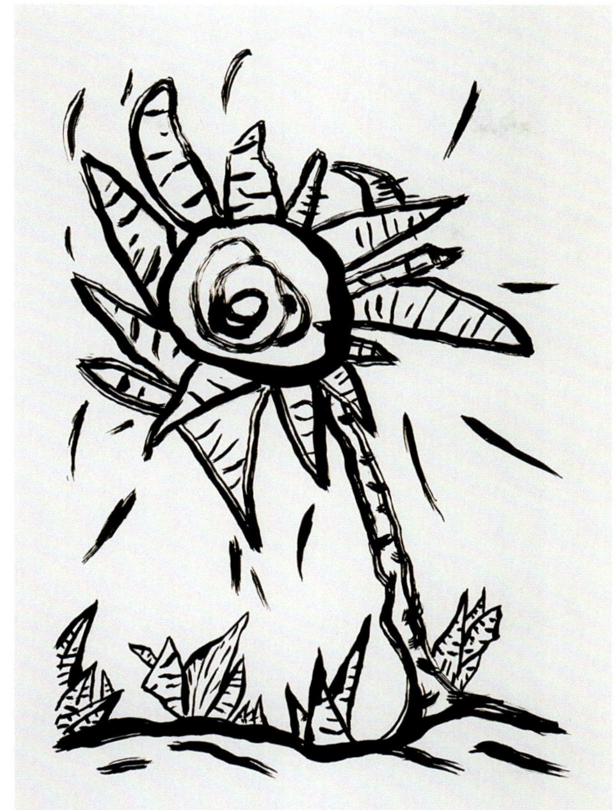

89

90.

Hi-Go

Date finished: 1992

Medium: lithograph

Paper size: 25 × 32⅛ in.

Image size: 23 × 23 in.

Paper type: Rives BFK White

Publisher: artist

Press: Tom Christison

Printer: Tom Christison

Edition: none

Proofs: 5 trial

Signature location: below image, LR

Chop location: none

Job number and location: none

Color printing order, execution of printing elements:

1. Aluminum printed with silver-green, flat-rolled.

2. Aluminum printed with warm black. Image drawn with recycled photocopy toner.

Note: Background color varies in proofs.

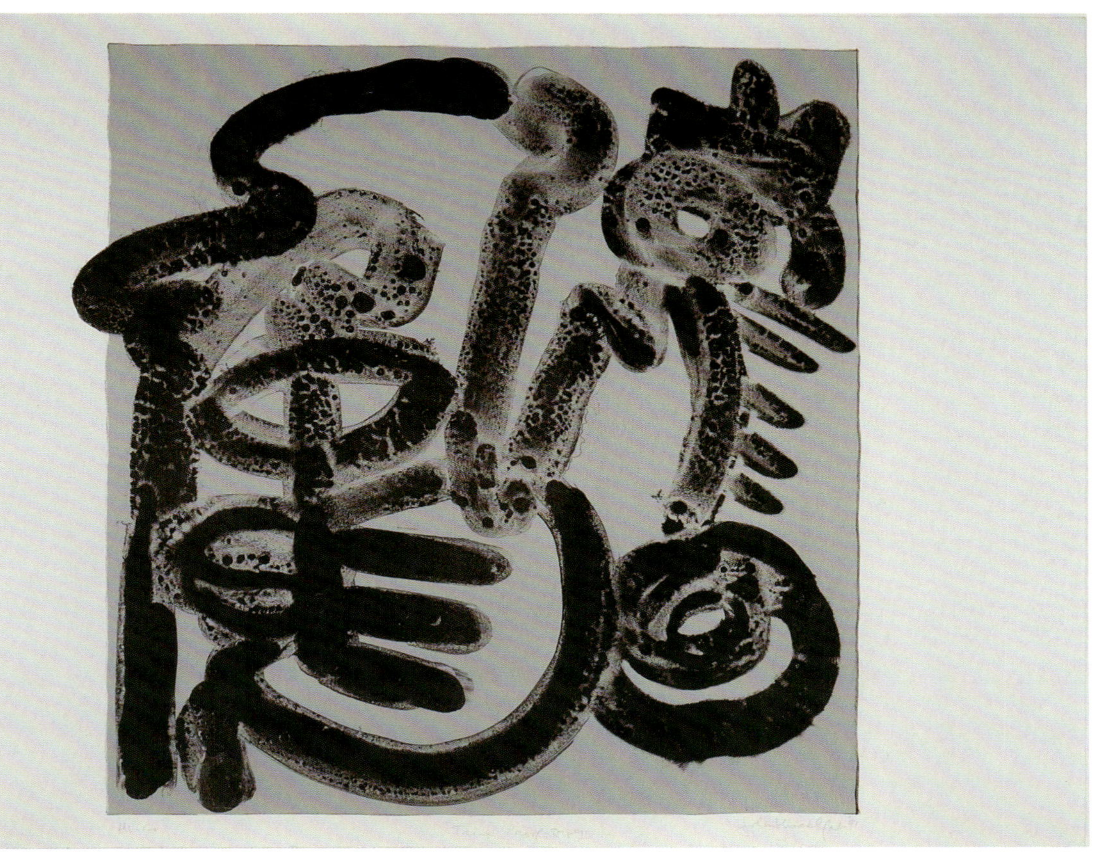

90

91

91.

Tabula Tabula Picta

Date begun: 2/17/1992

Date finished: 2/8/1993

Medium: lithograph

Paper size: 40 × 25 in.

Image size: same

Paper type: Rives BFK Gray

Publisher: Normal Editions Workshop, Illinois State University

Press: Normal Editions Workshop, Illinois State University

Printer: Veda Rives

Printer's assistants: Nicholas De Peder, Richard D. Finch, Theresa Gall, Ryan Scott McCullar, Meda Rives

Edition: 24

Proofs: 1 bon à tirer, 2 Illinois State University, 4 press, 1 ready to print

Signature location: LR

Chop location: publisher, LL; printer, LR

Job number and location: 93–102, reverse LL

Color printing order, execution of printing elements:

1. Aluminum printed with black, noir à monter. Print element transferred from run #1 of *Proof Copy* (no. 83) with additions drawn with brush and autographic ink.

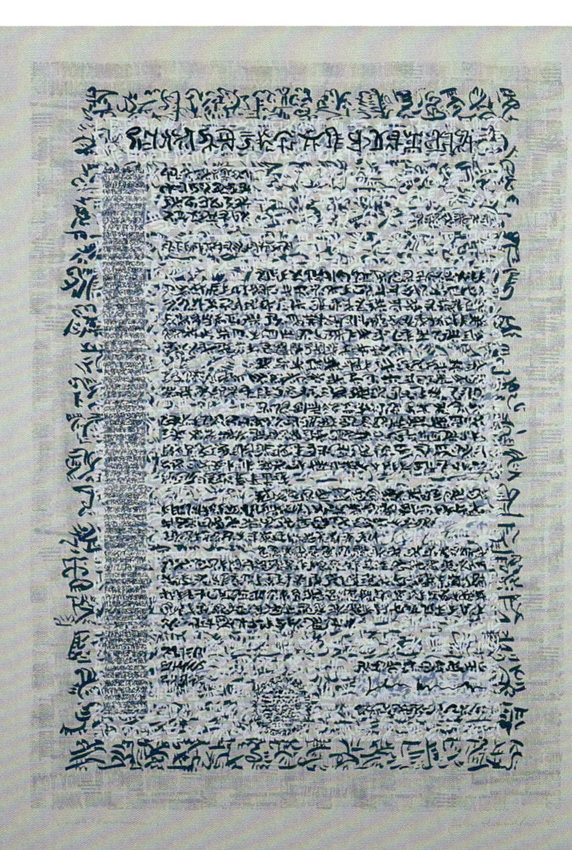

92

92.

Double Transmission

Date begun: 10/11/1993

Date finished: 11/2/1993

Medium: screenprint

Paper size: 29¾ × 21¾ in.

Image size: 26 × 18 in.

Paper type: Rives BFK Gray

Publisher: Stewart & Stewart

Press: Stewart & Stewart

Printer: Norman Stewart

Printer's assistant: artist

Edition: 1

Proofs: none

Signature location: below image, LR

Chop location: LR corner

Job number and location: © John Himmelfarb stamp in black, reverse LL

Color printing order, execution of printing elements:

No documentation of color order. Each original color separation drawn on mylar, then screenprinted using an indirect sensigraphic stencil system.

Note: Print element used in *Fax Appeal* (no. 93), *First Draft* (no. 94), and *Note of Appeal* (no. 95).

93.

Fax Appeal

Date begun: 10/11/1993

Date finished: 11/2/1993

Medium: screenprint

Paper size: 29¾ × 21¾ in.

Image size: 26 × 18 in.

Paper type: Rives BFK Gray

Publisher: Stewart & Stewart

Press: Stewart & Stewart

Printer: Norman Stewart

Printer's assistant: artist

Edition: 4

Proofs: 1 press, 1 publisher

Signature location: below image, LR

Chop location: LR corner

Job number and location: © John Himmelfarb stamp in black, reverse LL

Color printing order, execution of printing elements:

1. Cool gray

2. Transparent white

3. Blue-black

Each original color separation drawn on mylar, then screenprinted using an indirect sensigraphic stencil system.

Note: Print element reused from *Double Transmission* (no. 92).

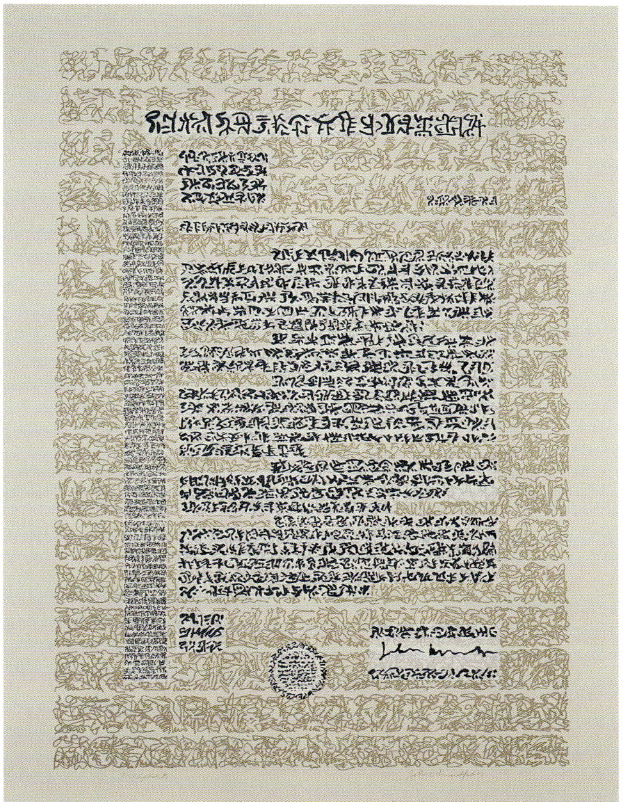

93

94.

First Draft

Date begun: 10/11/1993

Date finished: 11/2/1993

Medium: screenprint

Paper size: 29¾ × 21¾ in.

Image size: 26 × 18 in.

Paper type: Rives BFK Gray

Publisher: Stewart & Stewart

Press: Stewart & Stewart

Printer: Norman Stewart

Printer's assistant: artist

Edition: 7

Proofs: 1 artist, 1 publisher

Signature location: below image, LR

Chop location: LR corner

Job number and location: © John Himmelfarb stamp in black, reverse LL

Color printing order, execution of printing elements:

1. Cool gray

2. Dark blue

Each original color separation drawn on mylar, then screenprinted using an indirect sensigraphic stencil system.

Note: Print element reused from *Double Transmission* (no. 92).

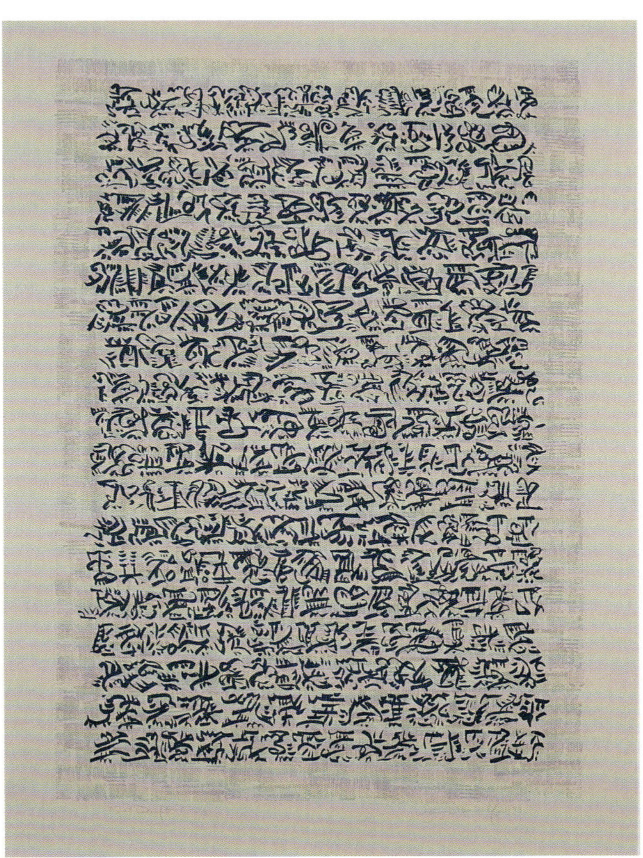

94

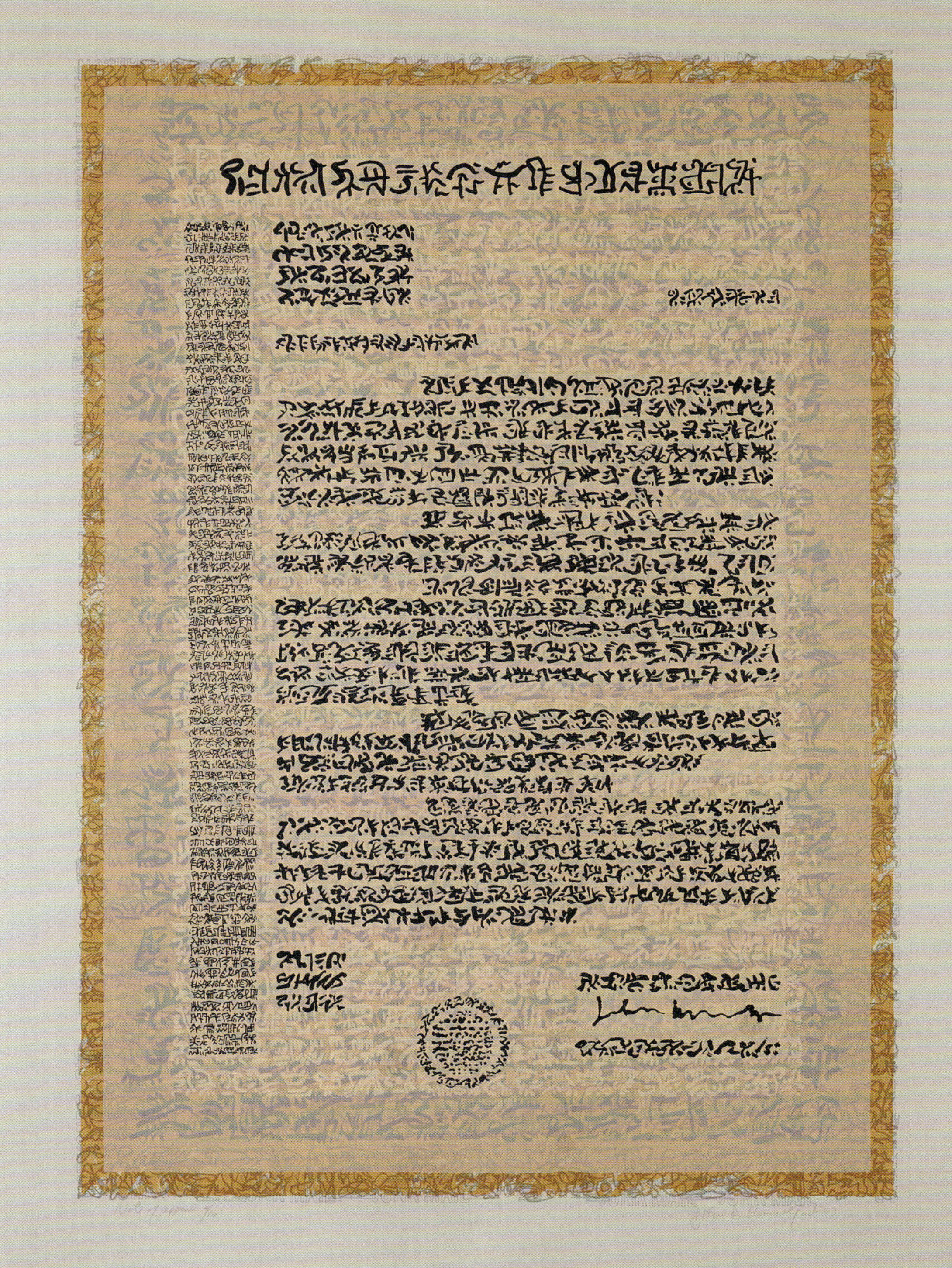

95.

Note of Appeal

Date begun: 10/11/1993

Date finished: 11/2/1993

Medium: screenprint

Paper size: 29¾ × 21¾ in.

Image size: 26 × 18 in.

Paper type: Rives BFK Gray

Publisher: Stewart & Stewart

Press: Stewart & Stewart

Printer: Norman Stewart

Printer's assistant: artist

Edition: 16

Proofs: 2 artist, 2 publisher

Signature location: below image, LR

Chop location: LR corner

Job number and location: © John Himmelfarb stamp in black, reverse LL

Color printing order, execution of printing elements:

1. Cool gray
2. Pale orange-red
3. Deep cool gray
4. Dark blue
5. White
6. Transparent white
7. White
8. Blue-black

Each original color separation drawn on mylar, then screenprinted using an indirect sensigraphic stencil system.

Note: Print element reused from *Double Transmission* (no. 92).

96.

Short Order

Date begun: 10/11/1993

Date finished: 11/2/1993

Medium: screenprint

Paper size: 29¾ × 21¾ in.

Image size: 26 × 18 in.

Paper type: Rives BFK Gray

Publisher: Stewart & Stewart

Press: Stewart & Stewart

Printer: Norman Stewart

Printer's assistant: artist

Edition: 17

Proofs: 2 artist, 2 publisher

Signature location: below image, LR

Chop location: LR corner

Job number and location: © John Himmelfarb stamp in black, reverse LL

Color printing order, execution of printing elements:

1. Cool gray
2. Pale yellow
3. Deep cool gray
4. Pale blue-green
5. Dark gray
6. Blue

Each original color separation drawn on mylar, then screenprinted using an indirect sensigraphic stencil system.

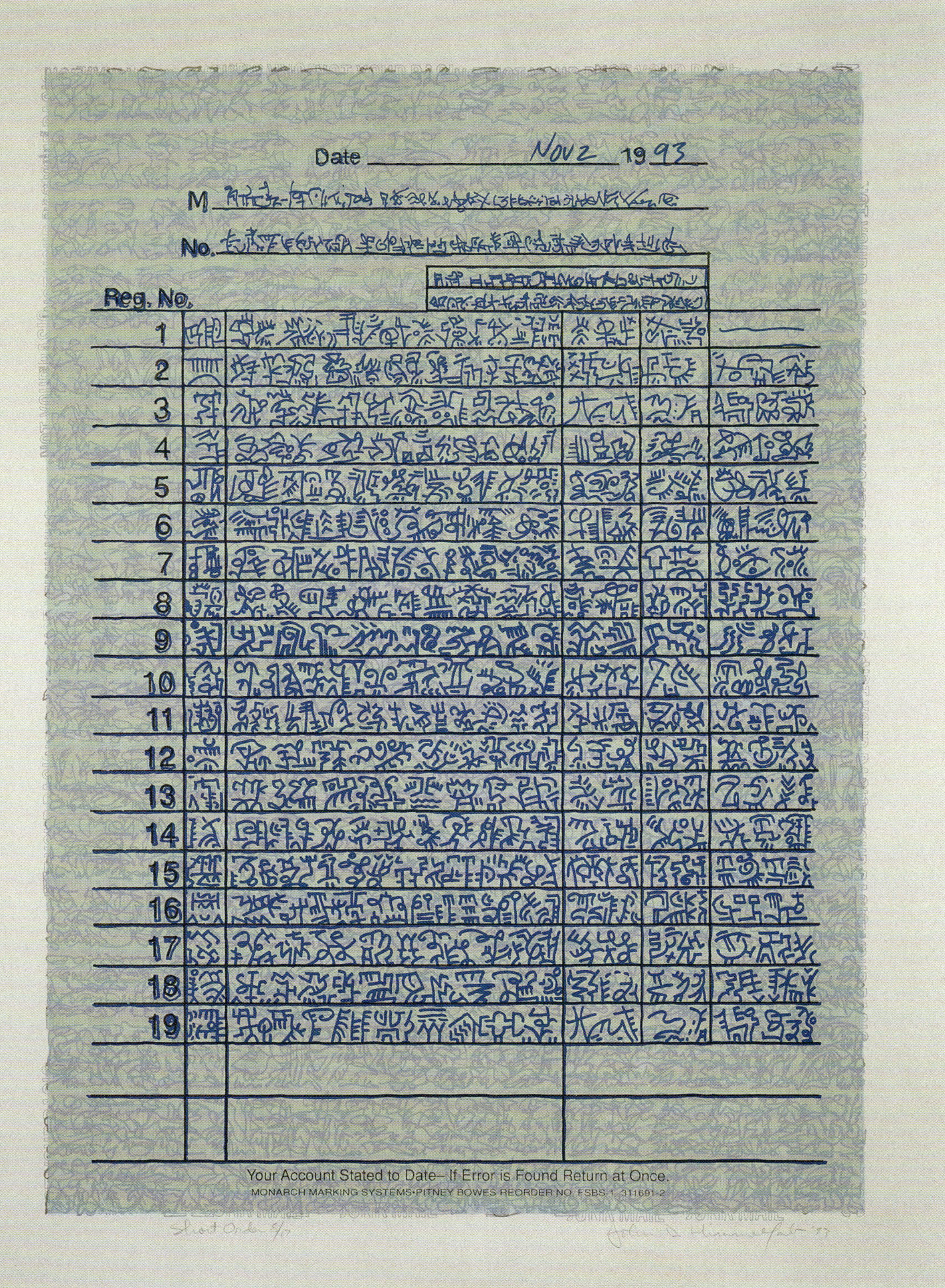

96

97.

White Out

Date begun: 10/11/1993

Date finished: 11/2/1993

Medium: screenprint

Paper size: 29¾ × 21¾ in.

Image size: 21¾ × 13¾ in.

Paper type: Rives BFK Gray

Publisher: Stewart & Stewart

Press: Stewart & Stewart

Printer: Norman Stewart

Printer's assistant: artist

Edition: 3

Proofs: none

Signature location: below image, R

Chop location: LR corner

Job number and location: © John Himmelfarb stamp in black, reverse LL

Color printing order, execution of printing elements:

1. White

Original color separation drawn on mylar, then screenprinted using an indirect sensigraphic stencil system.

98.

Cipher

Date begun: 9/10/1994

Date finished: 10/3/1994

Medium: screenprint

Paper size: 41 × 28½ in.

Image size: 36 × 24 in.

Paper type: Rives BFK White

Publisher: Stewart & Stewart

Press: Stewart & Stewart

Printer: Norman Stewart

Printer's assistant: Joe Keenan

Edition: 25

Proofs: 2 artist, 1 documentation, 1 printer, 3 publisher

Signature location: below image, LR

Chop location: LR corner

Job number and location: © John Himmelfarb stamp in black, reverse LL

Color printing order, execution of printing elements:

1. Black
2. Masking-tape yellow
3. Cadmium yellow light
4. White
5. Half-tone black
6. Blue-black

Each original color separation drawn on mylar, then screenprinted using an indirect sensigraphic stencil system.

Note: Print element in run#1 used in *Understatement* (no. 101).

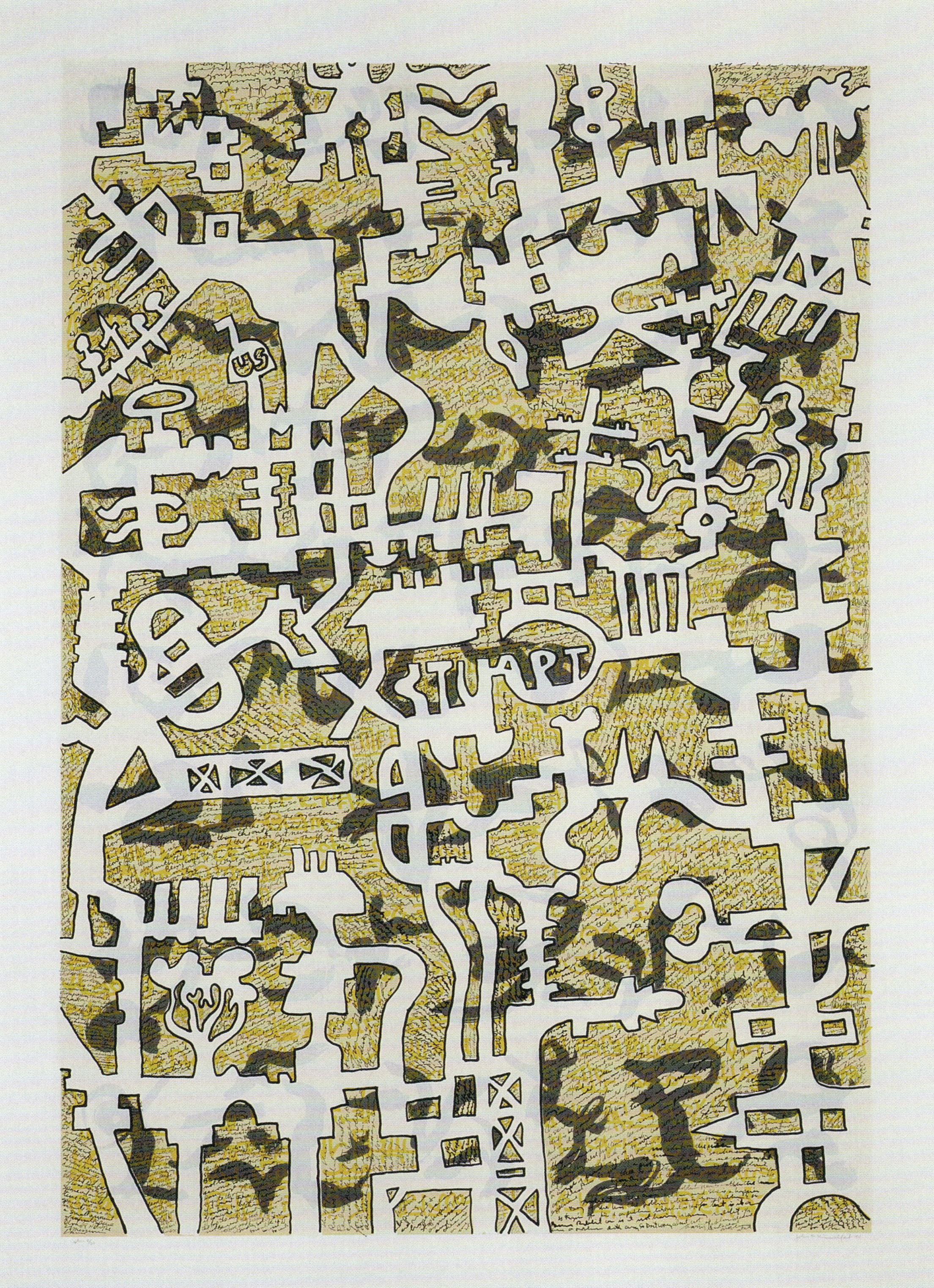

98

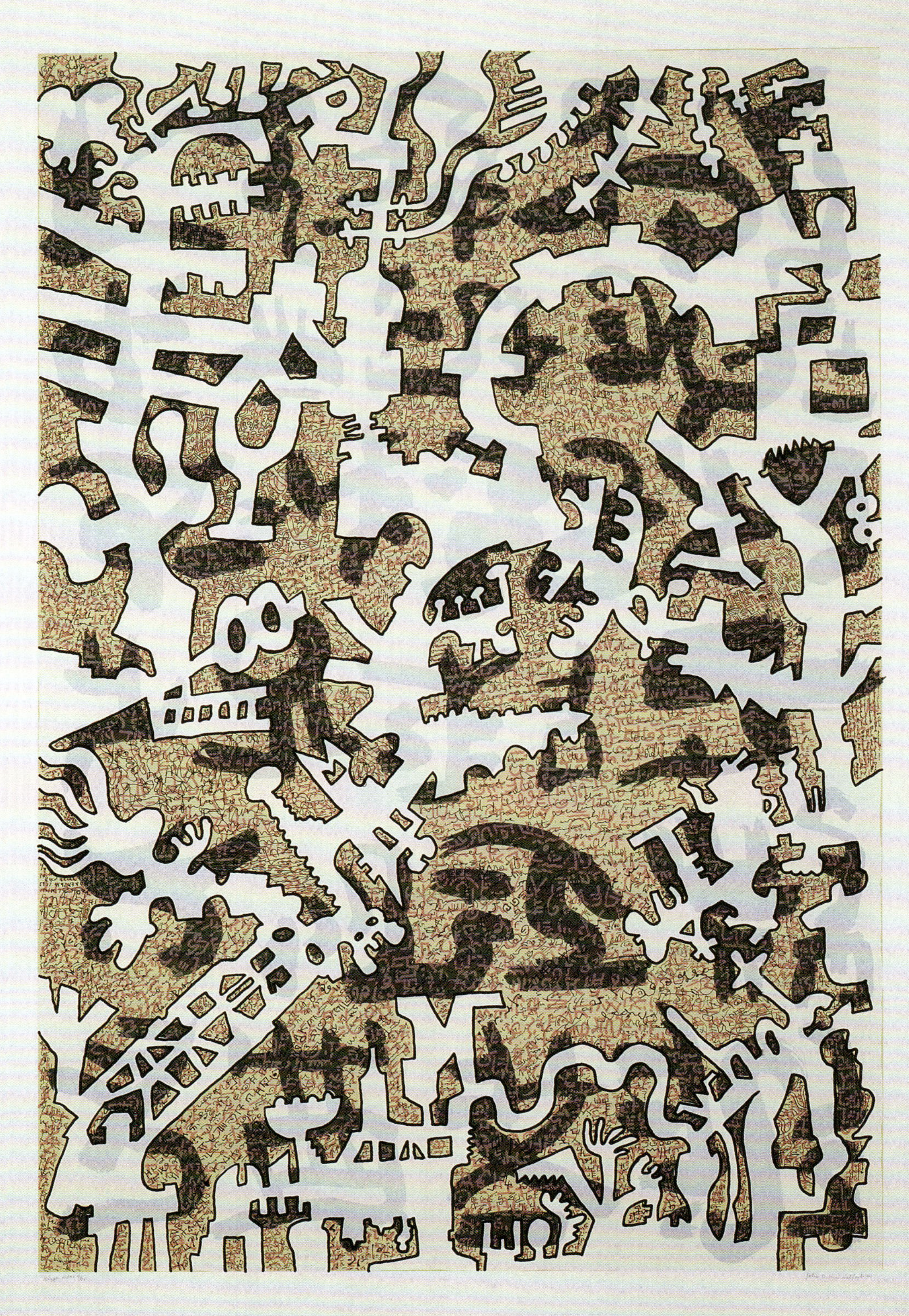

99.

Glyph Notes

Date begun: 9/10/1994

Date finished: 10/3/1994

Medium: screenprint

Paper size: 41 × 28½ in.

Image size: 36 × 24 in.

Paper type: Rives BFK White

Publisher: Stewart & Stewart

Press: Stewart & Stewart

Printer: Norman Stewart

Printer's assistant: Joe Keenan

Edition: 25

Proofs: 3 artist, 1 documentation, 1 printer, 3 publisher

Signature location: below image, LR

Chop location: LR corner

Job number and location: © John Himmelfarb stamp in black, reverse LL

Color printing order, execution of printing elements:

1. Black
2. Easter yellow
3. White
4. Cheap pink
5. Half-tone black
6. Black with scarlet red

Each original color separation drawn on mylar, then screenprinted using an indirect sensigraphic stencil system.

Note: Print element in run #1 used in *Top This* (no. 100).

100.

Top This

Date begun: 9/10/1994

Date finished: 10/3/1994

Medium: screenprint

Paper size: 41 × 28½ in.

Image size: 35¼ × 24 in.

Paper type: Rives BFK Gray

Publisher: Stewart & Stewart

Press: Stewart & Stewart

Printer: Norman Stewart

Printer's assistant: Joe Keenan

Edition: 10

Proofs: 2 artist, 1 documentation, 1 printer, 2 publisher

Signature location: below image, LR

Chop location: LR corner

Job number and location: © John Himmelfarb stamp in black, reverse LL

Color printing order, execution of printing elements:

1. Black

Original color separation drawn on mylar, then screenprinted using an indirect sensigraphic stencil system.

Note: Print element used in *Glyph Notes* (no. 99).

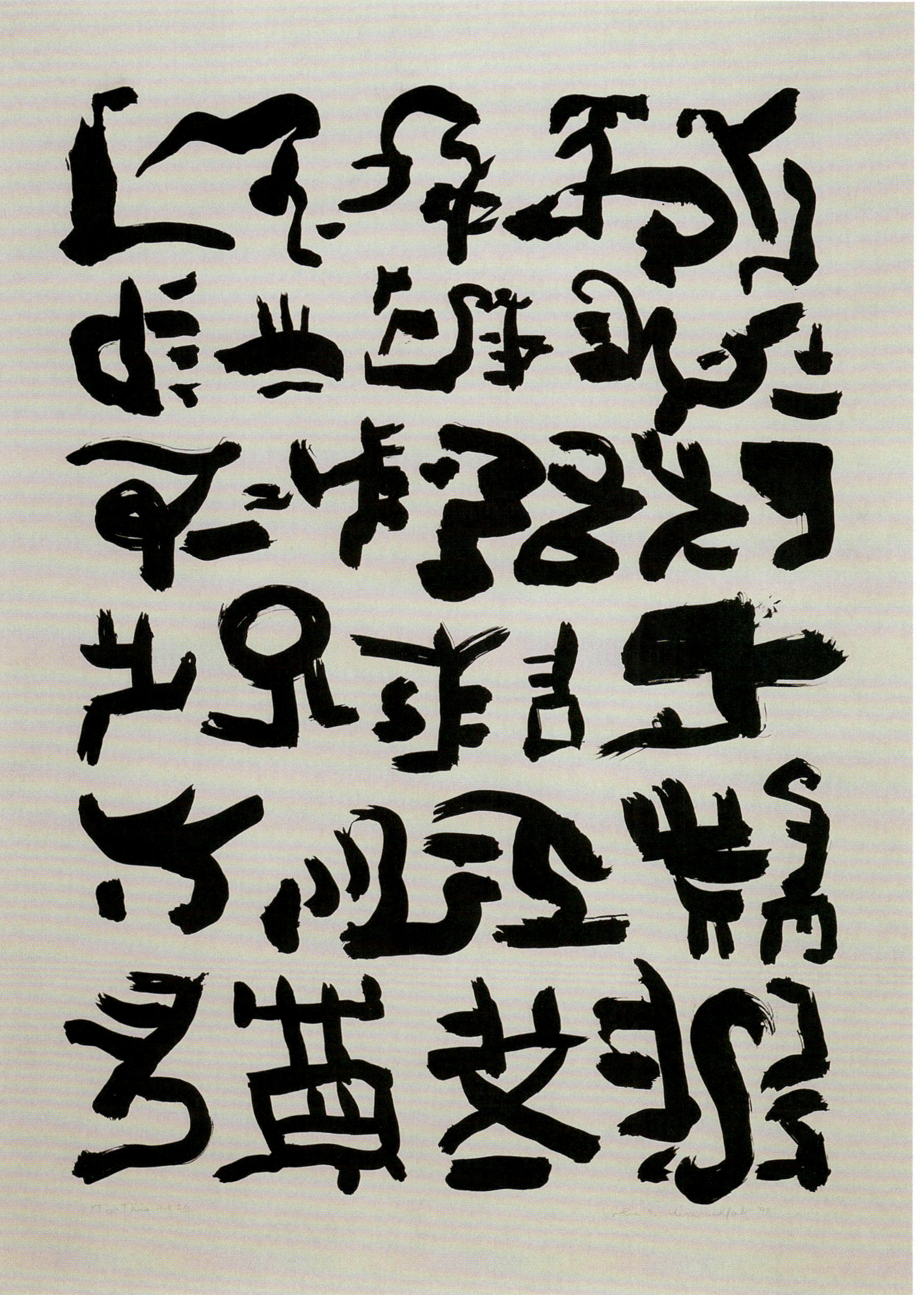

100

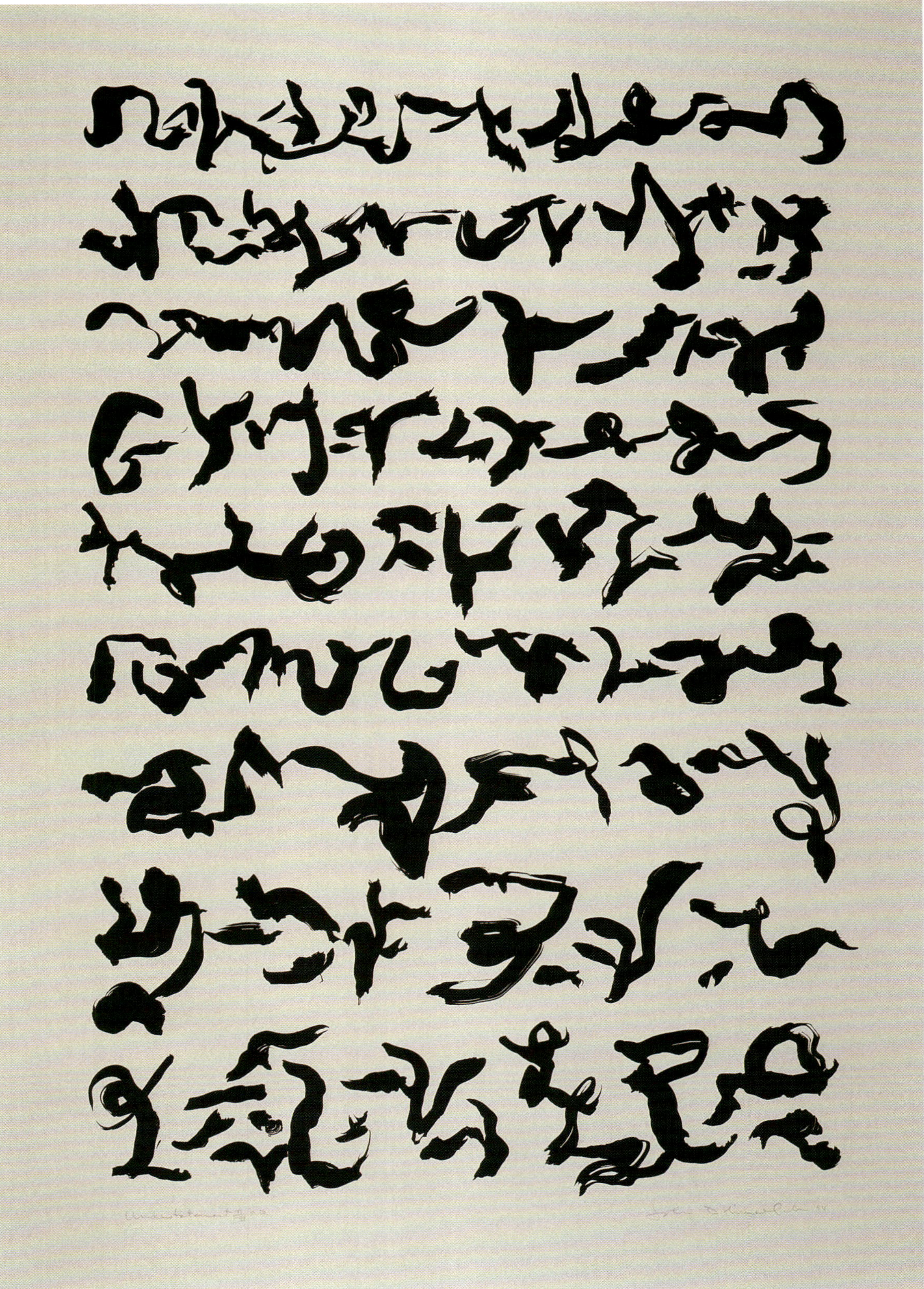

101

101.

Understatement

Date begun: 9/10/1994

Date finished: 10/3/1994

Medium: screenprint

Paper size: 41 × 28½ in.

Image size: 35¼ × 23¾ in.

Paper type: Rives BFK Gray

Publisher: Stewart & Stewart

Press: Stewart & Stewart

Printer: Norman Stewart

Printer's assistant: Joe Keenan

Edition: 10

Proofs: 2 artist, 1 documentation, 1 printer, 2 publisher

Signature location: below image, R

Chop location: LR corner

Job number and location: © John Himmelfarb stamp in black, reverse LL

Color printing order, execution of printing elements:

1. Black

Original color separation drawn on mylar, then screenprinted using an indirect sensigraphic stencil system.

Note: Print element used in *Cipher* (no. 98).

102.

Female Voice-Male

Date begun: 3/18/1996

Date finished: 4/15/1996

Medium: lithograph

Paper size: 22¼ × 13¾ in.

Image size: same

Paper type: Rives BFK Gray

Publisher: artist

Press: Normal Editions Workshop, Illinois State University

Printer: Veda Rives

Printer's assistants: Dennis Applebee, Eva Belmonte, Ian Butterfield, Richard D. Finch, Meda Rives, Feng Xie

Edition: 40

Proofs: 4 artist, 1 bon à tirer, 2 Illinois State University, 6 press, 3 proof (stamped, reverse), 1 Normal Editions Workshop, 1 ready to print

Signature location: LR

Chop location: LL

Job number and location: 96–103, reverse LL

Color printing order, execution of printing elements:

1. Aluminum printed with black. Image drawn with technical pen filled with plate etch (diluted with water).

102

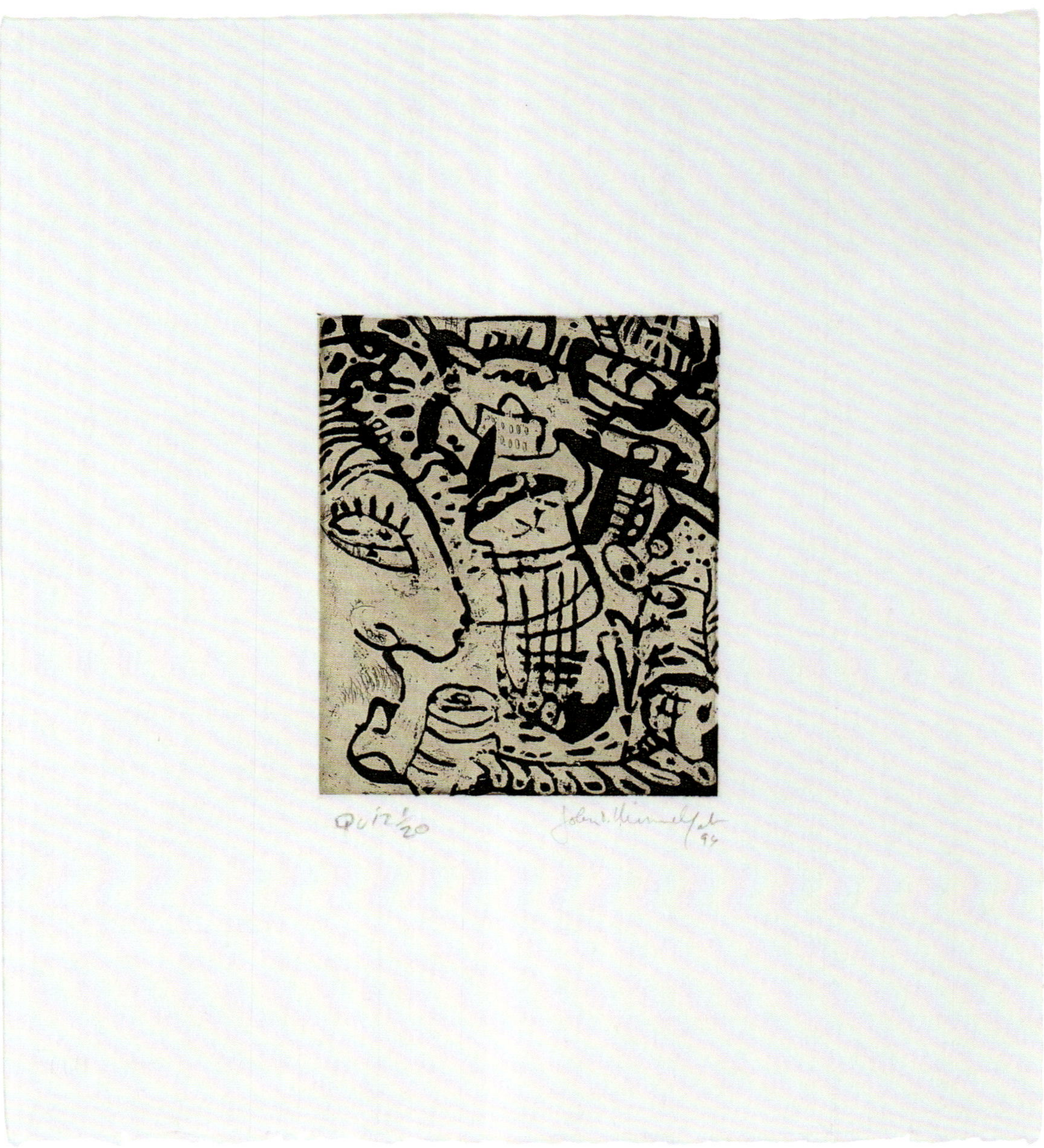

103

103.

Quiz

Date begun: 1996

Date finished: 1996

Medium: intaglio

Paper size: 11 × 10 in.

Image size: 5 × 4 in.

Paper type: Arches Cover White with Kitakata Chine Collé

Publisher: artist

Press: Normal Editions Workshop, Illinois State University

Printer: Dennis Applebee

Edition: 20

Proofs: 2 artist, 1 press, 1 ready to print with Kitakata Chine Collé, 1 trial without Kitakata Chine Collé

Signature location: LR

Chop location: LL

Job number and location: 96–104, reverse LL

Color printing order, execution of printing elements:

1. Copper printed with black. Image drawn with intaglio line-etch and sugar-lift techniques.

104.

Veneer Court

Date begun: 3/18/1996

Date finished: 3/3/1997

Medium: lithograph and woodcut

Paper size: 26¼ × 20⁵⁄₁₆ in.

Image size: same

Paper type: Rives BFK White

Publisher: Normal Editions Workshop, Illinois State University

Press: Normal Editions Workshop, Illinois State University

Printers: Richard D. Finch, Veda Rives

Printers' assistants: Dennis Applebee, Eva Belmonte, Ian Butterfield, Keith Domescik, Meda Rives, Feng Xie

Edition: 40

Proofs: 4 artist, 1 bon à tirer, 2 Illinois State University, 2 presentation, 7 press, 3 proof (stamped, reverse), 1 publisher, 1 ready to print

Signature location: LR

Chop location: LR

Job number and location: 96–105, reverse LL

Color printing order, execution of printing elements:

1. Aluminum printed with dark gray (white, tint base, Senefelder's black). Image drawn with brush and tusche.

2. Aluminum printed with light blue (white, pthalo blue peacock, tint base). Image drawn with rubbing ink, litho crayon, and tusche.

3. Stone printed with violet blue (white, pthalo blue-red, rhodamine red, tint base). Image drawn with photocopy toner washes.

4. Aluminum printed with red-orange (leaf brown, lemon yellow, tint base). Image drawn with litho crayon.

5. Aluminum printed with blue-gray (pthalo blue-red, rhodamine red, white, tint base). Image drawn with brush and tusche.

6. Woodblock printed with cream (white, lemon yellow, fire red, Senefelder's black). Image drawn and cut.

7. Aluminum printed with blue-black (pthalo blue-red, Senefelder's black). Drawn with brush and tusche.

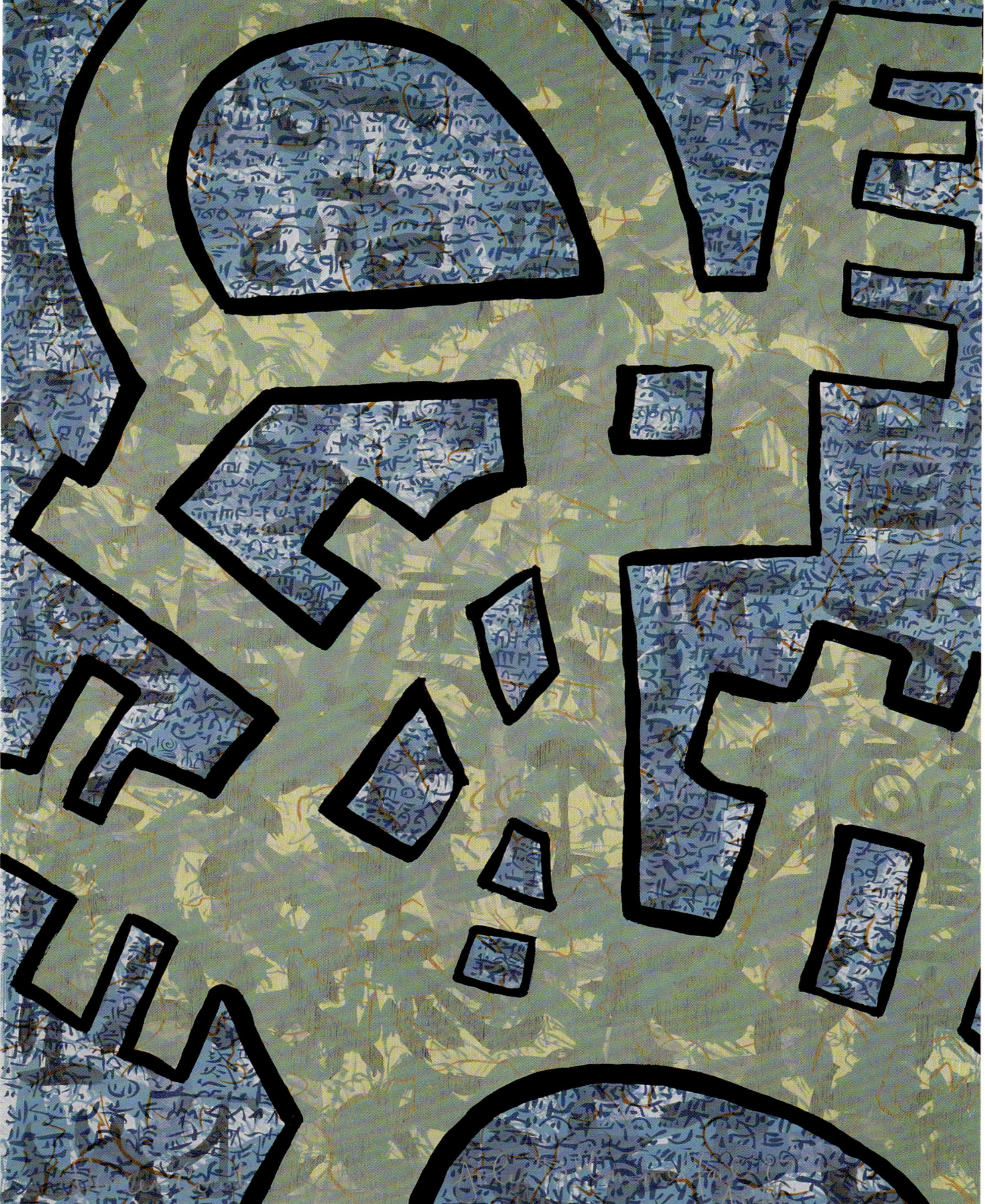

104

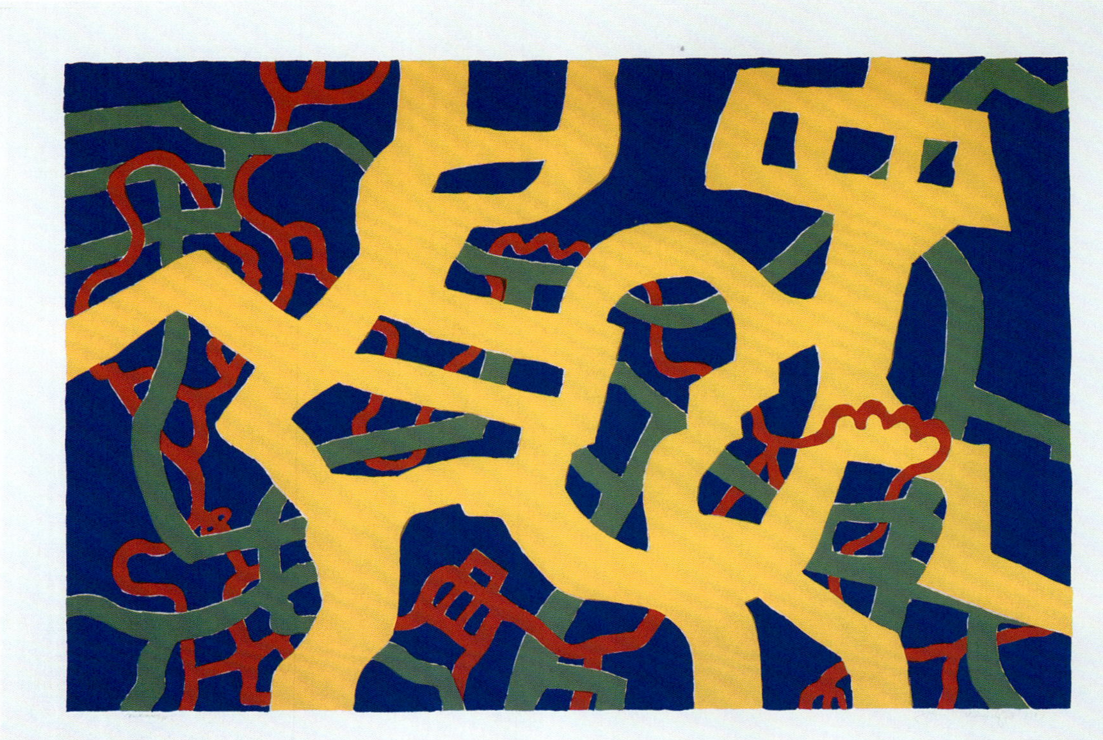

105

105.

Crinkum

Date begun: 5/1997

Date finished: 5/21/1997

Medium: screenprint

Paper size: 28½ × 41 in.

Image size: 24 × 36 in.

Paper type: Rives BFK White

Publisher: Stewart & Stewart

Press: Stewart & Stewart

Printer: Norman Stewart

Printer's assistant: Lanny Jardine

Edition: 35

Proofs: 4 artist, 1 documentation, 1 printer, 4 publisher

Signature location: below image, R

Chop location: LR corner

Job number and location: © John Himmelfarb stamp in black, reverse LL

Color printing order, execution of printing elements:

1. Transparent gray
2. Yellow-orange
3. Green
4. Red
5. Deep blue-black
6. Red #2

Each original color separation drawn on mylar, then screenprinted using an indirect sensigraphic stencil system.

106.

Crankum

Date begun: 5/1997

Date finished: 5/21/1997

Medium: screenprint

Paper size: 28½ × 41 in.

Image size: 24 × 36 in.

Paper type: Rives BFK White

Publisher: Stewart & Stewart

Press: Stewart & Stewart

Printer: Norman Stewart

Printer's assistant: Corey Stewart

Edition: 35

Proofs: 4 artist, 2 documentation, 1 printer, 4 publisher

Signature location: below image, LR

Chop location: LR corner

Job number and location: © John Himmelfarb stamp in black, reverse LL

Color printing order, execution of printing elements:

1. Transparent gray
2. Cobalt, midnight blue
3. Cobalt, midnight blue
4. Yellow
5. Red

Each original color separation drawn on mylar, then screenprinted using an indirect sensigraphic stencil system.

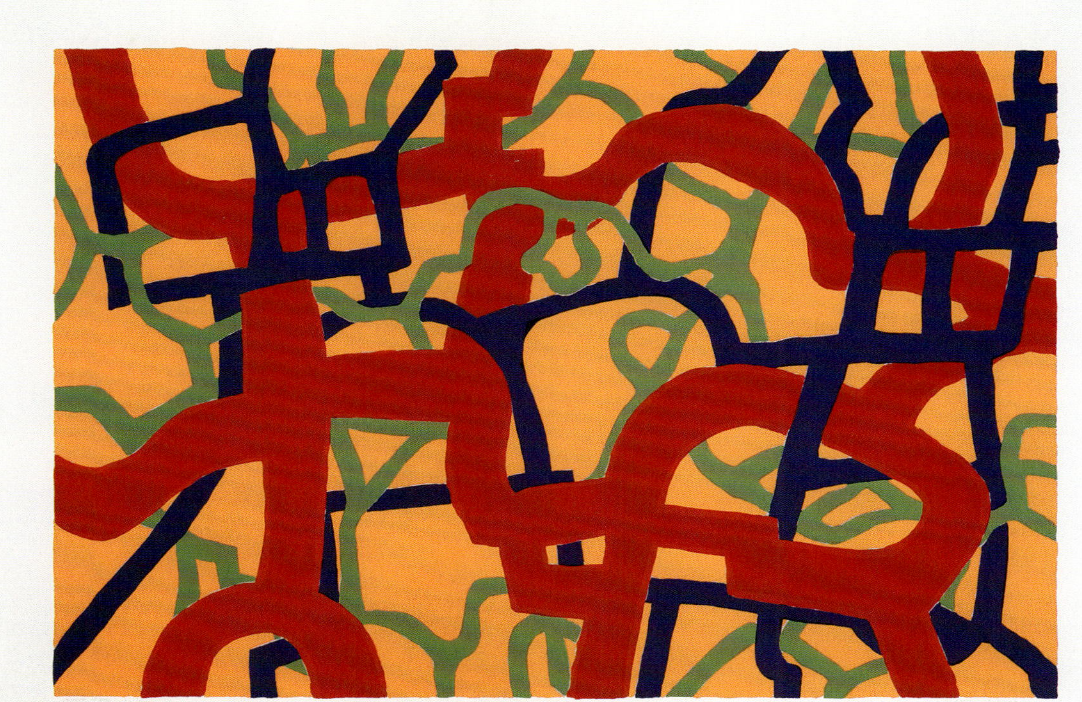

106

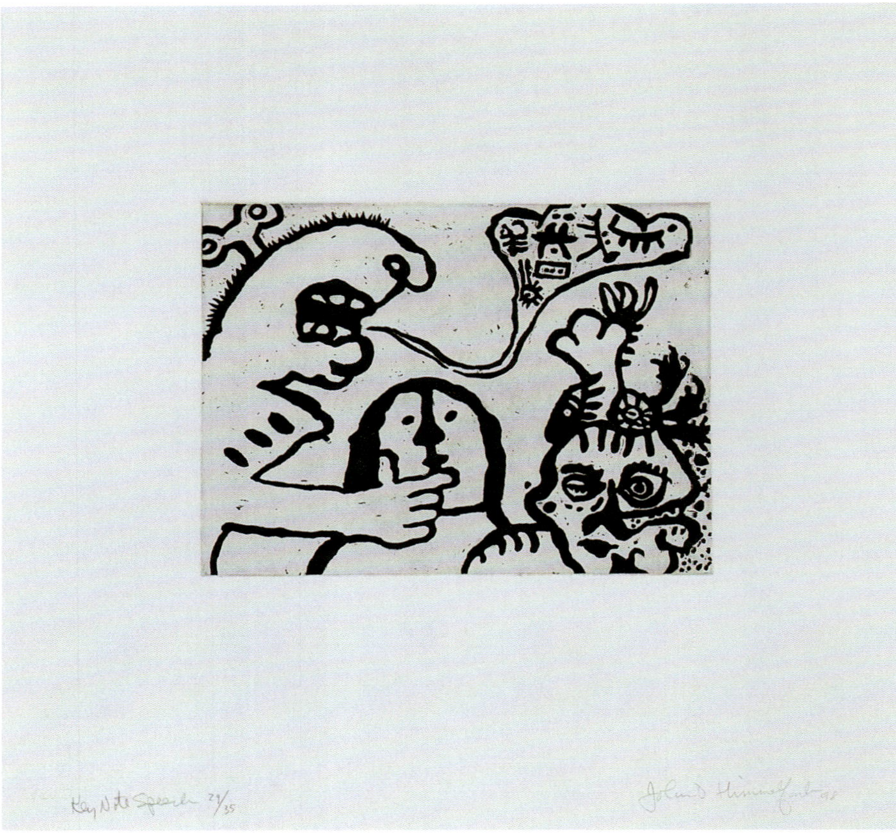

107

107.

Key Note Speech

Date begun: 12/17/1997

Date finished: 4/21/1998

Medium: intaglio

Paper size: 13 × 14 in.

Image size: 5⅞ × 7⅞ in.

Paper type: Arches Cover White

Publisher: artist

Press: Normal Editions Workshop, Illinois State University

Printer: Richard D. Finch

Printer's assistants: Amy Schmierbach, Meda Rives, Veda Rives

Edition: 35

Proofs: 1 artist, 1 bon à tirer, 2 Illinois State University, 3 press, 1 Normal Editions Workshop, 1 ready to print, 1 trial on Arches Cover White and Kitakata Chine Collé

Signature location: LR

Chop location: press, LL; printer, LR

Job number and location: 98–101, reverse LL

Color printing order, execution of printing elements:

1. Copper printed with black (Charbonnel #55985, Graphic Chemical etching black #514). Image drawn with sugar-lift and aquatint techniques.

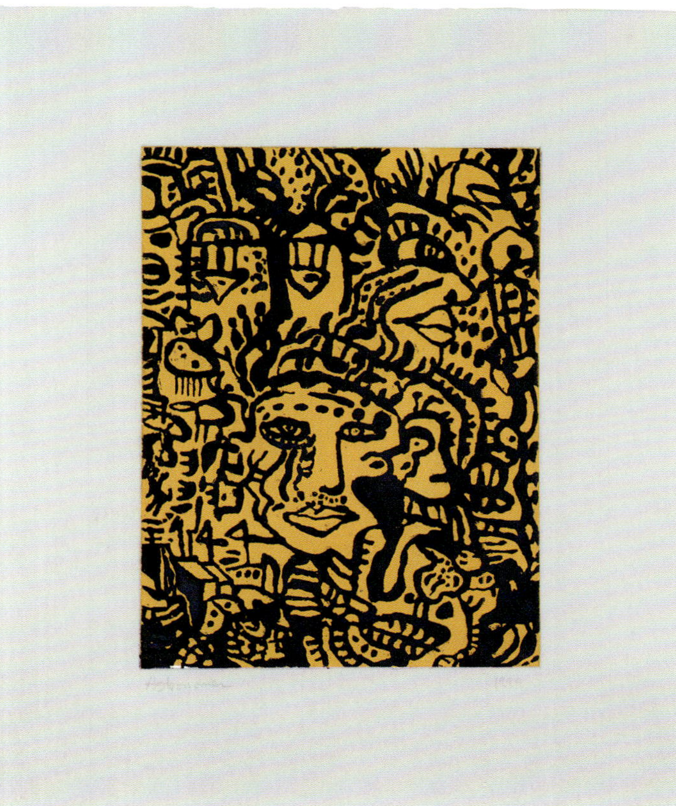

108

108.

Astronomer

Date begun: 12/17/1997

Date finished: 4/28/1999

Medium: intaglio

Paper size: 12 × 10 in.

Image size: 7⅞ × 5⅞ in.

Paper type: Arches Cover White

Publisher: artist

Press: Normal Editions Workshop, Illinois State University

Printer: Jessica Gomula-Colvin

Printer's assistants: Jessica Benjamin, Richard D. Finch, Mike Hornyak, Veda Rives

Edition: 40

Proofs: 4 artist, 1 bon à tirer, 2 Illinois State University. 1 Normal Editions Workshop, 1 presentation, 4 press, 2 proof copies (stamped, reverse), 1 ready to print

Signature location: LR

Chop location: LL

Job number and location: 98–104, reverse LL

Color printing order, execution of printing elements:

1. Copper printed with blue (Graphic Chemical etching blue #2346, etching magenta #2347) and relief-printed with yellow (Handschy lemon yellow). Image made with sugar-lift and aquatint techniques.

109.

Colorado

Date begun: 12/17/1997

Date finished: 1999

Medium: intaglio

Paper size: 5 × 15 in.

Image size: 2 × 11⅞ in.

Paper type: Arches Cover White

Publisher: artist

Press: Normal Editions Workshop, Illinois State University

Printer: Mike Hornyak

Printer's assistants: Richard D. Finch, Jessica Gomula-Colvin, Veda Rives, Amy Schmierbach

Edition: 30

Proofs: 3 artist, 1 bon à tirer, 2 Illinois State University, 1 presentation, 4 press, proof (stamped, reverse), 2 Normal Editions Workshop, 1 ready to print, 3 scholarship

Signature location: LR

Chop location: press, LL; printer, LR

Job number and location: 98–102a, reverse LL

Color printing order, execution of printing elements:

1. Copper printed in intaglio with black (Charbonnel noir #55985 and Graphic Chemical etching black #514) and in relief printed with red (fire red, Charbonnel noir #55985, Graphic Chemical etching black #514, tint base). Image drawn with sugar-lift and aquatint techniques.

Note: This is color version of *Silencio* (no. 110).

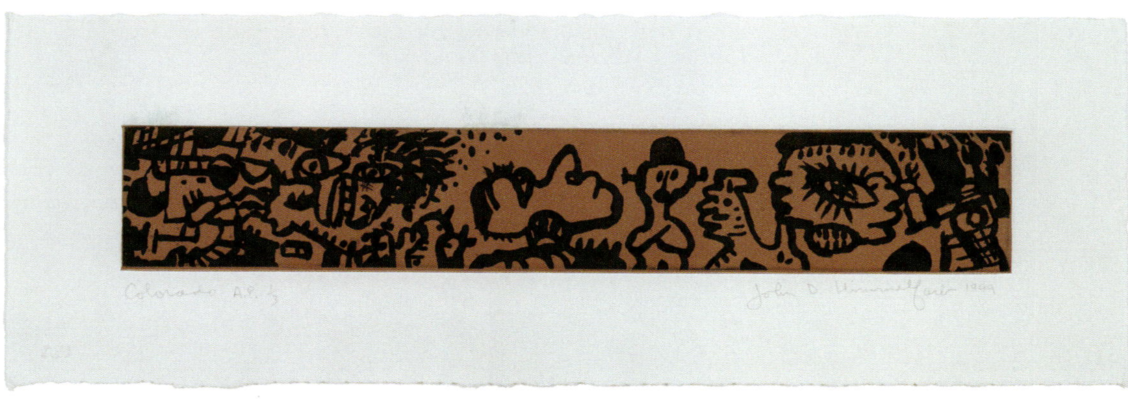

109

110.

Silencio

Date begun: 12/17/1997

Date finished: 1999

Medium: intaglio

Paper size: 5 × 15 in.

Image size: 2 × 11⅞ in.

Paper type: Arches Cover White

Publisher: artist

Press: Normal Editions Workshop, Illinois State University

Printer: Mike Hornyak

Edition: 5

Proofs: 1 Normal Editions Workshop

Signature location: LR

Chop location: press, LL; printer, LR

Job number and location: 98–102b, reverse LL

Color printing order, execution of printing elements:

1. Copper printed with Charbonnel noir #55985 mixed with Graphic Chemical etching black #514. Drawn with sugar-lift and aquatint techniques.

Note: This is black version of *Colorado* (no. 109).

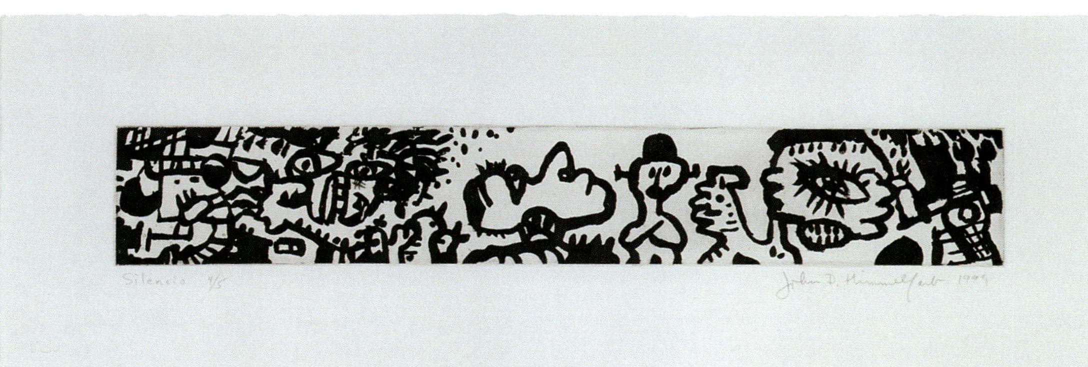

110

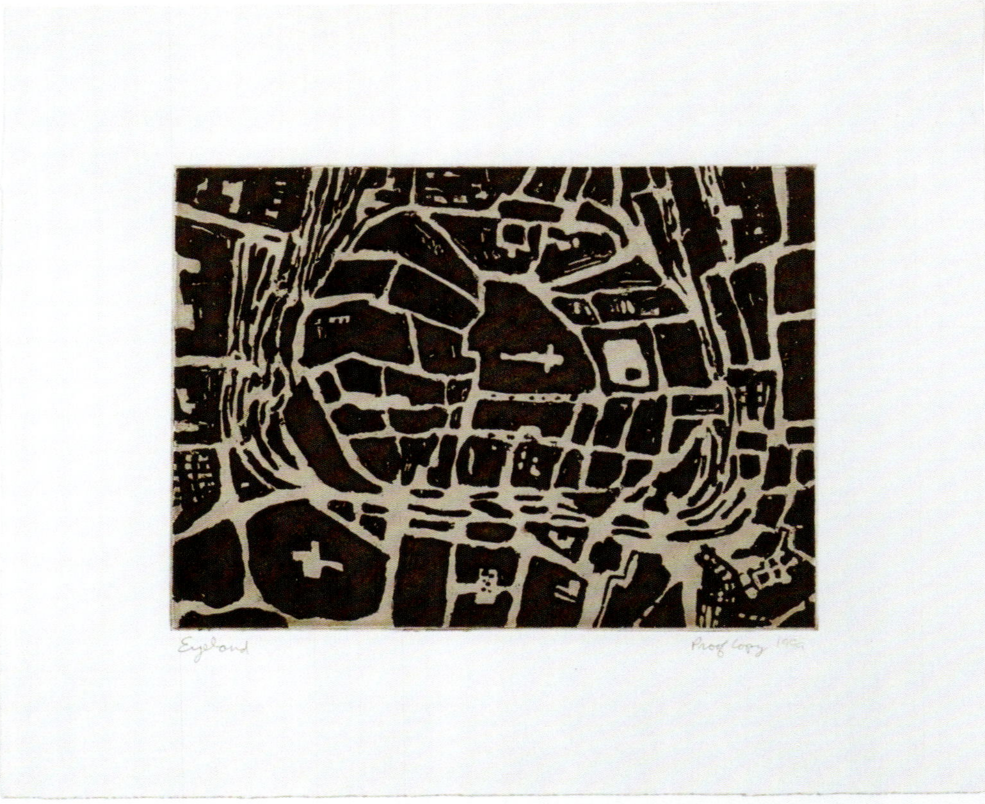

111

111.

Eyeland

Date begun: 12/17/1997

Date finished: 5/12/1999

Medium: intaglio

Paper size: 10 × 12 in.

Image size: 5⅞ × 7⅞ in.

Paper type: Arches Cover White, Kitakata Chine Collé

Publisher: artist

Press: Normal Editions Workshop, Illinois State University

Printers: Jessica Benjamin, Richard D. Finch, Matt Pulford, Veda Rives

Printer's assistants: Jessica Gomula-Colvin, Mike Hornyak

Edition: 40

Proofs: 4 artist, 1 bon à tirer, 2 Illinois State University, 1 Normal Editions Workshop, 5 press, 2 proof copies (stamped, reverse), 1 ready to print

Signature location: LR

Chop location: LL

Job number and location: 98–103, reverse LL

Color printing order, execution of printing elements:

1. Intaglio and collé printed with Graphic Chemical's etching sepia #2265C. Image etched with sugar-lift and aquatint techniques.

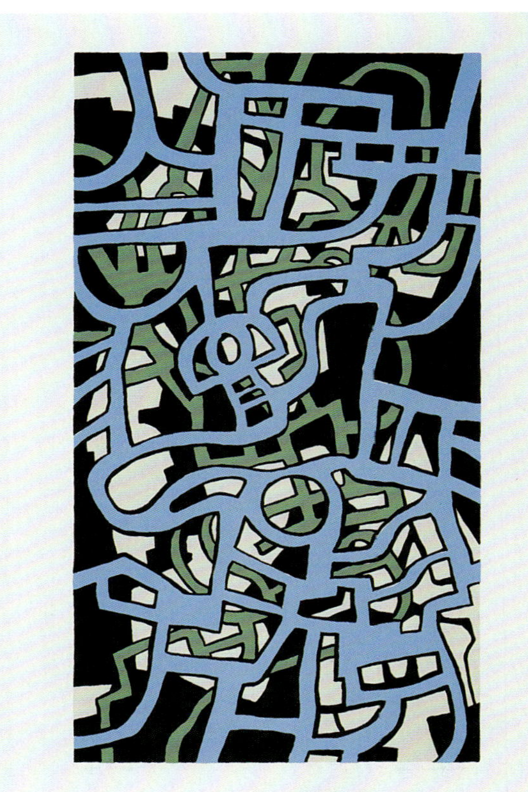
112

112.

Gizmo

Date begun: 6/1998

Date finished: 6/26/1998

Medium: screenprint

Paper size: 41 × 28½ in.

Image size: 36 × 20 in.

Paper type: Rives BFK White

Publisher: Stewart & Stewart

Press: Stewart & Stewart

Printer: Norman Stewart

Printer's assistants: Ryan Kelly, Sean Stewart

Edition: 38

Proofs: 4 artist, 1 documentation, 1 printer, 4 publisher

Signature location: below image, LR

Chop location: LR corner

Job number and location: © John Himmelfarb stamp in black, reverse LL

Color printing order, execution of printing elements:

1. Blue

2. Green

3. Light beige

4. Transparent black

Each original color separation drawn on mylar, then screenprinted using an indirect sensigraphic stencil system.

113.

Whiz-Bang

Date begun: 6/1998

Date finished: 6/26/1998

Medium: screenprint

Paper size: 41 × 28½ in.

Image size: 36 × 20 in.

Paper type: Rives BFK White

Publisher: Stewart & Stewart

Press: Stewart & Stewart

Printer: Norman Stewart

Printer's assistants: Ryan Kelly, Sean Stewart

Edition: 38

Proofs: 4 artist, 1 documentation, 1 printer, 4 publisher

Signature location: below image, LR

Chop location: LR corner

Job number and location: © John Himmelfarb stamp in black, reverse LL

Color printing order, execution of printing elements:

1. Yellow orange

2. Cool red

3. Light blue

4. Black

Each original color separation drawn on mylar, then screenprinted using an indirect sensigraphic stencil system

114.

Just Follow These . . .

Date finished: 6/26/1998

Medium: lithograph

Paper size: 10½ × 6⅞ in.

Image size: same

Paper type: Rives BFK White

Publisher: artist

Press: Richard D. Finch Workshop

Printer: Richard D. Finch

Printer's assistant: Molly Finch

Edition: 20

Proofs: 2 artist, 1 bon à tirer, 1 press, 1 ready to print, 5 scholarship

Signature location: LR

Chop location: press, reverse LL; printer, reverse LR

Job number and location: 98–103a, reverse LL

Color printing order, execution of printing elements:

1. Aluminum printed with black (Senefelder's crayon black, noir à monter, transparent base). Image drawn with plate etch, and black areas developed with vinyl plate lacquer.

Note: Printing element used in *Easy Assembly* (no. 115).

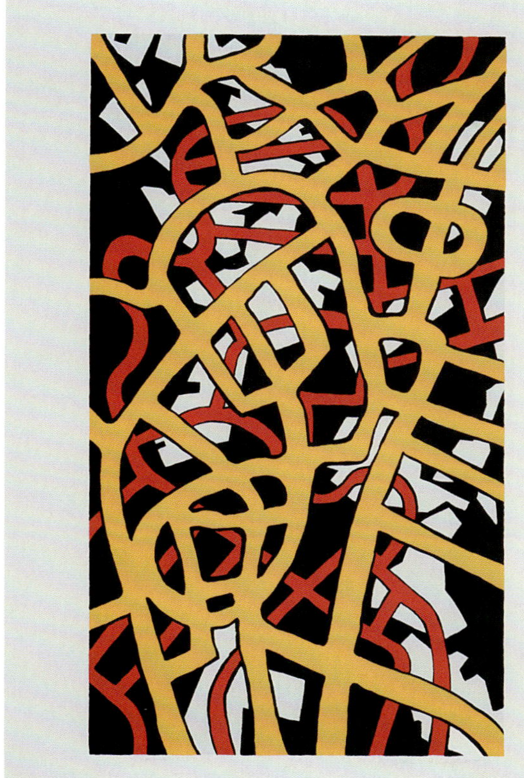

113

114

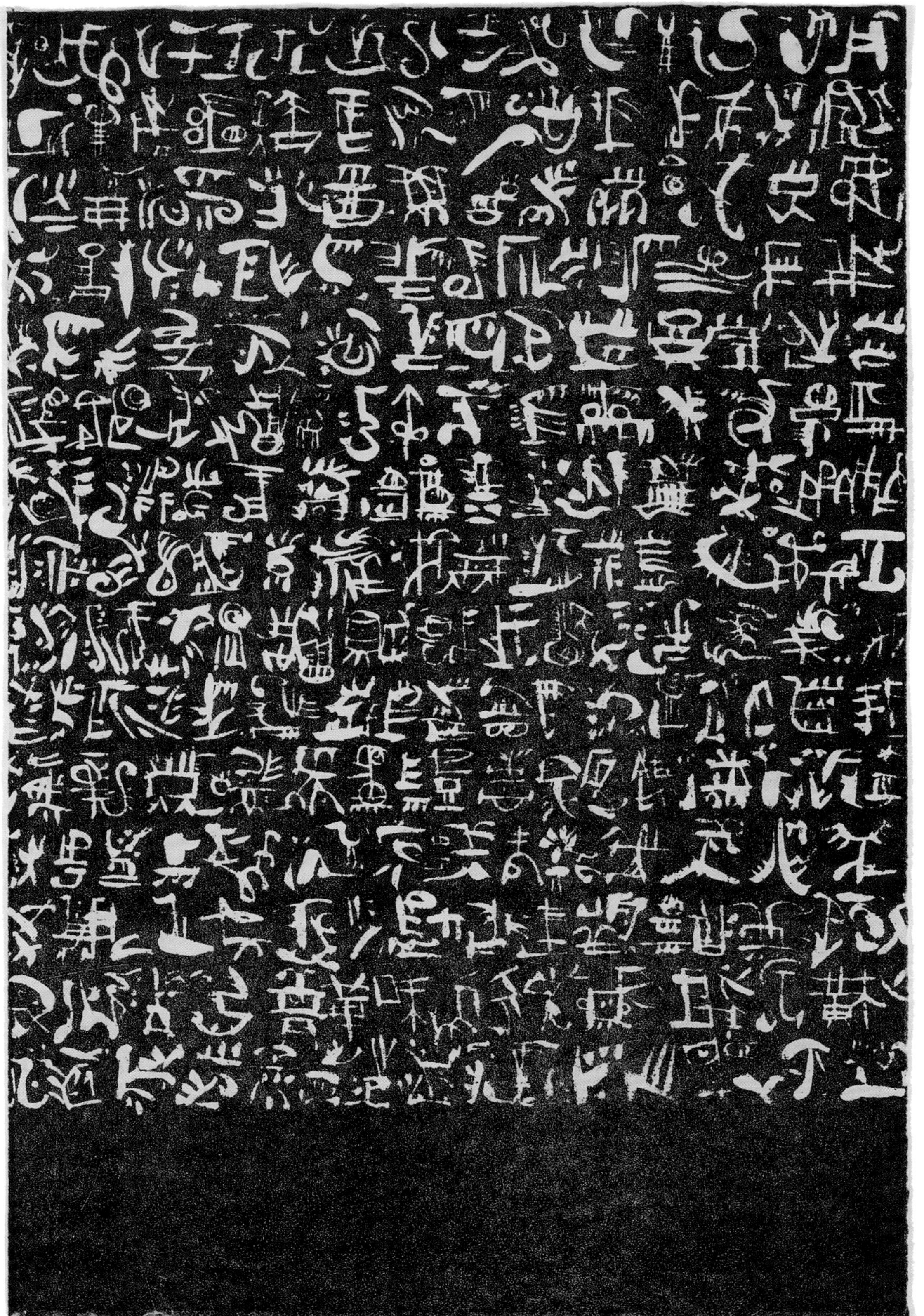

115.

Easy Assembly

Date finished: 8/5/1998

Medium: lithograph

Paper size: 10½ × 6⅞ in.

Image size: same

Paper type: Rives BFK Gray

Publisher: artist

Press: Richard D. Finch Workshop

Printer: Richard D. Finch

Printer's assistant: Molly Finch

Edition: 40

Proofs: 4 artist, 1 bon à tirer, 1 press, 1 ready to print, 3 scholarship

Signature location: LR

Chop location: press, reverse LL; printer, reverse LR

Job number and location: 98–103b, reverse LL

Color printing order, execution of printing elements:

1. Aluminum printed with black (Senefelder's crayon black, noir à monter, transparent base). Image drawn with plate etch, and black areas developed with vinyl plate lacquer.

Note: Printing element used in *Just Follow These . . .* (no. 114).

No photograph available.

116.

Lecture Notes

Date begun: 1998

Date finished: 1998

Medium: lithograph

Paper size: 17¾ × 11¾ in.

Image size: same

Paper type: Rives BFK Gray

Publisher: artist

Press: Art Department, Buena Vista University

Printer: Mac Hornecker

Printer's assistants: Julie Blodgett, Adam Paulek

Edition: 16 Roman numerals

Proofs: 3 press

Signature location: LR

Chop location: none

Job number and location: none

Color printing order, execution of printing elements:

1. Stone printed with black. Image drawn with brush and gum arabic.

117.

Plank

Date finished: 4/6/1999

Medium: lithograph

Paper size: 11 × 6⅞ in.

Image size: same

Paper type: Rives BFK White

Publisher: artist

Press: Richard D. Finch Workshop

Printer: Richard D. Finch

Printer's assistant: Veda Rives

Edition: 40

Proofs: 4 artist, 1 bon à tirer, 3 presentation, 1 press, 2 proof copies (stamped, reverse), 1 ready to pull, 1 trial

Signature location: LR

Chop location: work stamp, reverse LL

Job number and location: 99–101, reverse LL

Color printing order, execution of printing elements:

1. Aluminum printed with black (Senefelder's crayon black, noir à monter, transparent base). Image drawn with pen and plate etch, and black areas developed with vinyl plate lacquer.

118.

Boca

Date finished: 4/13/1999

Medium: lithograph

Paper size: 8⅜ × 13⅞ in.

Image size: same

Paper type: Rives BFK Gray

Publisher: artist

Press: Richard D. Finch Workshop

Printer: Richard D. Finch

Printer's assistant: Veda Rives

Edition: 40

Proofs: 4 artist, 3 presentation, 2 press, 2 copy proofs (stamped, reverse), 1 ready to print, 1 trial on Rives BFK White

Signature location: LR

Chop location: work stamp, reverse LL

Job number and location: 99–102, reverse LL

Color printing order, execution of printing elements:

1. Aluminum printed with black (Senefelder's crayon black, noir à monter, transparent base). Image drawn with plate etch (diluted with water), and black areas developed with vinyl plate lacquer.

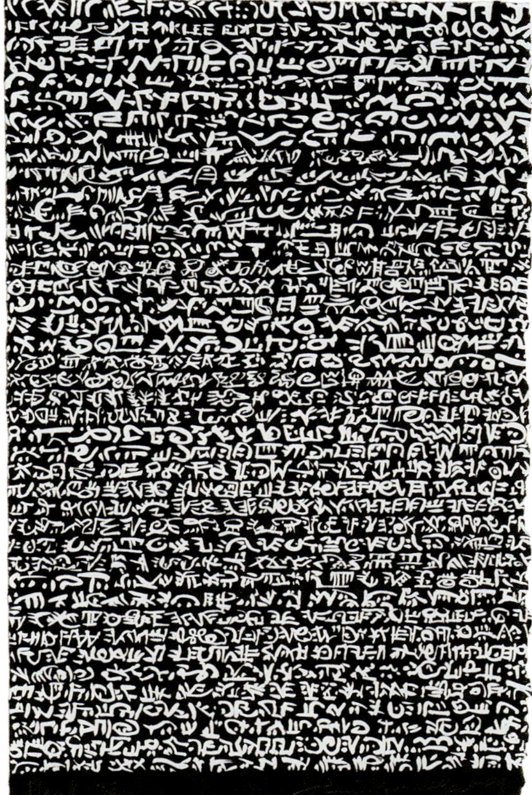

117

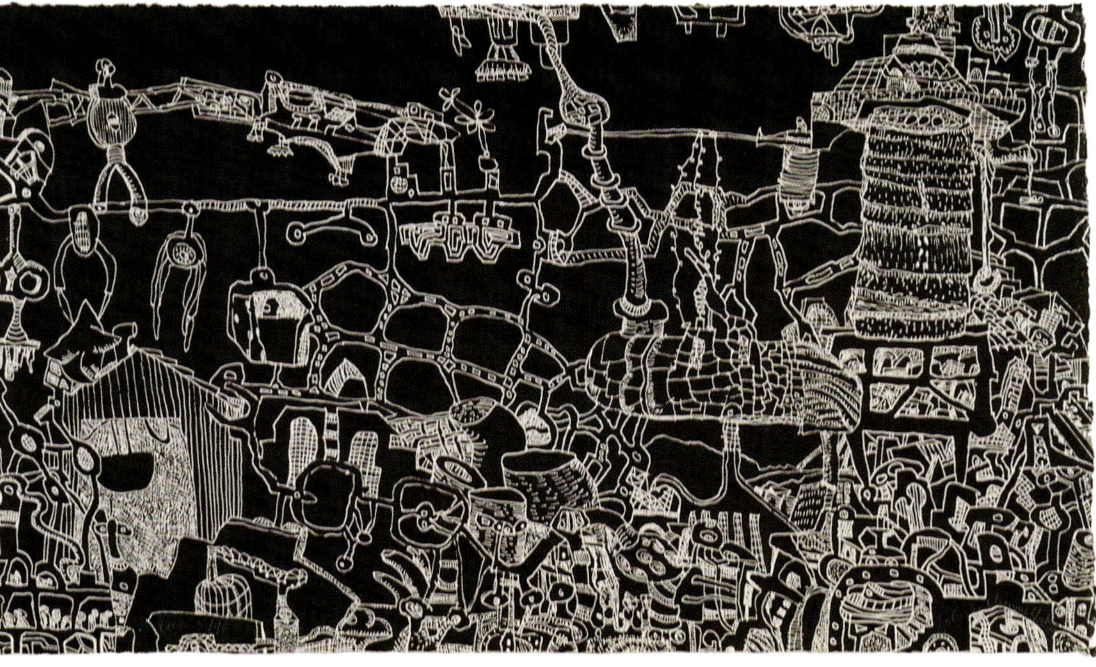

118

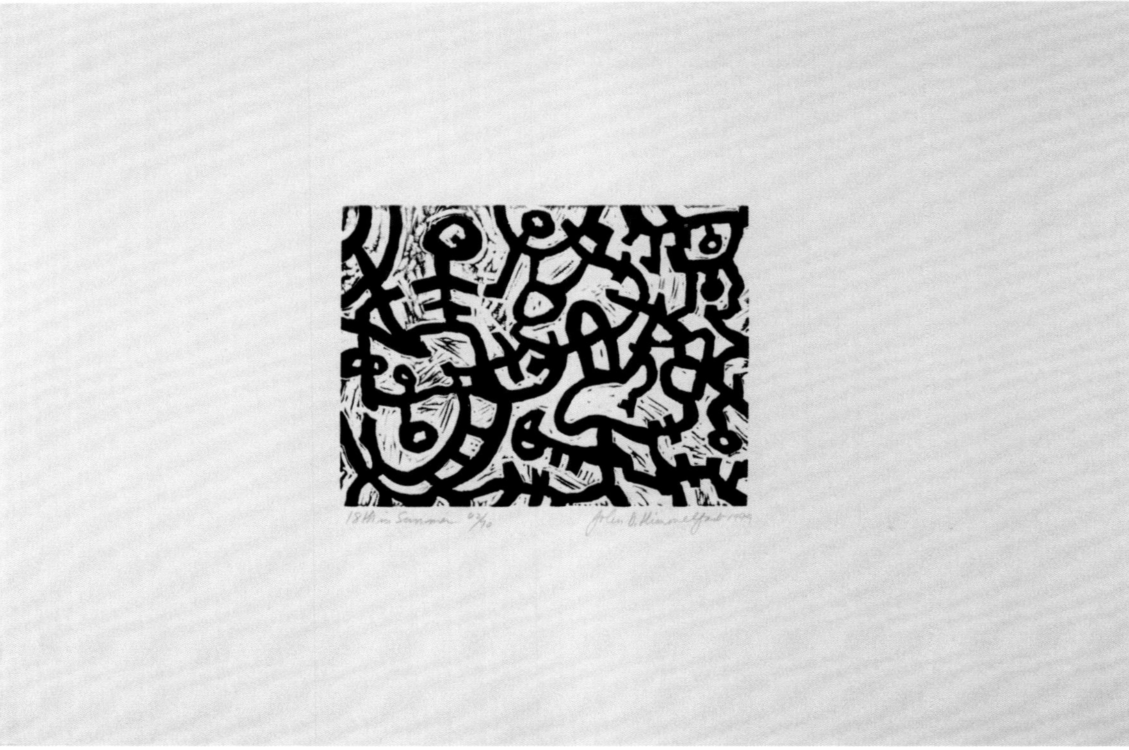

119

120

119.

18th in Summer

Date begun: 1999

Date finished: 1999

Medium: linoleum cut

Paper size: 15 × 20 in.

Image size: 6 × 8 in.

Paper type: Arches Cover White

Publisher: Tallers Mestizarte

Press: Tallers Mestizarte

Printer: Thomas Bringas

Edition: 70

Proofs: 20 artist

Signature location: below image, LR

Chop location: none

Job number and location: none

Color printing order, execution of printing elements:

1. Linoleum block printed with black. Image drawn with pencil and cut.

120.

RGB Good

Date begun: 6/2000

Date finished: 6/19/2000

Medium: screenprint

Paper size: 41 × 28½ in.

Image size: 35¼ × 23¾ in.

Paper type: Rives BFK White

Publisher: Stewart & Stewart

Press: Stewart & Stewart

Printer: Norman Stewart

Printer's assistants: Ryan Kelly, Sean Stewart

Edition: 8

Proofs: 1 artist, 1 documentation, 1 publisher

Signature location: LR

Chop location: publisher and printer, LR

Job number and location: © John Himmelfarb stamp in black, reverse LL

Color printing order, execution of printing elements:

1. Transparent raw umber. Original color separation drawn on mylar, then screenprinted using an indirect sensigraphic stencil system.

Note: To create screen for this print, a master digital drawing was executed and then rotated and repeated. Drawing also used as stencil for run #2 of each of the other prints in *RGB* series (nos. 120–23).

121.

RGB Cool

Date begun: 6/2000

Date finished: 6/19/2000

Medium: screenprint

Paper size: 41 × 28½ in.

Image size: 36 × 24 in.

Paper type: Rives BFK White

Publisher: Stewart & Stewart

Press: Stewart & Stewart

Printer: Norman Stewart

Printer's assistants: Ryan Kelly, Sean Stewart

Edition: 32

Proofs: 3 artist, 1 documentation, 1 press, [illegible] publisher

Signature location: below image, LR

Chop location: publisher and printer, LR

Job number and location: © John Himmelfarb stamp in black, reverse LL

Color printing order, execution of printing elements:

1. Cobalt blue
2. Transparent raw umber
3. Deeper cobalt blue
4. Deepest cobalt blue
5. Translucent white

Each original color separation drawn on mylar, then screenprinted using an indirect sensigraphic stencil system.

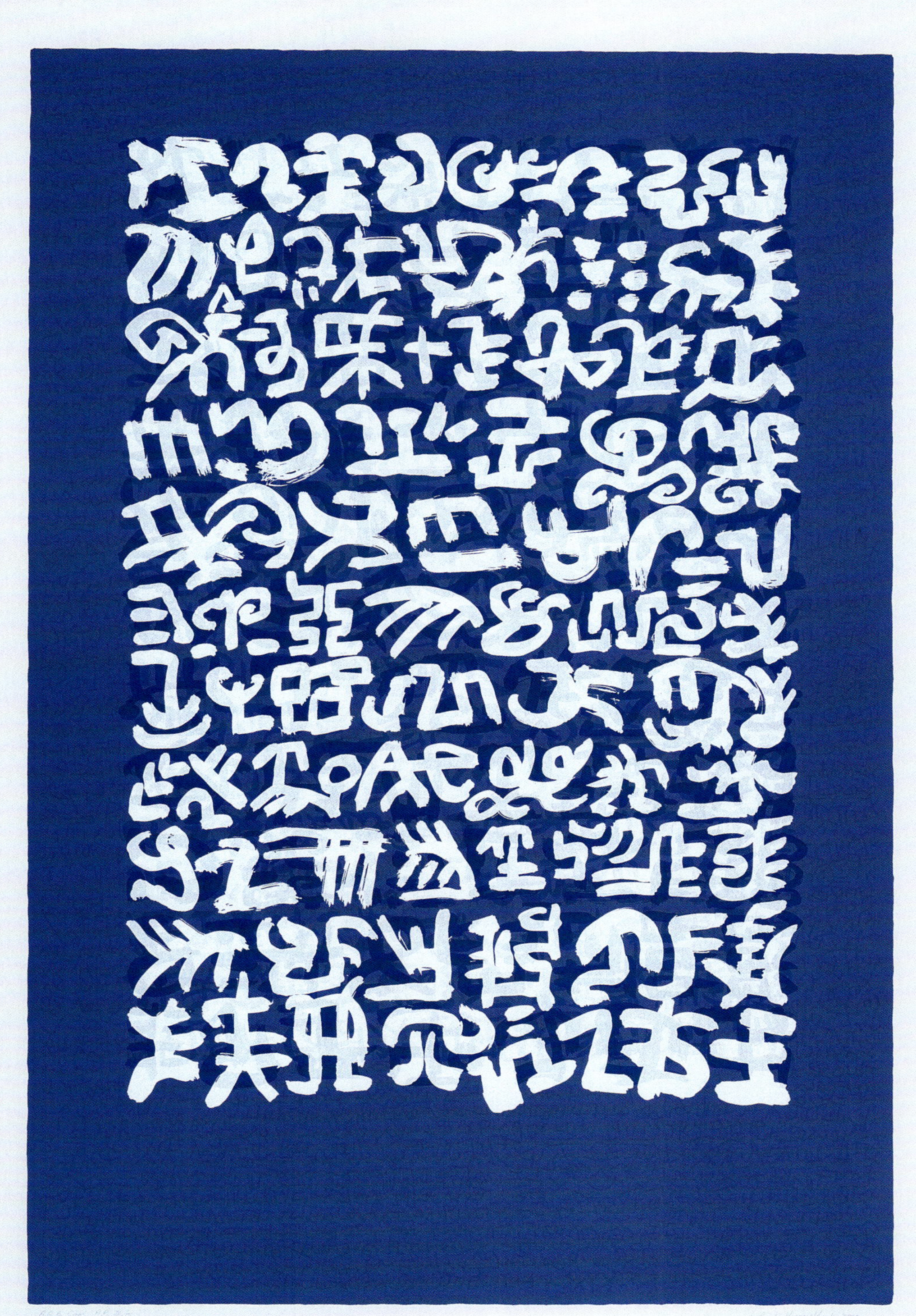

121

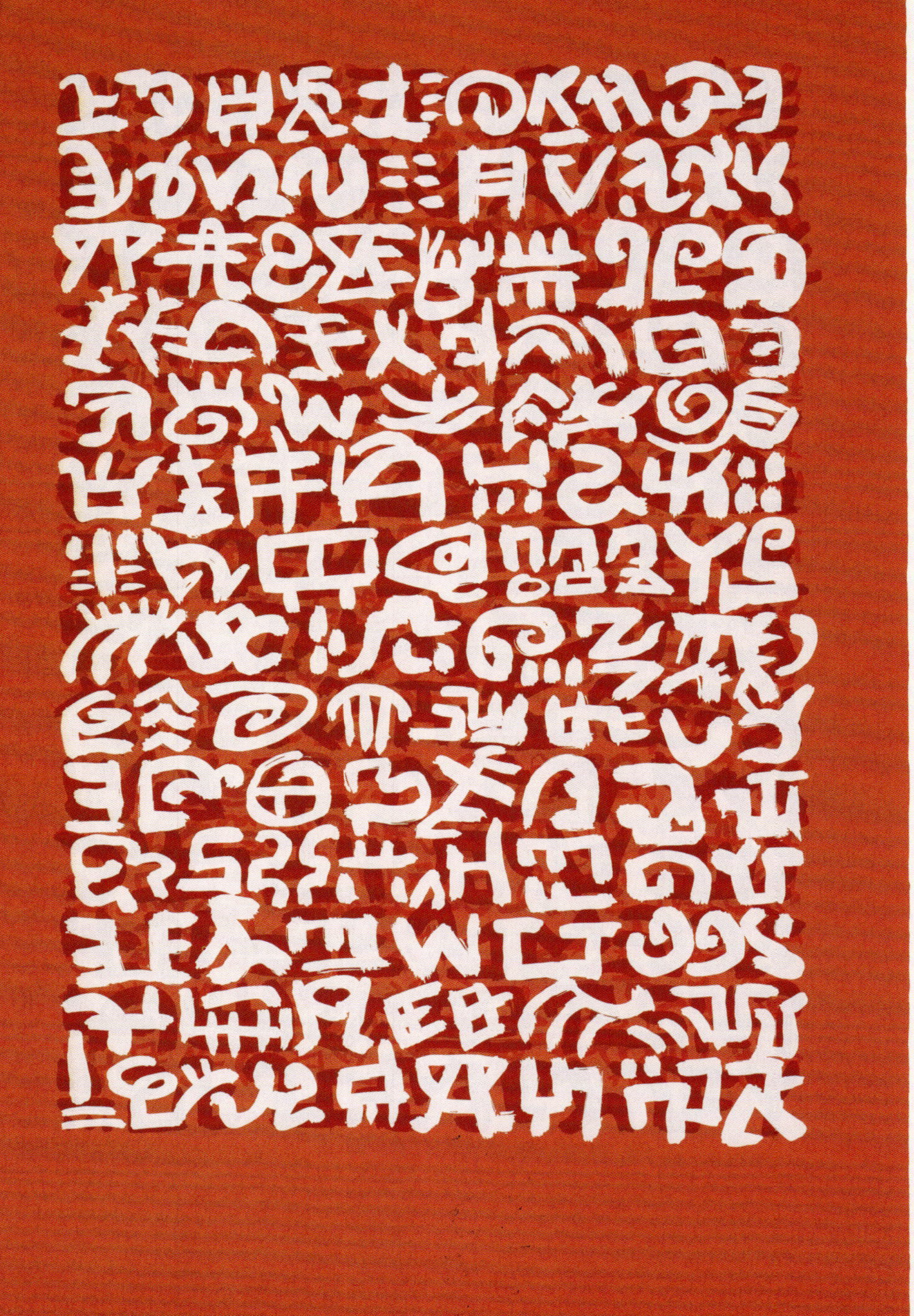

122.

RGB Happy

Date begun: 6/2000

Date finished: 6/19/2000

Medium: screenprint

Paper size: 41 × 28½ in.

Image size: 36 × 24 in.

Paper type: Rives BFK White

Publisher: Stewart & Stewart

Press: Stewart & Stewart

Printer: Norman Stewart

Printer's assistants: Ryan Kelly, Sean Stewart

Edition: 32

Proofs: 4 artist, 1 documentation, 3 publisher

Signature location: LR

Chop location: publisher and printer, LR

Job number and location: © John Himmelfarb stamp in black, reverse LL

Color printing order, execution of printing elements:

1. Iron red
2. Transparent raw umber
3. Deeper red
4. Deepest red
5. Translucent white

Each original color separation drawn on mylar, then screenprinted using an indirect sensigraphic stencil system.

123.

RGB Mine

Date begun: 6/2000

Date finished: 6/19/2000

Medium: screenprint

Paper size: 41 × 28½ in.

Image size: 36 × 24 in.

Paper type: Rives BFK White

Publisher: Stewart & Stewart

Press: Stewart & Stewart

Printer: Norman Stewart

Printer's assistants: Ryan Kelly, Sean Stewart

Edition: 32

Proofs: 3 artist, 1 documentation, 3 publisher

Signature location: below image, LR

Chop location: publisher and printer, LR

Job number and location: © John Himmelfarb stamp in black, reverse LL

Color printing order, execution of printing elements:

1. Green
2. Transparent raw umber
3. Deeper green
4. Dark green
5. Translucent white

Each original color separation drawn on mylar, then screenprinted using an indirect sensigraphic stencil system.

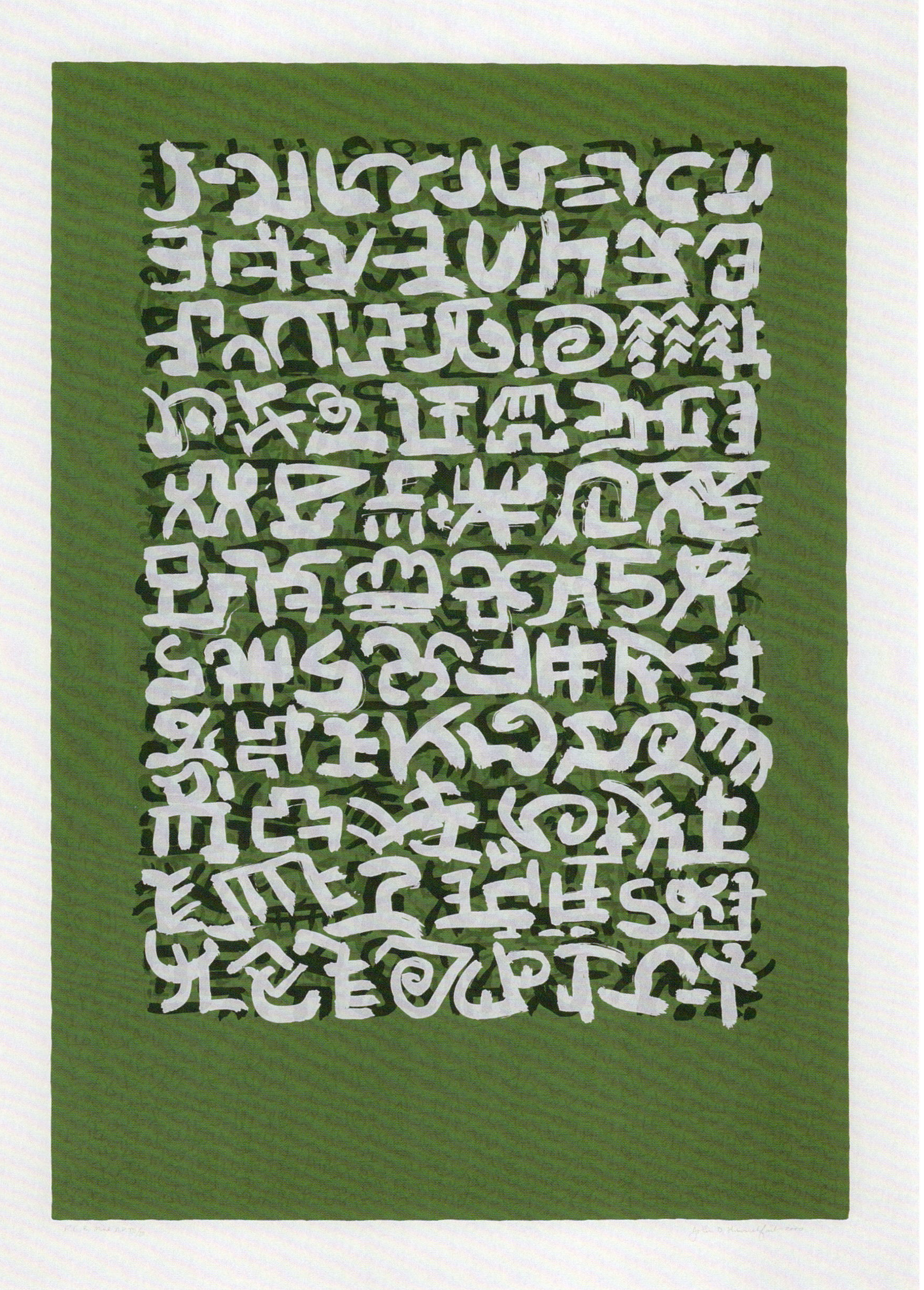

123

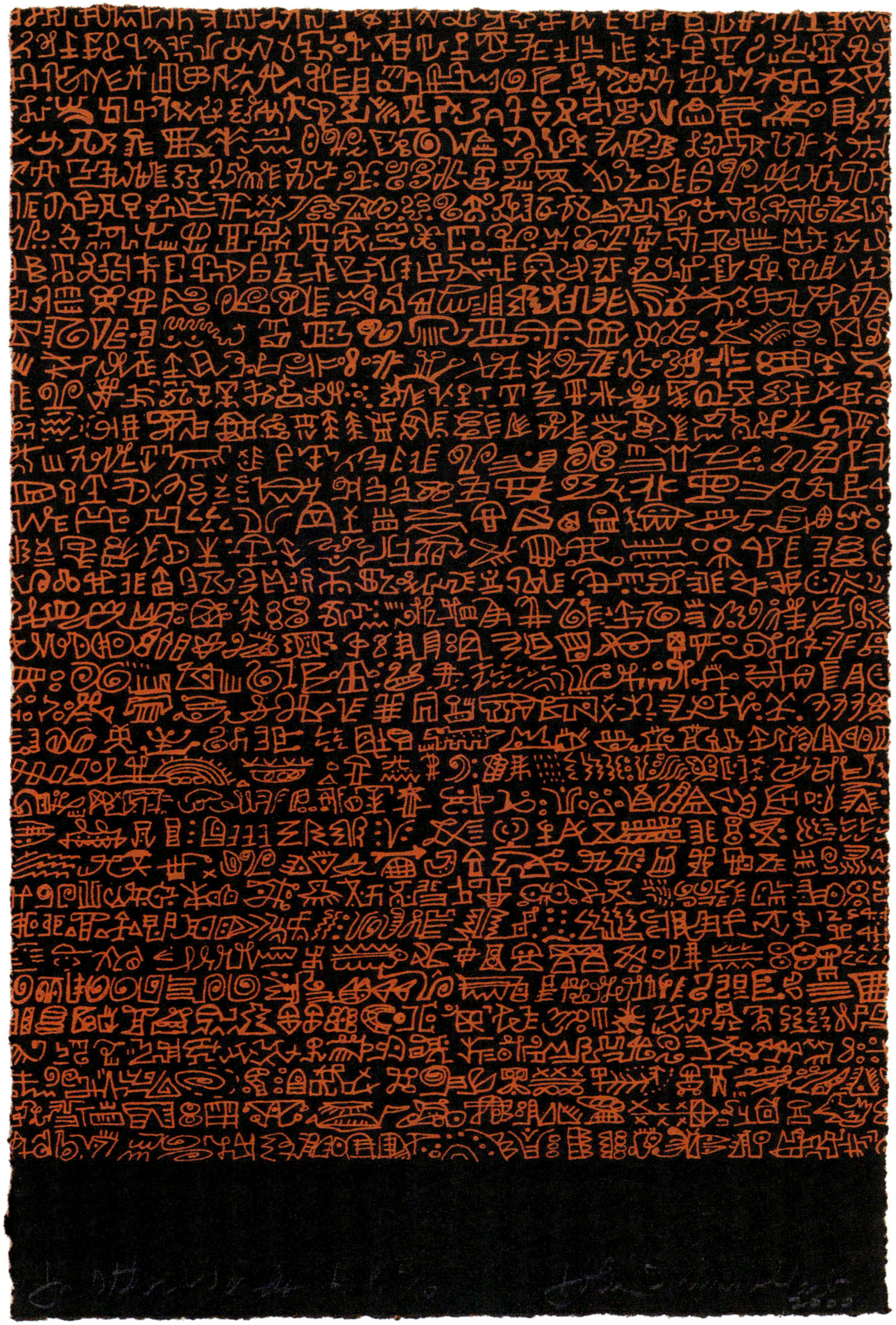

124.

In Other Words

Date begun: 6/2000

Date finished: 7/2000

Medium: lithograph

Paper size: 10½ × 6 13/16 in.

Image size: same

Paper type: Rives BFK White

Publisher: University of Wisconsin Press

Press: Richard D. Finch Workshop

Printer: Richard D. Finch

Printer's assistants: Amanda Finch, Diana Finch

Edition: 100

Proofs: 10 artist, 1 bon à tirer, 10 hors commerce (Roman numerals), 2 press, 1 ready to print

Signature location: LR

Chop location: printer, reverse LL

Job number and location: 00–102, reverse LR

Color printing order, execution of printing elements:

1. Plexiglass printed with fire red and transparent base. Ink rolled on and printed from plexiglass.

2. Aluminum printed with black (Senefelder's crayon black, noir à monter, transparent base). Image drawn on Toray plate.

125.

Uzzle

Date begun: 2000

Date finished: 2/16/2001

Medium: intaglio

Paper size: 24 × 20 in.

Image size: 24 × 20 in.

Paper type: Rives Buff

Publisher: UNO Print Workshop

Press: UNO Print Workshop

Printer: Gary Day

Edition: 30: 25 Arabic numerals, 5 Roman numerals (see Note)

Proofs: 3 artist, 1 bon à tirer

Signature location: LR

Chop location: none

Job number and location: none

Color printing order, execution of printing elements:

1. Plywood printed with brown. No image

2. Zinc printed with white. Image created with sugar-lift and aquatint techniques.

3. Zinc printed with red. Image created with sugar-lift and aquatint techniques.

4. Zinc printed with black. Image created with line-etching and aquatint techniques.

Note: Roman-numeral proofs printed with rubine red.

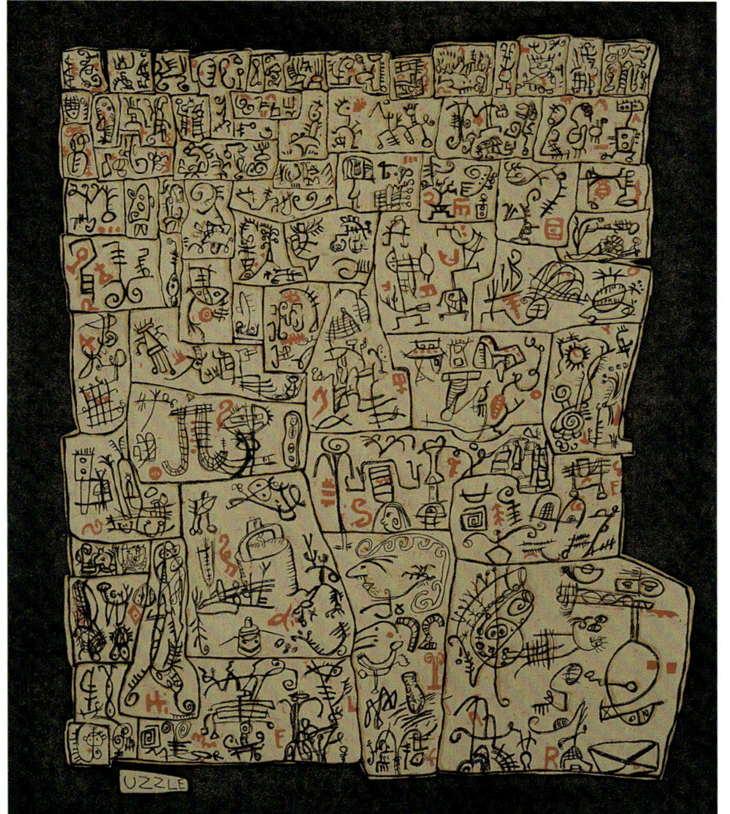

125

126.

Cow Phone

Date begun: 2000

Date finished: 2001

Medium: archival inkjet

Paper size: 9 × 6 in.

Image size: 6½ × 6 in.

Paper type: Schollershammer Velvet

Publisher: artist

Press: UNO Print Workshop

Printer: Gary Day

Edition: none

Proofs: 5 trial

Signature location: LR

Chop location: none

Job number and location: none

Color printing order, execution of printing elements:

1. Printed with Epson 9500 Inkjet with archival pigment-based inks. Image drawn in Photoshop on Macintosh computer.

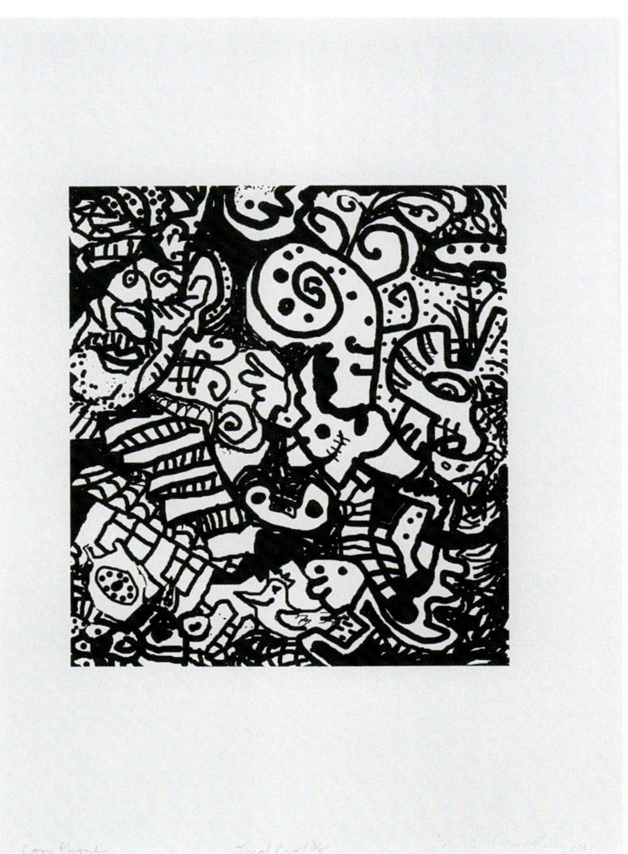

126

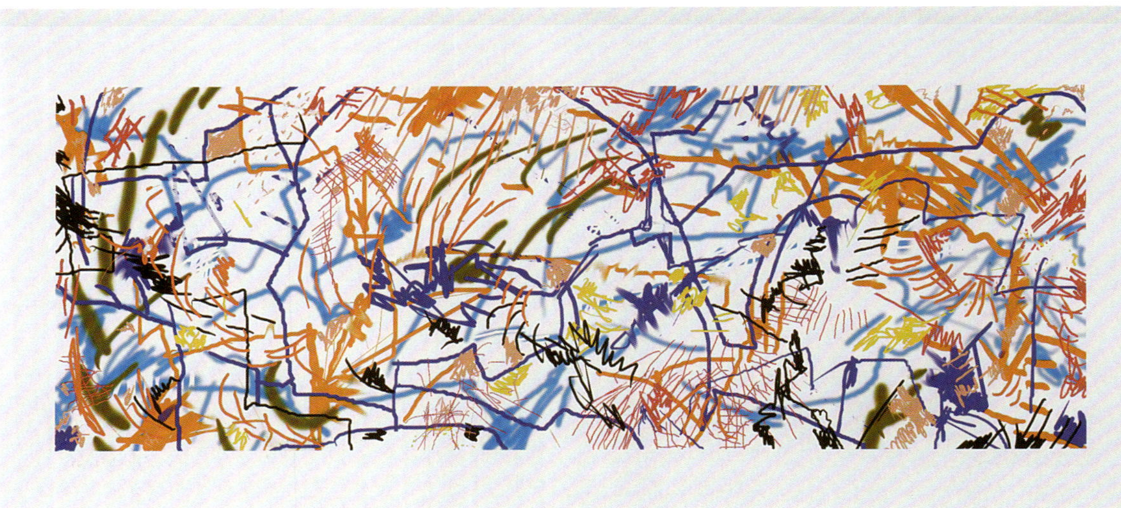

127

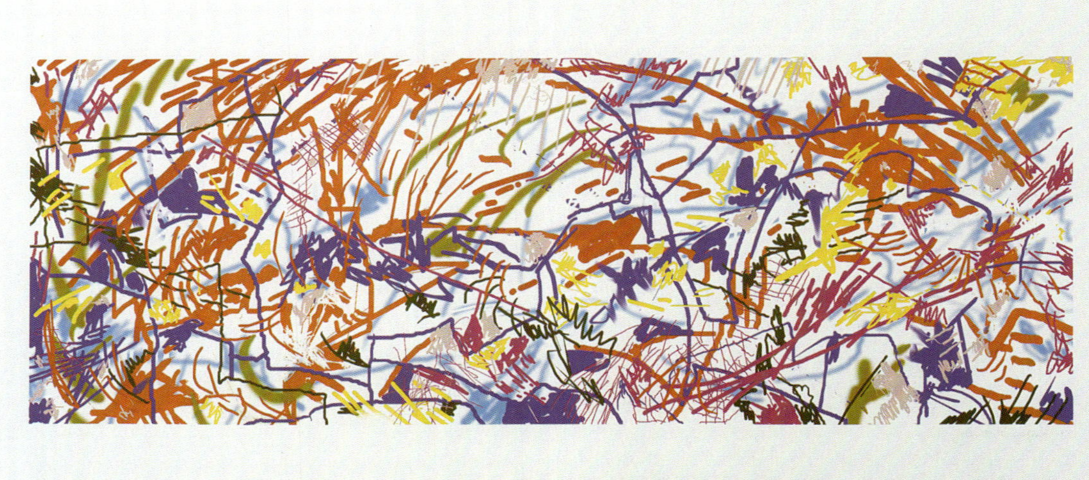

128

127.

Portrait of Molly

Date begun: 2000

Date finished: 2001

Medium: archival inkjet

Paper size: 16½ × 36 in.

Image size: 11½ × 32½ in.

Paper type: Schollershammer Velvet

Publisher: artist

Press: UNO Print Workshop

Printer: Gary Day

Edition: none

Proofs: 3 trial (see Note)

Signature location: LR

Chop location: none

Job number and location: none

Color printing order, execution of printing elements:

1. Printed with Epson 9500 Inkjet with archival pigment-based inks. Image drawn in Photoshop on Macintosh computer.

Note: Several proofs of a second version of this print, entitled *Very Last Picture*, were made. Print element of this version reused in *Zone* (no. 128).

128.

Zone

Date begun: 2000

Date finished: 2002

Medium: archival inkjet

Paper size: 17 × 36 in.

Image size: 11½ × 32½ in.

Paper type: Schollershammer Velvet

Publisher: UNO Print Workshop

Printer: Gary Day

Edition: 15

Proofs: 1 bon à tirer

Signature location: LR margin

Chop location: none

Job number and location: none

Color printing order, execution of printing elements:

1. Printed with Epson 9500 Inkjet with archival pigment-based inks. Image drawn in Photoshop on Macintosh computer.

Note: Developed from second version of *Portrait of Molly* (no. 127), entitled *Very Last Picture*.

129.

Suspension

Date finished: 1/15/2001

Medium: lithograph

Paper size: 14 × 11 in.

Image size: 8 × 6 in.

Paper type: Rives BFK White

Publisher: artist

Press: Richard D. Finch Workshop

Printer: Richard D. Finch

Printer's assistant: Diana Finch

Edition: 40

Proofs: 4 artist, 1 bon à tirer, 2 presentation, 1 press, 1 ready to print

Signature location: LR margin; some also appear below image, LR

Chop location: LR corner

Job number and location: 00–104, reverse LL

Color printing order, execution of printing elements:

1. Aluminum printed with black (Senefelder's crayon black, pthalo blue peacock, transparent base). Image developed on a positive-working photo plate from image drawn in MacPaint 88 on Macintosh computer.

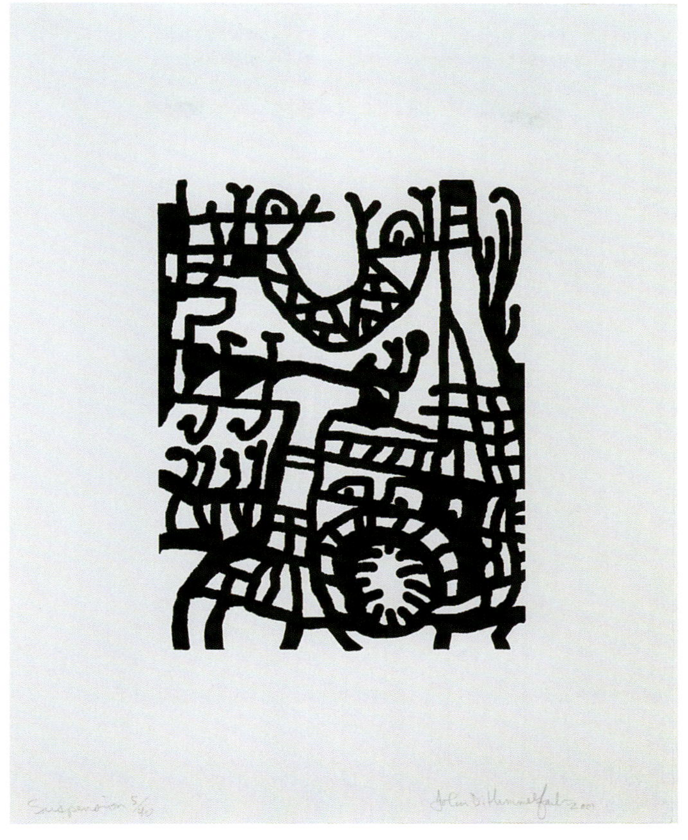

129

130.

Order Form

Date begun: 2001

Date finished: 2001

Medium: archival inkjet

Paper size: 18 × 24 in.

Image size: 14 × 21 in.

Paper type: Hannemuhle "Albrecht Dürer" Watercolor

Publisher: artist

Press: UNO Print Workshop

Printer: Gary Day

Edition: 24

Proofs: 1 printer, 1 UNO Print Workshop

Signature location: LR

Chop location: none

Job number and location: none

Color printing order, execution of printing elements:

1. Printed with Epson 9500 Inkjet with archival pigment-based inks. Image created in five layers flattened and converted to a TIFF image, using Photoshop on Macintosh computer.

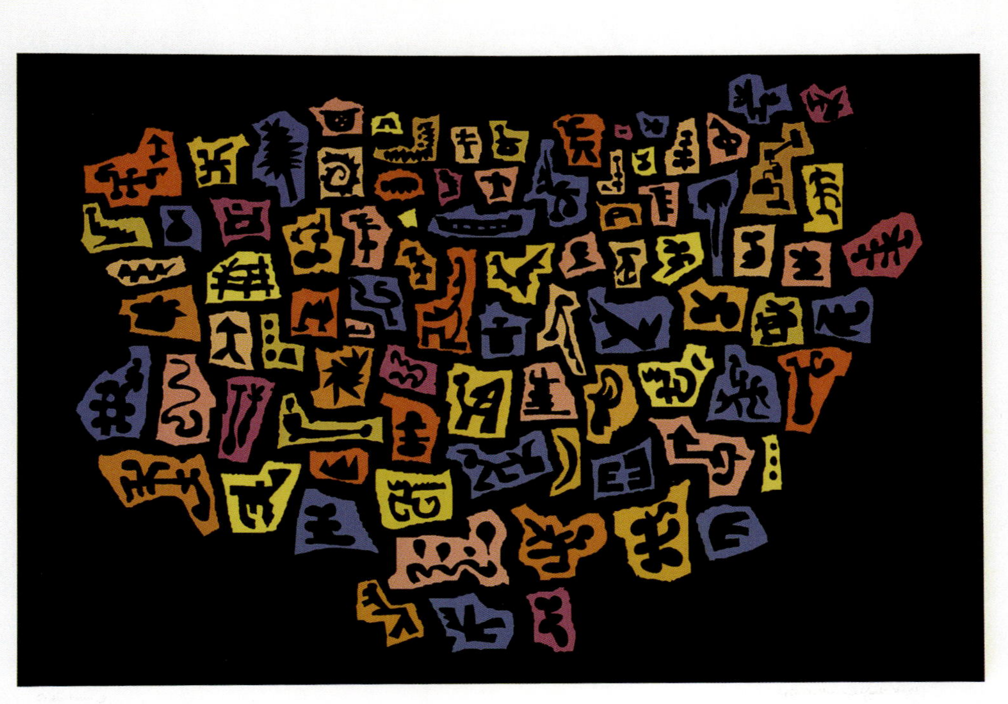

130

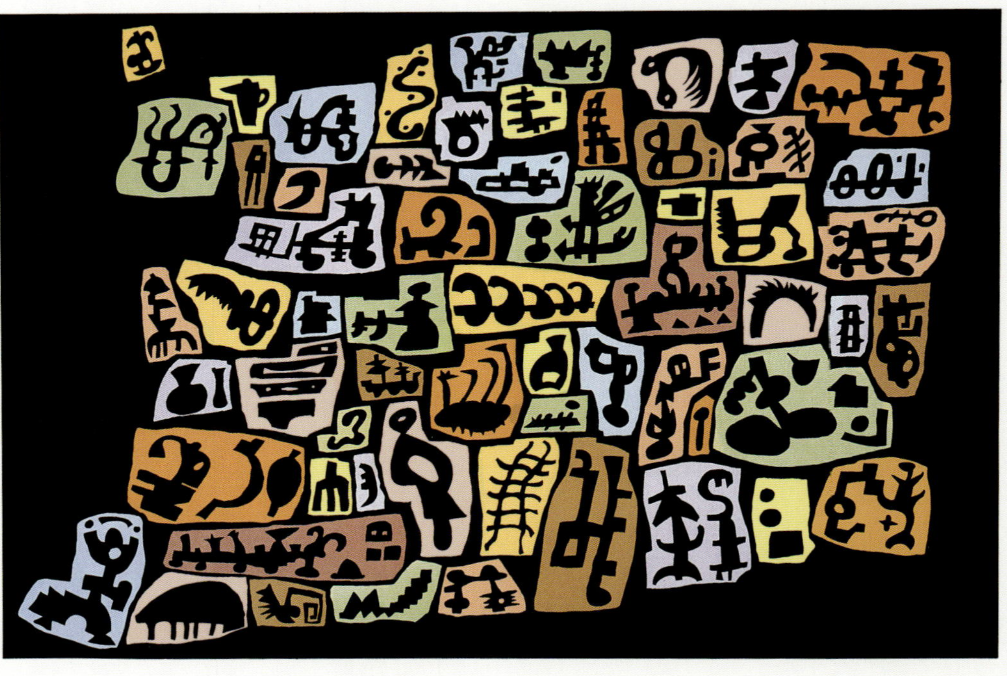

131

132

131.

Theory

Date begun: 6/2001

Date finished: 6/29/2001

Medium: screenprint

Paper size: 28½ × 41 in.

Image size: 24 × 36 in.

Paper type: Rives BFK White

Publisher: Stewart & Stewart

Press: Stewart & Stewart

Printer: Norman Stewart

Printer's assistant: Lanny Jardine

Edition: 40

Proofs: 4 artist, 1 documentation, 4 publisher

Signature location: below image, LR

Chop location: publisher and printer, LR

Job number and location: © John Himmelfarb stamp in black, reverse LL

Color printing order, execution of printing elements:

1. Transparent ultra-radiant blue
2. Rich red-brown
3. Transparent sign red
4. Yellow
5. Black

Each original color separation drawn on mylar, then screenprinted using an indirect sensigraphic stencil system.

132.

Song

Date begun: 6/2001

Date finished: 6/29/2001

Medium: screenprint

Paper size: 28½ × 41 in.

Image size: 24 × 36 in.

Paper type: Rives BFK White

Publisher: Stewart & Stewart

Press: Stewart & Stewart

Printer: Norman Stewart

Printer's assistant: Lanny Jardine

Edition: 9

Proofs: 1 artist, 1 documentation, 1 publisher

Signature location below image, LR

Chop location: publisher and printer, LR

Job number and location: © John Himmelfarb stamp in black, reverse LL

Color printing order, execution of printing elements:

1. Black

Original color separation drawn on mylar, then screenprinted using an indirect sensigraphic stencil system.

133.

Practice

Date begun: 6/2001

Date finished: 6/29/2001

Medium: screenprint

Paper size: 28½ × 41 in.

Image size: 24 × 36 in.

Paper type: Rives BFK White

Publisher: Stewart & Stewart

Press: Stewart & Stewart

Printer: Norman Stewart

Printer's assistants: Lanny Jardine, Sean Stewart

Edition: 40

Proofs: 4 artist, 1 documentation, 1 printer, [illegible] publisher

Signature location: below image, LR

Chop location: publisher and printer, LR

Job number and location: © John Himmelfarb stamp in black, reverse LL

Color printing order, execution of printing elements:

1. Transparent ultra-radiant blue
2. Rich red-brown
3. Transparent sign red
4. Yellow
5. Black

Each original color separation drawn on mylar, then screenprinted using an indirect sensigraphic stencil system.

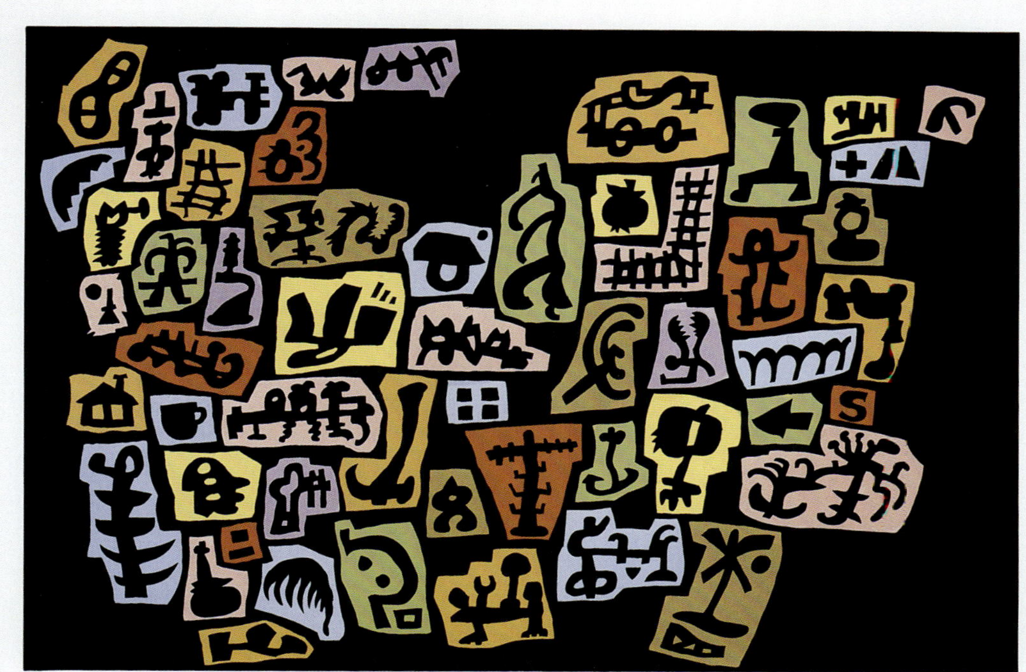

133

134.

Dance

Date begun: 6/2001

Date finished: 6/29/2001

Medium: screenprint

Paper size: 28½ × 41 in.

Image size: 24 × 36 in.

Paper type: Rives BFK White

Publisher: Stewart & Stewart

Press: Stewart & Stewart

Printer: Norman Stewart

Printer's assistant: Lanny Jardine

Edition: 9

Proofs: 1 artist, 1 documentation, 1 publisher

Signature location: below image, LR

Chop location: publisher and printer, LR

Job number and location: © John Himmelfarb stamp in black, reverse LL

Color printing order, execution of printing elements:

1. Black

Original color separation drawn on mylar, then screenprinted using an indirect sensigraphic stencil system.

134

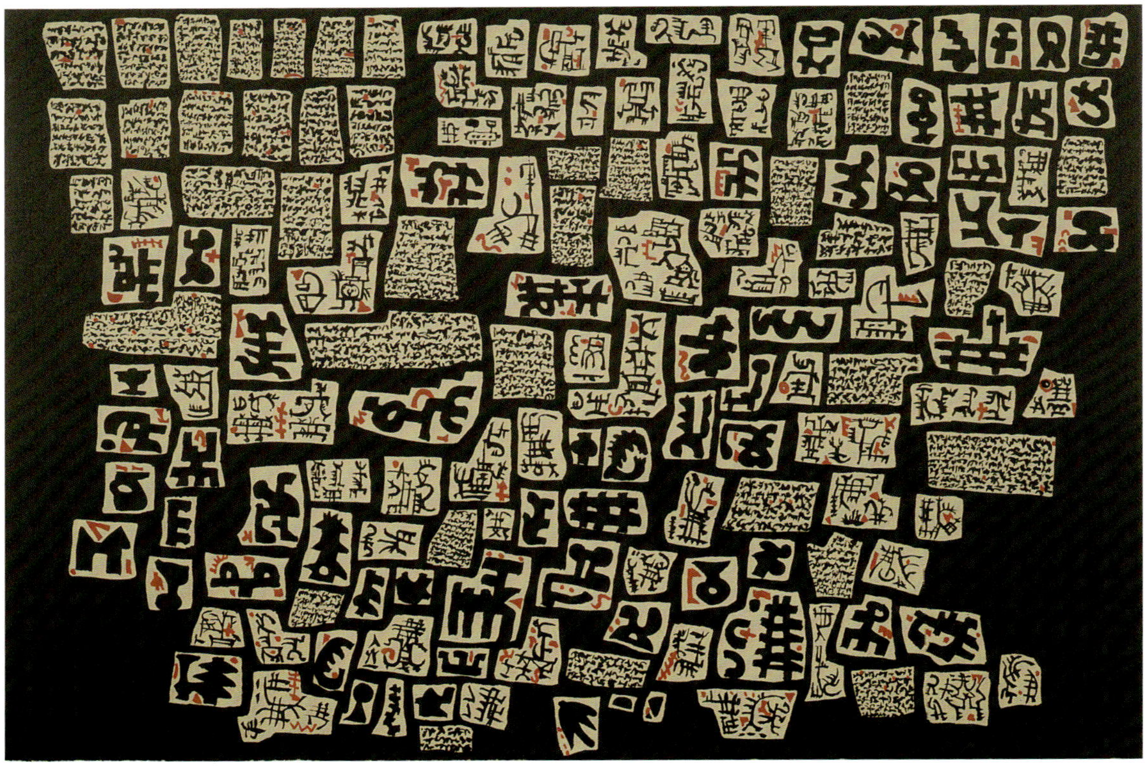

135

135.

Turandot's Riddles

Date finished: 7/3/2001

Medium: lithograph

Paper size: 15 × 22 in.

Image size: same

Paper type: Rives BFK Tan

Publisher: artist

Press: Richard D. Finch Workshop

Printer: Richard D. Finch

Printer's assistants: Diana Finch, John Finch

Edition: 25

Proofs: 2 artist, 1 bon à tirer, 1 presentation, 2 press, 1 ready to print, 2 trial (black) on Kitakata Chiri Large, 1 trial (red and black) on Kitakata Chiri Large

Signature location: LR

Chop location: printer, reverse LR

Job number and location: 01–101, reverse LL

Color printing order, execution of printing elements:

1. Aluminum printed with rubine red and transparent base. Image drawn with Korn's autographic ink.

2. Aluminum printed with Senefelder's crayon black. Image drawn with brush and tusche.

Note: Printing element used in *Language Arts* (no. 136).

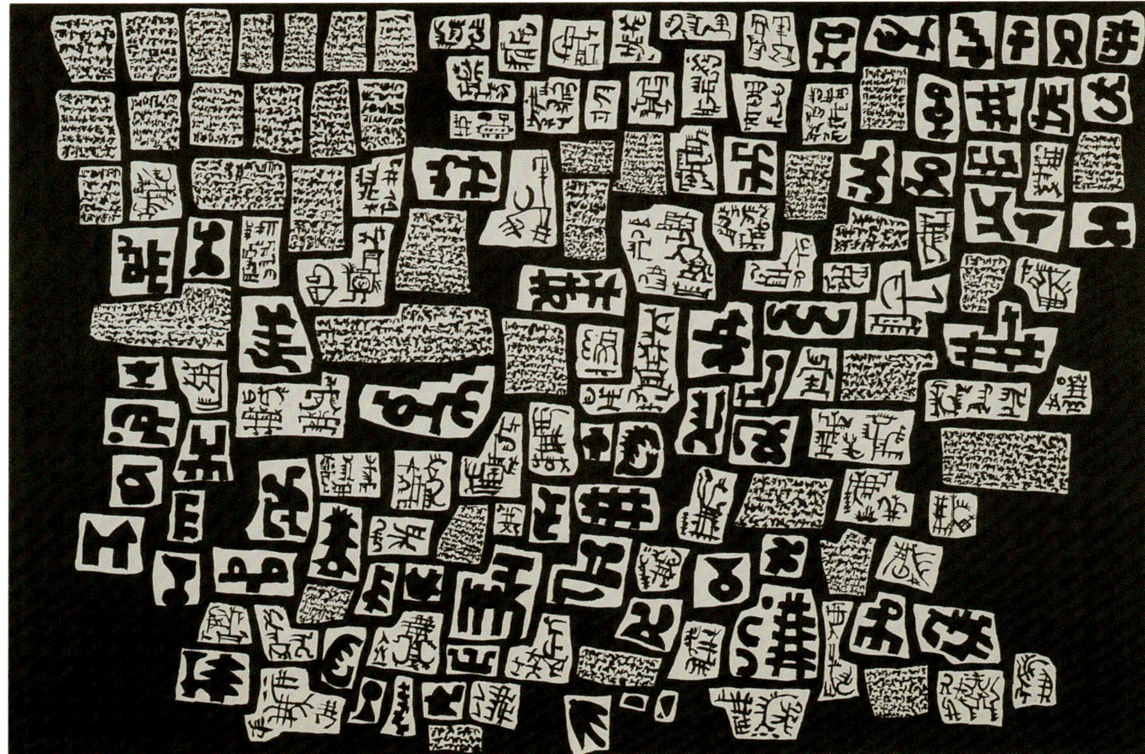

136

136.

Language Arts

Date finished: 7/4/2001

Medium: lithograph

Paper size: 15 × 22 in.

Image size: same

Paper type: Rives BFK Gray

Publisher: artist

Press: Richard D. Finch Workshop

Printer: Richard D. Finch

Printer's assistant: Diana Finch

Edition: 20

Proofs: 1 bon à tirer, 1 presentation, 1 press, 1 ready to print

Signature location: LR

Chop location: LL

Job number and location: 01–102, reverse LL

Execution/printing elements:

1. Aluminum printed with Senefelder's crayon black. Image drawn with brush and tusche.

Note: Printing element reused from *Turandot's Riddles* (no. 135).

137.

Actually Undoing

Date finished: 2001

Medium: archival inkjet

Paper size: 6 × 8 in. (variable)

Image size: same

Paper type: Schollershammer Velvet

Publisher: artist

Press: UNO Print Workshop

Printer: Gary Day

Edition: none

Proofs: 7 trial

Signature location: LR

Chop location: none

Job number and location: none

Color printing order, execution of printing elements:

1. Printed with Epson 9500 Inkjet with archival pigment-based inks. Image drawn in Photoshop on Macintosh computer.

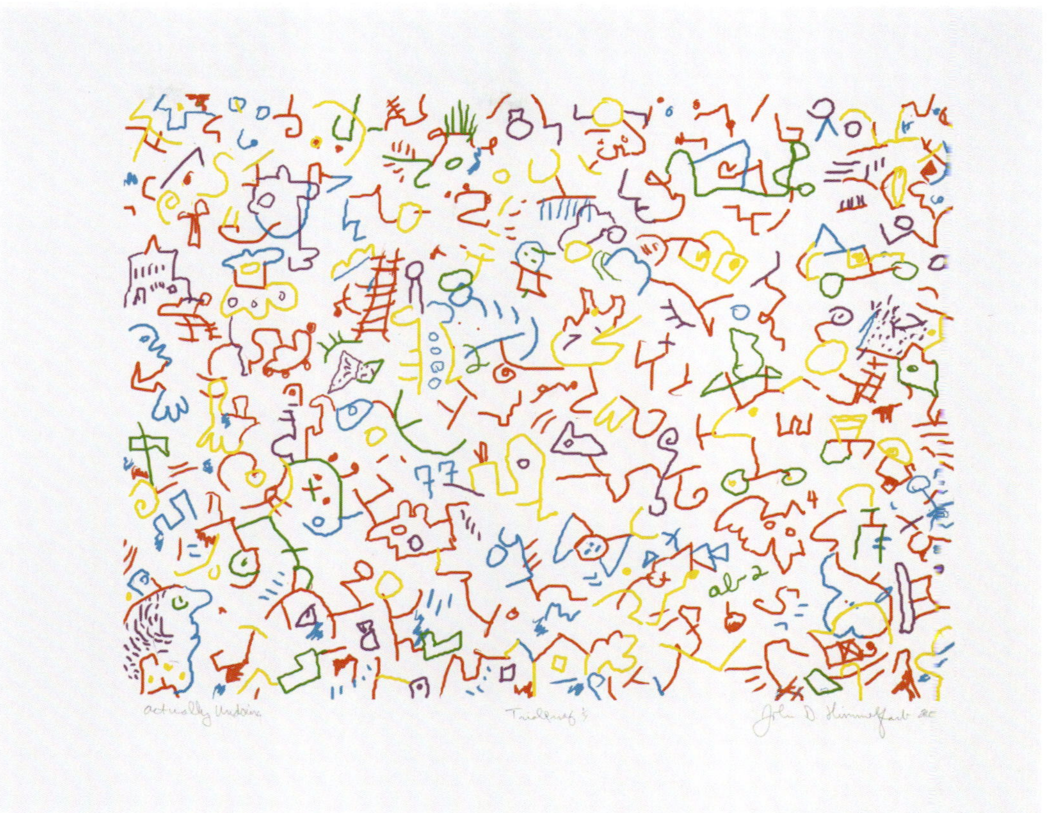

137

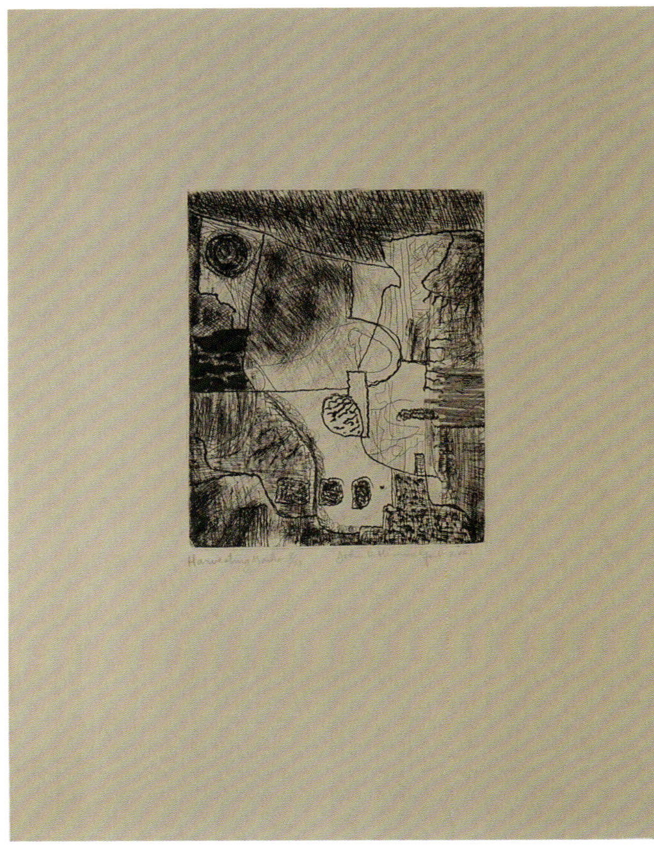

138

138.

Harvesting Marks

Date begun: 2002

Date finished: 2002

Medium: intaglio

Paper size: 12⅝ × 9¾ in.

Image size: 5½ × 4½ in.

Paper type: Rives BFK Tan

Publisher: Peck School of the Arts, University of Wisconsin–Milwaukee

Press: Peck School of the Arts, University of Wisconsin–Milwaukee

Printer: Brian Novak under supervision of Cheryl Olson-Sklar

Edition: 25

Proofs: 5 artist on Arches White with Kitakata Chine Collé

Signature location: below image, LR

Chop location: none

Job number and location: none

Color printing order, execution of printing elements:

1. Aluminum coated with silicone printed intaglio with black waterless litho ink.

Note: Also printed without Kitakata Chine Collé on Rives BFK White as *Farm and Fleet* (no. 139).

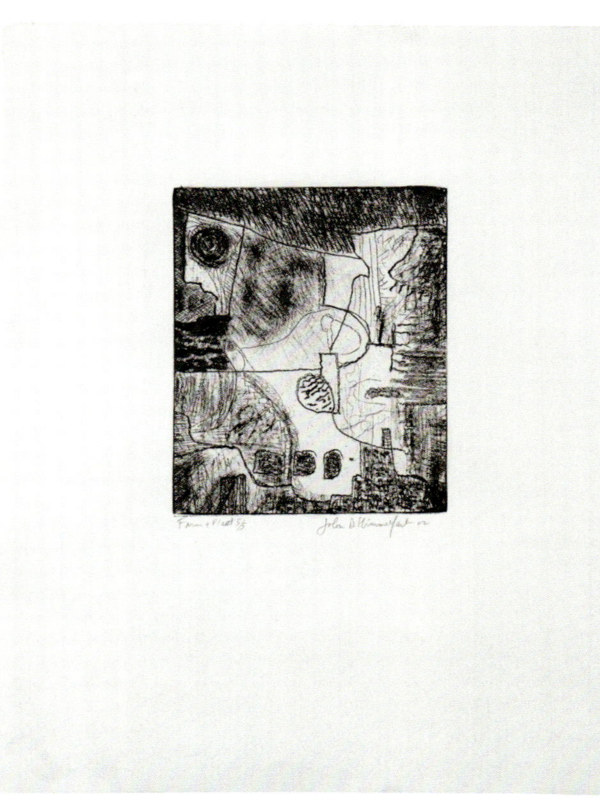

139

139.

Farm and Fleet

Date begun: 2002

Date finished: 2002

Medium: intaglio

Paper size: 12⅝ × 9¾ in.

Image size: 5½ × 4½ in.

Paper type: Rives BFK White

Publisher: Peck School of the Arts, University of Wisconsin–Milwaukee

Press: Peck School of the Arts, University of Wisconsin–Milwaukee

Printer: Brian Novak under supervision of Cheryl Olson-Sklar

Edition: 5

Proofs: none

Signature location: below image, LR

Chop location: none

Job number and location: none

Color printing order, execution of printing elements:

1. Silicone printed with black waterless litho ink.

Note: Printing element reused from *Harvesting Marks* (cat. 138).

140.

Chapeau

Date begun: 2/4/2002

Date finished: 3/4/2003

Medium: lithograph

Paper size: 22 × 30 in.

Image size: same

Paper type: Arches Cover Buff

Publisher: Normal Editions Workshop, Illinois State University

Press: Normal Editions Workshop, Illinois State University

Printers: Richard D. Finch, Veda Rives

Printers' assistants: Nathan Bailey, Chad Collofello, Todd DeVriese, John Disco, Yoko Kawazoe, Tanisha Redict, Meda Rives, Chris Shepard

Edition: 36

Proofs: 1 bon à tirer, 2 Illinois State University, 4 proof copies (unsigned, but stamped, reverse), 1 publisher, 1 ready to print

Signature location: LR

Chop location: LL

Job number and location: 02–102, reverse LL

Color printing order, execution of printing elements:

1. Stone printed with light brown (benz yellow, bismarck brown, chocolate crown, pthalo blue-red, tint base). Image created using monotype technique.

2. Aluminum printed with medium brown (benz yellow, bismarck brown, chocolate brown, pthalo blue-red, tint base). Image created using photo-lithography.

3. Aluminum printed with off-white (white, light brown from run #1, tint base). Image created with brush and toner washes on mylar using photographic techniques.

4. Aluminum printed with blue (white, pthalo blue-red, rhodamine red, tint base). Image created with brush and toner washes on mylar using photographic techniques.

5. Aluminum printed with green (white, pthalo blue-green, benz yellow, tint base). Image created with brush and toner washes on mylar using photographic techniques.

6. Aluminum printed with Senefelder's crayon black. Image created with Stabilo pencil on mylar using photographic techniques.

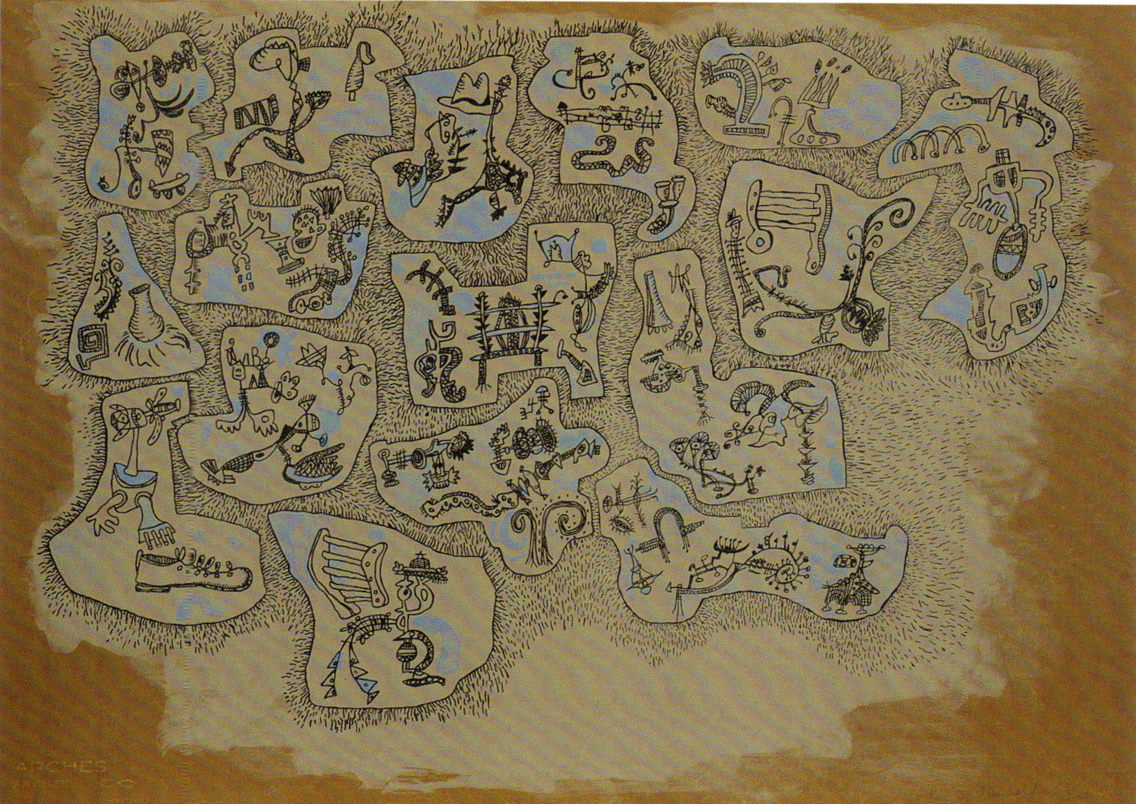

140

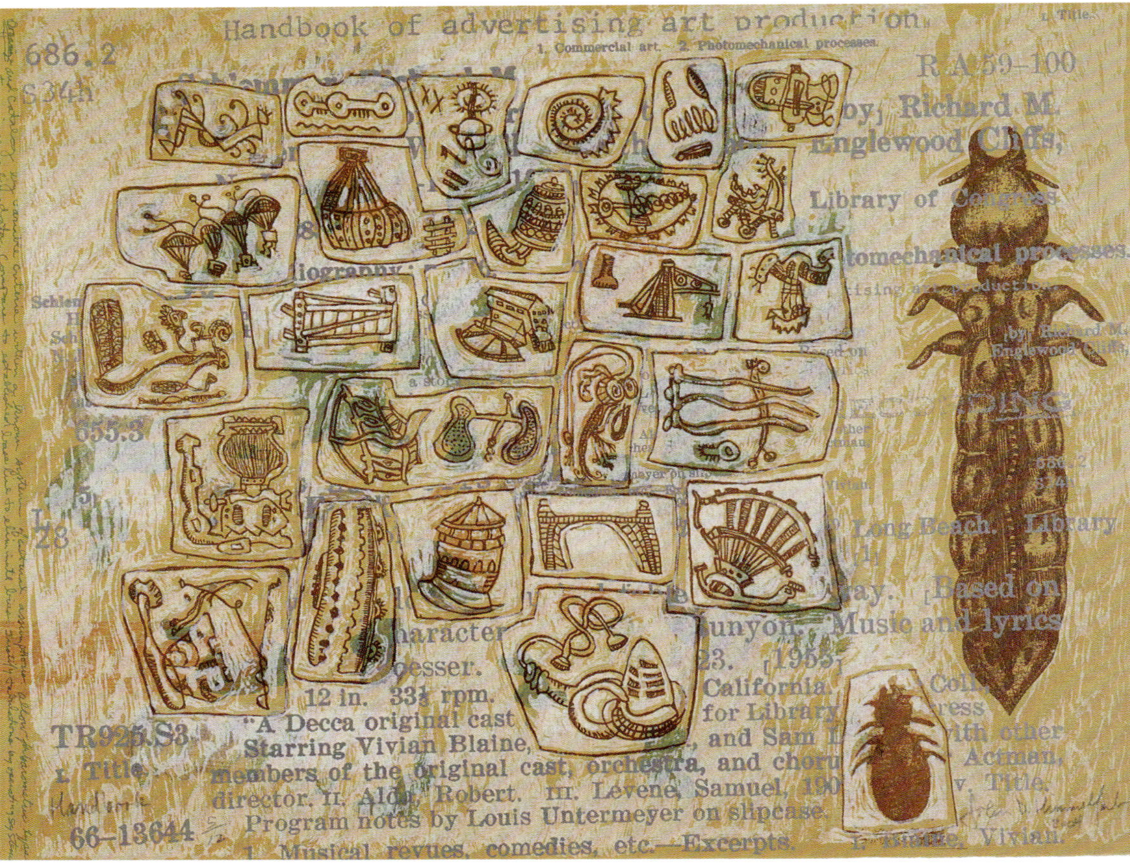

141

141.

Handbook

Date begun: 2/18/2002

Date finished: 2004

Medium: lithograph

Paper size: 15 × 19 in.

Image size: same

Paper type: Rives BFK Buff

Publisher: Peck School of the Arts, University of Wisconsin–Milwaukee

Press: Peck School of the Arts, University of Wisconsi–Milwaukee

Printers: Brian Novak and printmaking students under supervision of Cheryl Olson-Sklar

Edition: 12

Proofs: 1 bon à tirer, 11 college, 2 trial of each run

Signature location: LR

Chop location: none

Job number and location: none

Color printing order, execution of printing elements:

1. Piece of wood with grain printed with salmon. Relief roll.

2. Toray plate printed with light gray. Image realized from photocopies of artist's collection of library catalogue cards collaged, scanned, and pulled up on laser vellum, exposed on aqua contact film transferred onto Toray plate.

3. Toray plate printed with white. Image drawn with rubbing crayon on vellum, exposed on aqua contact film onto Toray plate.

4. Toray plate printed with transparent yellow. Image created with nib pen and opaquing liquid on art film exposed on Toray plate (white line, key plate reversal).

5. Aluminum printed with blue. Image drawn with litho coal on art film transferred and silicone-processed on aluminum.

6. Toray plate printed with green. Image drawn with brush and acrylic washes and opaque marker on art film photocopied on vellum, exposed on aqua contact film onto Toray plate.

7. Toray plate printed with orange and transparent off-white. Image made with inked wood-grain shapes, half-tone wood grain, and manipulated wood-grain illustrations photocopied on vellum, exposed on aqua contact film onto Toray plate.

8. Toray plate printed with off-white. Image made with inked wood-grain shapes, half-tone wood grain, and manipulated wood-grain illustrations photocopied on vellum, exposed on aqua contact film onto Toray plate.

9. Toray plate printed with white. Image drawn with acrylic washes on art film exposed on Toray plate.

10. Toray plate printed with red-brown. Image created with nib pen and opaquing liquid on art film photocopied on vellum, exposed on aqua contact film on Toray plate.

11. Toray plate printed with dark gray. Image drawn with opaque film markers applied to aqua contact film for run #2, exposed onto Toray plate.

Note: A second edition of *Handbook* was done as well (*Handbook II*, no. 142).

142.

Handbook II

Date finished: 1/2004

Medium: lithograph

Paper size: 15 × 19 in.

Image size: same

Paper type: Rives BFK Gray

Publisher: Peck School of the Arts, University of Wisconsin–Milwaukee

Printer: Brian Novak under supervision of Cheryl Olson-Sklar

Printer's assistant: Clark Rendall

Edition: 18

Proofs: 3 artist (Roman numerals), 1 bon à tirer, University of Wisconsin-Milwaukee (titled *College Handbook*)

Signature location: LR

Chop location: none

Job number and location: none

Color printing order, execution of printing elements:

Five-color multiple-plate silicone chemistry/photo-lithograph using runs #2, 3, 4, 9, and 10 of *Handbook* (no. 141) printed as follows:

1. Toray plate printed with pink. Image drawn with nib pen and opaquing fluid on art film exposed onto Toray plate (white line, key plate reversal).

2. Toray plate printed with red and green. Photographs of artist's collection of library catalogue cards cut and collaged, scanned, and pulled up on laser vellum, exposed on aqua contact film onto Toray plate.

3. Toray plate printed with chartreuse. Image drawn with rubbing crayon on vellum, exposed on aqua contact film onto Toray plate.

4. Toray plate printed with light blue. Image drawn with brush and acrylic washes on art film exposed onto Toray plate.

5. Toray plate printed with warm black. Image drawn with nib pen and opaquing fluid on art film photocopied on vellum, exposed on aqua contact film onto Toray plate.

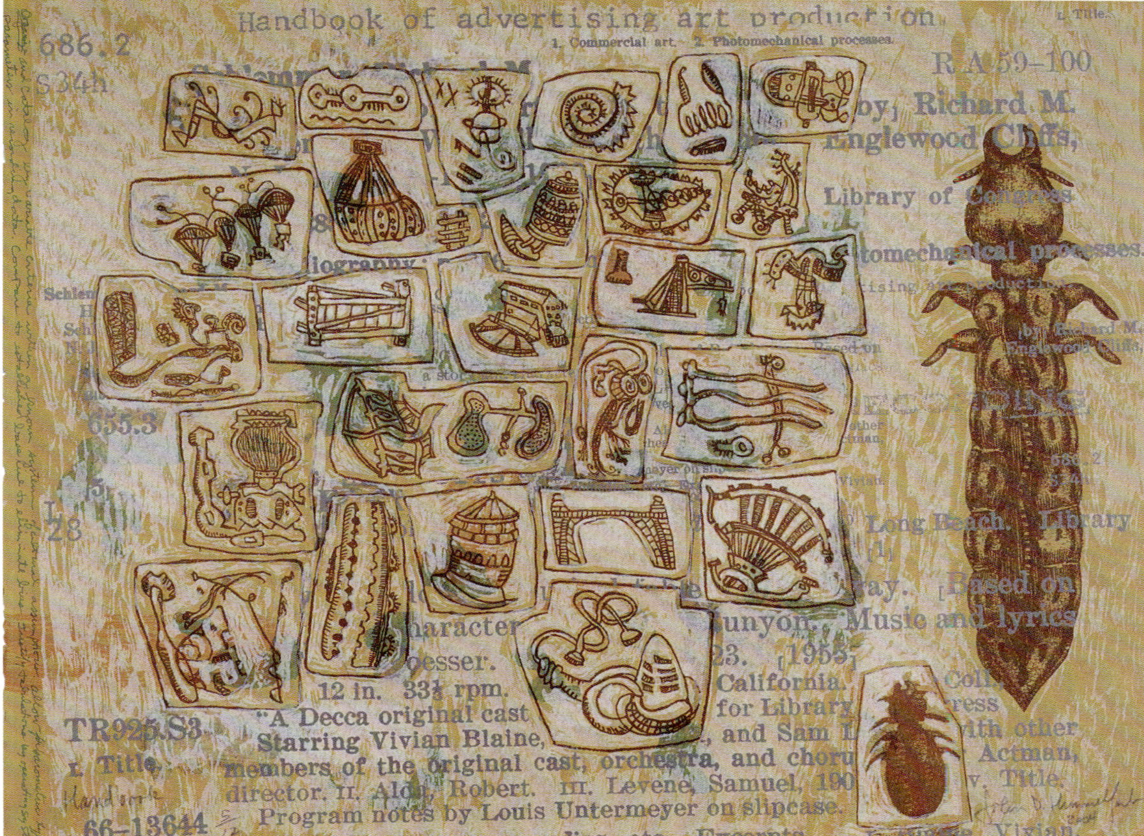

142

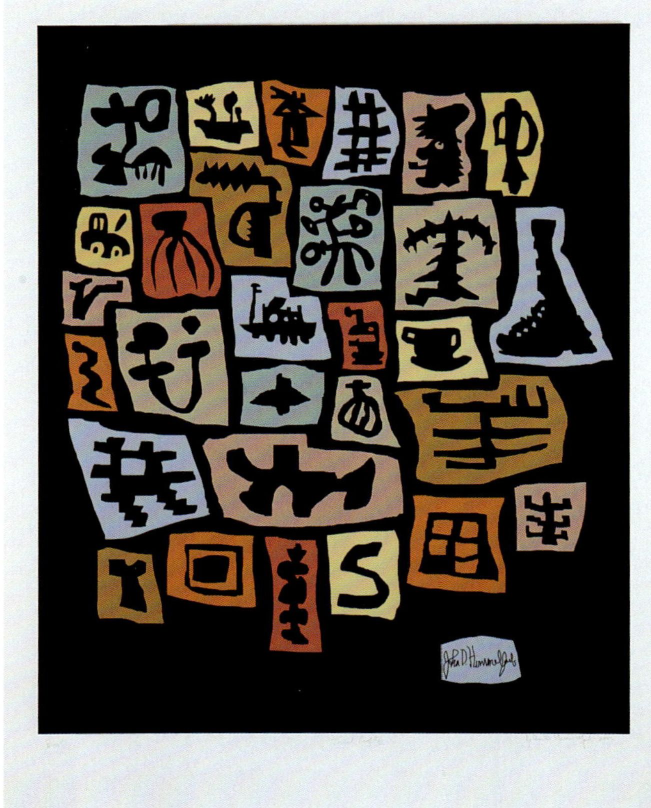

143

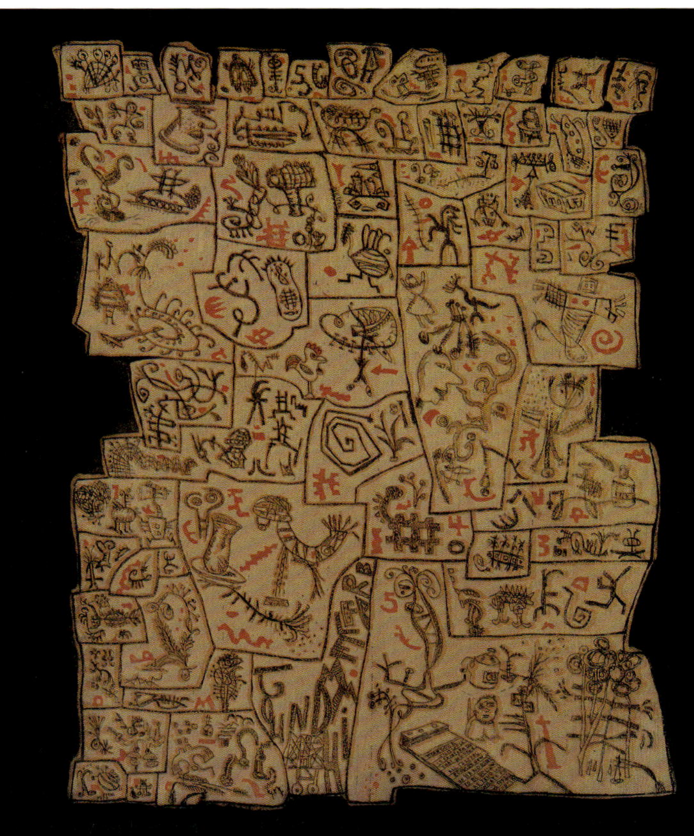

144

143.

Boot

Date finished: 2003

Medium: archival inkjet

Paper size: 23½ × 18 in.

Image size: 20 × 16 in.

Paper type: Schollershammer Velvet

Publisher: artist

Press: UNO Print Workshop

Printer: Gary Day

Edition: 20

Proofs: 1 bon à tirer, 1 UNO Print Workshop

Signature location: LR

Chop location: none

Job number and location: none

Color printing order, execution of printing elements:

Printed with Epson 9500 Inkjet with archival pigment-based inks. Image created using Photoshop on Macintosh computer.

144.

Xtra Xtra

Date begun: 2003

Date finished: 2004

Medium: intaglio

Paper size: 24 × 20 in.

Image size: same

Paper type: Rives BFK Tan

Publisher: UNO Print Workshop

Press: UNO Print Workshop

Printer: Gary Day

Printer's assistants: Melissa Corwin, Hannah Marchio, Julie Sopscak

Edition: 25

Proofs: 5 artist, 1 bon à tirer, 3 press

Signature location: LR

Chop location: none

Job number and location: none

Color printing order, execution of printing elements:

1. Plywood printed with brown. No image.

2. Zinc printed with white. Image created with sugar-lift and aquatint techniques.

3. Zinc printed with red. Image created with sugar-lift and aquatint techniques.

4. Zinc printed with black. Image created with etching and aquatint techniques.

145.

Zklee

Date begun: 2003

Date finished: 2004

Medium: intaglio

Paper size: 23¾ × 35¾ in.

Image size: same

Paper type: Kitakata Chiri Large

Publisher: UNO Print Workshop

Press: UNO Print Workshop

Printer: Gary Day

Printer's assistants: Melissa Corwin, Hannah Marchio, Julie Sopscak

Edition: 21

Proofs: 2 artist, 3 press, 11 trial

Signature location: LR

Chop location: none

Job number and location: none

Color printing order, execution of printing elements:

1. Zinc printed with iron-oxide red. Image drawn with aquatint.

2. Zinc printed with black. Image drawn with line etching.

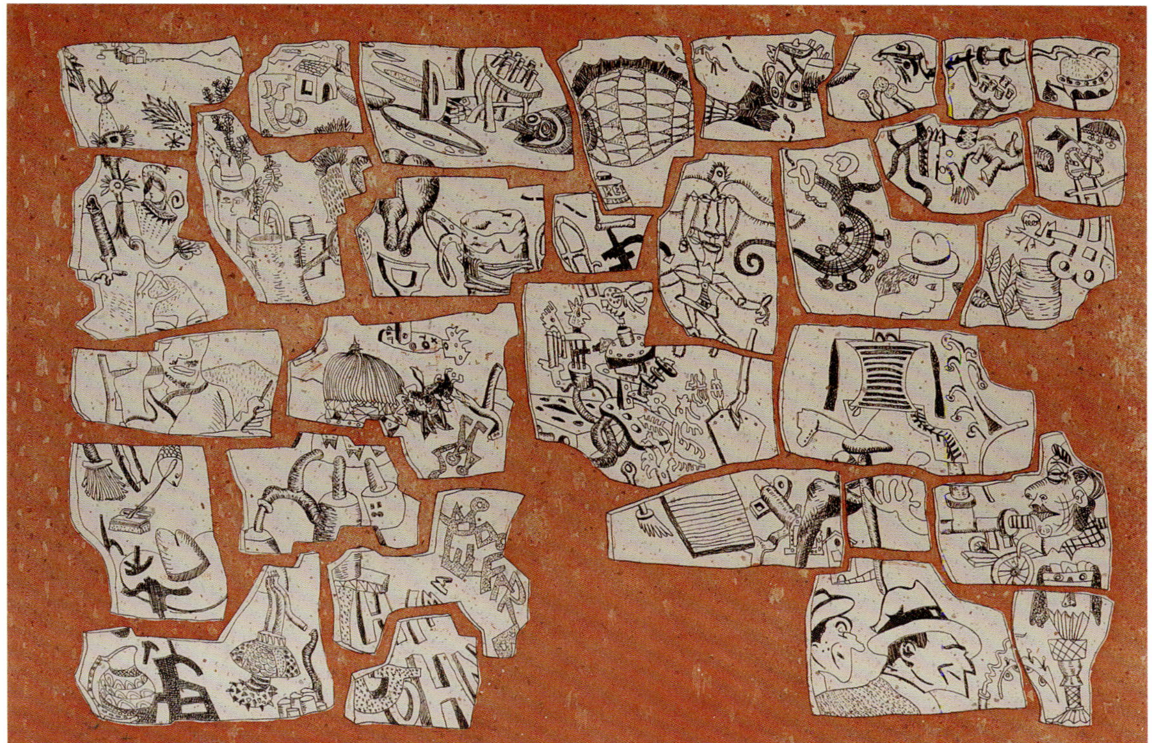

145

146.

Under the Palm

Date begun: 2004

Date finished: 4/13/2004

Medium: lithograph

Paper size: 14 × 10½ in. (variable)

Image size: 8 × 6 in.

Paper type: Dieu Donné Charcoal Double Laminate

Publisher: artist

Press: Chicago Printmakers Collaborative

Printer: artist

Printer's assistant: Carrie Iverson

Edition: 30

Proofs: 4 artist, 1 cancellation on Arches Buff, 1 Chicago Printmakers Collaborative, 2 press, 1 trial on Arches Buff

Signature location: LR

Chop location: LL

Job number and location: none

Color printing order, execution of printing elements:

1. Aluminum printed with black. Image drawn with litho crayon.

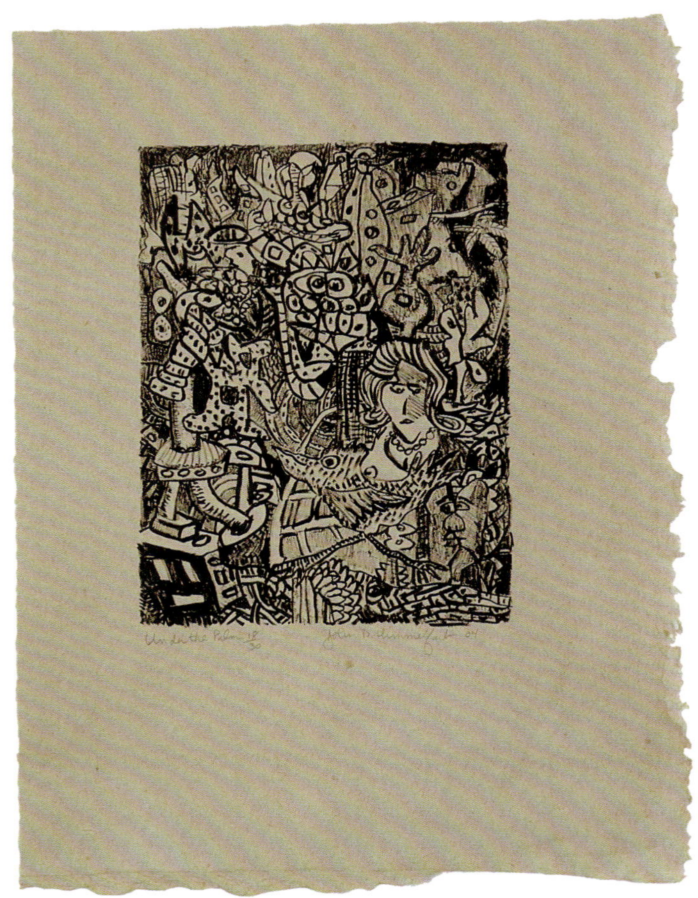

146

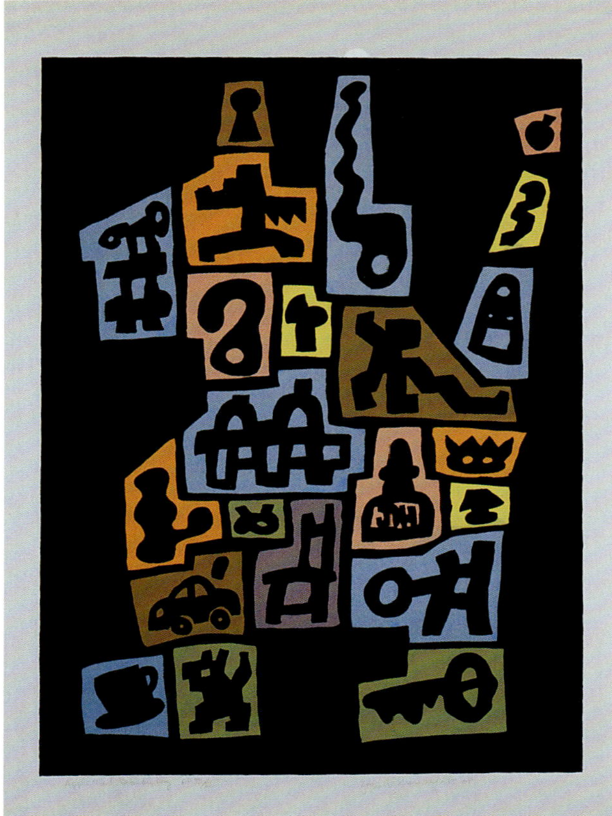

147

147.

Apple Tail Double Dog

Date begun: 5/2004

Date finished: 5/21/2004

Medium: screenprint

Paper size: 29¾ × 21¾ in.

Image size: 26 × 19 in.

Paper type: Rives BFK White

Publisher: Stewart & Stewart

Press: Stewart & Stewart

Printer: Norman Stewart

Printer's assistants: Joe Ermalovich, Sean Stewart

Edition: 30

Proofs: 3 artist, 1 documentation, 1 printer, 3 publisher

Signature location: beneath image, LR

Chop location: publisher and printer, LR

Job number and location: © John Himmelfarb stamp in black, reverse LL

Color printing order, execution of printing elements:

1. Blue
2. Red
3. Yellow
4. Deep cool gray

Each original color separation drawn on mylar, then screenprinted using an indirect sensigraphic stencil system.

Note: Print element in run #4 used in *Dalmation* (no. 148).

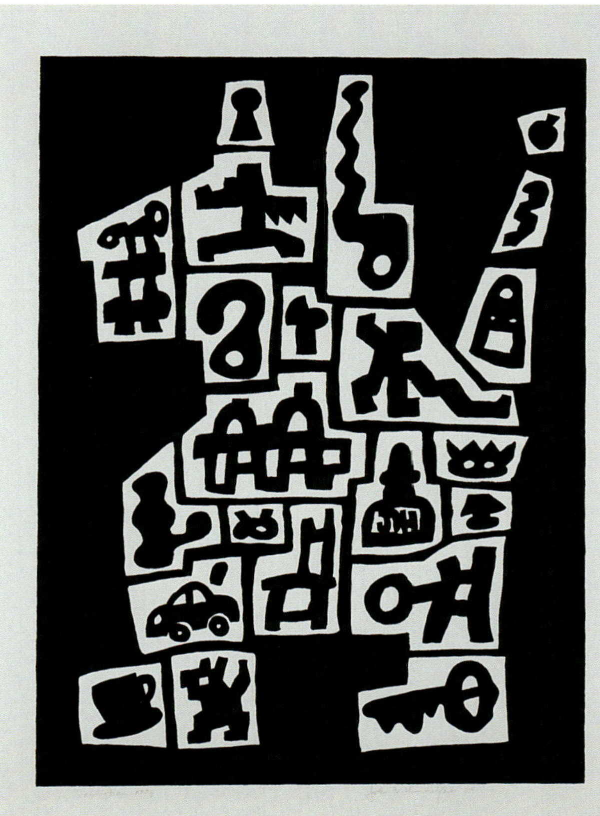

148

148.

Dalmation

Date begun: 5/2004

Date finished: 5/21/2004

Medium: screenprint

Paper size: 29¾ × 21¾ in.

Image size: 26 × 19 in.

Paper type: Rives BFK White

Publisher: Stewart & Stewart

Press: Stewart & Stewart

Printer: Norman Stewart

Printer's assistant: Joe Ermalovich

Edition: 10

Proofs: 1 artist, 1 publisher

Signature location: below image, LR

Chop location: publisher and printer, LR

Job number and location: © John Himmelfarb stamp in black, reverse LL

Color printing order, execution of printing elements:

1. Deep cool gray. Original color separation drawn on mylar, then screenprinted using an indirect sensigraphic stencil system.

Note: Print element reused from *Apple Tail Double Dog* (no. 147).

149.

Pie & Coffee

Date begun: 5/2004

Date finished: 5/21/2004

Medium: screenprint

Paper size: 29¾ × 21¾ in.

Image size: 26 × 19 in.

Paper type: Rives BFK White

Publisher: Stewart & Stewart

Press: Stewart & Stewart

Printer: Norman Stewart

Printer's assistants: Joe Ermalovich, Sean Stewart

Edition: 33

Proofs: 3 artist, 1 documentation, 3 publisher

Signature location: below image, LR

Chop location: publisher and printer, LR

Job number and location: © John Himmelfarb stamp in black, reverse LL

Color printing order, execution of printing elements:

1, Blue

2. Red

3. Yellow

4. Deep cool gray

Each original color separation drawn on mylar, then screenprinted using an indirect sensigraphic stencil system.

Note: Print element in run #4 used in *Cream & Sugar* (no. 150).

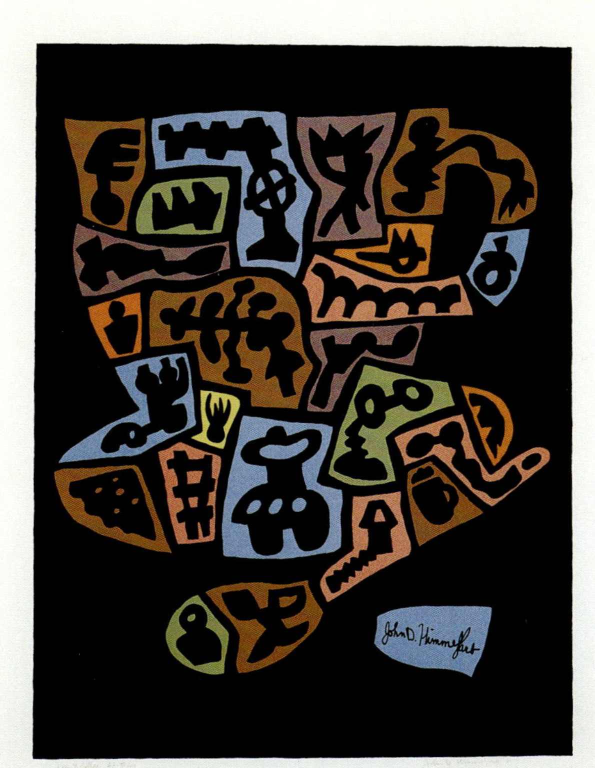

149

150.

Cream & Sugar

Date begun: 5/2004

Date finished: 5/21/2004

Medium: screenprint

Paper size: 29¾ × 21¾ in.

Image size: 26 × 19 in.

Paper type: Rives BFK White

Publisher: Stewart & Stewart

Press: Stewart & Stewart

Printer: Norman Stewart

Printer's assistant: Joe Ermalovich

Edition: 10

Proofs: 1 artist, 1 publisher

Signature location: beneath image, LR

Chop location: publisher and printer, LR

Job number and location: © John Himmelfarb stamp in black, reverse LL

Color printing order, execution of printing elements:

1. Deep cool gray. Original color separation drawn on mylar, then screenprinted using an indirect sensigraphic stencil system.

Note: Print element reused from *Pie & Coffee* (no. 149).

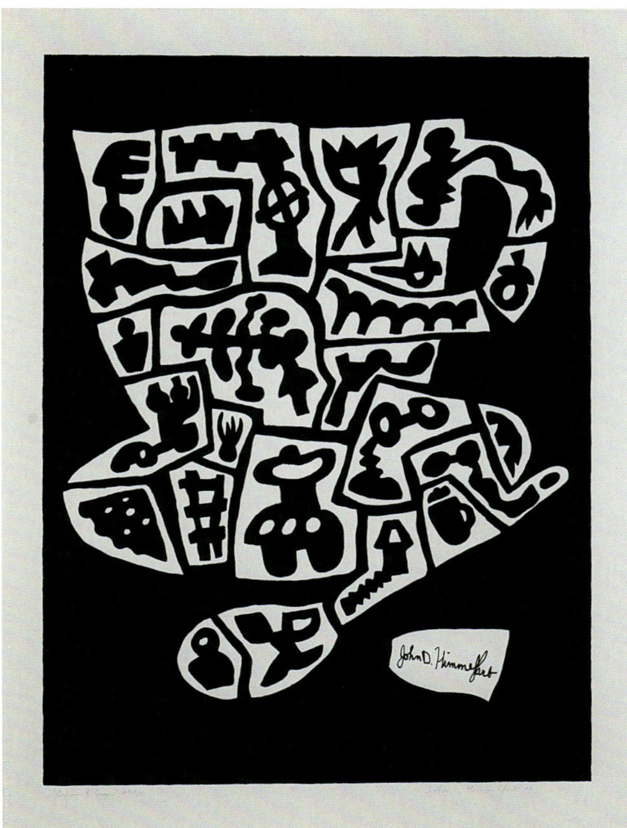

150

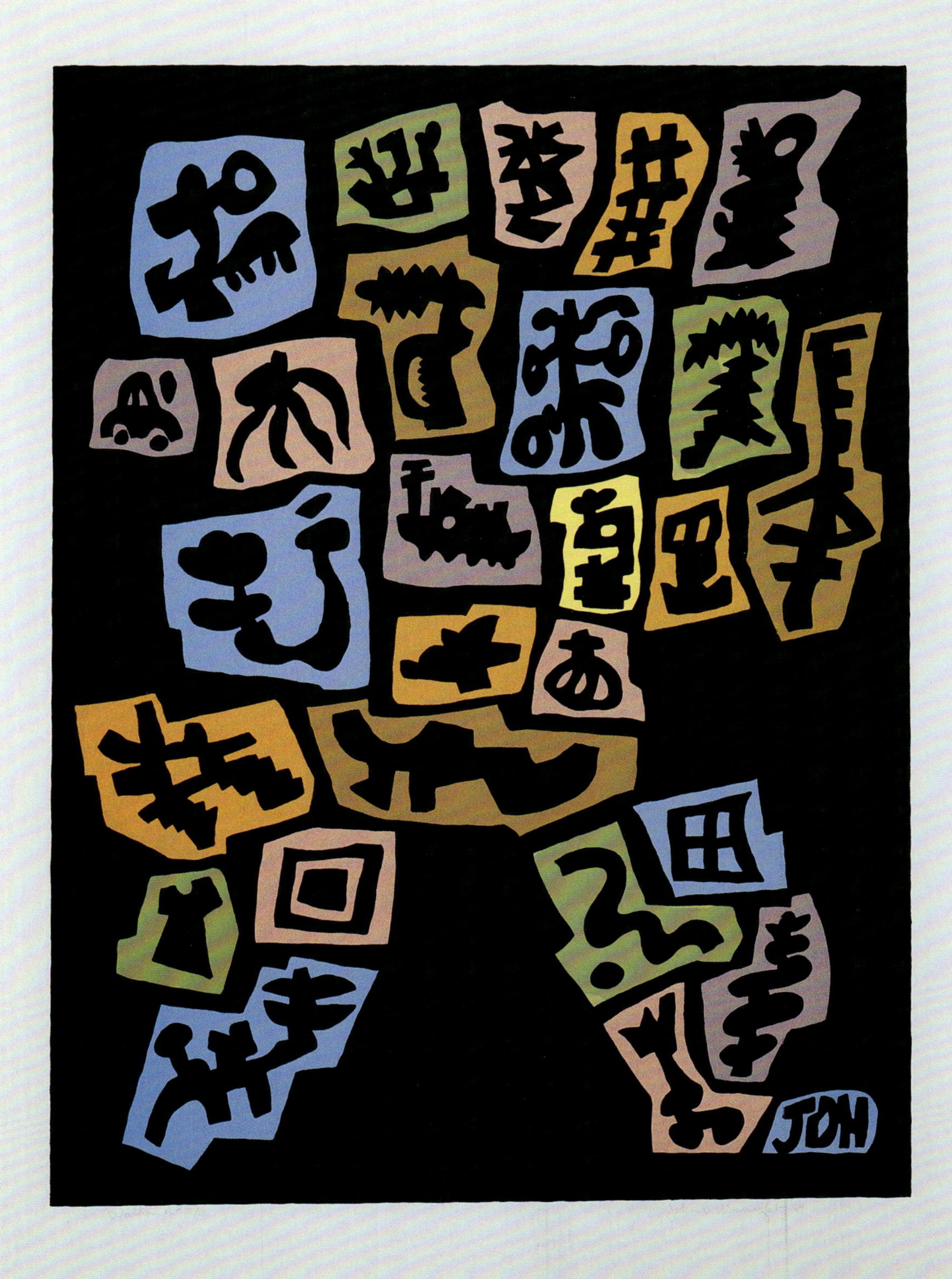

151.

Walker

Date begun: 5/2004

Date finished: 5/21/2004

Medium: screenprint

Paper size: 29¾ × 21¾ in.

Image size: 26 × 19 in.

Paper type: Rives BFK White

Publisher: Stewart & Stewart

Press: Stewart & Stewart

Printer: Norman Stewart

Printer's assistants: Joe Ermalovich, Sean Stewart

Edition: 30

Proofs: 3 artist, 1 documentation, 3 publisher

Signature: below image, LR

Chop location: publisher and printer, LR

Job number and location: © John Himmelfarb stamp in black, reverse LL

Color printing order, execution of printing elements:

1. Blue
2. Red
3. Yellow
4. Deep cool gray

Each original color separation drawn on mylar, then screenprinted using an indirect sensigraphic stencil system.

Note: Print element in run #4 used in *Walker B* (no. 152)

152.

Walker B

Date begun: 5/2004

Date finished: 5/21/2004

Medium: screenprint

Paper size: 29¾ × 21¾ in.

Image size: 26 × 19 in.

Paper type: Rives BFK White

Publisher: Stewart & Stewart

Press: Stewart & Stewart

Printer: Norman Stewart

Printer's assistants: Joe Ermalovich, Sean Stewart

Edition: 10

Proofs: 1 artist, 1 publisher

Signature: below image, LR

Chop location: publisher and printer, LR

Job number and location: © John Himmelfarb stamp in black, reverse LL

Color printing order, execution of printing elements:

1. Deep cool gray. Color separation drawn on mylar, then screenprinted using an indirect sensigraphic stencil system.

Note: Print element reused from *Walker* (no. 151).

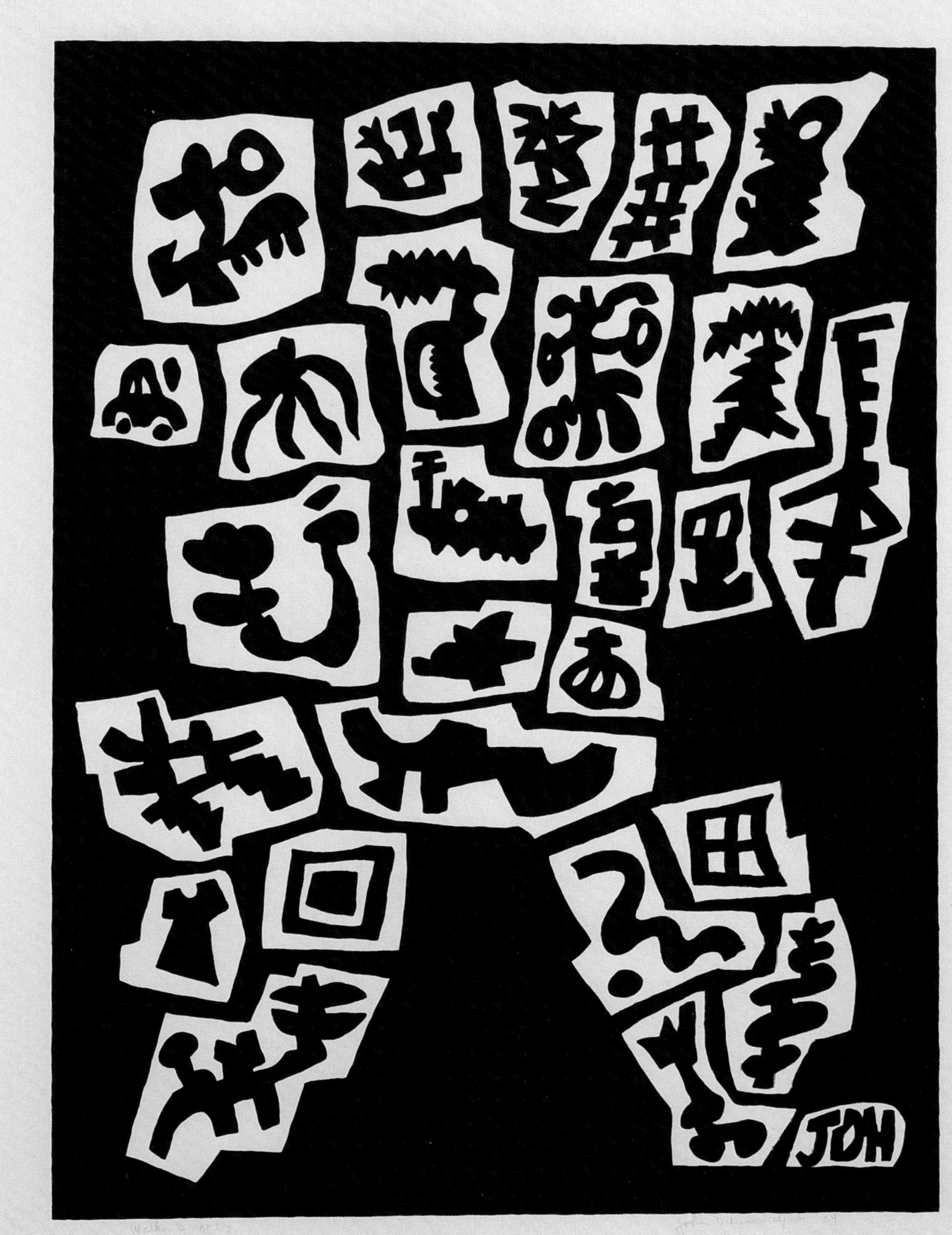

152

Chronology

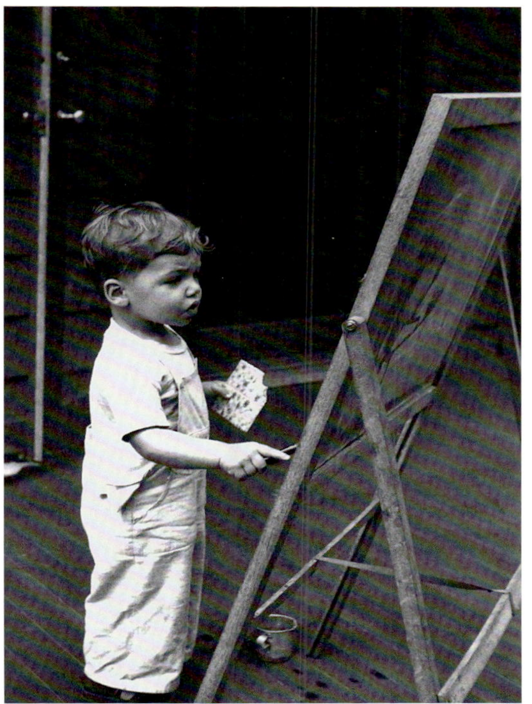
The young John Himmelfarb at his easel, c. 1950.

1946
Born to artists Samuel and Eleanor Gorecki Himmelfarb, in Chicago; raised in Winfield, Ill.

1960–64
Attends Wheaton (Ill.) Community High School.

1964–68
Attends Harvard University, Cambridge, Mass. In freshman year, takes two-dimensional class with Albert Alcalay. In sophomore year, takes three-dimensional class with Wil Reimann, and drawing with Robert Neuman. Continues with Reimann in an independent study in drawing, and learns basic etching with Mirko Basadella.

1968
Work shown in first national exhibition, "Drawings USA," at Minnesota Museum of American Art, St. Paul.

1968–69
Studies at Harvard Graduate School of Education.

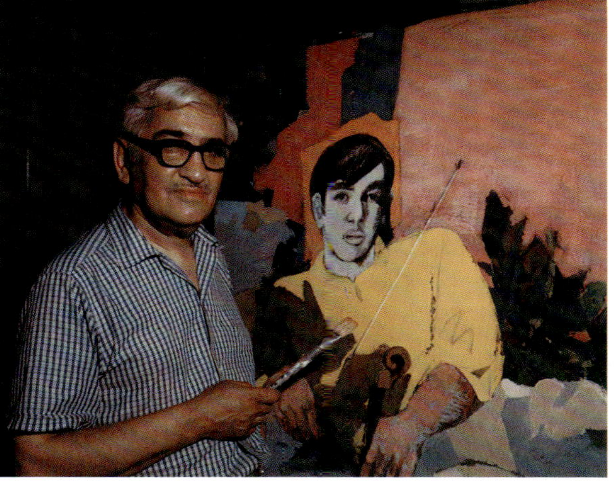
Samuel Himmelfarb with a portrait of his son, John, holding his violin, c. 1963.

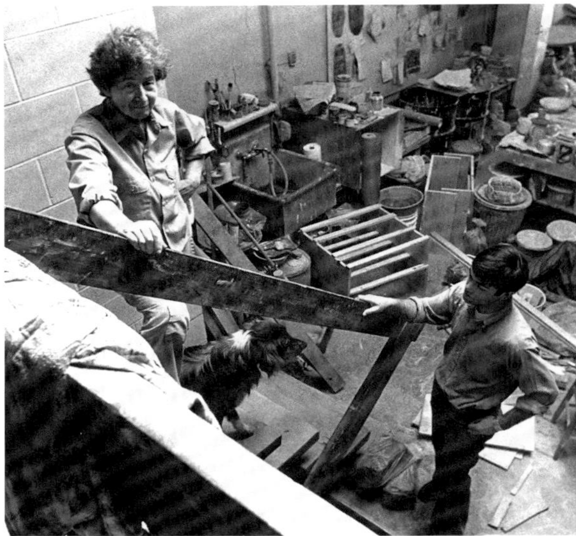

Ruth Duckworth and John Himmelfarb, Chicago, c. 1975.

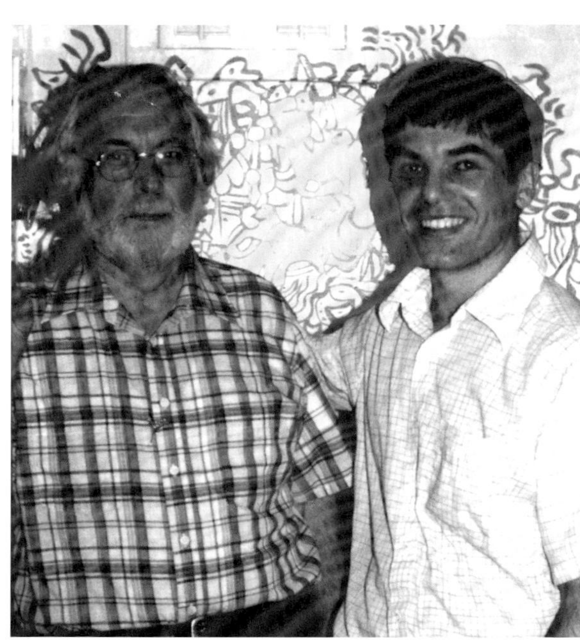

The art dealer Bob Rogers and John Himmelfarb, Omaha, 1980.

1969–70
Does education internship in New York City and consults with Newton Public Schools.

1970
Meets future wife, Molly Day. Returns to Chicago. Sets up work area in parents' studio. Through artist Misch Kohn, introduced to Landfall Press, Chicago, where he begins to make prints. Also assists ceramist/sculptor Ruth Duckworth and executes sculptures.

1971
Begins series of lithographs at Landfall Press. Prints included in "Brooklyn Museum Fence Show." Lives for short time outside New York City.

1972
Marries Molly Day. Couple moves into studio in Chicago's Pilsen neighborhood.

1974
Work included in "19th National Print Exhibition" at Brooklyn Museum of Art.

1976
Father, Samuel, dies.

1977
Begins to show with Terry Dintenfass Gallery, New York, and Gallery 72, Omaha. Himmelfarb and Day take up residence in Hyde Park area of Chicago.

1978
Work selected for "Works on Paper: 77th Exhibition by Artists of Chicago and Vicinity" at Art Institute of Chicago.

1979
Works at Yaddo artists' community, Saratoga Springs, N.Y. Has first solo exhibitions at Gallery 72 and Dintenfass. Son, Forest, born.

1980
Begins black paintings on raw canvas, leading to *Boatman* series.

1981
Begins to make prints with Cynthia Archer and Will Petersen at Plucked Chicken Press, Chicago.

1982
Shows *Boatman* series at Barbara Balkin Gallery, Chicago. Receives grant from National Endowment for the Arts.

1983
Lives and works for ten months on Maryland farm owned by in-laws. Begins showing at Brody's Gallery, Washington, D.C.

1984
During trip to Europe, meets ceramist Juan Gardy Llorens Artigas (son of ceramist Josep Llorens Artigas) in Gallifa, Spain. Leaves Chicago studio, working in new family residence in Chicago suburb of Oak Park.

1985
Arts Magazine runs five-page article, "An Interview with John Himmelfarb," by artist-writer Matthew Rose.

1986
Including eighty works, "Himmelfarb: Black on White" staged at Davenport (Iowa) Art Museum. Appointment as visiting artist at Illinois State University, Normal, leads to working relationship with Normal Editions Workshop and printer Richard D. Finch. Receives Pollock-Krasner Foundation and Illinois Arts Council grants. Daughter, Serena Aurora Day, born.

1989
Works at Tandem Press in Madison, Wis., and at Fundació Tallers Josep Llorens Artigas in Gallifa. Retrospective exhibition, "Meetings in the Garden: The Art of John Himmelfarb," opens at Kalamazoo Institute of Arts.

1991
Buys nineteenth-century department store in area known as Heart of Chicago and converts it into artists' studios, including a floor for himself. Does first prints with Norman Stewart at Stewart & Stewart, Bloomfield Hills, Mich. Begins showing at Spaightwood Gallery, Madison, Wis.

1994
Travels to Gallifa to participate in exhibition "Plats d'Artistes."

1995
Chicago Cultural Center mounts exhibition "Inland Romance: Paintings by John Himmelfarb," which includes drawings from his *Calligraphic* series.

1999
Family moves back to Hyde Park.

2001
"American Graffiti," solo exhibition at Centre of Contemporary Art, Christchurch, New Zealand.

2002
Receives second grant from Pollock-Krasner Foundation.

2003
Creates two ceramic-tile murals for the Graduate School of Education, University of Nebraska, Lincoln.

2004
Second exhibition at Centre of Contemporary Art, Christchurch, New Zealand. Wins competition for ceramic-tile mural for Kedzie station of the Chicago Transit Authority's Douglas branch Blue Line.

2005
Creates two large paintings for new Delta Airlines Terminal A at Logan Airport, Boston.

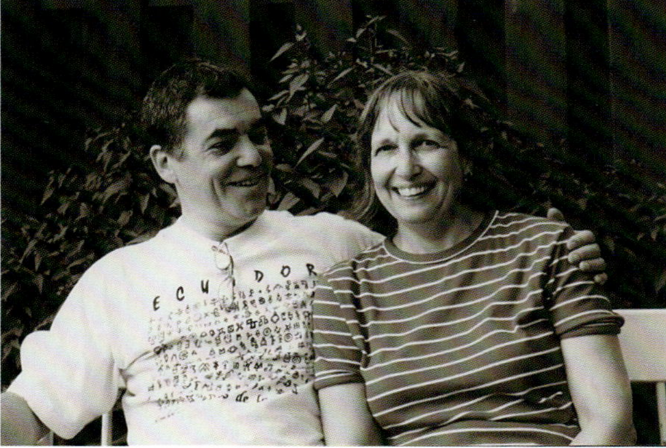

Molly Day and John Himmelfarb, 2002.

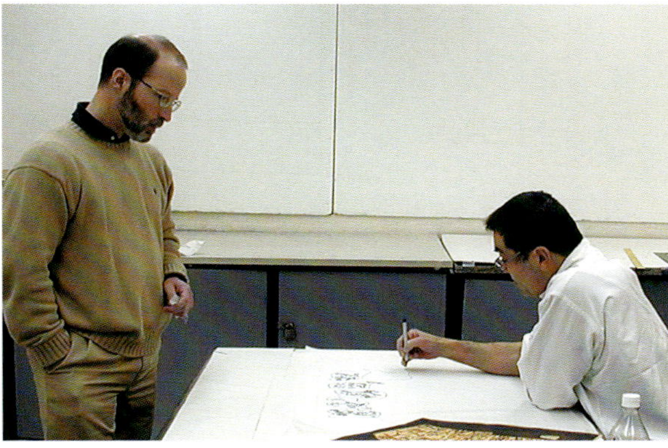

John Himmelfarb working with master printer Richard D. Finch, Normal, Illinois, 2002.

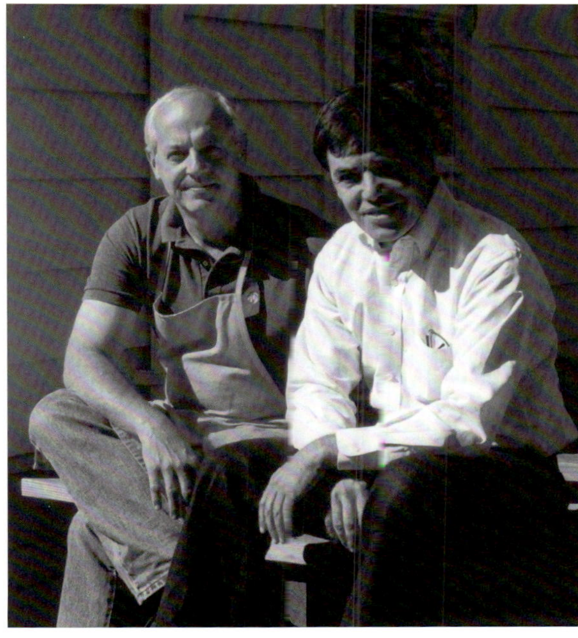

The print publisher Norman Stewart and John Himmelfarb, Bloomfield Hills, Michigan, 1994.

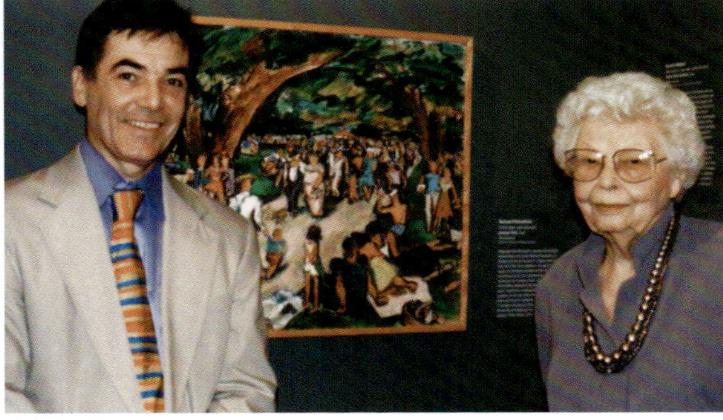

Eleanor Himmelfarb with her son, John, in front of Samuel Himmelfarb's painting Jackson Park, *which was included in the exhibition "Chicago Modern 1893–1945, Pursuit of the New," at the Terra Museum of American Art, Chicago, 2004.*

Public Collections, Exhibitions, Public Projects, Visiting Artist, Awards

Public Collections

Albrecht-Kemper Museum of Art, St. Joseph, Mo.

Arkansas Arts Center, Little Rock

Art Institute of Chicago

Baltimore Art Museum

Bibliothèque Nationale, Paris

Blanden Memorial Art Museum, Fort Dodge, Iowa

Boston Public Library Print Collection

British Museum, London

Brooklyn Museum of Art

Chazen Museum of Art (formerly Elvehjem Museum of Art), University of Wisconsin–Madison

Cleveland Museum of Art

Columbus Museum, Columbus, Ga.

Danforth Museum of Art, Framingham, Mass.

Davenport (Iowa) Museum of Art

Des Moines Art Center

Fogg Art Museum, Harvard University, Cambridge, Mass.

Frances Lehman Loeb Art Center, Vassar College, Poughkeepsie, N.Y.

Frederick R. Weisman Art Museum, University of Minnesota, Minneapolis

Grunwald Center for the Graphic Arts, UCLA Hammer Museum and Cultural Center, Los Angeles

High Museum of Art, Atlanta

Huntington (W. Va.) Museum of Art, Inc.

Illinois State Museum, Springfield

Indiana University Art Museum, Bloomington

Indianapolis Museum of Art

Jordan Schnitzer Museum of Art at the University of Oregon, Eugene

Kalamazoo Institute of Arts

Madison (Wis.) Art Center

Mary and Leigh Block Museum of Art, Northwestern University, Evanston, Ill.

Miami University Art Museum, Oxford, Ohio

Milwaukee Art Museum

Minneapolis Institute of Arts

Mitchell Museum at Cedarhurst, Mt. Vernon, Ill.

Montgomery (Ala.) Museum of Fine Arts

Museo d'Arte Contemporaneo, Palazzo Massari, Ferrara

Museum of Contemporary Art, Chicago

New York Public Library

Portland (Ore.) Art Museum

Rose Art Museum, Brandeis University, Waltham, Mass.

Sackner Archive of Visual & Concrete Poetry, Miami Beach

Sheldon Memorial Art Gallery and Sculpture Garden, University of Nebraska–Lincoln

Sioux City (Iowa) Art Center

Smithsonian American Art Museum, Washington, D.C.

Tarble Arts Center, Eastern Illinois University, Charleston

Toledo Museum of Art

Total Museum of Contemporary Art, Seoul

University Galleries, Illinois State University, Normal

University Museum, Southern Illinois University, Carbondale

University of Arizona Museum of Art, Tucson

University of Iowa Museum of Art, Iowa City

Western Illinois University Art Gallery, Macomb

Zimmerli Art Museum, Rutgers University, New Brunswick, N.J.

Solo Exhibitions

2005

Gallery 72, Omaha

"The Borrower's Name," Phyllis Stigliano Gallery, Brooklyn

"Gary, Indiana," Salena Gallery, Long Island University, Brooklyn

"New Work," Jean Albano Gallery, Chicago

"Recent Paintings and Prints," College of Lake County, Grays Lake, Ill.

2003

"The Card Catalog Drawings," Southern Methodist University, Dallas

"Icons: John Himmelfarb," Gallery 72, Omaha

2002

"A Decade of Prints." Northern Indiana Arts Association, Cultural Center, Munster

"A Visual Language: John Himmelfarb Prints," Christopher Art Gallery, Prairie State College, Chicago Heights, Ill.

"John Himmelfarb," Jean Albano Gallery, Chicago

2001

"John Himmelfarb (Inland Romance)," William A. Koehnline Gallery, Oakton Community College, Des Plaines, Ill.

"John Himmelfarb," Lukacs Gallery, Fairfield (Conn.) University

"American Graffiti," Centre of Contemporary Art, Christchurch, New Zealand

"People and Places," Gallery 72, Omaha

2000

"John Himmelfarb: Floor to Ceiling," Sioux City (Iowa) Art Center

"John Himmelfarb: Drawings and Paintings," Jean Albano Gallery, Chicago

"John Himmelfarb: Paintings and Works on Paper," Riverside (Ill.) Arts Center

1999

"John Himmelfarb," Spaightwood Gallery, Madison, Wis.

Gallery 72, Omaha

1998

Jean Albano Gallery, Chicago

1997

"Work, Work, Work," Gallery 72, Omaha

1996

"John Himmelfarb Mixed-Media," Jean Albano Gallery, Chicago

"Recent Drawings," Evanston (Ill.) Art Center

"John Himmelfarb: Recent (and Not So Recent) Work on Canvas and Paper," Spaightwood Gallery, Madison, Wis.

1995

"Inland Romance: Paintings by John Himmelfarb," Chicago Cultural Center (continued into 1996)

"Letters, Documents, and Suspicious Characters," Gallery 1756, Chicago

1994

"John Himmelfarb: Images, Graven and Otherwise," Spaightwood Gallery, Madison, Wis.

"Small Works," Gallery 72, Omaha

1993

"The Letters," Kamerick Art Center Gallery, University of Northern Iowa, Cedar Falls

1992

"John Himmelfarb Selected Prints," Anchor Graphics, Chicago

Gallery 72, Omaha

1991

"The Non-Objective Paintings," Terry Dintenfass, New York

"John Himmelfarb Paintings and Prints," Cissie Peltz Gallery, Milwaukee

1990

"John Himmelfarb Some Goodies," Gallery 72, Omaha

"New Masters." Huntington (W. Va.) Museum of Art, Inc.

"About Faces: Paintings and Works on Paper," Brody's Gallery, Washington, D.C.

1989

"Meetings in the Garden: The Art of John Himmelfarb," Kalamazoo Institute of Arts (traveled in 1990 to Madison [Wis.] Art Center; Miami University Art Museum, Oxford, Ohio; and Arkansas Arts Center, Little Rock)

"Selected Work," Terry Dintenfass, New York

"New Drawings" Fundació Tallers Josep Llorens Artigas, Gallifa, Spain

1987

Blanden Memorial Museum of Art, Fort Dodge, Iowa

"John Himmelfarb, An Exhibit of New Work," Evanston (Ill.) Art Center

1986

"John Himmelfarb Recent Work," Terry Dintenfass, New York

"Monumental Meetings," John Nichols, New York

"Himmelfarb: Black on White," Davenport (Iowa) Museum of Art

"Paintings, Drawings, Prints," Southwest State University, Marshall, Minn.

1985

Gallery 72, Omaha

"Paintings and Ceramics 1975–1985," Area X Gallery, New York

"Prints and Drawings 1970–1985," Sioux City (Iowa) Art Center

1983

"John Himmelfarb Paintings, Drawings, and Prints," Terry Dintenfass, New York

"John Himmelfarb Paintings, Drawings, Prints," Gallery 72, Omaha

1982

"John Himmelfarb Recent Work," Barbara Balkin Gallery, Chicago

1980

"John Himmelfarb Prints and Drawings," Fountain Gallery, Portland, Ore.

"John Himmelfarb Paintings, Drawings, Prints, and Sculpture," Hull Gallery, Washington, D.C.

1979

"John Himmelfarb Drawings," Terry Dintenfass, New York

"Paintings, Drawings, Watercolors, and Prints," Gallery 72, Omaha

Barbara Balkin Gallery, Chicago

"John Himmelfarb," Merwin Gallery, Illinois Wesleyan University, Bloomington

1978

"John Himmelfarb," Ball State University Museum of Art, Muncie, Ind.

"John Himmelfarb," Sheldon Memorial Art Gallery and Sculpture Garden, University of Nebraska–Lincoln

"Recent Paintings and Drawings" (also included prints), Albrecht-Kemper Museum of Art, St. Joseph, Mo.

"Recent Paintings and Drawings," Dorothy Rosenthal Gallery, Chicago

1976

"Paintings, Drawings and Prints," Dorothy Rosenthal Gallery, Chicago

"John Himmelfarb," Sheldon Memorial Art Gallery and Sculpture Garden, University of Nebraska–Lincoln

1974

Illinois Arts Council Gallery, Chicago

"Prints, Drawings and Paintings," Graphics I and Graphics II, Boston

1973

Studio Exhibit, 1825 S. Halsted, Chicago

1968

"An Exhibition of Drawings," Adams House, Harvard University, Cambridge, Mass.

"Pen and Ink Drawings," Milles (Mass.) Public Library

Group Exhibitions

2005

"New Prints," International Center for the Print, New York

"N.E.W. Selected Works," West Virginia University–Mesaros Galleries, Morgantown

2004

"New Prints," International Center for the Print, New York

"Sound and Vision: John Himmelfarb and Philip Trusttum," Centre of Contemporary Art, Christchurch, New Zealand

"Rivers and Other Bodies of Water," River Gallery, Chelsea, Mich.

2003

"New Prints," International Center for the Print, New York

"Himmelfarb, Himmelfarb, Himmelfarb," Haydon Gallery, Lincoln, Neb.

"77th Annual International Competition: Printmaking," Print Center, Philadelphia

"The Boston Printmakers 2003 North American Print Biennial," Boston University

2002

"Paper 5," John Woodward Gallery, New York

2001

"Abstract Art in the New Century," Crossman Gallery, University of Wisconsin–Whitewater

1999

"Large Drawings from the Arkansas Art Foundation Collection," Butler Institute of American Art, Youngstown, Ohio (also traveled to Columbus [Ga.] Museum; Hunter Museum of American Art, Chattanooga; and Mississippi Museum of Art, Jackson)

1998

"Minnesota National Print Biennial," Katherine E. Nash Gallery, University of Minnesota, Minneapolis

1996

"Cultured Pearl," Total Museum of Contemporary Art, Seoul

"Second Sight: Printmaking in Chicago, 1935–1995," Mary and Leigh Block Museum of Art, Northwestern University, Evanston, Ill.

"Large Drawings and Objects," Arkansas Arts Center, Little Rock

"7th Annual Davidson National Print Exhibition," Davidson (N.C.) College Visual Arts Center

1994

"Plats d'Artistes," Fundació Tallers Josep Llorens Artigas, Gallifa, Spain

"Tandem Press: Five Years of Collaboration-Experimentation," Elvehjem Museum of Art (now Chazen Museum of Art), University of Wisconsin–Madison

"20th Century Prints: The Last 50 Years," Jane Haslem Gallery, Washington, D.C.

1993

"Prints from Normal Editions Workshop," Carlsten Art Gallery, University of Wisconsin-Stevens Point

"Artists and Designers Alumni Show," Carpenter Center for the Visual Arts, Harvard University, Cambridge, Mass.

"SAGA 65th National Print Exhibition," Society of American Graphic Artists, New York

"Alechinsky, Miró, and Himmelfarb," Spaightwood Gallery, Madison, Wis.

"Recent Prints from Stewart & Stewart," Arnold Klein Gallery, Royal Oak, Mich.

1992

"Drawing on Experience," Miami University Art Museum, Oxford, Ohio

"Prints from Stewart & Stewart," Images Gallery, Toledo

"Postcards—Then and Now," Brody's Gallery, Washington, D.C.

1991

"Recent Acquisitions in Graphic Art," National Museum of American Art (now Smithsonian American Art Museum), Washington, D.C.

"Cobra and Friends," Spaightwood Gallery, Madison, Wis.

"A Matter of Scale," Spaightwood Gallery, Madison, Wis.

1990

"Diversity of Line: A Selection from the Permanent Collection," Des Moines Art Center

"Echo Press: A Decade of Printmaking," Indiana University Art Museum, Bloomington

"Coming Attractions," Terry Dintenfass, New York

"Tandem Press," Pace Gallery, New York

"Works on Paper," Terry Dintenfass, New York

1989

"Prints from Landfall Press," San Antonio Museum of Art

"July Prints," Brody's Gallery, Washington, D.C.

1988

"The Face: National Drawing Invitational," Arkansas Arts Center, Little Rock

"New Editions," Landfall Press, New York

"International Prints II," Silvermine Guilds Arts Center, New Canaan, Conn.

"Boston Printmakers 40th North American Print Exhibition," Brockton Art Museum, Boston

"Prints from Three Continents," Brody's Gallery, Washington, D.C.

1987

"Brought Up on Asphaltum," National Lithograph Invitational, Contemporary Crafts Museum and Gallery, Oregon College of Arts and Crafts, Portland

"V.E.S. Graduates," Carpenter Center for the Visual Arts, Harvard University, Cambridge, Mass.

"Recent Graphics/American Print Shops," Virginia Museum of Fine Arts, Richmond

"Recent Fine Prints," Brody's Gallery, Washington, D.C.

1986

"Monumental Drawings: Works by 22 Contemporary Americans," Brooklyn Museum of Art

"Contemporary Prints," Brody's Gallery, Washington, D.C.

"Blockbusters: The Big Impression," John Nichols, New York

"Faces," Area X Gallery, New York

"Recent Graphics from American Print Shops," Mitchell Museum at Cedarhurst, Mt. Vernon, Ill. (traveled).

1985

"Prints from Soho," Fuji Salon, Tokyo

"Prints and Multiples: 81st Exhibition byArtists of Chicago and Vicinity," Art Institute of Chicago

John Nichols, New York

1984

"Too Hot for New York," Area X Gallery, New York

"Summer Exhibit," Brody's Gallery, Washington, D.C.

"Original Lithographs from Plucked Chicken Press," Fairweather-Hardin Gallery, Chicago

1983

"Contemporary Chicago Lithography: Prints from the Four Brothers Press and Plucked Chicken Press", Illinois State Museum, Springfield (traveled)

"Director's Choice," Des Moines Art Center

"Rockford International '83," Rockford (Ill.) College Art Gallery/Clark Arts Center

1982

Barbara Balkin Gallery, Chicago

"Invitational Print Exhibition," Sykes Gallery, Millersville (Penn.) University

1981

"Permanent Collection: Artists' Books," Museum of Contemporary Art, Chicago

"Prints and Multiples: 79th Exhibition by Artists of Chicago and Vicinity," Art Institute of Chicago (traveled)

1980

"American Drawings in Black and White: 1970–1980," Brooklyn Museum of Art

"Annual International Competition," Philadelphia Print Club

1979

"Chicago and Vicinity Prizewinners Revisited," Art Institute of Chicago

"Rockford International Print Exhibition," Rockford (Ill.) College Art Gallery/Clark Arts Center

1978

"Works on Paper: 77th Exhibition by Artists of Chicago and Vicinity," Art Institute of Chicago

1977

"19th Annual Exhibition of Prints and Drawings," Oklahoma Arts Center

1975

"Davidson National Prints and Drawings Exhibition," Davidson (N.C.) College Visual Arts Center

"Three Lithographers," Sheldon Memorial Art Gallery and Sculpture Garden, University of Nebraska–Lincoln

"Third Hawaii National Print Exhibition," Honolulu Academy of the Arts

1974

"19th National Print Exhibition," Brooklyn Museum of Art (continued into 1975)

"Print and Drawing Show," Artists Guild of Chicago

"Art for Young Collectors," Renaissance Society, University of Chicago

1973

"Printmakers: Midwest Invitational," Walker Art Center, Minneapolis

"Drawings USA," Minnesota Museum of American Art, St. Paul

"Fourth Annual Colorprint U.S.A.," Museum of Texas Technical University, Lubbock

1971

"Prints from Landfall Press," Smithsonian Institution Traveling Exhibition

"Drawings in St. Paul," Minnesota Museum of American Art, St. Paul

"Drawings USA," Minnesota Museum of American Art, St. Paul

"Brooklyn Museum Fence Show," Brooklyn Museum of Art

1968

"Drawings USA," Minnesota Museum of American Art, St. Paul

Public Projects

2005

Boston, Logan Airport, Delta Airlines Terminal A. Two paintings.

2004

Chicago Transit Authority, Kedzie Station. Ceramic-tile mural.

2002

University of Nebraska, Graduate School of Education, University of Nebraska at Omaha. Two ceramic-tile murals.

1992

Art Omaha. Two ceramic-tile murals for Omaha Public Schools.

Visiting Artist

2003

Western Institute of Technology at Taranaki, New Plymouth, New Zealand

University of Canterbury, Christchurch, New Zealand

2002

University of Wisconsin–Milwaukee

Illinois State University, Normal

2000

University of Nebraska at Omaha

1998

Centre for Contemporary Art, Christchurch, New Zealand

Buena Vista University, Storm Lake, Iowa

Southern Illinois Univerity, Carbondale

University of South Dakota, Vermillion

1997

Sioux City (Iowa) Art Center

1992

Indiana University, Northwest, Gary

1991

Illinois State University, Normal

1990

"New Masters Workshop," Huntington (W. Va.) Museum of Art, Inc.

Kalamazoo Institute of Arts

Miami University, Oxford, Ohio

University of Wisconsin–Madison

1989

Ball State University, Muncie, Ind.

1988

Southern Illinois Univerity, Carbondale

1987

Whitman College, Walla Walla, Wash.

Blanden Memorial Art Museum, Fort Dodge, Iowa

1986

Southern Illinois University, Carbondale

Midway Studios, University of Chicago

Illinois State University, Normal

1985

Augustana and Sioux Falls Colleges, Sioux Falls, S.D.

Balzekas Museum of Lithuanian Culture, Chicago

Briar Cliff College, Sioux City, Iowa

Dordt College, Sioux Center, Iowa

Northwestern College, Orange City, Iowa

Sioux City (Iowa) Art Center

University of Northern Iowa, Cedar Falls

University of South Dakota, Vermillion

University of Wisconsin–River Falls

1978

Albrecht-Kemper Museum of Art, St. Joseph, Mo.

1976

Joslyn Art Museum, Omaha

Awards

2003

Illinois Arts Council

2002

Pollock-Krasner Foundation

1989

Chicago Artists Abroad

1986

Illinois Arts Council

Pollock-Krasner Foundation

1985

National Endowment for the Arts

1982

National Endowment for the Arts

1979

Yaddo artists' community, Saratoga Springs, N.Y.

Selected Bibliography

2005

Lisa Stein, "Art Scene: John Himmelfarb's One-Man Renaissance." *Chicago Tribune*. March 11. Section 7. Page 25.

Artner, Alan. "Art Galleries Review: . . . John Himmelfarb." *Chicago Tribune*, February 25. Section C7. Page 21.

Blue Line Art Project. Chicago: Chicago Transit Authority and City of Chicago. Pages 12–13.

2004

Parker, Daniel. *African Art, The Diaspora + Beyond: The Daniel Texidor Parker Collection*. Chicago: self-published. Page 75.

Stewart & Stewart. "New John Himmelfarb Editions." *Journal of the Print World* (fall).

2003

Moore, Christopher. "Doubly Expressive." *Christchurch (New Zealand) Press*. October 22. Arts Section. Page C2.

"Visual." *Christchurch (New Zealand) Press.* October 19. Art Beat Section.

77th Annual International Competition: Printmaking. Exhibition catalogue. Essay by Mark Pascale. Philadelphia: Print Center. Page 12.

United States Embassy, Port-au-Prince, Haiti. *Art in Embassies*. Essay by Brian Dean Curan. Washington, D.C.: Art in Embassies Program. Pages 16–17.

The Boston Printmakers 2003 North American Print Biennial. Exhibition catalogue. Introduction by Clifford Ackley. Boston: Boston University. Page 11.

2002

Rose, Matthew. "Wall to Wall: John Himmelfarb." *Arts Magazine* 7, 2 (December). Page 20.

Swafford, Jan. "Remembering John Himmelfarb," *Graven Images: Studies in Culture, Law, and the Sacred*. Volume 5. Edited by Andrew D. Weiner and Leonard V. Kaplan. Madison: University of Wisconsin Press. Pages 284–85 (and front- and back-cover illustrations).

2001

Plucked Chicken Press: The Oakton Community College Collection of Stone Prints by Will Petersen and His Contemporaries. Essay by Nathan Harpaz. Des Plaines, Ill.: Oakton Community College. Page 24.

Stewart & Stewart. "New John Himmelfarb Editions." *Journal of the Print World* (fall).

Peers, Robyn. "Smorgasbord of Glorious Images." *Christchurch (New Zealand) Press*. August 22. Arts Section. Page 40.

Moore, Christopher. "American Beauty." *Christchurch (New Zealand) Press*. August 15. Arts Section. Pages 33–34.

2000

Hawkins, Margaret. "Gallery Glance." *Chicago Sun-Times*. November 10. Page 55.

"John Himmelfarb Astronomer." *Art on Paper* 4, 5 (May–June). Page 67.

1999

Seventeenth Open Studios Competition. Volume 3, number 5. Wellesley, Mass. Open Studio Press. Pages 42–43.

1998

Hawkins, Margaret. "John Himmelfarb." *Chicago Sun-Times*. June 26. Arts Section. Page 18W.

Barandiaran, Mariá José. "Small Presses Leave Their Mark on Chicago." *Dialogue Magazine* (May–June). Pages 32–33.

Hawkins, Margaret. "Exhibits Explode in Splashes of Color." *Chicago Sun-Times*. January 9. Arts Section.

1997

"Meet the Artist." *Sioux City (Iowa) Journal*. July 4.

Brunetti, John. "John Himmelfarb." *New Art Examiner* (December 1996–January 1997).

1996

Buchholz, Barbara. "Gallery Scene." *Chicago Tribune*. September 27. Section 7. Page 47.

Second Sight: Printmaking in Chicago, 1935–1995. Exhibition catalogue. Essays by James Yood, Mark Pascale, and David Mickenberg. Evanston, Ill.: Mary and Leigh Block Museum of Art, Northwestern University. Pages 10, 45, 48–50, 59, 127–28.

Artner, Alan. "Gallery Scene." *Chicago Tribune*. August 23. Section 7. Page 48.

———. "Gallery Scene." *Chicago Tribune*. January 25. Section 5. Page 9C.

1995

"In Motion." *Echo Imprint* 2, 1 (fall). Page 2.

1994

"Five New Prints by Artist John Himmelfarb." *Journal of the Print World* 17, 1 (winter).

Stewart, Susan. "John Himmelfarb." *Contemporary Impressions: Journal of the American Print Alliance* 2, 2 (fall). Pages 16–19.

Stevens, Andrew. *Tandem Press: Five Years of Collaboration-Experimentation*. Exhibition catalogue. Madison: Elvehjem Museum of Art (now Chazen Museum of Art), University of Wisconsin. Pages 26, 47, 67, 77–78, 97–100.

"John Himmelfarb, 'Tabula, Tabula Picta.'" *Print Collector's Newsletter* 25, 2 (May–June).

"John Himmelfarb, 'Fax Appeal,' 'First Draft,' 'Note of Appeal.' 'Short Order,' 'White Out.'" *Print Collector's Newsletter* 25, 1 (March–April).

1993

SAGA 65th National Print Exhibition. Exhibition catalogue. Introduction by Michael Di Cerbo. New York: Society of American Graphic Artists. Pages 6, 19 (and back-cover illustration).

Norris, Scott. "Himmelfarb Drawings at Arts Center." *Iowa City Press Citizen*. September 15.

Hess, Harvey. "Exhibition of Japanese Artwork Snaps Stereotype." *Waterloo (Iowa) Courier*. September 15.

Maass, Mary R. "Cultural Detour to Kamerick Art Gallery." *Northern Iowan (Cedar Falls)*. September 3.

"Juggler on Stage." *Art Business News*. June.

"John Himmelfarb's 'Juggler and Juggler on Stage.'" *Print Collector's Newsletter* 24, 1 (March–April).

1992

Postcards—Then and Now. Exhibition catalogue. Essay by Tom and Judy Brody. Washington, D.C.: Brody's Gallery. Pages 19, 22.

MacMillan, Kyle. "Chicagoan Rejoices in His Art." *World-Herald (Omaha)*. June 12.

Huntington Museum of Art Biennial Report 1990–1992. Huntington, W. Va.: Huntington Museum of Art, Inc.

1991

Rowe, Jessica. "A Diversity of Line: A Selection from the Permanent Collection." Des Moines Art Center *Gallery Guide*. November.

Auer, James. "Art Exhibits: Paintings, Prints, Dolls among Items on Exhibit." *Milwaukee Journal*. September. Page D8.

1990

Echo Press: A Decade of Printmaking. Exhibition catalogue. Essays by Rudy Pozzatti, Kathleen A. Foster, Peagram Harrison, Barry Walker, Nan Esseck. Bloomington: Indiana University Art Museum. Pages 11, 67.

"Inside Artworks." *Inside Chicago* 4, 5 (September–October). Page 50.

Lynch, Kevin. "Meetings in the Garden: Artist Paints Turmoil." *The Capital Times (Madison, Wis.)*. August 11–12.

Laskin, Tom. "City Notes on Art and Entertainment: Animal Magnetism. Living Large with John Himmelfarb." *Isthmus (Madison, Wis.)*. August 10. Page 32.

Madison Art Center *Newsletter* (summer). Page 3.

Kukla, Cynthia M. "John Himmelfarb." *Dialogue* (May–June). Page 30.

MacMillan, Kyle. "Painter Himmelfarb Moves in New Direction." *Sunday World-Herald (Omaha)*. March 25.

1989

"The Gallery." *The World Journal of the Unitarian Universalist Association* 3, 5 (September–October). Pages 14–15.

"Meetings in the Garden." Kalamazoo Institute of Arts *Forum* 2, 1 (September). Page 1.

Meetings in the Garden. The Art of John Himmelfarb. Exhibition catalogue. Helen Sheridan with essay by Michael Bonesteel. *Kalamazoo Institute of Arts Bulletin* 75.

Bonesteel, Michael. "Diversions: Art Goes to School." *Pioneer Press (Winnetka, Ill.)*. June 1.

The Chicago Art Review. An Illustrated Survey of the City's Museums, Galleries, and Leading Artists. Chicago: American References Publishing Corp. Pages 199–201.

1988

Wolfe, Townsend. *The Face: National Drawing Invitational*. Exhibition catalogue. Little Rock: Arkansas Arts Center. Pages 15, 24–25, 111–12.

Boston Printmakers 40th North American Print Exhibition. Exhibition catalogue. Essay by Peter J. Baldaia. Brockton (Mass.) Art Museum. Page 5.

"1987 Acquisitions." Mitchell Museum at Cedarhurst *Cedarhurst Quarterly* (February–April 1988). Page 5.

1987

Castle, Frederick Ted. "John Himmelfarb at Terry Dintenfass and John Nichols." *Art in America* 75 (December). Pages 161–62.

Matranga, Victoria. "A Meeting with John Himmelfarb." *Nit & Wit* 8, 3 (June). Pages 14–16 (and front-cover illustration).

Nusbaum, Eliot. """The Visual Arts: Challenges by Himmelfarb." *Des Moines Sunday Register*. May 17. Page 5C.

Argy, Andy. "John Himmelfarb—Evanston Art Center." *New Art Examiner* 14 (March). Page 44.

1986

"John Himmelfarb, 'Lengthy Meeting.'" *Print Collector's Newsletter* 17, 4 (September–October). Page 141.

Kotik, Charlotta. *Monumental Drawings: Works by 22 Contemporary Americans.* Exhibition catalogue. Brooklyn: Brooklyn Museum of Art. Pages 22–23.

Rose, Matthew. "John Himmelfarb." *Art Gallery International* 7, 6 (September–October).

First Three Years. Washington, D.C.: Brody's Gallery. Page 12.

"Bigger *is* Better." *Print Collector's Newsletter* 17, 3 (July–August).

Butler, Charles Thomas, and Laufer, Marilyn. *Recent Graphics from American Print Shops.* Exhibition catalogue. Mt. Vernon, Ill.: Mitchell Museum at Cedarhurst.

Stegmaier, Mark. "Gallery Exhibit—A Veritable *Tour de Force*." *Quad City (Davenport) Times*. February 2.

"Too Hot for New York and Warming Up the Season Here / John Himmelfarb: The Artist as Translator." *Davenport (Iowa) Art Gallery Newsletter* (January–February).

Himmelfarb: Black on White. Exhibition catalogue. Introduction by L. G. Hoffman and essay by Frederick Ted Castle. Davenport, Iowa: Davenport Museum of Art.

1985

Rose, Matthew. "An Interview with John Himmelfarb." *Arts Magazine* 60 (October). Pages 68–72.

"John Himmelfarb: 'Grand Street Meeting.'" *Print Collector's Newsletter* 16, 4 (September–October). Page 140.

"Goings On About Town: John Himmelfarb." *The New Yorker.* April 8.

Butler, Charles Thomas, and Laufer, Marilyn. "John Himmelfarb: Prints and Drawings 1970–1985." *Artifact* (March–April). Pages 5–12.

Prints and Multiples: 81st Exhibition by Artists of Chicago and Vicinity. Exhibition catalogue. Chicago: Art Institute of Chicago. Page 12.

Krantz, Les. *American Artists: An Illustrated Survey of Leading Contemporary Americans* Chicago: Les Krantz; New York/Oxford, England: Facts on File Publications. Page 154.

1983

Catlin, Roger. "Des Moines Art Center." *World-Herald (Omaha)*. November 6.

Demetrion, James. *Director's Choice.* Exhibition catalogue. Des Moines: Des Moines Art Center.

Contemporary Chicago Lithography: Prints from the Four Brothers Press and Plucked Chicken Press. Exhibition brochure. Springfield: Illinois State Museum.

Rockford International '83. Exhibition catalogue. Essay by Gordon Gilkey. Rockford, Ill.: Rockford College. Page 10.

"Goings On About Town: John Himmelfarb." *The New Yorker.* January 26–February 5.

1982

Murman, Lydia. "John Himmelfarb." *New Art Examiner* 9 (October). Page 72.

"Veteran Artists Exhibit." *Chicago Sun-Times.* June 25.

"John Himmelfarb, 'Trio.'" *Print Collector's Newsletter* 13, 2 (May–June).

1981

Artner, Alan. "Pictures at an Exhibition: 'Chicago' Opens." *Chicago Tribune.* July 3. Section 4, page 12.

Flint, Janet. *Prints and Multiples: 79th Exhibition by Artists of Chicago and Vicinity.* Exhibition catalogue. Chicago: Art Institute of Chicago. Pages 12, 32.

Chicago Art Review, An Art Explorer's Guide. Chicago: Les Krantz. Page 49.

Alexis, Karin. "John Himmelfarb." *New Art Examiner* 8 (January).

1980

American Drawings in Black and White, 1970–1980. Exhibition catalogue. Essay by Gene Baro. Brooklyn: Brooklyn Museum of Art. Page 5.

Chicago Artists. Exhibition catalogue. Essay by Allen S. Weller. Mt. Vernon, Ill.: Mitchell Museum at Cedarhurst. Page 4.

Sparks, Esther. *Chicago and Vicinity Prizewinners Revisited*. Exhibition catalogue. Chicago: Art Institute of Chicago.

Chicago Art Prospective. Exhibition catalogue. Chicago: City of Chicago. Page 18.

"John Himmelfarb, 'Words Cannot Describe.'" *Print Collector's Newsletter* 11, 1 (March–April).

1978

Sparks, Esther. *Works on Paper: 77th Exhibition by Artists of Chicago and Vicinity.* Exhibition catalogue. Chicago: Art Institute of Chicago. Pages 4, 12.

"John Himmelfarb." *Accessions 1976–1978. University of Iowa Museum of Art Bulletin* 2, 2. Pages 10–12.

1977

19th Annual National Exhibition of Prints and Drawings. Exhibition catalogue. Essay by Lowell Adams. Oklahoma City: Oklahoma Arts Center. Page 10.

1976

Haydon, Harold. "Chicago Art Abundant, but Unappreciated." *Chicago Sun-Times.* June 20.

22nd Annual Drawing and Small Sculpture Show. Exhibition catalogue. Essay by Norman Geske. Muncie, Ind.: Ball State University Art Gallery. Pages 2, 9.

Haydon, Harold. "His Images Reflect Our Hectic World." *Chicago Sun-Times.* April 11.

1975

Davidson National Prints and Drawings Exhibition. Exhibition catalogue. Statements by Herb Jackson and Marcia Tucker. Davidson, N.C.: Stowe Gallery, Davidson College. Pages 9, 30.

Third Hawaii National Print Exhibition. Exhibition catalogue. Essay by James W. Foster. Honolulu: Honolulu Academy of Arts. Page 13.

1974

"Graphics with a Bias toward Significance." *Chicago Sun-Times.* November 7.

1973

Larson, Philip. *Printmakers: Midwest Invitational.* Exhibition catalogue. Minneapolis: Walker Art Center. Pages 2, 4, 6, 11, 27.

Drawings USA. Exhibition catalogue. Essay by Alan Fern. St. Paul: Minnesota Museum of American Art. Page 12.

Fourth Annual Colorprint U.S.A. Exhibition catalogue. Statement by Charles Morgan. Lubbuck: Museum of Texas Technical University. Page 4.

Transport, Darryl Licht [John Himmelfarb]. *The Family Dog: Drawings by John Himmelfarb.* Chicago: self-published.

1971

Drawings in St. Paul. Exhibition catalogue. Introduction by A. Hyatt Mayor. St. Paul: Minnesota Museum of American Art. Page 36.

Drawings USA. Exhibition catalogue. Essay by Cleve Gray. St. Paul: Minnesota Museum of American Art. Pages 11, 20.

Prints from Landfall Press. Exhibition catalogue. Essay by Harold Joachim. Washington, D.C.: Smithsonian Institution. Page 22.

1968

Drawings USA. Exhibition catalogue. St. Paul: Minnesota Museum of American Art. Page 13.

Index of Works

Publishers, Printers, and Their Locations

Allyn Print Shop, Department of Art, Southern Illinois University, Carbondale: nos. 62–65, 69–71

Anchor Graphics, Chicago: no. 74

Artist: nos. 1–50, 58, 61–66, 69–71, 74–75, 81, 90, 102–03, 107–11, 114–18, 126–27, 129–30, 135–37, 143, 146

ARZ NOVA, Chicago*: nos. 54a–c, 55–56

Buena Vista University, Art Department, Storm Lake, Iowa: no. 116

Ruth Bauman, Chicago: nos. 36–38

Chicago Printmakers Collaborative: no. 146

Tom Christison, Madison, Wis., currently Knoxville, Tenn.: no. 90

Echo Press, Indiana University, Bloomington*: no. 67

Richard D. Finch Workshop, Bloomington, Ill.: nos. 114–15, 117–18, 124, 129, 135–36

Four Brothers Press, Chicago*: nos. 52–53

Full Court Press, Morton Grove, Ill.*: no. 85

Anita Jung, Madison, Wis., currently Knoxville, Tenn.: no. 61

Landfall Press, Chicago until 2004; currently Santa Fe: nos. 5–25, 33, 66, 68

John Nichols, New York, currently Princeton, N. J.: no. 57

Normal Editions Workshop, Illinois State University, Normal: nos. 60, 75, 80, 82–84, 91, 102–04, 107–11, 140

Peck School of the Arts, University of Wisconsin–Milwaukee: nos. 36–38, 138–39, 141–42

Plucked Chicken Press, Chicago*: nos. 39–51

Andrew Rubin, see Tandem Press

Stone Roller Press, Chicago*: nos. 26–31

Stewart & Stewart, Bloomfield Hills, Michigan: nos. 77–79, 86–89, 92–101, 105–06, 112–13, 120–23, 131–34, 147–52

Tandem Press, University of Wisconsin–Madison: nos. 59, 72–73

Tallers Mestizarte, Chicago: no. 119

Teaberry Press, Chicago, currently San Francisco: no. 32

University of Northern Iowa, Art Department, Cedar Falls: no. 58

UNO Print Workshop, University of Nebraska at Omaha: nos. 76, 125–28, 130, 137, 143–45

**No longer in operation*

Acknowledgments and Photo Credits

The following individuals are among those who contributed in a variety of ways to the realization of this catalogue raisonné:

Cindy Arnson
Sue Atkins
William H. Bengtson
Judith and Bruce Clark
Ruth Crnkovich
Gary Day
Molly Day
Karen and Robert Duncan
Catherine and Terry Ferguson
Richard D. Finch
Aline Hill
Eleanor Himmelfarb
John Himmelfarb
Carrie Iverson
Henry Joseph
Norm and Lucinda Katz
Peter Millock
Kate and Bill Morrison
Stan Ries
Peggy Ross
Nell and Paul Schneider
Gerald Serotta
Eban Shapiro

Photo credits
All prints by John Himmelfarb were photographed by William H. Bengtson, Chicago.
Photograph on page 137, LL, © 1994 www.StewartStewart.com